The Military in Chilean History

The Military
in Chilean History

Essays on Civil-Military Relations, 1810-1973

Frederick M. Nunn

UNIVERSITY OF NEW MEXICO PRESS
Albuquerque

For My Parents

Contents

Acknowledgments

I want to thank again the Henry L. and Grace Doherty Charitable Foundation, the American Philosophical Society, and the Portland State University Committee on Research and Publication for support which has enabled me since 1962 to carry out continued research on Chilean civil-military relations. Much of the initial research for parts I and II of this book, for example, was done during 1962 and 1969 in Santiago, Chile and Washington, D.C. Sabbatical leave granted by Portland State University made it possible for me to return to Santiago in 1972 to gather material for part III.

A number of historians merit acknowledgment for the ways in which they have contributed to this work. Professor Edwin Lieuwen of the University of New Mexico has continued to offer advice, suggestions, and comments long after I ceased to be his student. Professors Michael C. Meyer of the University of Arizona, William Sherman of the University of Nebraska, and Joan Connelly Ullman of the University of Washington often have discussed with me aspects of civil-military relations, and some of their ideas have influenced my thinking over the years. Professor Jesse L. Gilmore, chairman, Department of History, and George C. Hoffman, dean, College of Social Science, both of Portland State University, have encouraged me in my efforts on many occasions. Professor Eugenio Pereira Salas of the University of Chile has never failed me when I needed assistance. To each of these scholars, my profound thanks.

During my years of attention to Chilean history and politics no one has contributed more to my endeavors than Gonzalo Mendoza Aylwin, director of the Biblioteca del Estado Mayor General, Ejército de Chile. I will never be able to express my gratitude to him adequately. To those many officers of the Ejército de Chile, active and retired, who have conversed with me on numerous occasions in Santiago and elsewhere, I extend a warm *¡mil gracias!*

I have been fortunate to have some exceptional student research assistants at Portland State University, and each has aided in the completion of this project. Craig E. Wollner, Ann M. Rosentreter, Sally Jones, Robert Schaefer, Nancy Salsbery Muñiz, and Juli Salmon all assisted in portions of the research. Barbara Madigan not only aided in the research stage, she carefully read and commented on the manuscript and helped in the last-minute typing chores.

Nancy Maurer, Karen Waters, Barbara Rossman, Linda Owen, Anita Swartout, and Lee Cummins, those intrepid Department of History secretaries and typists, rendered invaluable assistance in typing the bulk of the manuscript, as did Patricia Stenaros and Beverly Ellis of the College of Social Science. Without the help of such students and staff the whole effort would have been most difficult.

Each member of my family has been most patient and understanding during some trying times when I was engaged in research and writing, too busy to be attentive or too engrossed to participate in family activities. My wife and colleague, Susan Karant-Nunn, consistently encouraged me in my work.

Deserving a paragraph of her own is my daughter Marianna. She was especially understanding at those times when her father stuck to his work schedule, and she was generous with her own time, rendering invaluable assistance in the final revision process. No father could ever ask more.

Without the numerous suggestions, concentrated attention, and competent supervision of Elizabeth Heist and Carl Mora of the University of New Mexico Press this book would be less than it is.

Though many have contributed to the preparation of this book, I, of course, am solely responsible for any errors in it.

Introduction

Chilean civil-military relations were abruptly altered on September 11, 1973, when the armed forces and the national police overthrew the government led by President Salvador Allende Gossens. The *golpe de estado* of September 11, 1973, was the first such military action since 1932, the first time in over four decades that civilian rule had been interrupted. That fact alone makes a study of Chilean civil-military relations necessary—and timely—for few seriously thought it possible that the Chilean armed forces could break tradition.

When I published my *Chilean Politics, 1920–1931: The Honorable Mission of the Armed Forces* (Albuquerque: University of New Mexico Press, 1970), I closed by stating:

> Since the end of the Honorable Mission and the restoration of civilian authority there have been isolated and insignificant political ventures by men in uniform, but no widespread movement like that which took form in 1920, matured in 1927, and died in 1931–32. With discipline and the apolitical tradition restored, the Chilean armed forces, particularly the army, remain concerned observers of national politics to this day.

In short, I believed at that time that tradition could be broken despite a body of "evidence" to the contrary.

Chilean Politics, 1920–1931 chronicled a brief period in Chilean history during which there developed a situation apparently uncharacteristic of that country's history, politics, and civil-military relations. But that situation always seemed to me to be but a segment of a greater history, a history beginning with the attainment of independence and continuing long past 1931. I decided, therefore, to undertake a more far-reaching treatment of Chilean civil-military relations.

The present book was begun before the accepted variables and constants of Chilean civil-military relations broke down in the face of recent developments. It began as an attempt to describe and interpret historical relations between state, nation, and society—and their components—and the armed forces, and to indicate the significance of Chile's confrontation with Marxism in its manifestation as a legitimately and constitutionally conceived expression of that state, nation, and society. Further, this book was designed to set forth possible alternatives to the essential Chilean civil-military relationship—military obedience to civilian authority—alternatives made possible, if not probable, by the political rise of Marxism. One of the possible alternatives included in the original conception was indeed the assumption of political power by the armed forces.

The possibility, the probability, then the golpe itself did not change to the slightest degree my interpretations of the 160 years of Chilean civil-military relations preceding the Allende regime. The golpe did make it vividly apparent, though, that the study of civil-military relations in Chile and Latin America (and elsewhere, for that matter) has a fruitful future because of the intricacies, exceptions, and contradictions involved.

In these essays I have emphasized relations of the Chilean armed forces with state, nation, and society, but I should point out that I consider the state, its components, and the nation to be especially significant. Therefore, I have endeavored both to describe and to interpret those characteristics of the state, especially the political system, which affect its relations with the military. I have also attempted to describe and interpret the military's own views of nation and society where such views have affected relations. Obviously the army receives more attention than the other branches of the military because of its size and greater propensity for political action.

These essays vary in the way they deal with the subject. Some are primarily interpretive; others are more descriptive and narrative, but include interpretive passages. There is, I believe, a need for both: for descriptive essays because there is no full-length study of the subject, and for interpretive discussions because some aspects already studied by Chileans and others need reexamination and reevaluation.

There are three parts to the study; each begins with an overview followed by three chapters on specific topics or themes. By using this method, I believe, I have been able to establish frameworks within which civil-military relations during different stages of Chilean history can be discussed, interpreted, and evaluated. These frameworks include the military's historical role and professional development; the incidence and characteristics of military political action;

reasons for military inaction and disinterest; military attitudes toward the state, the nation, and the society of which the military is a part or subsystem; and the forces that bind or unbind civilian and military institutions.

Part I is devoted to the nineteenth century until 1891. It was during those years that Chile established an enviable record among Latin American countries for a harmonious civil-military relationship and role definition. It was the essential relationship of those years that conditioned historians and others, I believe, to consider the 1920–31 situation as uncharacteristic of Chile. Certain qualities of nineteenth-century relations, however, either underwent change or ceased to be applicable, and these are pointed out both in the later stages of part I and at the beginning of part II.

Part II is concerned both with the confrontation of a professionalizing army with a stagnating society and polity, and with the resultant inversion of relations. It was during the years 1891–1931 that the military, especially the army, began to act as a professional group. The strains of professional development began to show as army officers began to question the social, political, and economic status quo and their own situation with respect to the country around them: Whom did they represent? Were they a part of Chilean society or a separate entity? Was their loyalty to a specific administration, a political system, the greater interests of the nation, a segment of society, or society as a whole? The various ways in which the military responded to these questions made for dramatic times in Chile.

Part III deals with the reestablishment of civil-military tradition and normalcy in a modern context, showing how out of the chaotic 1931–32 debacle civilians emerged triumphant as they had done a century before. It is at this point in the study that the reader may begin to see points of comparison in the history of Chilean civil-military relations. Indeed, on more than one occasion I asked myself about cycles, constants, and variables. Was the revived political party system of the years after 1932 simply a modern version of the Basque-Castilian aristocracy—a modernized form of oligarchy? Was the restoration of military subservience to civilian rule after 1932 based on essentially the same things that it was based on in the 1830s? Was the breakdown of civil-military relations between 1970 and 1973 comparable to what occurred between 1920 and 1924? The questions were numerous, the answers never totally satisfactory; these essays may in the end raise more questions than they answer. There is still room for much speculation on the subject, and I hope this book will encourage scholars to reexamine Chilean civil-military relations in greater depth.

For Chile may now be entering "part IV" of its civil-military history. Various writers have posited that the age of liberal democracy, whatever its achievements or shortcomings, may have ended for Brazil in 1964 and Peru in 1968 because of military assumption of political leadership. May this also obtain for Chile because of what happened in 1973? I believe these essays may offer some points of departure for continued study of the subject.

PART I: The Nineteenth Century

1

The Army and the Autocratic Republic: An Overview

Civil-military relations in Chile have been characterized by civilian control of the armed forces throughout the republican period, with only two exceptions. Between independence and 1831 the army played a leading political role and was responsible—at times solely so—for the creation and destruction of government. One hundred years later, in the political crisis of 1924, the military—this time all the armed forces rather than just the army—assumed responsibility for conduct of national affairs. But between 1831 and 1924 Chile established an enviable record among Latin American states with regard to military obedience to civilian authority.

Like her Spanish South American neighbors, Chile inherited her army from the early nineteenth-century independence campaigns and witnessed unbridled military political action in the wake of those campaigns. But there the similarity between Chile and her sister republics ended. For by the 1830s Chile's army had been restricted to functions strictly concerned with the "military imperative,"[1] which might better be called the "external imperative." Even when the Chilean military was used in the years after 1830 to assure order within Chile—thus fulfilling the "civil" or "internal" imperative—it did so for, never against, the state.

In this chapter we shall explore the nineteenth-century Chilean need for an army which would be capable of fulfilling the military imperative, but which, after 1830, was not to engage in the civil imperative in the same way that armies in other Latin American countries did. Alone among Latin American republics of the past

3

century, Chile possessed a truly functional army and a civilian political system capable of containing it as such.

We will discuss here the justifiable existence in South American countries of a military organization for the maintenance of national security. Another important matter is the presence of specific conditions or factors which collectively enabled Chile to avoid the civil-military tragedies so prevalent throughout the Spanish-speaking portion of South America. For most of the nineteenth century, whether Conservatives or Liberals managed national affairs in Chile, they did so within the structural framework of the "Autocratic Republic." We will use this same structural framework to describe and explain civil-military relations in the four chapters constituting part I of this study.

On Armies and War in Nineteenth-Century South America: The External Imperative[2]

Latin American armies were not involved in the kinds of dynastic struggles which historically lent weight in Europe to the idea that armies should exist.[3] In South America, however, armies did exist for the purpose of assuring territorial integrity at a time when diplomacy (when used) could not.

When Argentina, Brazil, Bolivia, Chile, Peru, Colombia, Ecuador, Venezuela, Paraguay, and Uruguay became sovereign states, their frontiers were uncertain. Boundaries were marked poorly during the colonial period, and not for the purpose of delineating zones of true sovereignty. Frontiers were shifted in the eighteenth century primarily to provide for better colonial administration, and it is significant that the major international armed conflicts in South America have occurred where old borders of colonial origin were contested.[4] In most cases the disputants claimed territory once governed or administered from their capital.[5] In two cases there was real fear that national territory might be gobbled up and governments overthrown by powerful neighbors with territorial designs or diplomatic and economic interests.[6]

Hence governments in Santiago and La Paz laid claim to the wastes of the Atacama, where once Diego de Almagro searched in vain for another Peru; and late in the nineteenth century Peru was sucked into the Bolivian-Chilean conflict by virtue of a secret treaty. A half-century later La Paz and Asunción contested possession of the Chaco, the heartland of southern South America.

Earlier in the century fear of encroachment, violations of sovereignty, concern over balance of power, and outright fear for survival led both Chile and Paraguay into wars against unfavorable odds. When the smoke cleared from the field at Yungay in 1839, Chile had bested Peru and Bolivia—only to have to fight again forty years later. Paraguay was less fortunate, for in the War of the Triple Alliance (1864–70) it was crippled beyond recovery. Both Paraguay and Chile were, nevertheless, militarized by their nineteenth-century experiences. Chileans later fought the same foes; Paraguayans would officially answer the call to arms again in the Chaco in 1932, this time not against the Empire of Brazil and the Argentine Confederation as in 1864, but against hapless Bolivia.

Far to the north of those heartland and Andean-coastal rivalries, another set of postindependence rivalries developed, leading to military conflict. In the twilight years of the Spanish American Empire, Madrid placed the Kingdom of Quito under the jurisdiction of the Viceroyalty of New Granada. Like Bolivia under the Viceroyalty of La Plata in the eighteenth century, Ecuador was thus placed under new and alien guidance. In the postindependence years borders were new, claims uncertain, and force the ultimate arbiter. The history of Ecuador since independence is, in part, a history of shame, defeat, and desperate struggle to hold onto a steadily decreasing share of continental territory.[7] Colombia and Peru—itself a loser twice over—are historically the predators. Only Venezuela of all the South American countries has not engaged in a major international conflict since independence.

There were, then, three interlocking zones of conflict, war, and territorial adjustment born in colonial times and only settled long after independence. The heartland zone included at one time or another Argentina, Brazil, Paraguay, and Uruguay; it consisted of two "great powers" and two buffers. The Pacific-Andean zone comprised Chile, the great power; Bolivia, a heartland buffer after loss of Pacific provinces in 1880; Argentina, Chile's trans-Andean rival; and Peru, the anomaly, the would-be great power. Finally, the Amazon Basin zone has consisted of Brazil, Venezuela, the buffers Ecuador and Bolivia, and the regional powers Peru and Colombia. Chilean foreign policy priorities involved the Santiago government in all these zones of conflict; militarily, however, Chile was active only in the Pacific-Andean area.

Situated on the western slopes of the Andean range, Chile became involved in two major territorial controversies in the nineteenth century, each indicating the need for an army for possible fulfillment of the external military imperative. Defense was desirable, too, for the frontier area which divided the country between Concepción and Valdivia to the south, on either side of which Araucanians and other tribes proved a menace to the Euro-American Chilean nation. The country's long coastline led the government to support and maintain a navy and a coastal defense system.

Chile contested her Andean frontier with Argentina throughout the nineteenth century (though no war ensued), and, as we will see, quarreled with Peru over borders for thirty years into this century. Military strategy was geared toward hostilities with Argentina until about 1910 and toward war with Peru until 1930 (and still is, for that matter). To the north lay Bolivia, whose western province of Antofagasta was Chile's northern frontier until 1880, and Peru, until the same year the power of the Pacific coast.

Potentially hostile neighbors to the north and east, savages to the south, and vast stretches of Pacific coast posed real threats. Like her sister South American states, Chile resorted to force to assert sovereignty and acquire that which she considered hers. Territorial designs in South America arising out of poorly defined frontiers suggest the value placed on territory. National values vary at different chronological points, but they have consistently been bound to economic and commercial desires and necessities. In this sense, Chile and South America differ little from any other part of the world.

"Argentina has no borders but the Andes in the west and the sea in the south," claimed those who participated in and supported the 1878–79 Conquest of the Desert, during which the Pampa Indians ceased to be a barrier to Argentine expansion. The Brazilian rubber boom and access to the cacao and rubber of the Andean watershed motivated Colombian and Peruvian seizure of Ecuadoran lands in the nineteenth and twentieth centuries; even during World War II, Peru fought for borderlands with Ecuador! Bolivia's own desires for access to the Atlantic Ocean and for the petroleum rumored to be found in the Chaco propelled that country into war with Paraguay from 1932 to 1936, forcing the latter to fight for its existence a second time.

Nitrates and copper fell to the victor in the War of the Pacific. Land, forests, river routes to the outside world, access to the sea, rubber, cacao, minerals, and hydrocarbons have meant much to the countries of South America. Military force assured possession of these riches between independence and World War II; lack of force precluded their exploitation.

It is a popular misconception that there has been a low incidence of war in Latin America. Every war causes untold grief, suffering, and loss, and what seems a minor war to today's world powers, because of its limited or negligible impact on world affairs, can be devastating to those involved. The comic-opera coverage of the "Soccer War" between El Salvador and Honduras in 1969 may have been the only way for journalists to gain column inches in reporting that conflict. The idea of P-51 Mustangs dueling in the skies above those two tiny countries may seem exotic to the impartial or vicarious observer, but not to the pilots or to those on the ground below. The duels of the ironclads of Chile and Peru in the 1880s titillate naval warfare buffs and lead to comparisons with the *Monitor* and the *Merrimac*. But those who died off the coast of the Atacama are national heroes. By world standards, therefore, past wars in Latin America may not seem important or serious, but by the standards of those involved they are major historical confrontations which sealed destinies.

Mobilization, transport, supply, equipment, and loss of life cost Chile dearly in the nineteenth century. In the years 1810–24, 1836–39, and 1879–84 Chileans were a people at war, or geared for it, because of international problems—independence and its maintenance, as well as conflicts with Bolivia and Peru. From roughly 1850 to 1885 Chilean forces struggled along both sides of the southern frontier zone, gradually pushing it inward at the expense of the hostile Indians. In 1891 the country was convulsed by a civil war, which, if not comparable in length to the American Civil War, was nevertheless a bloody, truncated political and economic catharsis.

Superficially, Chile differs but little from its neighbors with regard to the postindependence military presence. The army helped to build the nation, expand it manifest destiny–style, and "bind it together"—so the victors would say—in times of civil discord. Whereas civilians were often beholden to the military for political power in South American countries during the nineteenth century, civilians in Chile maintained a firm grip on the military for three-quarters of the century. Historians do not dispute this fact, but it is not the truism it appears to be. Many factors were responsible for Chile's civil-military relationship, and now we turn to them.

In probable order of importance, these factors are: a fusion of civil and military leadership in the form of the Basque-Castilian oligarchy that dominated Chilean government and politics for ninety years (1830–1920); the peculiarities of Chilean demography, ethnic composition, and geopolitics which made Chile expand in an orderly fashion; a highly developed sense of nationalism, bordering on chauvinism and xenophobia, shared by the civilian and military sectors; a competent, responsible, and responsive governing class, the Basque-Castilian aristocracy itself;[8] a docile, subservient lower class; a national sense of mission; and a cumulative reverence, respect, and appreciation for the services rendered by the military. In addition, a disgust for military meddling in civilian affairs developed after the 1823–31 period of political turbulence. Let us examine these forces, which were conducive to civilian control of the military, Chilean style.

Military Subservience in Chile: The Basque-Castilian Oligarchy[9]

It has been written that in France, prior to the disaster of 1871, military and civilian leaders came from the same class and consequently both represented the interests of that class.[10] In nineteenth-century Chile, as in other neocolonial Latin American republics, this was also the case. An elite social group, the Basque-Castilian aristocracy, held a fast grip on government and politics after 1830 and on land and business throughout the century. By means of intermarriage, the aristocrats governed the nation as an oligarchy through a succession of elected chief executives and national congresses, beginning as early as 1831.

There are only two exceptions to the dominance of this group, whose unbroken control was unprecedented in republican Latin America. For ten years, from 1851 to 1861, Manuel Montt Torres, of Catalan ancestry, was president; but even he was elevated to that position by the Basque-Castilian clique. And in 1891 the incumbent member of that clique, José Manuel Balmaceda, was unseated in a civil war which in one sense was but a struggle within his own peer group.

The Basque-Castilian aristocracy included a majority of the great landlords of the Central Valley, many of whom were also active in commercial affairs. Thus the government of Chile was under the control of an extended sociocultural family which also controlled major activities in mining and agribusiness.

So, too, did the Basque-Castilian elite influence military affairs. Evidence of their influence—which should not be taken to indicate total civil-military fusion—can be seen during the first twenty years of nineteenth-century Chilean political normalcy. Generals Joaquín Prieto Vial and Manuel Bulnes Prieto governed Chile for two successive five-year presidential terms each (1831–41, 1841–51). Prieto was the Conservative military leader responsible for the smashing of Liberal forces in the important battle of Lircay (1830). Bulnes was the military hero of the 1836–39 war against Peru and Bolivia. Significantly, he was also Prieto's nephew. Prieto and Bulnes personified Basque-Castilian civil-military fusion and political conniv-ance. They established a pattern of executive strength, civilian rule, and military subservience to both. Prieto, the hero of a civil conflict, and Bulnes, hero of an international conflict, were responsible for the elevation of the officer class to a position of high esteem in the nineteenth century. Their own prestige and the ability of their advisers and confidants established the Basque-Castilian aristocracy as Chile's ruling class and made oligarchic civilian supremacy over the military the rule, not the exception, in nineteenth-century Chile.

Until 1920 this Basque-Castilian elite ran Chilean affairs, with Montt the only real exception. As noted, Montt can be considered a member of the elite; he was related by marriage to the elite, and his elevation to the presidency came about because he was acceptable to the ruling class. Almost every Chilean president was related (if only by marriage) to at least one other chief executive until the 1920 election of Arturo Alessandri Palma, whose Italian ancestry set him apart like a proverbial sore thumb from his predecessors in La Moneda, the presidential palace. Figure 1 illustrates Chile's nineteenth-century "presidential genealogy."

Civil-military fusion and class identity within that fusion both weakened considerably between 1891 and 1920. For some of the same reasons—and for other reasons—so did military submission to civil authority. The erosion process which broke apart the fusion, altered

10

FIGURE 1.
The Chilean Presidential Families, 1831-1920

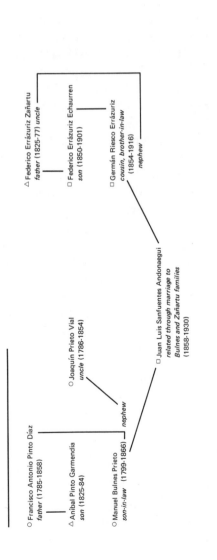

○ Bernardo O'Higgins y Riquelme (1778-1842)

○ Ramón Freire y Serrano (1787-1851)

○ Francisco Antonio Pinto Díaz
father (1785-1858)

△ Aníbal Pinto Garmendia
son (1825-84)

○ Joaquín Prieto Vial
uncle (1786-1854)

○ Manuel Bulnes Prieto (1799-1866)
son-in-law   nephew

□ Juan Luis Sanfuentes Andonaegui
related through marriage to
Bulnes and Zañartu families
(1858-1930)

△ Federico Errázuriz Zañartu
father (1825-77) uncle

□ Federico Errázuriz Echaurren
son (1850-1901)

□ Germán Riesco Errázuriz
cousin, brother-in-law
(1854-1916)
nephew

○ Manuel Montt Torres
father (1809-80)
distant relative
through Pérez-Montt
family

□ Pedro Montt Montt
son (1848-1910)

○ José Joaquín Pérez Mascayano
distant relative (1800-1889)

□ Ramón Barros Luco
brother, Nicolás m. Teresa
Pérez Flores (1835-1919)

□ Jorge Montt Álvarez
distant relative through
Pérez-Montt and Montt-
Goyenechea families
(1845-1922)

△ Domingo Santa María González
children, siblings married
into branches of various
presidential families
(1825-89)

□ José Manuel Balmaceda
no close blood ties
(1840-91)

○ Penquista-South Central Valley Dynasty—Independence Generation
△ Postindependence Generation
□ Midcentury Generation

class identity, and challenged civil authority over the military is best considered in another context, and we will reserve it for pages to come.

Military Subservience in Chile: Geopolitical and Demographic Considerations[11]

At the beginning of the nineteenth century, Chile was roughly one-third its present size.[12] The population clustered in the Central Valley, was homogeneous by Latin American standards, Spanish speaking, with mestizo and European elements and little African or Oriental mix. Through the century such relative homogeneity helped create a myth of racial and cultural superiority. The Santiago area was the core of the geographic and demographic area known as Chile. Other population clusters or urban areas were politically and economically influential only in a secondary capacity.

Concepción, to the south, was a frontier city, and until the last quarter of the century, Penquistas (a name derived from Penco, the original site of the Spanish settlement there) lived apprehensively, one eye on the Araucanian Indians to the south and the other on politicians and businessmen up north in Santiago. Farther south, on the other flank of Indian Chile, tiny Valdivia was merely a frontier village. La Serena, in the northern end of the central valley, was neither big enough nor the center of enough wealth or commercial activity to stand as a rival to the capital. Copiapó, on the southern fringe of the Atacama Desert, was, like Valdivia, a village. Valparaíso, perched between the coastal hills and the sea, just barely rivaled Santiago in wealth and population. Valparaíso was (and still is) Chile's main seaport, but it was not a political center above the provincial level. The fact that the Central Valley landlords had business interests in common with their *porteño* brethren and the fact that Valparaíso was quite close to the capital tended to weld the two centers together. When commercial interests centered in Valparaíso and Santiago clashed with governmental policy, however, as they did in 1891, Chilean political stability yielded.

The vast majority of Chileans, then, lived in a seven-hundred-mile-long valley in a national territory less than one hundred and fifty miles wide. The easily traversible valley floor was no impediment to transport or communications, even by early nineteenth-century conveyance. There were many passes though the hills along the coast. Even the southern forests were not difficult to penetrate, except those of the coastal foothills and the Andes, where indigenous hostiles lived.

The Andes and the Pacific were frontiers as effective as the borders of any other South American republic. Until the final destruction of Araucania and the northern movement of the 1880s, the Bío-Bío River south of Concepción and the fringes of the Atacama Desert commencing around Copiapó were also effective natural limits for Chile. Thus national loyalties were influenced by centripetal forces and not by the centrifugal provincialism rampant in Argentina and Brazil.[13] The concepts of frontier and boundary were firmer in Chile than in Argentina, Peru, Bolivia, or Paraguay in the early part of the century. Chile, in short, was more a nation—an identifiable cultural and ethnic aggregation—than its neighbors were. This did not obviate the need for organized armed force; it increased and propitiated it. The northern and southern frontiers and the coastline had to be defended, and the Andes bore watching, for through their passes had marched the Argentine-Chilean liberation army of 1817.

One look at a map of Chile in 1830 in comparison with a 1930 map indicates the dramatic change in the nation's boundaries. Lands were *claimed* to the north and south early in the century, but forceful expansion ultimately gave the republic a *hold* on the Strait of Magellan and Patagonian territory, and on the wealth of Antofagasta, Tarapacá, and Arica. Losses by Araucanians, Argentines, Bolivians, and Peruvians were gains for Chileans, and those "expanding frontier" gains assured by force of arms must be considered contributory to the overall political, social, and economic development of Chile.

Origins of Chilean Nationalism: Civil-Military Commonality

The armed forces maintained order within the heartland after 1830, but not through oppression, for by that time the maintenance of order was not so difficult as to make harsh measures and widespread violence necessary. One reason for this is the early development of nationalistic feeling.

Nationalism in Chile became important first in the independence period, though it is not at all certain that it was a factor in the winning of independence. At that time it meant little more than a spirit of togetherness, a belief in the geographic and cartographic entity as a homeland rather than just a cultural extension of Spain. Nationalism also meant a hostility toward those who would try to limit or deny the existence of Chile and its development. For many Chileans at the end of the eighteenth and beginning of the nineteenth centuries, Spain was anathema. Many were Basques, a number Navarrese, and some really thought of themselves as Castilians, not Spaniards. To Basques and Navarrese, to Catalans and Asturians, Spain was an unpleasant memory or image, although only one-third of the Chilean elite was ever committed to severing ties. [14]

Dislike for outsiders—notably for the Peruvian merchants and officials who operated out of Lima and Callao between 1780 and 1820—was widespread. It took the form of commercial rivalry, chafing at restrictions set down by the Hapsburgs and Bourbons and their colonial officials, and profound shock at the savage behavior of Spanish military officials in the Spanish reconquest of 1814–17. [15]

The Republic of Chile was born after the second expulsion of the Spaniards (1817–18), when the Army of the Andes surged through the Andean passes to do battle at Chacabuco and then at Maipú. The last Spanish forces were not dislodged from republican territory until 1823, however. In the meantime, Peru—imperial Spain's last bastion —posed a threat to the new nation's very existence.

José de San Martín, soon to be the Protector of Peru, and Bernardo O'Higgins, the Supreme Director of Chile, knew that Spanish power on the Pacific Coast had to be eliminated if Chile were to survive. They and their aides, the new Chilean government, and the wealthy members of the Central Valley aristocracy devoted much effort between 1817 and 1820 to the liberation of Peru. As institutions and national organization were established and internal order maintained—no small tasks—anti-Peruvian spirit developed throughout the country.

Even after Peru was wrested from Spanish control, Chileans still could not rest easy. Small, thinly populated, comparatively poor, the Republic of Chile might have been easy prey for the leaders of the new Andean nation to the north. Memories of viceregal domination died slowly in Santiago, Valparaíso, and Concepción. Furthermore, O'Higgins fell from power in 1823, before all of Peru was free, and for a decade at least O'Higginista plots emanated from Lima.

The alleged desire of Marshal Andrés de Santa Cruz y Calahumana, leader of confederated Peru and Bolivia (1833–39), to absorb Chile in his sphere led to war in 1836. The defeat of the Confederation in 1839 only spurred Chilean hostility toward Peru. By that time Chile, in the firm grip of the Basque-Castilian aristocracy, had emerged as a commercial power in South America. Chilean leaders were loath to cede their hegemony to Peru. Furthermore, the vicissitudes of postindependence Peruvian and Bolivian governments led the Santiago regime to consider Chile superior to the Andean countries. The fact that Peru and Bolivia were both heavily Indian in ethnic composition, whereas Chile was mestizo-European, contributed to the Chilean myth of racial and cultural superiority, which has never vanished.

To the east the Argentine Confederation sank further into the barbarism so colorfully described by Esteban Echeverría, Domingo F. Sarmiento, and others. Concurrently Chile became a haven for Argentine exiles, and the plight of these unwilling travelers confirmed Chileans' belief in their own good fortune.

Chilean hostility toward neighboring Argentina, Bolivia, and Peru can best be understood from the point of view of a diplomatic historian, such as Burr, examining the decades 1850–90. During those forty years Chilean diplomacy was alternately designed to protect the nation's interests in the Atacama and to assure its frontiers in the Andes and in Patagonia where it bordered Argentina. Chilean statesmen and ministers therefore had to balance the Andean powers against Argentina, a process which made them wary of contiguous countries.

But Chilean nationalism implies more than the xenophobic tendencies of the past century. The internal development of central Chile made possible by able leadership and lack of topographic or ethnic barriers was something in which articulate Chileans took pride. In addition, Chile's regulated, orderly political process, while by no means free from arbitrariness and highhanded action, was remarkable in comparison to Argentina's prior to 1862, Peru's—with the exception of the years 1845–62—and Bolivia's during the entire period since independence.

Military might allegedly kept Chile from being absorbed by the Andean Confederacy, saved it from disgrace at the hands of the Spanish Pacific fleet in 1864–66, enabled it to defeat Peru and Bolivia in 1879–84, helped it to pacify and settle Araucania, and met all

Argentine Patagonian challenges. As a result, the national spirit and identity were closely linked to the civilian-controlled army and navy.

Chile's Competent Ruling Class: A Further Note on Oligarchy

The competence of the civilian elite in nineteenth-century Chile was not the result of military subservience but a cause of it. To make the latter responsible for the former is to express an untenable value judgment resulting from assumptions about norms of civilian-military relationships that are not applicable in a nineteenth-century Latin American context.[16]

The Chilean Constitution of 1833; the twenty-year control over the executive branch of government by the Concepción-based, Santiago-supported Prieto-Bulnes machine (1831–51); the superb management of financial and state affairs by Diego Portales (1831–37); the successful conduct of national affairs by successive regimes after 1851—these examples of smooth civil government provided few pretexts for action by the military. Diplomacy, commercial activities, agriculture, mining, and cultural development all have rich histories in the years 1831–91. Most of the chief executives during this period were better than average administrators. Flexibility rather than dogmatism was the rule for a protective economic policy which served the interests of most of the ruling class.

It may be that the absence of doctrinaire political and economic thought from elite circles helped to preclude civil-military conflict; it certainly reduced conflict within the civilian sphere until mid century.[17] Near the end of the decade 1851–61, however, what we can call political parties began to form. These parties reflected developing clashes over the form of the national government more than the emergence of firmly delineated class or interest groups or economic issues. They were parties, in other words, but parties within the elite. That elite still enveloped the military, which persisted in its apolitical stance. "Political" clashes, then, did not involve a challenge to the oligarchic control of the national administration, and because of this the aristocracy's ability to govern was not subverted. Indeed, ability continued to mark civilian government after 1851. The cumulative effect of decade upon decade of able, responsible government, responsive to ruling-class interests made this tradition increasingly stronger, so that by 1891 the possibility of overt military intervention was virtually nonexistent.

The absence of doctrinaire politics until quite late in the century does not signify an absence of hard issues. From mid century to 1891, a consistent campaign was waged to circumscribe the powers of the executive branch. Twice, in 1851 and in 1859, the opposition involved itself in rebellions against the constituted authority; on both occasions the prime issue was executive prerogatives in the designation of a successor. In 1863 the Radical Party was organized for the purpose of whittling away at existing executive power and reducing the influence of the Church. The Radicals had no monopoly on the desire to reduce presidential power during the second half of the century. A fusion coalition (La Fusión) of ultramontanist Conservatives and parliamentarist Liberals—the extremes of the political spectrum—joined forces in Congress to balance executive powers.

The rise of the coal, copper, and nitrate mining industry helped to produce a new protoaristocracy in mid-nineteenth-century Chile, and complicated the developing political issues. But although specific economic issues might divide the ruling elite, that elite absorbed new wealth readily. Wealth itself, marriage, or sheer prestige in conjunction with financial success proved sufficient for entrance to Chilean high society, and high society was composed largely of the ruling class in the Central Valley. Because absorption rather than exclusion was the rule, a steady flow of new talent helped to determine Chile's future. This continued through the post-1861 administrations of José Joaquín Pérez (1861–71), Aníbal Pinto Garmendia (1871–76), Federico Errázuriz Zañartu (1876–81), Domingo Santa María González (1881–86), and José Manuel Balmaceda (1886–91).

The Lower Classes: Subservient and Quiescent

There was little violence among the populace in nineteenth-century Chile. Not until the first two decades of this century were the lower classes sufficiently urbanized or mobilized to pose any threat of violence to the constituted order. Conservative writers usually portray agrarian Chile as bucolic, self-contained, and removed from political issues; and there were few social issues. The fear of Araucanian hostiles in sparsely settled areas did much to unite society. Writers also note the discipline of the Chilean lower classes, their sobriety (these writers make no mention of wine consumption!), and the "dignity of work." Marxist Chilean historiography, however, has presented the Chilean peasant and later the working-class Chilean as oppressed and subjugated by the landlords. Both these views are too biased and subjective to be acceptable.

Chilean peasants of the nineteenth century were apolitical; whether because of ineligibility or apathy, the vast majority did not vote or render opinions on national issues. When they did vote—after property qualifications were dropped and literacy qualifications relaxed—they voted as they were told. (This became more significant politically as the nineteenth century moved toward the clash of 1891.) The apolitical existence of the peasants did mean that they accepted their lot—if for no other reason, because they knew no other way of life. The paternalistic, seigneurial, manorial style of life (usually incorrectly termed "feudal") in Chile's Central Valley tended to perpetuate the apolitical, obedient nature of the masses. And leftist writers have held that this system worked to the detriment of the peasant.[18] Held in thrall by the landlord, the Chilean peasant worked his life away in the fields, ignorant of his potential, simply trusting or fearing his mayordomo and *patrón*.

Whatever the real reasons—racial homogeneity, ignorance, lack of issues, electoral exclusivism—the peasant provided no threat to the oligarchy ruling from Santiago or to the aristocracy clustered about Concepción and Valparaíso. The peasants had no political advocate until the twentieth century, and thus they went unpoliticized. The same was true of other workers, or *rotos* ("broken" or "cut loose" from agrarian paternalism), until quite late in the century. Copper, coal, and nitrate miners, lighter crews, dock workers, and workers in warehouses, small factories, railroads, wholesale commercial houses, and urban service positions were only rudimentarily organized by syndicate leaders until the 1910s. Up to that time, jobs depended on one's willingness and ability to endure harsh working conditions. In the copper and coal pits and tunnels, and in the nitrate fields, lower-class Chileans toiled long hours for low pay. They lived in hovels and spent their meager earnings at stores where prices were high and credit was an enslaving device. But they earned money, which they found far preferable to earning the right to cultivate a strip of land in return for labor on one of the fundos, the large estates in the Central Valley.

It is generally agreed that labor in the mines or on the docks or jobs in the cities transformed the peasant into a conscious citizen, giving him an awareness of his world and ultimately a sense of identity. Such labor also ruptured the paternalistic relationships of the old Chile. In the cities, mines, and nitrate fields and on the docks, individualism and harsh conditions were the only reality. This urbanization did not result in any remedial, progressive legislation on the part of the government, however, nor did it make organized labor politically significant during the nineteenth century.

National Consciousness: A Sense of Mission

Chilean workers felt a strong national consciousness. Far up in the nitrate fields, and later in the northern copper mines, whenever miners got out of hand, there was always the threat of imported Bolivian labor. Chile's enemies were the worker's enemies, too, for economic rivalries affected the worker's livelihood.

Some Chileans regard themselves as the British of South America; most are deeply proud of their historical and political legacy. Statements about the country's character that sound like introductory material for a travel folder are nevertheless true. Chileans are not reluctant to discuss the "psychological inadequacies" and "political immaturity" of Argentines—and Argentines, of course, regard the Chileans as "undernourished," "dull," and uncultured. The view from Peru is much the same. Chileans offer comments freely about Andean "political passions" and the "inability of Bolivians and Peruvians to govern themselves." The fact remains that "practical," "plodding" (in relative terms, of course) Chileans made the Atacama produce copper and nitrates for the world, populated and developed much of Argentina's far south, and provided ships passing through the Strait of Magellan with a base for supply and repair. Chileans have no sense of national guilt. From the 1830s on, Chilean leaders did not doubt that their country should be the most powerful on the Pacific side of the Andes. And Chile led through military force when reason could not prevail. It is not by chance that the legend on the national escutcheon reads *"por la razón o la fuerza"* ("by reason or force").

The Chilean Army played an important role as guarantor of

sovereignty and provider of territory through conquest. Its mission
was to defend, and to attack and conquer when it had to. It fulfilled its
mission in the external imperative sense. That sense of mission, with a
heavy admixture of nationalism, patriotism, distrust of adjacent states,
and confidence in civilian political institutions, maintained the army
in a state of respectful obedience, with minor exceptions, in the
nineteenth century after 1830.

We must now consider the disgust of Chilean leaders at the
national political scene between 1823 and 1830, a scene dominated by
men in uniform. Between the fall of Bernardo O'Higgins in 1823 and
the Battle of Lircay in 1830, Chile showed few signs of achieving the
prerequisites noted above for the civil-military balance she achieved
and maintained during the rest of the nineteenth century. *Because* of
the turbulent 1820s, not despite them, the political system embodied
in the Constitution of 1833 was developed and the army relegated to
its 1831–91 role. In short, the landholders and business and political
leaders of Chile in the late 1820s included a firm antimilitarism in
their thinking on national issues and elaborated upon it so as to
preclude the possibility of, and obviate the necessity for, military
intervention.

2 | The Postindependence Years, 1823–30

Chile underwent thirty separate changes of national administration between January 23, 1823, and April 1, 1830, a period of seven years and two months, or a change of administration on the average of every two and a half months. Military figures held power for most of the period—over four years—and civilians ruled for the remaining three years and two months. Force was the key to political power for politician and general alike. At the beginning of those troubled years, the Chilean Army consisted of the remainders of the expeditionary force assembled for San Martín's assault on Spanish Peru, a force financed and equipped by the Chilean aristocracy and the Buenos Aires government. The expeditionary force achieved no great successes in the Peruvian campaign, and by late 1822 San Martín was no longer the commander in the viceregal core. San Martín yielded to Simón Bolívar, the entire campaign bogged down, and the days of the liberators in Chile consequently were numbered.

By 1823, when O'Higgins fell, the army's thirteen-year history was one of privation, poor organization, inconsistent support, and generally incompetent leadership. Seven years later the situation was worse. There was no tradition of civilian rule to adhere to, few interludes during which officers could be given the rudiments of training, but almost constant military-political action or preparation for it.

Thirty years into the nineteenth century, then, the Chilean Army was in a sorry state. As a military force capable of defending the nation from foreign powers, it was still of questionable value, and it is probably a very good thing that Chileans did not have to make war during the 1820s. As a force capable of maintaining internal order and security, the army was still unquestionably incompetent. In fact, the army was the major cause of political turmoil, making and breaking each government between the fall of O'Higgins in 1823 and the battle of Lircay in 1830.

Origins of El Ejército De Chile, 1810–23: A Modest Beginning[1]

A Chilean army of sorts did exist early in the nineteenth century, since the Cabildo Abierto in Santiago created a volunteer militia of 630 men and officers in 1810. Despite fears that the viceroy in Lima would send a restoration force (or punitive expedition), popular opinion was not strongly in favor of creating a militia at that time. Few funds were immediately available to support a standing army or to finance a navy, so Chile's first defense system was based primarily on coastal fortifications manned and backed by volunteers. The Cabildo Abierto, however, with an eye to the future, did enter into negotiations for the purchase of 2,000 uniforms, 2,000 sabers, 10,000 rifles, and 10,000 braces of pistols. The engineer Juan MacKenna drew up plans for new fortification of Valparaíso, Talcahuano, Concepción, and Coquimbo and proposed the founding of a school to train military officers. The Cabildo Abierto adopted his proposals, but little headway was made toward their implementation before the Chilean reconquest campaign was launched from Lima. When Spanish troops came again to Chile, popular support for a militia grew.

Molding a cohesive, competent officer class capable of national defense is never an easy task where resources are lacking and where training consists at best of periodic paramilitary instruction. During the Patria Vieja (the term applied to Chile between the independence movement of September 1810, and the Spanish reconquest in 1814), there was no shortage of officer volunteers, but few effective measures were taken to raise funds for the military or to sign volunteer soldiers.

Between 1810 and 1814, young men of distinguished families eagerly sought commissions, and many received them despite their lack of previous experience or qualifications for command positions. Family name, connections—in short, influence—were the best means of obtaining a commission. As a result, some entirely incompetent persons were placed in command positions while men with some training, but without connections, served as subalterns. O'Higgins, who proved to be a better-than-average tactician and strategist, served under a known incompetent in the early days of the Patria Vieja.

At the same time, those without distinguished ancestry or connections were understandably less than enthusiastic about volunteering for rank-and-file duty in an army so poorly equipped, organized, and commanded. Uniforms and equipment were in bad condition, abuses were frequent, and pay was low and irregular. Forced conscription—*la leva*—did not endear the military to Chilean commoners. Further, the military's financial woes were public knowledge, and the government's resort to tobacco and playing-card taxes, reduced salaries in other agencies, and confiscation of merchants' funds were not popular. Less than six months after the official founding of the militia, the Chilean armed forces began the succession of coups that culminated at Lircay. Lieutenant Colonel Tomás de Figueroa pronounced against the government in March 1811, surrendered on April 1, and went unpunished. Six months later José Miguel Carrera overthrew the government and created a new *junta de gobierno*. On November 25, 1811, Carrera destroyed his own creation by surrounding the government house with infantry and artillery. Carrera's *golpes* resulted in the formation of a triumvirate consisting of himself representing Santiago, Gaspar Marín from Coquimbo, and O'Higgins from Concepción. Within a week Carrera was in sole control of the government.

Carrera's power grab did not meet with popular approval; that is to say, it did not have the support of the politically articulate. Nevertheless, Carrera, those he commanded in the army, and his few civilian supporters were the most active participants in Chilean politics between 1810 and 1814. Carrera's failure to solidify political support in Coquimbo and Concepción and the reluctance of O'Higgins to consort with the demagogic Carrera—viewed as a Chilean Jacobin by some historians—resulted in divisions that facilitated the reconquest when General Mariano Ossorio invaded Chile in 1814. Not until 1817 did Chileans and the army reassert their desire for independence. The record of the Chilean Army during the Patria Vieja clearly was not an enviable one.

The story of the independence campaign of 1817–18 has been told over and over, and to chronicle it again here is not our purpose.[2] It was an epic event in national history, and it did restore prestige to men in uniform. The heroism displayed by the commanders and men of the grandiloquently named Army of the Andes at the battles of Chacabuco and Maipú and the other clashes of 1817–18 in the Central Valley gave the army a new purpose and a new strength. From early 1817, when the Army of the Andes invaded the Central Valley from San Martín's Mendoza stronghold, until the eclipse of San Martín in 1822, the Chilean Army was a triumphant and widely praised organization. In embryo it had poured from the Andean passes at Uspallata, Los Patos, and Planchón; it had driven the Spaniards out of the valley, restored independence, and then, with hundreds of Argentine volunteers, embarked on the great task of hastening the end of Spain's power in South America. Finances were now forthcoming, and commanders at last were more experienced. Bernardo O'Higgins saw to that.

Don Bernardo O'Higgins y Riquelme combined several rare talents found in varying degrees in the other Spanish-American leaders of the immediate postindependence period.[3] By virtue of the provisional Constitution of 1818, he was Supreme Director of Chile. A skillful organizer, he was also extremely arbitrary in matters of policy and administration. He had the wisdom to establish a formal training program for army officers. On February 21, 1817, barely a week after the battle of Chacabuco, which gave the Army of the Andes access to Santiago, O'Higgins decreed the establishment of Chile's first military school, the Military Academy, whose purpose it would be to train officers for a standing army.[4] On March 16 he proclaimed that only academy graduates were to be eligible for officer rank. Contemporary French training manuals were used at the academy, and the staff had sole control over the internal organization and administration of the army. Significantly, funds were set aside for scholarships to be given to humble applicants and sons of deceased officers and men. Thus it was possible at this early stage for persons other than aristocrats to become cadets and officers. Because academy staff members had sole responsibility for ordinances, the army was to a degree autonomous from civilian control and responsible for its own governance. By the end of 1817 nearly five thousand men and officers wore the uniform of El Ejército de Chile. An institution was born.

With the exception of activities directed against the few Spanish troops remaining in Chile, notably a royalist contingent on the southern island of Chiloé, Chile's first venture into warfare after 1818 was the aforementioned liberation of Peru. It was a solemn yet festive day when the expedition, some sixty-five hundred strong, sailed from

Valparaíso on August 18, 1820. That unfortunate campaign was a major cause of the Supreme Director's downfall and the reentry of men on horseback (literally, in some instances) into the political arena.

Less than two years after the expedition left Valparaíso, San Martín resigned. Lord Thomas Cochrane, the British "sailor of fortune" who organized the Chilean Navy, returned to Chile, blaming San Martín for failing to liberate all of Peru. Having taxed Chileans heavily to support the expedition, and having proved excessively zealous as a reformer, owing particularly to his 1818 decree abolishing entailed estates (*mayorazgos*)—a decree later rescinded by Congress—O'Higgins also fell from grace. Late in 1822 he yielded to pressure and convened a constituent assembly to write a new constitution. The constitution was never written. In November General Ramón Freire y Serrano, commander of the garrison at Concepción, pronounced against the Santiago government. In so doing, he initiated a period of military intervention that was to end only with the destruction of the army as an interfering force nearly eight years later.

The Army as Political Tool: The Fall of O'Higgins[5]

The downfall of Bernardo O'Higgins is a typical example of the resort by civilians to the threat of armed force to bring about political change. It resembled the many other golpes perpetrated in other new Latin American nations during the first postindependence generation, for in the 1820s Chile was remarkably similar to her sister states with regard to civil-military relations. In 1822–23 political parties were ephemeral, and liberal and conservative appellations signified little. The terms *democracy, republic,* and particularly *independence* were not universally understood. The army, such as it was, did not function as an extension of the state; rather, the state functioned as an extension of those persons, civilian and military, who could muster the armed support to gain power and hold it.

Ramón Freire, by all accounts, was a *distinguido caballero,* a gentleman of distinction. He had served valiantly during the fight for independence in command of a detachment of San Martín's Army of the Andes. It was Freire who had crossed the Andes south of Santiago, successfully engaged a Spanish force near Talca, and then swept up the valley toward the capital. After Chacabuco and Maipú, Freire took command of the Concepción garrison on the southern frontier. He owned land there and had well-placed friends among the Penquista aristocracy.

The southern part of the Central Valley was a depressed area after the expulsion of Spanish troops. Towns had been sacked, fields had been burned repeatedly, and cattle herds thinned during the fighting. The southern economy did not improve markedly by 1822. The export of wheat, the prime source of income for the owners of southern estates, or fundos, was sharply reduced between 1818 and 1822. Most of the export wheat was shipped or carted north to the capital, to be sold there at a higher price or sent to the expeditionary force in Peru. Freire intervened with O'Higgins to place restrictions on wheat exports so that some would be held for sale in Concepción at a price favorable to producers. In September 1822 Freire was given powers to restrict wheat exports from southern Chile, but this did not pacify the southerners. Economic policy was but one edge of their sword of opposition to the central government.

When pressed to promulgate the new constitution in 1822, O'Higgins stubbornly responded by proposing changes that would give Santiago more administrative control over the provinces. Ever protective of their newly won local autonomy, the Penquista oligarchs convinced Freire that O'Higgins had to go. Freire's troops were no better off than southern peasants, and more than once mutiny had become a possibility. When friends warned him of O'Higgins's centralist designs—and reminded him of the Supreme Director's hostility toward *mayorazgo*—he pronounced on November 22. A week later an assembly of notable Penquistas appointed him civil governor of the province. From Santiago O'Higgins dispatched a contingent of troops; then, realizing his weakness in the capital itself, he resigned on January 28, 1823. Freire did not recognize the junta assembled in Santiago to replace O'Higgins, and two months later he entered the capital as provisional supreme director.

The overthrow of O'Higgins, though relatively peaceful, was certainly more than a personal struggle between two generals. Nevertheless, it was achieved through personalistic control of armed force. It was popular at the time in that it had the support of many civilian politicians. While O'Higginistas continually sought a restoration until don Bernardo's death in 1844, their influence dissipated during the 1820s and was minimized by the ascendency of the Portalian clique from 1830 on. The overthrow of O'Higgins reflects the enormous importance of regional interests in providing impetus for action by military leaders. It also foreshadows the impending struggle between what can be termed "centralist" and "federalist" tendencies and their conservative and liberal exponents.

Freire and Pinto: Caudillos and Politicos, 1823–30[6]

Ramón Freire, champion of conservative federalist interests, remained the dominant political figure in Chile from his assumption of the directorship in 1823 until mid 1827. During that period of just over four years he served as provisional supreme director, provisional president, and president on nine separate occasions! His longest period of tenure was nine and one-half months, June 14, 1824, to March 26, 1825; his shortest was a three-week provisional presidency in early 1827.

Chileans are fond of pointing out that their political history has been free from personalism, caudillismo, and militarism. Regardless of the exact definition of such terms, Chilean scholars are reluctant to admit that their country was ever plagued by the same political ills that assumed epidemic proportions in, say, Peru, Bolivia, and Argentina after their independence from Spain. Yet if Freire and General Francisco Antonio Pinto were not caudillos, what were they?

As civilians, both were respected citizens. Both were propertied men, and Pinto was a lawyer by profession. Neither, however, was adept at political leadership. Neither, as a military-political figure, was at all sophisticated in dealing with civilians; neither was a skilled organizer or administrator. Both, on the other hand, commanded personal followings of troops and could count on influential civilian supporters. Both were used by civilians hungry for power or sincerely concerned for their country's existence. And both were called upon repeatedly by civilian leaders to head the government after civilians foundered (Pinto was chief executive three times, for a total of two years and two months). Their comings and goings to and from La Moneda, the presidential palace, punctuated the political life of the 1820s in dramatic fashion.

A detailed chronicle of Chilean politics and civil-military relationships during the years between 1823 and 1831 would be almost indescribably tedious. Several points about this period, however, are important to the theme of our discussion. First is the awesome and continual presence of the military leaders and their allies in power. Second, and interwoven with the first, is the almost slavish civilian reliance on these men as generators or guarantors of order, men who could be trusted, even saviors. Third is the utter failure of the emerging civilian political factions either to inspire confidence or to provide economic and political order. And finally, there is the scandalous (by Chilean standards) behavior of other men in uniform. By examining these points we can see how the experience of the 1820s gave rise to the consensus among political leaders of the post-1830 years that the army should be kept out of political affairs. That consensus is as significant as the other forces, noted in the first chapter, that led to civilian control of the state from 1831 on.

After the 1824 battles of Junín and Ayacucho in Peru, the Spanish presence on the Pacific coast of South America ceased to be the strictly defined raison d'être of the Chilean army. The Bolivarian forces moved into southern Peru and under Sucre marched into Bolivia (originally Alto, or Upper, Peru). By the end of 1826 Spain's power in South America had come to an end. What, then, became the role of the Chilean Army? Quite simply, its role became a political one associated with the "civil imperative." Technically this meant the maintenance of internal order and defense against outside aggression—the preservation of sovereignty.

The only menace to sovereignty from 1826 until 1836 came not from the north but from the south. The Araucanians (a general term applied to Chilean Indians) still posed a barrier to potential southern expansion as they continued their marauding in the southern valley and forest lands. The major southern garrison at Concepción was Chile's northern bulwark against the indigenous hostiles.

But in fact most of the army's activities were of a political nature, and control of the garrisons at Santiago and Concepción was of paramount importance to the determination of national affairs. Freire and Pinto were the two men who more often than not could gain that control.

Ramón Freire y Serrano (1787–1851) was born in Santiago in comfortable surroundings. When the Spanish reconquest stifled rebellion in 1814, Freire was a cavalry captain. He served under San Martín and was responsible for the liberation of Talca in 1817. He went south to Concepción as intendant and military chief in 1818, broke Spanish resistance in the south, and became a popular figure in the process. It was from his southern power base that Freire surged into national prominence as a political leader. Francisco Antonio Pinto Díaz (1785–1858) came from a distinguished Central Valley family. He served the Patria Vieja as emissary to Buenos Aires and London between 1810 and 1817, and returned to serve under San Martín and Bolívar in southern and Upper Peru. He did not become a figure of national significance, though, until he had served as interior and foreign minister, and as intendant of Coquimbo (1824–26). His first experience as a national leader came when he succeeded Freire as chief executive in 1827.

Freire and Pinto were not unlike their counterparts in other Spanish American states. They were influential citizens by birth and connections, patriotic military men by necessity, revolutionaries in the sense that they had fought for their country's existence. Freire and Pinto represented the fusion of the aristocracy and the military at a time when this fusion provided political leadership through use of force. Military men were still heroes, though the aura faded during the 1820s, and decisions affecting all facets of national life had been made by patriotic revolutionary military figures since 1810. So the presence of Freire and Pinto and their followers, both civilian and military, was consistent with Chile's 1810–18 revolutionary heritage.

Although civil-military fusion in Chile became a positive influence on civilian control of government and politics after 1831, it was plainly the decisive negative influence between 1823 and 1830. In a new country like Chile in the 1820s, where only a few solid ideas influence politicians in their efforts to organize, but where liberty, independence, and freedom mean much, politics is often chaotic and government is usually ineffective. Individual thought and collective agreement gradually produce new ideas, and would-be leaders seek ways to put those ideas into action. When new ideas are contrary to prevalent ones, or impinge upon liberties and freedoms recently won, the advocates of those ideas frequently resort to force for the purpose of seizing power, holding it, or turning ideas into policy. Alien political theories and systems, which appeal to new leaders, also contribute to the use of force, for the emulation, adoption, and even adaptation of a nonindigenous ideology or system can prove disastrous and thus necessitate reliance on military might. The naked lust for power also calls for the control of organized (sometimes just barely) force.

In Chile between 1823 and 1830 the development of political ideas, the formation of factions (not yet genuine political parties), the attempts to turn the ideas of a faction into action or policy, the adoption of nonindigenous philosophies, and the lust for power were all dependent on control of, or good relations with, the military.

The Military and Government: Federalism and Centralism, Liberalism and Conservatism[7]

For most of the years between 1823 and 1830, federalism and liberalism were major influences on Chilean political thought and action. In embracing these ideas, Chileans were expressing their distaste for the legacy of centralized rule under Spain—the viceroy in Lima, the captain general in Santiago, and the autocratic behavior of O'Higgins—as well as showing their approval of the United States Constitution. Advocacy of federalism—political rights for the provinces—was not limited to areas removed from Santiago. After the fall of O'Higgins, the province of Santiago itself joined Concepción and Coquimbo in electing a provincial assembly and municipal council, which in turn gave notice that congressional legislation could be scrutinized at the local level. If not approved by representatives from the provinces, it would not be in effect. When Freire, back in power, called for congressional elections in 1825, Coquimbo and Concepción refused to participate. During 1825 and 1826 a national administration was possible only because of Freire's prestige and through the threat of violence; Coquimbo and Concepción remained autonomous within the federal government.

In 1826 Freire marched off to southern Chile, where a few remaining Spanish royalists continued to make trouble. Back in Santiago, a provisional government set about to "federalize" the country through legislation. Provincial assemblies and autonomy were legalized; the government in Santiago functioned, according to law, to conduct foreign policy and to provide for national defense. As a result, the national government was impotent as well as incompetent. The experiment was unsuccessful, and by March 1827 Santiago leaders had begun to lose faith in any system but a centralized one. In 1827 Freire resigned (again) and his vice-president, General Pinto, became chief executive for the first time.

It was Pinto who championed the cause of liberalism in the 1820s. Political liberalism was associated with federalism, but by 1827 provincial autonomy had proved so disastrous that ideologies were realigned and Liberals became known chiefly for their advocacy of civil liberties and anticlericalism. These Liberals were known as Pipiolos, or "novices," and they acted the part.

In the euphoria of national independence, many Chileans embraced liberal egalitarian ideals as symbolic of newly won liberties and optimism for the future. Chilean Liberals in the 1820s occupied a unique place in the developing political spectrum. By 1827 Conservative centralism was quiescent and Conservative federalism had proven unworkable, and the Liberals, who appealed to some centralists and some federalists, were able to gather support at elections for a constitutional convention in 1828. The Liberals won a majority and wrote a liberal constitution, which was promulgated that year. Pinto was at best an unwilling and uncomfortable Liberal for most of 1828–29, for the new constitution, in an effort to satisfy everyone, guaranteed the rights of provincial assemblies but expanded the powers of the executive branch. What appeared to be compromise resulted in stalemate in Chile because of geography, economics, and provincial antipathy toward Santiago.

Out of the welter of Chilean political thought in the 1820s one small and cohesive force developed—a coalition of landowners, businessmen, centralists, authoritarians, and proclerical and military interests united by their opposition to both federalism and liberalism. Unlike the Liberals and federalists, this force did not look to military figures for leadership, but did use military leaders to achieve its ends. At its inception the group was known fittingly as Los Estanqueros (concessionaires or monopoly holders) and its unquestioned leader was the calculating businessman Diego Portales Palazuelos. The Estanqueros formed the basis of the Conservative Party that emerged after the brief civil war of 1830. The rise of the Estanqueros is more fittingly discussed, however, in connection with the Portalian system.

The blurring of Liberal-federalist–Conservative-centralist lines in the post-O'Higgins period made the military a necessary power group. Shifts in military allegiance were frequent and sometimes extreme. A Liberal who favored a centralized form of government might realize that liberalism and centralism were not compatible, and thus become a Liberalist-federalist or, even more bizarre, a Conservative-federalist! The political dilemmas were innumerable and do not bear recounting in full. Yet a few examples will serve to illustrate the politico-military woes of Chile between 1823 and 1831.

The Military and Government:
Caudillismo, Irresponsibility, and Antimilitarism

In April 1825, while Freire was temporarily out of office again and in the field, a group of colonels demanded back pay and salary increases from the provisional government. Claiming that they had not received their salaries since the end of 1824, they threatened to lead their troops into the countryside to forage for food and supplies. The government responded that the colonels had no right to make such a demand because other government employees were also without salaries—a pitifully weak response considering the belligerence of the officers. One member of Congress allegedly (and courageously) stated that the army was an unnecessary burden and ought to be put to work in the fields to earn pay instead of staying in the barracks! Three colonels, Jorge Beauchef, José Rondizzoni, and Benjamín Viel, were relieved of their commands. Freire returned to Santiago in late May, and the crisis passed because of his presence in the capital. But Freire soon broke with the Congress himself when legislators attempted to limit the powers of the supreme director to military and foreign policy matters only. When he attempted to suppress a rebellion in Valparaíso in October, Congress again attempted to thwart him. The April conspirators pronounced for Freire, but the Valparaíso rebellion sputtered and internal order prevailed only by default.

Freire again left office in November 1825, only to reassume his duties in March 1826! When Congress reconvened as scheduled in July 1826, Freire formally presented his resignation. His successor, Admiral Manuel Blanco Encalada, served two months before resigning, unable to govern the provinces or to provide an economic policy suitable to federalist demands. Blanco's successor was deposed on January 20, 1827, by former colonel Enrique Campino, a self-appointed federalist caudillo.

The Campino coup was Chile's most flagrant example of predatory, calculated militarism in the 1820s. Campino was a member of Congress, but he had been expelled from the army for dereliction of duty and scheming during 1825 and 1826. In January 1827 he conspired with Colonel Ambrosio Acosta, who was "always disposed to enter into seditious enterprises and adventures," and Sergeant Major Nicolás Maruri, "a valiant soldier . . . absolutely ignorant of the complications and perplexities of politics."[8] Campino forced the Santiago garrison commander, General Francisco Calderón, to turn over his troops to Maruri and then arrested some members of the government on January 20. That evening Campino declared himself chief of state but received no ovation from the citizens of the capital or from fellow congressmen. In fact, legislators demanded that he release his prisoners and send Maruri and the troops back to the barracks (better the barracks than the fields at this point!). Campino's response to this was to attend the evening congressional session on horseback with an infantry company behind him. He ordered his men to level their guns on the legislators, whereupon the chamber was cleared rapidly. The next morning Freire announced that he would march on Santiago, and on January 24 Maruri imprisoned his erstwhile fellow-conspirators and pronounced for Freire! On January 25 the hero of Talca was back in the capital for his eighth essay at government. In May he characteristically resigned again, this time, as noted, in favor of the vice-president, General Pinto. Conservative federalism had failed and Liberalism was about to have its day. The army continued to be the prime source of political power.

During 1827, however, steps were taken to bridle the army. A law of August 24 retired permanently, with a generous severance pay, all officers not actually on active duty. Over one hundred officers left the service with honorable discharges. For the first time the government limited the number of troops on active duty, formally divided the army into corps, standardized uniforms, and established minimum sanitation codes for barracks. This attempt at civil authority over the military may have been a small first step, but it represented a more thoughtful attitude on the part of the civilians toward the army as a political interest group and instrument of national defense. The legislation did little to keep the army out of government, however, for in 1828 there were three more instances of major insubordination.

In July, while the Liberal-dominated Congress was preparing a new constitution, former captain Pedro Urriola led the San Fernando garrison (Colchagua Province) in a revolt against the Liberals after being convinced by some federalists that Pinto had betrayed their interests. The response in Santiago to Urriola's rebellion was similar to the reaction to Campino's revolt early the previous year; Urriola capitulated, but pronounced again in August, only to capitulate a second time. Still in August, Lieutenant Gregorio Murillo, an obscure junior officer, declared against Pinto; he too capitulated after a week of marching his troops through the valley south of Santiago.

In all three 1828 pronunciamentos no one was cashiered or punished. Urriola and Murillo received amnesty. All three revolts were directly against the Liberals, who, it was assumed, were betraying federalist interests, notably those of Coquimbo and the provinces of Concepción and Colchagua. The fact that no one was punished for seditious actions kept violence to a minimum and undoubtedly moved Urriola and Murillo to lay down their arms like Campino before them, but the absence of reprisals also amounted to license to revolt.

As noted, the Liberal Constitution of 1828 provided for a compromise between centralism and federalism, establishing provincial legislatures or assemblies and giving more power to the executive branch. In addition it was an advanced social document, for had it been promulgated, it would have abolished *mayorazgo*, a bulwark of the landed aristocracy. Despite constitutional compromise and military reforms, though, Chile suffered from a series of political and civil-military woes for another two years.

The Development of Political Factions and Continued Military Presence: 1828–30[9]

By 1828 there were five distinguishable political factions in Chile: the Conservatives (now called Pelucones, or "Bigwigs"), the still important O'Higginistas, the federalists, the Estanqueros, and the Liberals. Conservatives and Estanqueros were authoritarian-minded centralists; most federalists represented conservative provincial interests; and O'Higginistas existed solely for the restoration of their namesake, who at this time lived modestly in Lima. The intertwining of philosophical, social, and economic points of view still precluded any clear-cut lines of differentiation, but Conservative-Estanquero interests did agree on centralism and governmental formulation of economic policy. Even some federalists whose social views did not coincide with those of Liberal-federalists were more properly Conservatives. These Conservatives, divided as they may have been, constituted formidable opposition to the egalitarian Liberals and their 1828 constitutional revision, but faith in the electoral procedure and democratic processes made it a loyal, if obdurate, opposition for the time being.

The new Constitution was promulgated on September 18, 1828, Independence Day in Chile, and if anyone can be blamed for its failure, or for the collapse of the Liberals, the Liberals themselves were responsible. There simply was no Liberal leader who inspired the confidence of Chileans: liberalism perhaps, and the Constitution maybe, but no individual leader, civilian or military. Personalism was still an important political style in Chile. The multifaction conservative opposition had leaders of stature, financial resources, and, predictably, friends in uniform. Once the leadership of the opposition came to rest in the hands of a small group, those military connections proved the key to national power.

Meanwhile military men continued to harass civilian government. Less than a month after the promulgation of the Liberal constitution, the Maipú infantry battalion revolted. Surprisingly, when the revolt collapsed, its leaders, two lieutenants, were summarily executed. In December 1828, Lieutenant Lorenzo Villegas faced a firing squad for conspiring against the Pinto government. Pinto then declared an amnesty in February 1829, making the government seem inconsistent in its responses to military plotting. This was a mistake. On June 6 the elite government escort led by Captain Felipe La Rosa went into revolt. La Rosa, claiming he was acting for General Freire, occupied the Plaza de Armas and demanded Pinto's resignation.

But the palace guard remained loyal, and La Rosa marched out of the capital that night. Then a rumor circulated that Campino and Urriola, the emeriti conspirators, were behind the whole affair, acting for opposition politicians. The next day, June 7, La Rosa surrendered to the intendant of Aconcagua Province, north of Santiago. He was pardoned, five subalterns were executed, Campino was banished, and Urriola went unpunished—the height of inconsistency, and of wishful thinking, on the part of the government. Clearly a stalemate existed. Ludicrous actions by army officers either resulted in shootings or got them quick amnesty; the Liberals made little sense in their dealings with the offenders or, for that matter, in their conduct of public affairs.

Presidential elections were held in 1829. They led to the decline of predatory militarism and Liberal power, and to the political rise of the Conservative-Estanquero clique with their military cohorts.

The Crisis of 1829–30: The Triumph of Conservatism

The crisis of 1829–30 came about in a curious way. General Pinto, the Liberal presidential candidate, let it be known that he was an unwilling standard-bearer and nothing more. Both the Liberals and the opposition knew that he would resign if elected. Therefore the principal office at stake in 1829 was really the vice-presidency. Liberals also supported an Aconcagua landowner, Francisco Ruiz Tagle Portales, "in appearance a Pipiolo, but Pelucón body and soul," and Conservatives flocked to his support as well. Two other candidates placed their names on the ballot: Liberal Joaquín Vicuña Larraín, a wealthy former army officer from Coquimbo, and General Joaquín Prieto Vial, the stern chief of the Concepción garrison and a Conservative associate of Diego Portales.

Technically there were no tickets, for the electoral code specified an open ballot with two votes for each elector. The two top candidates would then vie for the presidency, and the second-place candidate would be the vice-president.

Pinto won and Ruiz ran second, but by election time Pinto was no longer even halfheartedly committed to the Liberal cause. Prieto was third, but his Conservative-federalist background did not endear him to the Pipiolos; the Liberal, Vicuña, was selected vice-president, and an unwritten rule was broken in the process. Congress had been expected to declare Ruiz vice-president, but, knowing Pinto's plans and Ruiz's leanings, the Liberal majority selected Vicuña, the fourth-place candidate! The loyal if obdurate opposition ceased to be loyal. Angered at the Liberals' breach of political etiquette, Pinto resigned in a huff early in November. Simultaneously the provincial assembly of Concepción disavowed allegiance to the newly constituted government. The provinces of Chillán and Maule followed suit as the southern valley went into revolt. By November 12 the southern army, commanded by Colonel Manuel Bulnes Prieto (a nephew of General Prieto) was camped on the outskirts of the capital. After an inconclusive skirmish at Ochagavía on December 14, an armistice was signed, placing the government under the control of General Freire, who had come out of retirement to serve his country (and himself) one last time. A week later Freire turned the government over to a Conservative junta and then began consorting with the Liberals!

Between December 1829 and April 1830, Liberals, Conservatives, followers of Freire, and those of the Prieto-Portales faction all went after the presidency and control of the government. The intricacies of conspiracy, association, personal rivalry, and deceit make those four months a veritable microcosm of the post-O'Higgins period. But it was the manipulation of the 1829 election that set these men and forces in motion, and it was General Prieto, a disappointed candidate, who proved the ultimate victor. On April 17 his southern army met and defeated Freire's Santiago garrison at Lircay, near Talca. Freire's force was shattered, and the Liberals were discredited, as much for having conspired with Freire as for their chronic political ineptitude. Chile was delivered into the hands of the Conservatives, who were in the hands of Prieto and Portales. The military-oligarchy fusion was born.

In this chapter we have seen, albeit briefly, how military insubordination, constant conspiracy, administrative weakness, and nebulous philosophical attachments took precedence over more prosaic national interests—trade, administrative organization, political compromise—in the immediate postindependence period. Repeatedly men in uniform stalked onto the political stage, uttered their lines, and then, like frustrated bit players anxious to steal a scene, attempted to upstage the stars. Indeed, Freire and Pinto achieved status by virtue of their constant availability as well as their peculiar form of patriotism.

Less sophisticated politicians relied upon other military figures—the Campinos, Urriolas, La Rosas of the 1820s—in their quest for power. Not once did Freire or Pinto commit an act as ludicrous or as outrageous as those of Campino or Urriola; and these latter never secured the kind of support necessary actually to take over the national government. By 1830, however, any military man was likely to be scorned, whether he was a distinguished hero of the independence campaigns or an outright adventurer.

Small and compact though Chile was in the 1820s, no one could maintain power without using brute force. Civilian methods such as constitutions, guarantees of assemblies to the provinces, or autonomy were not sophisticated or functional enough to ensure the extension of national authority throughout the Central Valley.

The army was small too; it numbered no more than four or five thousand poorly trained and equipped officers and men during those years. It was enough though, to tip the balance or intimidate any of the thirty administrations. The fact that Freire and Pinto were irresolute in nature, and that Freire was seemingly forever in the field, did nothing to endear them and their brand of caudillism to Chileans. By mid 1830, Chile was an exhausted little nation. Landlords, businessmen, and politicians wanted order, and they got it on terms satisfactory to an articulate majority. With it they received a civil-military relationship established by Portales and Prieto, constructed of materials that would last for nearly a century. How that construction took place and how it endured, despite political, economic, and social change, for the better part of the nineteenth century is the subject of the following chapter.

3

Civil-Military Relations, 1830–66

What happened at Lircay on that April day in 1830 was of momentous importance for Chile's future. Prieto's defeat of Freire cannot be considered a landmark in military history, but the victory allowed Prieto's civilian allies unimpeded access to power in Santiago. Military force brought into the national government new civilian political elements which for the next seven years influenced the shaping of institutions and governmental policy.

Authority and Power Groups in Early Nineteenth-Century Chile: An Interpretation

In 1830 Chile was still small enough in size and population to be controlled by a few capable men. In this context, *control* implies authority to organize and administer without fear of effective political opposition based on philosophical premise, military force, regional interests, or any of the combinations of these three that were so prevalent in the preceding decade. During the 1820s, it is true, an equally small percentage of the total population exercised any authority at all, but that small percentage perpetually faced opposition and was thus unable to claim absolute authority. Thirty changes of government, scandalous military behavior, wavering caudillos, and continual domestic disorder convinced many citizens that leadership needed to be absolute. Not all military figures were committed to political adventurism, and some reacted negatively to the stigma attached to their vocation—or their avocation if they were not career officers.

Authority is rarely absolute. Monarchs, caudillos, and dictators in the Hispanic world from Philip II to Francisco Franco and António de Oliveira Salazar have never held total power. Neither did the Chilean Diego Portales. No man in history, no matter how much power he has held, has ruled without some form of consent by individuals or groups who may be associated with him for their own purposes. Nevertheless, the smaller the geographic unit and the population, the easier it probably is to approach true personal absolutism; this is almost certainly so if the ruler is associated with interest groups of an absolutist or authoritarian nature.

In Chile during the early nineteenth century there were three principal interest groups: the army, the Church, and the landed and commercial aristocracy. All had absolutist-authoritarian tendencies at this time. The army had a monopoly on armed force and, of course, a potential for violence. The Church held sway in the spiritual, moral, and cultural spheres. The aristocracy led the way in social and economic life and contributed its talents to the political and financial organization and administration of Chile.

The size, topography, shape, and population of the country; the cooperation for various reasons of associated interest groups; a dislike for the preceding years of confusion; and the efforts of a skillful leadership group combined to produce absolutist rule in Chile. Furthermore, until quite late in the century, neither the extent of national territory nor the goals of associated interest groups grew too large or complex for the maintenance of authority by the political system constructed by Diego Portales and his cohorts.

Do men make history or does history make men? That question, of course, can be answered only tentatively. Portales's contemporaries believed that he made history. He was a guiding genius, an event maker, an institution maker. Well into this century many Chileans regarded Portales as the country's creator. More sophisticated observers—outsiders interested in Portales, or Chilean social scientists of recent years—considered Portales merely a representative of interest groups who became a major historical figure by virtue of his dispassionate but adamant personality, his powers of persuasion, and his organizational and administrative talents. Chilean government and politics in the Portalian era really reflect more of a cult of government than one of personality, but personality never vanished entirely from politics or from the military.

Portales: Personification of Authority[1]

Don Diego José Víctor Portales Palazuelos was born in Santiago in 1793, and gave up a law career for business in his early years. He was not involved in the 1810–18 independence struggle. By 1824, at the age of thirty-one, he was a successful merchant with no avowed interest in political questions. As head of the Casa Mercantil Portales, Cea y Compañía, he was one of Santiago's most influential businessmen. In 1824 Portales and his firm became involved in politics, and from that involvement would grow his conviction that his country needed firm government.

Portales secured from the Freire government a monopoly on importation of spirits and tobacco for his firm in return for pledging to meet the service on a loan contracted by the government in England. The plan failed, Portales, Cea y Compañía lost money, and don Diego became convinced that business could not survive without domestic order. From this experience sprang Los Estanqueros—really more a businessmen's political clique or lobby than a party or faction, at least until 1829–30. Portales and his associates were conservative by temperament, but they did not adhere to Conservative-federalist ideals. They were centralists, more interested in business, profits, and law and order than in civil liberties and republican ideals. They gave the Conservatives organizational and administrative expertise, and the Conservatives gave them, after 1830, a willing, if at times truculent, following of Central Valley land and commercial interests.

Under the leadership of Diego Portales, the Basque-Castilian oligarchs joined the military chieftains to become the Chilean ruling class; they did not cede administrative control of the country until 1920, yet only for a brief decade (1830–40) would this combination go completely unchallenged. The group's significance lies more in the fact that for ninety years it adjusted to changing times, compromised, absorbed potential dissidents, and remained capable of effective leadership than in any supposed omnipotence or unchallenged status. For most of the 1830s, though, challenges to the new order were misbegotten or short-lived, and the civil-military relationship designed during that period endured. In a Latin American context this last accomplishment must be credited as a major feat by Chileans, their leaders, and especially Portales.

Historically, where political change has been accomplished through armed force, it behooves the inheritors of authority to subject that armed force to their will. This was the task of United States leaders in the late eighteenth century, and they performed it successfully. In Latin America, only Brazilians and Chileans during the past century approximated the achievements of England's former Atlantic Seaboard colonists.

The inability of Freire or the Liberal government to regroup in the aftermath of Lircay aided Portales's endeavor greatly, as did the subjection of the victorious forces to the iron discipline of Prieto and his nephew Bulnes. With Portales as overseer, the provisional government (1830–31) began the work of reorganizing the army, thus creating the basis for a civil-military relationship that endured intact until 1891 and lasted with some strain until 1920.

The Establishment of Civilian Hegemony: The Demilitarization of Chile[2]

Reorganization was performed first through purge. Freire was exiled to Peru, and his officers were cashiered or pensioned. Officers with Liberal connections (family or close friends) were retired, and Liberal public officials were dismissed. Members of Prieto's command whose absolute loyalty could not be assured were dismissed or retired. A garrison command could no longer be an easy route from obscurity to notoriety. From the Battle of Lircay on, salaries were paid on time; fiscal matters would no longer be a pretext for political action.

Portales suggested, and his associates agreed, that in the future the army officer class be composed of reliable young men of respectable, trustworthy families, and that officers be subjected to strict regulations and training. Another suggestion of Portales's resulted in the creation of the Guardia Civil, a rural- and urban-based militia under the supervision of local landowners and wealthy city dwellers, which served as a counterpoise to the standing army. One year after Lircay the Guardia numbered 25,000 men and officers. Portales commanded a Guardia infantry battalion (quartered in La Moneda), trained with it, and marched in uniform on festive and patriotic occasions until his death in 1837. Guardia officers were recruited from leading families;

troops came from peasant and worker stock. The militia was a militarized microcosm of Chilean political society, sober, disciplined, and organized on a nationwide scale. The Guardia had no occasion to interpose itself between state and military, so we cannot appraise its true effectiveness. There is little doubt, however, that its sheer size could have blunted a large-scale military insurrection.

Two years after Lircay, the sporadically operated and financed military school founded by O'Higgins reopened as the War Academy (a short-lived appellation and not to be confused with the staff school founded in 1886).[3] The entrance requirements were prohibitive to all but the best-educated aspirants to cadet status. Cadets were no longer recruited from the more modest sectors of society, and this helped to create an extremely homogeneous and ingrown cadet and officer corps. Because neither the Guardia nor the regular army officer corps was far removed from civilian high society, neither could conceivably represent social, economic, or political interests at variance with those of the aristocracy. The reopening of the military school and the formation of the Guardia also lent a tone of respectability to military and paramilitary activity. This was service born not of opportunism, desperation, or political interests, but of patriotism and responsibility; it was service to the state.

The state now became the domain of civilians—civilians close to the military through Guardia service or relations to the officer class. Prieto as president and Portales alternately as minister of finance, minister of the interior, and minister of war (and foreign relations minister for a time in 1830) insisted that those who served the state be absolutely trustworthy and loyal to it. It can thus be said that Prieto and Portales expected as much from civilian leaders as they did from men in uniform. This consistency in thought and action when dealing with civilian and military leaders aided in the fusion of the two between 1831 and 1841, the Prieto decade.

Organization and pacification were not overnight accomplishments. The provisional government dominated by Portales and the first Prieto administration (1831–36) were buffeted by conspiracy and revolt involving Liberals, former army officers, and adventurers. Centralization of authority did not please all Chileans, and the residue of conspiracies from the preceding decade dissipated only gradually. Ostracized Liberals and O'Higginistas bore grudges for personal and political reasons.

In March 1831, just under a year after Lircay, a revolt broke out south of Concepción, where sentiment for autonomy ran high. The rebellion was snuffed out quickly, with little bloodshed, and the guilty parties were relegated to Más Afuera in the Juan Fernández Islands (the setting for Daniel Defoe's *Robinson Crusoe*). In December the exiles (together with their guards!) embarked for Coquimbo, where they were to join O'Higginista rebels from Lima. Like Concepción, Coquimbo was a center of autonomous sentiment. The rebels made a bloody stand, but government forces prevailed and the rebel leaders were finally captured and executed.

During 1832 and 1833 more plotting was discovered. Because of the 1832 conspiracy, Prieto authorized the funding and organization of a secret police, which remained in existence for thirty-two years. The 1833 plot, uncovered by the secret police, involved cashiered officers and some members of the government, all of whom were exiled for two years. Old ways, it has been said again and again, die slowly. But by the end of 1833 secret police activities and heavy-handed justice diminished the attractiveness of antigovernment activity.

The Creation of the Portalian System: Responsibility, Discipline, Probity[4]

The Portalian system that evolved during the Prieto administrations was no less resourceful and forceful in putting Chilean civil affairs in order. Portales's forte was organization and management; in another time and place he might have been an entrepreneur par excellence. In the years alloted to him, he gave his country an enduring political and economic structure, no mean accomplishment in postindependence Latin America.

Two Chilean institutions had come through the 1820s unchanged —though not entirely unaffected—by revolt, reconquest, independence, and politics: the Church and the Central Valley aristocracy. The third element of the postindependence society, the army, had obviously lost its solidarity and, as noted, had to be reconstituted to function as a complement to the other two. Portales dealt exclusively with the great families of the Basque-Castilian aristocracy. He both forced them to accept and convinced them of the importance of their obligations to their country, and he succeeded in making responsibility more praiseworthy and profitable than idle privilege. During the 1830s, in particular, the rolls of government, diplomatic, and military leadership read like the Chilean social register.

It is much more difficult for a military organization to oppose a system than to oppose an individual, particularly when the system has the support of a close-knit interest group to which the military leaders themselves belong. The cult of government fostered trust and belief on the part of civilians, but Portales was not above using intimidation, which proved a valuable tool. The Chilean cult of government rested on two primary bases: law and order, and effective administration.

Unflinching use of punitive law during the 1830s and 1840s nearly eradicated banditry and civil disorder. Prior to Lircay, the army had been employed with varying degrees of success in the maintenance of internal order and the persecution of criminals. Outlaws were commonplace in rural Chile and even in Santiago during the turbulent 1820s, and looting and robbery were widespread. From their sanctuaries in the southern forests and the Andean foothills, bandits like the notorious Pinchera brothers plundered and pillaged until national reorganization began under Portales. At the command of his uncle, the president, Colonel Bulnes defeated Pablo and José Pinchera in southern Chile in 1832, and subsequent army action eliminated other predators from the countryside. Offenders—both leaders and followers—were executed or exiled (yet fewer executions took place after Lircay than before).

The army became increasingly important and effective in maintaining internal order. This lessened the possibility of frustration on the part of army leaders, for they felt that they were as competent in their military role as civilian leaders were at managing the government.

Probity and conscientiousness in the national administration assured public respect. No government riddled with corruption or hobbled by incompetence commands admiration. Under the Portales government, those suspected of graft, malfeasance, or laxity were dismissed; if proved guilty, they were punished. Government salaries were modest; those of high-ranking officials were purposely low, so that only wealthy Chileans sought high office. Portales contributed his salary to the army. However mundane it may seem in retrospect, the fact that Portales personally supervised the cleanliness and orderliness of government offices—to the point of demanding that cigar butts be

properly disposed of!⁵—lent an aura of order and respectability to
Chile's developing government.

Institutionalization of the Portalian System:
The Constitution of 1833[6]

The greatest achievement of the Portales age was the writing and
promulgation of the Constitution of 1833, the codification of the
Portalian ideals of law, order, organization, and efficiency that
remained the fundamental charter of the land until 1925. Thirty-six
eminent citizens met during 1831 and 1832, technically to reform the
1828 document; the family names of those involved attest to the
eminence of the Basque-Castilian aristocracy: Tocornal, Viel, Rengifo, Astorga, Carrasco, Larraín, Echevers, Pérez, Puga, Egaña, Gandarillas, Elizalde, Arriarán, Meneses, Vicuña, Irarrázaval, Errázuriz,
Barros, Correa de Sáa, Argüelles, Aldunate. Mariano Egaña Fabres,
Anglophile, theorist, and reactionary, and Manuel José Gandarillas, a
progressive-minded Estanquero, guided the notables in their work.

The Constitution of 1833 need not be summarized here in detail. It
retained elements of the much-maligned 1828 document regarding
organization of the state and rights of citizenship. Provincial rights
and privileges were eliminated, however, and the executive branch
overshadowed the legislative and judicial branches and extended into
the affairs of the provinces. Executive powers were particularly
extensive in the maintenance of internal order; the armed forces were
declared "essentially obedient" and denied the right to political
pronouncements. The chief executive served for five years, could be
immediately reelected for one additional term, controlled appointment and dismissal of the cabinet and the administration of elections,
and was empowered to maintain order through state of siege and
declaration of martial law with the concurrence of Congress.

This autocratic document centralized government and concentrated power in the executive branch. As long as the executive branch
represented the Basque-Castilian aristocracy of land and commercial
interests, those interests did not protest loudly. The fact that both
Prieto and Bulnes, whose presidencies took up two full decades, were
prestigious generals welded the army to the state. The Church,
patronized by the state, similarly supported the new order. The

Constitution of 1833 created an omnipotent state; Portales oversaw the functions of that state; the state controlled, rather than being controlled by, the army.

"La Segunda Independencia": The War of 1836–39[7]

By 1836 Prieto was in his second presidential term. The state had asserted itself under the guidance of Prieto and Portales, and internal calm was no longer a goal but a fact. That year the Bolivian president, Andrés de Santa Cruz y Calahumana (formerly one of San Martín's and Bolívar's better aides), forced Peru to join Bolivia in a confederacy. Santa Cruz had many enemies in Lima, but his greatest enemies were Portales and Prieto.

Until 1776 Bolivia had been a province of the Viceroyalty of Peru, and until independence part of the Viceroyalty of La Plata. The alliance of Bolivia and Peru alarmed the Santiago government, for it confronted Chile with two powerful neighbors (Argentina under Rosas was the other). It also exacerbated the Valparaíso-Callao commercial rivalry.

Four years earlier, in June 1832, the Peruvian government had raised the tariff on Chilean wheat, the major export of the Central Valley. In reprisal Chile raised the tariff on imports of Peruvian sugar. Safe, orderly Valparaíso by this time was challenging Callao as the major commercial port on the Pacific coast. Peru's tariff policy was obviously designed to put an end to that challenge by cutting into Valparaíso's export business and reducing it to secondary status. The Peruvian tariff and the threat posed by the alliance between Bolivia and Peru goaded the Prieto administration into assuming a belligerent stance.

In addition, the Santiago government feared that Santa Cruz would try to reestablish the Inca Empire. Chileans saw Santa Cruz as a schemer, a sinister latter-day Inca militarist. He was, after all, a cholo, son of a Spaniard and a Colla noblewoman, he even looked like an Indian, with dark skin and black hair, and he "had the air of a simple Indian of the Bolivian mountains." Portales, upon hearing of the formation of the confederacy, is reported to have said, "This cholo is going to give us much trouble."[8]

And that he did. Santa Cruz made no secret of his plans to incorporate Ecuador into the Confederation, but he did not commit himself regarding northeastern Argentina and Chile, the southern fringes of the Inca area. Until 1836 he limited his activities in Santiago to financing the activities of spies and to supporting an ill-fated invasion of southern Chile by the disgraced General Freire.

In 1836, the same year the Confederation was formed, Chile called for indemnities for Freire's venture, as well as overdue payment for the costs of Chilean participation in the independence expedition, and demanded that the Confederation be dissolved. Santa Cruz refused on all points, and Chile made warlike threats. The Chilean armed forces were about to undertake their first defense of national honor and sovereignty. Their success was by no means assured.

On a special mission to Lima, Mariano Egaña, the constitution writer, failed to persuade Santa Cruz to dissolve the Confederation, and Chile declared war in December 1836. Congress gave Prieto the authority to exercise all public power during the emergency. Like the army, the state was about to face its first major crisis, for the concentration of power in the executive branch under emergency conditions created a virtual dictatorship.

Both the state and the armed forces, then, met supreme tests in 1836. War and its effects could either bind Chileans to the Santiago government or bring about political collapse in the event of military reversal, governmental abuse of power, or both. The Constitution, the Portalian insistence on administrative probity and efficiency, and the reorganization of the army proved, however, to be enlightened policies. A decided underdog in 1836, Chile emerged triumphant, its civil institutions tested under wartime extremes.

Early in 1837 the Peruvian propaganda mongers spread the word among Chilean army officers that Portales wanted the war in order to "send them off to the Atacama and the Altiplano where they would die and their bones [would] bleach in the high deserts of the Andes."[9] For his own evil purposes, they said, Portales wanted to do away with the heirs of O'Higgins. They apparently did not say what the alternatives to war would be: absorption of Chile by the Andean powers or a negotiated peace. Among the civilian populace there was trepidation at the thought of extraordinary presidential powers, mobilization, a long campaign, maybe defeat. Chilean exiles in Lima were responsible for much of this propaganda, so great was their hatred for Portales and Prieto.

Throughout the summer and fall of 1837 (January–May) mobilization went ahead amidst grumbling and discontent. Portales (as interior and war minister) and President Prieto made full use of their powers, punishing their opponents severely. Then tragedy struck; Chile sustained a national insult so great that partisan quarrels gave way temporarily to aggressive nationalism. On June 3 Portales was in Quillota, on the Aconcagua River near the road from Santiago to Valparaíso, to inspect the garrison there. The garrison's commander, Colonel José Antonio de Vidaurre, took Portales prisoner. Vidaurre pronounced against the government and marched toward Valparaíso with his prisoner-hostage. Though the record is not clear, he probably planned either to attack the port city or, with his men, to take ship for Callao. But loyal troops pursued him. Fighting broke out on the morning of June 6, and Portales was forced from his carriage, shot twice, and bayonetted thirty-five times. Vidaurre and his henchmen were soon captured and executed, but their punishment was an anticlimax. Chilean public opinion demanded war as revenge on Santa Cruz, who may or may not have induced Vidaurre to treachery. The incident overshadowed domestic issues; the martyred Portales became a nationalistic symbol to Chileans.[10]

Mobilization continued through the winter months, and on September 15 an expedition left Valparaíso for Lima under the command of Admiral Blanco. The Chileans were defeated soundly at Arequipa. Blanco agreed to recognize the Confederation but when he returned south his act was disavowed by the Santiago government. Like Santa Anna after San Jacinto, Blanco bought his freedom and that of the Chilean survivors, but the government, like that of Mexico in the wake of the Texas rebellion, would have none of his decision. Mobilization continued.

In January 1838 a second expedition, commanded by General Bulnes, left Valparaíso. The Chilean expeditionary force occupied Lima with the support of northern Peruvian rebels who opposed Santa Cruz. After a year of waiting, the armies of Chile and the Confederation met at Yungay, in Ancash Province, north of the capital, on January 20, 1839. The war ended there, for the Chileans, despite their inferior numbers, defeated the Santa Cruz forces.

From the standpoint of tactics and strategy the 1836–39 war was nothing for the Chileans to be proud of. Bulnes and his troops did not fare well in Lima, and the struggle at Yungay could easily have been a disaster for Chile. Massed cavalry charges and a desperate assault on the Peruvian artillery saved the day, for the Chileans were under pursuit and turned at Yungay only to make a stand.

Yungay: Reaffirmation of Civilian Hegemony

From the standpoint of Chilean civil-military relationships, however, the war that culminated at Yungay was extremely significant in that it strengthened the relationship molded by Portales: a military obedient to civilian authority and designed to defend as well as maintain order. When the war began the Chilean Army, comprising perhaps 3,000 trained men and officers, appeared hopelessly outnumbered. Santa Cruz could muster nearly four times that number, but the majority of his troops were poorly trained. At Yungay, Bulnes had 5,200 under his command and Santa Cruz at least 6,000. This indicates that mobilization in Chile rapidly provided nearly 2,000 trained men. It also shows that the army of the Confederation was not nearly as large as propaganda claims made it appear.

The triumph at Yungay made the Chilean Army a source of national pride as a legitimate means of preserving and extending Chilean power and dignity: "Sing the glory of the martial triumph won by the Chilean *people* at Yungay," begins the "Canción de Yungay" written by José Zapiola and Ramón Rengifo, to commemorate the triumph.

Chilean victory was assured by good communications with the homeland, which in turn were made possible only by control of the sea, because South Peru was Santa Cruz's stronghold. The occupation of Lima-Callao was difficult, but sea communications made it possible. Thus the navy, such as it was, shared in the army's glory and remained an important fixture in Chile's national defense plans. Forty years after Yungay, the navy would be the main contributor to victory in the War of the Pacific.

The fact that the fighting was done abroad did nothing to diminish interest in the war. The army had defeated the enemy on his own ground at great risk and a cost of many lives, and Chile remained intact. Successful mobilization, maintenance of lines of communication, military victory in a foreign land were to the credit of the government. As the war feeling mounted, Andean propaganda lost its appeal, and opposition died down. President Prieto willingly relinquished emergency powers soon after the fighting ceased, and his earlier abuses of power and dictatorial measures were nearly forgotten (but not necessarily forgiven). The cult of government was strengthened; the Portalian system had proved itself under the most trying circumstances.

It functioned well and efficiently during the political honeymoon from 1830 to 1832. Between 1832 and 1834 it successfully instituted a constitutional regime, put an end to most antigovernment conspiracies, and organized a responsible bureaucracy. With Portales as interior and war minister, from 1832 to 1835, the regime maintained firm control over organized armed force through purge, reorganization, and training; from 1837 to 1839, after his departure, it shared credit with the armed forces for the defeat of Santa Cruz.

The cause of the army officers was best served by internal stability and obedience to civil authority. By 1840 their goal—to defend Chile from her enemies, foreign and domestic—was identical with that of the ruling Basque-Castilian aristocracy. In 1841 Bulnes, the hero of Yungay, became president. He perpetuated the Chilean civil-military fusion for another ten years; by mid century Chile would have been governed for two decades by men who had first made their mark on the battlefield and who were widely respected for it.

The Bulnes Decade: A Decade of Growth[11]

The Bulnes decade was one of domestic tranquillity, cultural and intellectual growth, and activity unequaled in the rest of Latin America. Talented exiles from Argentina and other countries inspired Chileans to cultural pursuits that would have been frowned upon by Portales. Anticlericalism, freedom of speech and press, criticism of the government and state were widespread but resulted in a respect for individual opinion and dissent rather than in sedition or revolt. Partisan politics, sedition, and revolt did develop in the next decade and seriously menaced the constitutional order, but during the 1840s Chile enjoyed economic progress and cultural growth.

Bulnes presided over a normalcy already restored by his uncle, President Prieto. Normalcy meant not only the return of constitutional guarantees after the war emergency had passed but, significantly for Chilean civil-military relationships, also the recall of numerous officers purged after Lircay. Some were brought back to serve their country during the war and some after. The officers' discontent was allayed by this indication of their continued value as military, if not political, figures. As an example of amnesty and respect for the military, Francisco Antonio Pinto was reincorporated in May 1839. To be sure, this type of maneuver also helped the government, for it brought certain people under military jurisdiction at a time when Prieto was preparing to impose Bulnes as his successor!

Some reincorporated officers received back pay, and widows and children of purged officers became eligible for pensions; this induced some officers to rejoin their regiments during the war. The majority of officers involved in plots between 1830 and the outbreak of the war who had been stripped of their rank and privileges returned to military service. Whatever the motive, these measures militated against plotting between the end of the war and the election of 1841.

Bulnes became the official candidate in 1840. The opposition, composed of oligarchs who chafed at the centralism of the Portalian system, supported General Pinto, only recently back in good graces. Soon after Pinto announced his candidacy, Manuel Bulnes virtually put an end to Pinto's chances by publicly announcing his engagement to doña Enriqueta Pinto Garmendia, Pinto's eldest daughter! Amnesty, reincorporation, and the matrimonial union of two great military families made the election a formality from the military point of view. Bulnes received a popular majority, 154 electoral votes to 9 for Pinto and 1 for noncandidate O'Higgins. The era of Bulnes had begun.

The awakening of culture, economic expansion in mining, commerce, and agriculture, and the democratic atmosphere of the Bulnes decade did little to alter the civil-military relationship established between 1830 and 1840. The resurgence of party politics, however, did have some effect in this area.

At no time during the Portalian era (1830–37) or the Prieto presidencies (1831–41)—and the two need not be synonymous—was opposition to the system or its leaders entirely absent. But at no time was it the kind of opposition capable of using, or willing to resort to, armed force. Opposition came from within the aristocracy, from the great families, from Estanqueros who had fought with Portales. Members of one branch of the Errázuriz family, Manuel José Gandarillas, Diego José Benavente, Manuel Camilo Vial, and others objected to autocratic and proclerical measures early in Prieto's first administration. They called themselves Filopolitas,[12] friends of the people, and criticized the government in speeches and articles.

"Filopolitismo" was the beginning of the new Chilean liberalism, which would become a loyal opposition after the 1836–39 war. In a purely sociopolitical sense it was the first manifestation of La Fronda (after the Fronde, the French aristocratic-parliamentary clique that struggled with Cardinal Mazarin prior to the majority of Louis XIV), which would seek to circumscribe the powers of the executive branch for the remainder of the century. Bulnes allowed some members of this budding opposition into his administration. Manuel Vial, for example, served briefly as interior minister. At mid century, Chilean politics began to show some signs of a Liberal-Conservative split and of division within the conservative group, based on Frondista opposition to autocratic centralism.[13] The storms of the 1820s had not abated entirely.

Meanwhile the army and navy loyally served the state. Early in the first Bulnes administration (1841–46) British and French ships reconnoitered the Strait of Magellan. Responding to this European challenge, Bulnes sent Admiral Juan Williams Rebolledo to establish a Chilean settlement on the strait. On September 21, 1843, Fuerte Bulnes was founded. Six years later the settlement moved north along the western shore of the strait to Punta Arenas. By the time Bulnes was elected to a second term, the army had pacified most of the area around Valdivia and around Lake Llanquihue in the south Central Valley. German settlers moved into the area after mid century and developed a moderate-sized landholding agricultural area. Bulnes saw to it that the military school was renovated, and a nautical school —forerunner to the naval school—was organized at Valparaíso in 1845.

As the decade wore on, the armed forces continued to provide protection for the colony on the Strait of Magellan, for settlers on the southern frontiers, and for guano entrepreneurs operating close to the Bolivian border (latitude 23° south). But late in Bulnes's second term, politico-military relations tensed as the chief executive prepared to impose a successor. There was great opposition to his official choice, Manuel Montt Torres.

Montt: A Decade of Dissent and of Military Obedience[14]

Montt was a self-made man. Of Catalan descent, as his surname indicates, he was an outsider to the Basque-Castilian aristocracy, but politically he was one of them. By temperament he was disciplined, serious, and a master organizer, as an administrator he was a stickler for detail. He served Bulnes as minister of the interior and minister of war, and, most significantly, as minister of justice, worship, and education. To Frondistas he was anathema. Liberals thought him a reactionary, and even some Conservatives considered him an unknown quantity. Montt, La Fronda, and the resurgence of party politics combined to bring the army into the political arena again.

At mid century the Chilean Liberal "party" had one goal: the defeat of Montt in 1851. The "party" was made up of three distinct groups. One group, Liberal in name only, was composed of Conservatives who disliked Montt and who supported Vial for the presidency; a second group was the "Society of Equality" and its followers, whose inspiration derived from the 1848 Liberal outbursts in Europe; the third was composed of superannuated Pipiolos, survivors of Lircay and the subsequent purges. Liberals supported the candidacy of Bulnes's cousin, General José María de la Cruz Prieto, a Yungay hero like Bulnes and a native of Concepción Province.

Cruz was extremely conservative, but he was a Frondista Conservative, a zealous partisan of federalism and provincial autonomy. Liberals, therefore, flocked to his standard out of their desire for provincial autonomy and because they believed he had a good chance to win. Penquista leaders believed the president should be a Penquista if centralism and authoritarianism were to be at all tolerable. Freire (and O'Higgins before him), Prieto, and Bulnes had all been from the South. Concepción "deserved" the presidency; if the vote went against Cruz, there was always the southern garrison, where he had many friends.

Two barracks revolts, one late in 1850, the other early in 1851, failed miserably, and Montt was duly elected. The government machinery obtained 132 electoral votes for Montt, with Cruz winning only 32, most of them from outlying areas. Cruz received all 21 electoral votes from Concepción; Maule, in the South, gave him 5 and Coquimbo, on the northern frontier, 3. Personalities aside, the election was primarily a contest between centralism and federalism, the latter very appealing to provincial Conservatives as well as to Liberals. Other issues would refine the political divisions of Chile during the Montt decade.

How was this contest reflected in politico-military matters and civil-military relationships? In the first place, General Cruz did not accept defeat in 1851. Unlike Pinto, he had no daughter to be wooed and won by the official candidate, and he had strong support among Frondistas, Liberals of the intellectual Generation of 1842, and Liberals inspired by the events of 1848. Allied, they opposed the continuation of Portalian autocracy and centralism. Separately, they stood for causes ranging from anticlericalism to provincial autonomy. Among the officer corps, however, the cult of government and military discipline was so strong that there was little political debate. Nevertheless, Cruz pronounced against the government in early September 1851, hoping to block Montt's inauguration.

Cruz's was not a true military pronunciamento, for he did not have wide support in the officer corps, and the officers who did not back him would not merely step aside. Rather, Cruz undertook a politico-military adventure akin to the golpes of Freire, Pinto, and Prieto. It smacked of regionalism and personal disgruntlement more than of liberalism or conservativism, and it had little effect on the officer corps. Bulnes took the field against his cousin and defeated him at Loncomilla, but not before a revolt led by the ultraliberal Society of Equality had briefly taken over the city of La Serena under the direction of the youthful, romantic Benjamín Vicuña Mackenna. When Cruz was defeated, the La Serena rebels capitulated.[15] Again the army had stood firm in the face of a challenge to its solidarity and its loyalty to the state.

Chile at Mid Century: The End of a Dynasty

The revolt of José María de la Cruz Prieto brought to an end the era of Penquista dominance of national affairs and terminated the close relationship between the Concepción garrison and the southern aristocracy. During the 1850s and 1860s the government sent larger numbers of fresh troops, commanded by northerners, southward to push back the frontiers of Araucania. The Cruz revolt had not swept military men along with it, for Cruz had promised them nothing. It also struck some military men as a family affair as much as or more than a matter of Penquista political jealousy. Bulnes was, of course, Prieto's nephew, and Cruz was his cousin; moreover, Bulnes was Pinto's son-in-law. Not many officers were interested in family squabbling, nor were many willing to go along with the strident anticlericalism, civil disobedience, and federalism of the new Liberals and their radical young cohorts of the Society of Equality.

After his ill-fated golpe of 1851 Cruz retired to private life
O'Higgins had been dead since 1842; Pinto was already sixty-six years
old and would die in 1858. Freire died in 1851; Prieto in 1854, at the
age of sixty-eight; and Bulnes also retired to private life. A generation
had yielded power politically and militarily, and a new type of officer
corps was coming to the fore.

With the passing of the southern politico-military dynasty, federalism grew less regional in quality and started to become a constitutional issue of major significance. By mid century neither Concepción
nor La Serena could pose a threat to Santiago's position as the
national center. The Central Valley population clustered about
Santiago had a centralizing effect politically; the Santiago-Valparaíso
commercial and economic axis concentrated vital national activities
in the capital area. The continued efficiency of the centralized
administrative structure also tended to enhance the position of the
capital.

Chile at Mid Century: A South American Power[16]

During the Montt decade Chile was politically advanced, more
stable constitutionally than any South American country with the
exception of Brazil, and more democratic than any of the neighboring
states. While democracy must be considered in restrictive and relative
terms for nineteenth-century Latin America (and in qualified terms
for the twentieth century), democratic processes were observed more
regularly in Chile than in troubled Argentina or in the Andean
countries. Consistency in governmental organization, institutional
functions, and national administration was the rule in Chile more
often than the exception, and that cannot be said of the other South
American republics, where institutional breakdown was common.
Regional interests were sublimated in Chile, and constitutional
processes were accepted by the majority of the politically articulate
as the proper means for gaining power and effecting any change.

Similarly, there were no threats of social disorder, no alienated
masses to be led into demagogic, violent political action. At mid
century, fully one-third of the population (Chile had 1,400,000
citizens in 1855 and fewer than 2,000,000 inhabitants as late as 1875)
was composed of self-employed workers—artisans, craftsmen, and
owners of family farms. Roughly a quarter of the population were

peasants who lived within the bounds of a paternalistic, agrarian system akin to feudalism, but by no means truly feudal. Fewer than 10 percent were domestics. There was no proletariat and no urban population pressure, though urbanization was taking place. Santiago had a population of nearly 100,000; Valparaíso nearly 60,000; Concepción and La Serena considerably less. Perhaps 15 percent, but no more, of the population were urban workers. Fewer than 5 percent were involved in mining. The rest of Chile's population was composed of bureaucrats, the clergy, the military, businessmen, landowners, and the self-employed. Apart from sporadic demonstrations, pressure from the lower classes simply did not exist; nor did excessive exploitation by the wealthy, at least in comparison with Chile's neighbors. Disorder and violence, then, posed no threat to the status quo.

Economically Chile was expanding. From the beginning of the first Prieto presidency, Chile exploited her mineral wealth. Silver at the Chañarcillo and Caracoles mines, coal at Lota and Coronel, nitrates from the fields on both sides of the Chilean-Bolivian frontier, and copper, of which Chile was the world's leading exporter, all contributed to prosperity—and to a heavy dependence on extractive industry which by the 1880s would have a negative effect on the economy.

The nouveaux riches had no trouble entering the aristocracy. This had a double-edged effect: it enlarged the ruling class but diluted its Basque-Castilian composition. Into the social register and the rosters of servants of the state crept decidedly non-Iberian names like Edwards, König, Subercaseaux, Gallo, and MacClure. Significantly, the broadening of the aristocracy did not lead to extraconstitutional conflict over control of the state. Changing social and economic patterns strengthened rather than weakened the civil-military relationship established during the Portalian age, but these changes did affect the political sphere.

The Beginnings of Change: Political Conflict, Economic Problems, and Military Glory

The revival of liberalism was due in part to socioeconomic change. It was facilitated by adherence to constitutional norms. The fact that liberalism was not dependent on military adventurism both militated against alteration of the civil-military relationship and ultimately contributed to its imbalance. This is true for several reasons. First, the Montt decade ended as it had begun, in an atmosphere of tension. Second, an economy based too heavily on extractive industry helped to involve Chile in a second war with Peru and Bolivia. Third, the army and the navy became exceedingly important as autonomous, professional, national institutions and ceased somewhat to be extensions of the aristocracy. The rest of this chapter will discuss political change in mid-nineteenth-century Chile, fostered by the rise of new liberalism. The other reasons for imbalance in civil-military relationships will be treated in the following chapter.

Manuel Montt was by no means inclined toward liberalism, but he was conscious of the need for modernization. His abolition of *mayorazgo* through laws passed in 1852 and 1858 fulfilled O'Higgins's earlier dream but it alienated many Conservatives. His autocratic policies did not endear him to Liberals. His "regalist" stand against the Church encouraged a split in the Conservative Party but did little to attract anticlerical Liberals to his autocratic standard.

By the end of Montt's second term, the Conservative Party had split. One sector, comprising primarily landowners and Pelucón-Penquistas, retained the Conservative appellation and was closely associated with the Church and traditionalism. The other branch fused with some members of the new business, banking, and mining elite and called itself the National Party or the Montt-Varistas (from the president's name and that of his trusted collaborator José Antonio Varas). By 1861, Conservatives were in league with a sizable portion of the Liberal Party in a coalition called La Fusión; despite the persistence of the divisive religious question, coalitions would dominate Chilean national politics until the end of the century. La Fusión was an unsteady alliance, and partly because of it the army would become politically restless in the years after the War of the Pacific (1879–84). La Fusión forced the election of José Joaquín Pérez Mascayano, a National acceptable to the coalition, in 1861 and in 1866, and until 1891 all the candidates it supported for president were elected.

The election of Pérez in 1861 is important with respect to civil-military relationships for two reasons. First, it began an era of bitter political fighting. The political struggles of 1861–91 over commercial and fiscal policy, Church-state relations, foreign policy, and constitutional change shook the foundations of the Portalian system. Indeed, to many historians, 1861 marks the end of the Autocratic Republic and the beginning of the Liberal Republic. And, in steps so gradual that they have never been considered significant, the army was drawn into political questions during these years. Second, the agreement between the administration party (Nationals or Montt-Varistas) and the opposition (Conservative-Liberal, La Fusión) to deliver the presidency to Pérez was the result of an attempted golpe in 1859. Although the army did not instigate the attempt, it was enmeshed in the political question.

But, to return to the close of the Montt regime, by 1859 it was clear to all that Montt had selected Varas as his successor. Varas, a Portalian autocrat, was acceptable neither to the Conservatives nor to the Liberals. He was an advocate of strong, centralized authoritarian government based in the executive branch, and this was anathema to Frondistas and Liberals, who championed civil liberties, freedom of the press, and parliamentary supremacy. Before Varas declined the nomination and paved the way for the compromise on Pérez, the golpe developed.

In January 1859, Pedro León Gallo, a wealthy Liberal mine owner in northern Copiapó whose family had interests in the Chañarcillo silver mine, raised an army of a thousand men and led Atacama Province into revolt.[17] The revolt was put down in March, and Gallo fled the country; nevertheless, the attempt had its consequences. Gallo and his followers demanded constitutional reform to increase the powers of Congress, and they clearly represented the mining and banking interests that felt restricted by the Portalian system. The revolt was actually nationwide, and only with difficulty did the Montt government stand firm. Hewing to the post-1830 tradition, the regular army supported the government. The masses were not involved.

The troops, only recently denied the right to vote while serving in the army, certainly did not stand to gain anything from the rebellion. The 1859 revolt was definitely not a popular movement; it came from within the ruling class (the Gallo family was related to Montt by marriage). Therefore the army's defense of the government was indicative only of obedience to the Constitution and rejection of extraconstitutional action; it was not a political stance by men in uniform. It did indicate, though, that within the ruling group the military was still to be considered. Whatever else it did, the revolt convinced the government that forcing a candidate on the electorate in 1861 might lead to further revolt. Varas, therefore, disavowed his candidacy, and the noncontroversial Pérez was agreed upon. This was tantamount to election, and Pérez was awarded all electoral votes.

It fell to the Pérez administration to deal militarily with Spain's last brief flash of power in the Pacific. The Spanish Pacific fleet appeared off the west coast of South America in 1863 for the purposes of scientific study and investigation of debt claims held by Spaniards against the Peruvian government. But blundering Spanish diplomats, generals, and admirals touched off an international scandal when the fleet occupied the guano-rich Peruvian Chincha Islands in 1864.[18] The next year the fleet appeared off Valparaíso, and the Spanish fleet commander, Admiral José Manuel Pareja, demanded a twenty-one-gun salute. The Pérez administration responded with a declaration of war; Ecuador, Peru, and Bolivia joined with Chile in an unexpected show of cooperation.

On March 31, 1866, the Spanish Pacific fleet bombarded defenseless Valparaíso. The bombardment destroyed the weak fortifications and the port installations and reduced Valparaíso to a shambles, in one blow wiping out the commercial position gained a quarter-century before at the expense of Peru. Ironically, Peru, part of whose territory had been occupied, suffered very little when the Spaniards attacked the port of Callao. The cost of reconstructing Valparaíso was high, and the government in Santiago resorted to tripling the public debt and issuing nonconvertible paper money (for the first time since the 1820s) in order to restore the city.

Chile and Spain ceased hostilities soon thereafter, but peace was restored formally only after fifteen years of negotiation. As a direct result of the War with Spain Chile embarked on a military buildup. Coastal defenses were modernized, and two new warships, the sloops O'Higgins and Chacabuco, were purchased. Krupp fieldpieces were purchased for the army, and the navy was expanded. Peru, for obvious reasons, also began a naval and military buildup. Barely a decade had passed before the short-term allies against Spain were involved in war with each other. That war began a new period in Chilean civil-military relationships.

In the three and one-half decades between Lircay and the bombardment of Valparaíso, the Chilean army and navy were obedient defenders of the nation's interests and of the legally constituted state. Nevertheless, Chile's political, economic, and social changes would be reflected in civil-military relationships during the remainder of the century. New types of relationships could be detected by 1891.

4

From the War with Spain to the Civil War of 1891

The quarter-century of Chilean history between the bombardment of Valparaíso in 1866 and the revolt of 1891 can be divided into two distinct periods with respect to civil-military relationships. The first period began in the late stages of the second administration (1866–71) of José Joaquín Pérez, as the presidential succession for 1871 was being arranged, and ended with the outbreak of war with Bolivia and Peru in 1879. The second includes the War of the Pacific (1879–84) and the subsequent military reforms (1885–91). In the first period the beginnings of the disruption of the Portalian concept of the state were quite visible; in the second, the beginnings of military professionalization coincided precisely with the definitive scrapping of the Portalian system.

Nineteenth-Century Civil-Military Relations in Retrospect: An Interpretation

During the first half of the century the state had maintained control over the army by a variety of means discussed and described in the previous chapters: vigorous, efficient, honest administration; fusion of the military with the aristocracy; successful articulation of national policy through the use of military force against both foreign and indigenous hostiles; and the primarily internal resolutions of political conflict surrounding the candidacy of Montt, his controversial administration, and the compromise of 1861 which gave the presidency to Pérez. By Latin American standards—the only ones that really should apply—the Chilean civil-military balance of power after 1830 decidedly favored the civilian sector.

Until the damages to Valparaíso, Chile's main seaport, caused financial setbacks, and until the worldwide recession of the mid 1870s reached South America, the Chilean economy was sound. The working classes—peasants, miners, laborers, and artisans—caused no problems. No class or interest group rose to challenge the flexible Basque-Castilian aristocracy for national leadership. Because the economy was expanding, until the 1890s nonaristocrats did not need to enter the army in large numbers as a way of gaining status. And in politics, although the development of parties—still factions really—during the 1850s did initiate a challenge to oligarchic rule, it did not cause sufficient instability to motivate military leaders to undertake political action.

But probably the most significant deterrent to political action by the military was the fact that the army officer corps still had no real identity other than the family connections that gave it the general character of an extension of the aristocracy, like the Church, the government, or business. Furthermore, because the officers were close to the civilian aristocracy in background and attitudes, they did not feel close to the troops. Army officers, whether aristocrats or not, held attitudes similar to those of civilian aristocrats who, however enlightened and reform-minded, considered themselves quite superior to the masses.

We will discuss the two periods of civil-military relationships noted in the first paragraph of this chapter with emphasis on the following major points. Whereas during the 1870s the military was not deeply involved with the civilian sector, subsequent developments in government, politics, and diplomacy created a situation in which military men did become concerned with their country's policies. The War of the Pacific, a major event in Chile's history, saw the army again defend the state against overwhelming odds. After the war the administration of President Domingo Santa María González (1881–86) tried to make Chile the leading military power west of the Andes in the southern part of the continent—the area Argentine geopoliticians call the Cono Sur, or Southern Cone.

More questions may arise from this chapter than can be answered at this point in our study of Chilean civil-military relations, and some of these will be addressed in the next part of the book. For example, was it in the 1870s and 1880s that military men first began to offer opinions on foreign policy, after nearly a half-century of participating in foreign affairs, if only in a secondary capacity? Did the War of the Pacific instill a kind of paranoia in those who determined military policy, so that defense activities assumed an inflated importance? Was the decision to reform and modernize the army and navy made for political reasons only, and did it drive a wedge between military and civilian aristocrats? Last, how important were intraarmy and interservice (army vs. navy) rivalries during the war and after, and to what extent did they contribute to the crisis of 1891?

Liberal Administrations of the 1860s and 1870s: Oligarchic Fission[1]

Most historians have seen the Pérez decade (1861–71) as a transition period between the height of the Autocratic Republic (1831–71) and the beginnings of the Liberal Republic (1861–91). This thesis may be historically sound in describing the composition of administrations, but it is misleading in indicating a definitive transition from autocracy to liberalism. For autocracy did not end with the Pérez years, despite the fact that Liberals supported by coalitions exercised most of the power from 1871 forward.

José Joaquín Pérez, a Liberal, started the last "presidential decade" in Chilean history as the official candidate of the National or Montt-Varista Party. He ended his second administration supported by La Fusión, the coalition of Conservatives and Liberals who advocated greater powers for parliament. La Fusión thus became the "official" or "administration" coalition, not through revolt, violence, or even elections but rather by political bargaining with the chief executive.

Pérez's successor was the Liberal Federico Errázuriz Zañartu, scion of one of Chile's great families and nephew of Archbishop Rafael Valdivieso Zañartu, with whom Manuel Montt had struggled bitterly in the mid-century contest between Church and state. Errázuriz gained the presidency with support from La Fusión and was opposed by an on-again, off-again Radical-National-Liberal coalition. As president he was supported in Congress by a Radical-Liberal coalition known as the Liberal Alliance.

The election of Errázuriz began a half-century of domination (not always total control) of Chilean politics by coalitions of parties seeking more power for legislators and less for executives, and advocating the secularization of the state. The National and Conservative parties ceased to figure prominently in politics, and after 1891 both parties functioned mainly as temporary allies on specific legislative or electoral issues. Nationals and Conservatives were by no means drawn to each other naturally, but they still represented those elements—the strong state and the prominent Catholic Church as extensions of the aristocracy—that had formed the basis of the Portalian state and maintained civil control of the military earlier in the century.

The Church by no means withered in the face of the anticlerical legislation of the late nineteenth century, but it ceased to form part of the triarchy. The state continued to be an extension of the aristocracy, but it became a weaker extension. Although supported by parliamentarist parties, Pérez, Errázuriz, and particularly Santa María and José Manuel Balmaceda (1886–91) were all quite autocratic, even despotic, in the conduct of executive affairs. Throughout this period, then, the chief executive remained a symbol of national government and power—and commander in chief of the army officer class.

In 1876 the Liberal Alliance elected Aníbal Pinto Garmendia to the presidency. It was Pinto's misfortune to have to deal with the worst effects of the economic recession visited upon Chile during the Errázuriz administration. He was forced also to deal diplomatically with hostile neighboring states and later to lead his nation during the war with Bolivia and Peru. Related to three former presidents—his father, General Francisco Pinto; Manuel Bulnes, his brother-in-law; hence by marriage even to Prieto—Aníbal Pinto was one of Chile's most erudite and talented leaders.[2] Nevertheless, his presidency (1876–81) was one of Chile's most stormy.

By the time Pinto had served five years, the Conservative Party was reduced to almost permanent minority opposition status, and the separation of executive and legislative powers—something Portales had sought to avoid—was under way. The rapid erosion of the traditional composition of the Chilean state did not immediately affect the military, for from the early 1870s on, army leaders' attention was focused on the possibility of war growing out of Chilean interests in the Atacama and Patagonia.

Chilean Foreign Affairs:
Frontier Conflict and International War[3]

In the 1870s Chile and Argentina both had barely plausible claims, based on colonial jurisdiction, to the part of Patagonia south of the Río Negro. After several war scares in the 1860s and 1870s, the two governments finally agreed to arbitrate the question in January 1879, thus averting almost certain naval conflict and possible land fighting. Army leaders and diplomats also looked north in the 1870s, as war with Bolivia and then Peru became imminent.

By 1873 the Antofagasta Nitrate Company (Compañía de Salitre de Antofagasta) was the major extraction operation on the Bolivian littoral. The company, a Chilean consortium, operated under agreements of 1866 and 1874 acknowledging 24° south latitude as the frontier and establishing Chilean rights, with long-term tax stability, to exploit nitrate deposits north of that line in Bolivian territory. Both countries hoped to share revenues accruing from nitrate production in the area between 23° and 25° south latitude. In 1876, military chieftain Hilarión Daza came to power in La Paz, and he recklessly or patriotically (we may never know which) challenged the validity of the treaties under which the Chilean consortium operated. Two years later, in February 1878, Daza unilaterally raised the duty on nitrate exports from Antofagasta, violating a section of an 1874 accord. Negotiations followed, with Bolivia holding in abeyance collection of the higher tax. Late in the year La Paz informed the Pinto government that the Antofagasta Nitrate Company would be required to pay higher rates retroactive for the entire year of 1878. Refusing to negotiate further, Daza also threatened to confiscate Chilean holdings in Antofagasta without payment.

The Chilean response was swift and forceful. Troops occupied Antofagasta on February 14, 1879, a relatively simple task since over 90 percent of the population was Chilean. The army was also directed to pacify Antofagasta and occupy coastal territory as far north as 23° south latitude—the old frontier occupied under Bulnes and only relinquished in 1866 in return for the mineral exploitation rights. Bolivian resistance was pathetic, more like Mexican resistance to the United States in 1847 than that of a nation with a vital stake in an invaded area. Even though armaments purchases, naval equipment, and service contingents had all been cut back during the first years of

Pinto's government, the Chilean army and navy could handle the Bolivian forces.

Bolivia, however, was not Chile's only foe. In a secret treaty Peru had pledged itself to aid Bolivia in the event of war. Financially and militarily weak, the Peruvians reluctantly came to the aid of Bolivia. Chile declared war on Peru on April 4, 1879. The lines were drawn. Though little has been written about civil-military relationships in Chile during this period, the crisis of 1879 figures as a major turning point for several reasons.

The Chilean economy was heavily dependent on nitrates and extractive industry. Bolivian threats to that industry—whether higher taxes, which would inhibit competition with Peru, or confiscation, which would damage investment-capital operations in Santiago and Valparaíso and impair Chile's international credit—were threats to the entire national economy and hence to the financial wherewithal for routine government expenditures. In addition, the economy was still reeling from the recession of the 1870s. In 1879 many workmen, miners, and dockers were unemployed. The questions were, Could the economy support a war and would the war receive popular support?

The economy did support the war as an expensive necessity for national survival, and the war did receive popular support. Opposition leaders temporarily quieted their foreign policy debates and pledged their all for victory over Peru. Where Peru was concerned, Chileans of all classes, parties, and factions tended to forget their differences temporarily. Where Peru and Bolivia were concerned, Chileans forgot their differences even faster. By the 1870s, when Argentina was also concerned (the Andean countries had attempted to associate themselves with Buenos Aires in an anti-Chilean pact), Chilean solidarity was incredible, though reports that young men flocked to enlist in the army and navy are not to be believed. To this day the War of the Pacific is probably revered more than any other episode in Chilean history except the struggle for independence.

The War of the Pacific:
Another Triumph for Chile on Land and Sea[4]

It took Chile less than four years to subdue completely her old enemies, less than eighteen months to defeat Bolivia, and less than two years to occupy Lima, then gradually complete the victory by establishing a puppet regime in Peru and eschewing confrontation with partisans in the Andes.

Because the War of the Pacific was a naval war, Chilean naval operations took on an unprecedented significance, and Chile therefore entered the 1880s as the foremost naval power on the continent, at a time when naval strength was generally considered the key to great-power status.

When war broke out in 1879 the Chilean Army consisted of fewer than 2,500 men on active duty, supported by 7,000 militia men. Rumor had it that the Peruvian army numbered 5,000 (some said 15,000) and the Bolivian army, 2,500; each nation reputedly had over 50,000 men in reserve. These were rumors and nothing more; as they had been in 1837, Peru and Bolivia were overestimated as military powers. The Andean reserves were unwilling Indian conscripts, untrained for effective, prolonged service in the field. Both nations were in financial plights as bad as or worse than Chile's. The small, disciplined Chilean Army was comparatively well armed and equipped. On land, then, Chile had an advantage.

It is over 1,800 miles from Santiago to Lima by land, 1,100 to Arica, 950 to Iquique, and 700 to Antofagasta. The transportation of an army to any of these strategic points would have been impossible in the 1880s without a navy. Moreover, even in the sparsely populated Bolivian and Peruvian Atacama, supply lines would have to be exterior. Tarapacá, Arica, and Tacna, where proportionately more Peruvians lived than Bolivians in Antofagasta, could not have been subdued by land alone.

At sea, however, Chile did not have the advantage in 1879.[5] On May 21, 1879, the Peruvian warships *Huáscar* and *Independencia* trapped the Chilean antiques *Covadonga* and *Esmeralda* at Iquique. The *Esmeralda* was lost, but the Peruvians lost the *Independencia*. The ironclad *Huáscar* ranged far south during the winter of 1879. But by the beginning of 1880 Chile did have the advantage at sea. A new Chilean ironclad, the *Almirante Cochrane*, hastily summoned from Europe before construction was finished, engaged the *Huáscar*, terror of the Pacific. At Punta de Angamos (Mejillones) the *Huáscar* was forced to surrender on October 8, 1879; the loss of the ship put an end to Peruvian naval supremacy. The *Cochrane* and her sister ship, the *Almirante Blanco Encalada*, dominated the Pacific coast for the rest of the war. The *Huáscar* became a historic relic, permanently docked in the Talcahuano naval yard in southern Chile.

In successive victories Chilean forces captured the Peruvian Atacama. The province of Tarapacá was invaded and occupied in 1879, and Arica and Tacna fell by mid 1880. The fall of Tarapacá caused revolt in Bolivia. Daza was ousted, and General Narciso Campero took the field at Tacna; his defeat led to his own fall and his country's withdrawal from the war. But negotiations failed to end hostilities with Peru in 1880. This led to the decision of the Santiago government to attack Lima. The War Ministry, ably directed by Domingo Santa María, drew up plans to invade the central coast of Peru late in 1880.

First at Chorrillos and then at Miraflores—at the time towns outside the capital, today pleasant suburbs of Lima—the Peruvian Army was totally defeated; by the end of January 1881 Chilean troops completed the occupation of Lima. In barely two years' time the combined forces of the Andean powers had been subdued. Antofagasta, Tarapacá, Tacna, and Arica were in Chilean hands, Lima was occupied, and resistance was confined to the Peruvian sierra. That resistance was never totally quelled, and until 1883 there was no definite conclusion to the war. Finally a collaborationist regime directed by General Manuel Iglesias convinced influential Peruvians that further resistance was more expensive and damaging than peace, and gained enough support to go to the treaty table. On October 20, 1883, Chile and Peru agreed to peace.

The Treaty of Ancón, signed at a village north of Lima, resulted in Chilean sovereignty in Tarapacá and called for a future plebiscite to determine the ownership of Tacna and Arica. (The plebiscite was never held. The Tacna-Arica question plagued both countries until 1929, when Peru reoccupied Tacna and Chile retained control over Arica in return for reparations.) A subsequent agreement with Bolivia in 1884 turned Antofagasta over to Chile, but it was not ratified by the Bolivians until 1904.

The War of the Pacific made Chile the undisputed Pacific power of South America. Chile had shattered Peruvian sea power and won stirring victories on the coastal flats outside Lima. The economy had revived, not suffered; nitrates were more important than ever, and textiles, railroads, construction materials, and food processing also grew in importance. The Pinto administration and its successor, that of former war minister Santa María, did not have to resort to extraordinary powers or major emergency measures. Government activities other than those related to defense were carried on in an atmosphere of normalcy. After decades of stalemate and frustration the southern army put an end to Araucanian depredations, thus opening fertile lands in the far southern Central Valley just as the international conflict was coming to an end in the North. Into these frontier lands moved new generations of farmers and ranchers whose interests, as one might expect, would not always coincide with established Central Valley interests. But for the moment calm prevailed. Even Santa María's election was carried out in regular fashion. Could there, wondered Chileans, be a greater country in South America?

A New Military Tradition: Martyrdom and Heroism[6]

Chileans were especially proud of their army and navy. War heroes were numerous, and some became legendary, among them Captain Carlos Condell de la Haza, who commanded the *Covadonga* (captured by him from the Spaniards in 1866) in the battle of Iquique and barely defeated the Peruvian ship *Independencia;* Captain Arturo Prat Chacón, the martyr of Iquique, who leaped from the deck of his sinking *Esmeralda* to the deck of the *Huáscar*, there to be felled by rifle fire; Sergeant Juan de Dios Aldea, who followed his captain; Captain Juan José Latorre Benavente, who captured *Huáscar* off Punta Angamos in October 1879 in the first high-seas confrontation of ironclads; Colonel Emilio Sotomayor Baeza, "Conqueror" of Antofagasta and of Iquique; General Erasmo Escala, hero of the Antofagasta and Tarapacá campaigns; General Manuel Baquedano, who directed the 13,000-man Chilean contingent that invaded Tacna-Arica and led the attack on Lima's southern districts; Colonel Pedro Lagos Marchant, a decorated veteran of the Araucanian wars who directed the assault on the *Morro* of Arica and who also marched on Lima; Araucanian veteran Orozimbo Barboza Puga, decorated at Tacna; Captain Patricio Lynch Zaldívar, terror of the northern coast of Peru and director of operations during the occupation of Lima; Colonel Estanislao del Canto Arteaga, another Araucanian veteran who fought brilliantly in the Peruvian campaign; the young Captain Ignacio Carrera Pinto, grandson of José Miguel Carrera, who died heroically trying to pacify the Peruvian interior.

The names of martyrs and heroes like Prat, Condell, Latorre,

Sotomayor, Escala, Baquedano, Lagos, Barboza, Lynch, Canto, Carrera are still spoken with respect and pride in Chile. And there are
seamen, sergeants major, cabin boys, and infantry men, both well
known and anonymous, to whom Chileans still pay homage. National
reverence for military martyrs and heroes may even have helped
make the military reluctant to change the essential civil-military
relationship.

The Consequences of Conflict:
Militarization, Militarism, and Oligarchic Fission[7]

The War of the Pacific was the most important war in nineteenth-
century South America. Its consequences were as momentous to its
participants as were those of the Mexican War to the United States
and Mexico, more consequential than those of the War of the Triple
Alliance to Argentina, Brazil, Uruguay, and Paraguay. Chile gained
immense wealth, new territory, citizens—and problems. Peru lost
much wealth and land; Bolivia lost an unexploited and indefensible
access to the sea. From the standpoint of relations between the
Chilean Army and the state, the results of the conflict were still being
felt a half-century later, for soon after the Treaty of Ancón, Chile took
measures to ensure its continued naval and military supremacy on the
west coast. The Santa María administration looked to Europe for
advice in molding the most highly trained and powerful army in
South America so that Chile's enemies would never again prove a
military threat. The age of military professionalization began, and
with it the age of military politics.

Military politics and military professionalization ultimately became inseparable in Chile, but the relationship was not the same
during the 1880s as it would be, say, forty years later. And while the
growth of military interest in political affairs after World War I was
indeed a long-range result of the military politics of the 1880s and
1890s, the differences in interests would prove extreme.

With the advent of peace in 1884, the Chilean Army, by this time
around 25,000 strong, obviously had to be reduced in size. This did
not meet with the approval of all military leaders, for the experiences
of wartime and the prewar diplomatic crises with Argentina and the
Andean powers had made them wary. In the 1881 accord with
Argentina, Chile ceded rights to Patagonia, but the Andean frontier

was still in question. In addition, former Argentine-Bolivian border disputes became "Chileanized" with the seizure of Antofagasta Province. Treaties notwithstanding, Andean revanche seemed a real possibility.

Some of the returning heroes became politically active officers, and some, on retirement, actually entered politics. Popular military men have repeatedly been sought as allies by politicians in the modern world, in France, Germany, England, and the United States, and late nineteenth-century Chile was no exception to this rule. The deterioration of the Portalian system and the proliferation of political parties, coalitions, temporary alliances, and arrangements created a situation in which members of the officer class were lured, or sought of their own accord, to associate themselves with parties. Never before had Chilean officers had so much prestige; any civilian politician who associated himself with a war hero could bask in reflected glory.

The presidencies of Santa María and his ill-fated successor Balmaceda were fraught with political squabbling. Both were headstrong autocrats who balked at every attempt by leaders in Congress to curb their powers. Balmaceda in particular was an unpopular leader; Radicals and Liberals only helped elect him in 1886 as the best candidate under the circumstances. The decline in prestige of these executives helped to erode the friendly executive-military relationship molded by Prieto and Bulnes.

The aristocratic oligarchy lost its cohesiveness during the 1880s, and this as much as any other late-nineteenth-century development helped to break the hitherto strong military-aristocracy link. No longer was the oligarchy the preserve of the Basque-Castilian group. Absorption of other elements,[8] however, tended to delay "class conflict" until late in the century, and when major political conflict came, it was based on political and economic issues rather than true class struggle. By 1890 the executive-legislative conflict had sharply divided the loyalties of the oligarchs, with those favoring the legislative side probably in the majority. The family and marriage ties that formerly linked the aristocracy to the military and the officer class to the ruling class forced many officers to choose sides, too. No longer did the aristocrat in uniform simply serve the state.

In short, the internal cohesion of two parts of the triarchy was weak by 1890 as the officer class and the aristocracy expanded and grew apart, as the cohesion of each broke down, and as both were faced with institutional change. Major changes in Chilean civil-military relationships resulted. Ultimately, when the oligarchy lost control of political power after World War I, the civil-military balance was inverted temporarily; but that remains to be discussed in part II.

What exactly were the institutional changes confronting the oligarchy and the officer class? Army leaders were faced with professionalization, reform, and modernization—changes which for several reasons did not please all members of the officer class. When the Santa María government announced in 1885 that it had obtained the services of a retired German captain to oversee army education and training, some officers (a minority) objected. They feared for their position and prestige. Others wondered what a retired German captain could teach those who had taken Antofagasta, Iquique, Arica, Tacna, and Lima. Still others saw military modernization—the overall term we shall apply to the program and process—as an attempt to weld the army to the executive branch of government by reshaping and purging it. High-ranking officers in particular feared that the army would be turned into a political creature to be manipulated by the high-handed Santa María and his probable successor, Balmaceda. The majority of lower-ranking officers, however, applauded modernization and eagerly awaited the arrival of the German captain.

Confronting civilian leaders at this point in Chilean history was the continual clash of political and economic interests. Balmaceda struggled against the advocates of parliamentary power, Radicals and Liberals mostly. His plans for what amounted to a step toward state economic planning, for new taxes, and for utilization of nitrate impost revenues in internal development schemes instead of normal government operations were also vigorously opposed. The clash was so involved that it merits a book of its own; it culminated in the death struggle known as the Civil War of 1891, Balmaceda's own death, and the final destruction of Portalian ideals. The military played an integral part in these events. By 1891 the army was bitterly divided, for its officers had already felt the first influences of institutional change at the hands of Captain Emil Körner.

Körner and Prussianization: Germano-Chilean Professionalism[9]

Emil Körner was a Saxon and a commoner. Born in 1846, he entered the army in 1866, studied and taught at the Artillery and

Engineer's School (Charlottenburg), and was decorated after Sedan. He graduated from the Kriegsakademie in 1876 and served in Italy, Spain, and Africa. When he was approached by the Chilean government he had spent nearly twenty years in the kaiser's army, had risen to the rank of captain, and had made a good record, but, like many non-Prussians and commoners, he had little future in the Imperial Army. Chile's minister to Germany, Guillermo Matta, met with Körner in 1885 and convinced him that his future lay in South America. Impressed with what he had read of Chile's recent victory, Körner, after considering a similar offer made by Japan, agreed to teach artillery, infantry, cartography, military history, and tactics and to serve as subdirector of the Escuela Militar for 12,000 marks annually, to be paid in Chilean gold. Körner began his awesome-sounding duties in 1886 and soon began to plan for a staff school—a Chilean Kriegsakademie.

On September 9, 1886, the Academia de Guerra was formally inaugurated and the Chilean Army began a new life. The decree creating the Academia stated that the purpose of the new institution was to improve "as much as possible the level of technical and scientific instruction of army officers, in order that they may be able, in case of war, to take advantage of new methods of combat and modern armaments in use today."[10] The Academia was to function as a staff school, and the army adopted the general staff system in order to be prepared for war at any time.

The founding of a staff school gave outstanding junior officers an opportunity for advanced and specialized training never before enjoyed by Chileans. In the Escuela's three-year (sometimes two-year) curriculum, cadets studied tactics and strategy, a little military history, some science (generally elementary physics and chemistry), mathematics, and courses of a purely military nature. When the Academia accepted its first students in June 1887 its projected three-year curriculum consisted of the following:

First Year
German
Mathematics or World History
Tactics
Fortification
Cartography
Ballistics

Military History
Geography
Military Science
Inorganic Chemistry
Physics

Second Year

German
Mathematics or World History
Tactics
Fortification
Cartography
Geography
Military Science
Physics
Chemistry
Topography
War Games

Third Year

German
Mathematics or World History
Chilean Military History
Latin American Military Geography
International Law
Hygiene
General Staff Service
War Games

Of the fifteen lieutenants and captains who completed the first three-year course in 1890, five were sent to Germany for further training. In less than five years Körner had molded an incipient military elite.

Military Fission:
Simultaneous with Oligarchic Fission

The new elite was composed of young officers who attended Körner's classes at the Escuela and Academia. Most Academia students by 1890 were veterans of the War of the Pacific and knew the rigors of both the battlefield and the classroom first hand. Their adulation of Körner was complete; he soon became known throughout Chile as "don Emilio" much as Colmar von der Goltz would be known throughout the Ottoman Empire as "Goltz Pasha." Körner's clique of students and former students was made up primarily of lieutenants and captains. Although none of them had held a command position prior to the civil war of 1891, the young lions identified with each other from the beginning far more than with any civilian sector. Ultimately this identity became a kind of cohesive force within the officer corps.

As noted, older officers had mixed feelings about Körner. General Emilio Sotomayor Baeza, the instigator of military modernization, was pleased. After the battles of Chorrillos and Miraflores and the occupation of Lima, Sotomayor became director of the Escuela. He urged that something be done to update manuals (Spanish translations of outdated French works were still being used), curriculum, and, of course, advanced training. But other figures, such as Canto and Baquedano, were not convinced that the army needed anything more than strengthening. Too, many senior officers who had been promoted rapidly during the war saw military modernization with emphasis on the Escuela and the new Academia as a threat to their recently acquired status.

Most Chilean sources agree that by 1890 the army officer class was made up of three distinct groups: the young, progressive junior officer group composed of lieutenants, captains, and some majors and lieutenant colonels; the older officers, the majority of whom were generals and colonels and who had little interest in Körner and military modernization or even opposed them outright; and the third group, majors, lieutenant colonels, and colonels, who owed their positions to the war (or to ties with the oligarchy).[11] The lines between these groups were blurred, and it was not at all rare for a man to belong to more than one—just as a politician might take various positions. In other words, the early impact of the reform program, following closely on the military triumphs of 1879–83, divided the army officer class along intraarmy professional lines.

By 1889 the outspoken Körner was advocating further reforms in military training. From that date forward official military publications —*informes*, annual reports (*memorias*), and special studies—began to reflect a growing consciousness of reform on the part of junior officers and those of all ranks involved in the modernization program, sometimes chiding the government—in general, for no specific leaders were ever taken to task—and the high command for professional inadequacies.

In his official *informe* prepared for the Ministry of War in 1889, for example, Körner was blunt in assessing Chilean military training. The physical plant, books, uniforms, and teaching materials were either in poor condition or nonexistent, he wrote. This was "an unnecessary and foolish economy" resulting in Escuela graduates who were ignorant in science and languages. Körner also lamented the archaic overspecialization of Escuela training, whereby cadets were funneled into the infantry, cavalry, artillery, or engineers and not given basic training in all arms. This would make coordinated action in wartime impossible. He even called for a new examination process whereby cadets would be required to show evidence of study several times a year and not just at the end of the course. Körner and his early supporter Colonel Jorge Boonen Rivera (who had initially opposed major changes) were the major pre–Civil War advocates of further and deeper reform. Their publications—Körner's *Informe pasado por el primer subdirector de la escuela militar sr. don Emilio Körner* (1889) and Boonen's *Estudio sobre la organización i planta del ejército* (1888)—were extremely influential among officers and politicians alike and rank as landmarks of Chilean military literature. They reflect German training and doctrine and advocate constant preparedness for war.

At this stage in his Chilean career, Emil Körner functioned in an instructional, administrative, and advisory capacity; he was not in actual command of troops. In theory, he had little more influence than did French and German military instructors and advisers in the Ottoman Empire, the Balkans, or Japan. Although European military advice achieved much in those areas, the Europeans never commanded troops there during peacetime except in maneuvers and war games. What made the military reform program in Chile distinct from other such European ventures of the time in Latin America, the Middle East, and the Orient was the fact that Körner *did* assume the role of a commander in 1891. He ultimately became a Chilean citizen and took his place in the pantheon of military heroes.

By the time Körner's and Boonen's studies became controversial in political and professional circles, Balmaceda's ill-fated presidency was more than half over. Through arrogance, self-righteousness, and autocratic measures, Balmaceda had succeeded by 1890 in alienating the very groups that had brought him to power and in dividing the

Basque-Castilian oligarchy. The nouveau riche mining barons, nitrate kings, manufacturers, and businessmen feared his advocacy of new fiscal policies and state planning. Reformers, Radicals, and Democrats considered him the reincarnation of Portales and Montt. Thus he faced widespread opposition on constitutional, political, and economic grounds. But this type of conflict had existed before; the key new ingredient, which precluded internalization of political disputes, was the military.

The Armed Forces and Oligarchic Fission: Military Motivations in 1891

We must now consider the navy. The Chilean Navy, Latin America's most powerful, had been, like the army, an extension of the state and of the aristocracy.[12] Within its officer class, however, cohesion was stronger than that of the army in the 1880s. Close to the conservative British Navy since the time of Cochrane and Williams Rebolledo, who by this time was active in politics, the Chilean Navy was still fused to the conservative Frondista aristocracy. Williams and others had been particularly critical of governmental interference in naval affairs during the War with Spain and blamed political interference for early reversals of the War in the Pacific, yet none of the great names of Chilean naval history figured in the revolt of 1891. Naval headquarters were in Valparaíso, and younger naval leaders mingled socially with the Porteño upper classes, who were involved in business and foreign trade. These people saw Balmaceda as a representative of an outmoded autocracy and as a threat to their interests because of his attempts to find new sources of revenue through tariffs and other taxes. Jorge Montt Álvarez (distantly related to the former president) became the maritime governor of Valparaíso in 1887 after returning from Europe with the recommendation that new ships for the navy be built in British yards. Balmaceda preferred French yards, and a squabble ensued. Neither Montt nor any other naval chief questioned Balmaceda's interest in a strong navy, and the influential Círculo Naval even praised his dedication to a strong sea defense system. The president, after all, had supported increased naval power and had pushed for the creation of an engineers' school, which had opened in 1887. Naval officers opposed Balmaceda because of their ties to civilians, for essentially political reasons. Promises of support from congressional leaders for further naval expansion also helped to sway the navy officer class which, to a man, went into revolt in January 1891.

The motivations of the army in the 1891 crisis are less clear, but we can draw some rather firm conclusions as to the stand of the officer class. Internal cohesion was weaker than ever before because of—not in spite of—the reform program. The already-divided officer class split into two groups in 1891. Among older officers the question was one of political loyalties versus constitutional dictates, aristocratic and oligarchic connections and relationships versus loyalty to the chief of state. Among middle-ranking and junior officers, the historical evidence shows that the divisions in 1891 were caused more by attitudes arising from the reform program: objection to Körner and German orientation on the one hand, and attachment to Körner and the "new army" on the other. In addition, Balmaceda was known to favor limitations on the size of the standing army; this was at once an economy measure and symptomatic of his recognition that naval power was more important to Chile's status. To many young army officers this was near treason!

Then, too, certain political motives overrode constitutional dictates at all levels; enough officer-class cohesion remained to influence some members of all ranks. Körner's case in 1890–91 illustrates this. Körner was not a political officer; he was a professional military man, and this forced him to take a political position. Balmaceda's favoritism toward the navy and his wish to limit the size of the army were unacceptable to Körner, who feared a setback to his own plans for the army. Körner was simply not accustomed to a political system that allowed civilian authority to dictate to military interests, much less favor sea power! Körner was, of course, the progenitor of military modernization, and a good case could be made that Balmaceda and the system for which he stood were anachronistic.

Some Chileans believed that Körner was self-seeking and megalomaniacal. This may be so, and we cannot discount the idea that Körner saw in revolt the chance to apply modern strategy and tactics in order to establish political conditions propitious to reforms he thought necessary. The United States minister to Chile during the Civil War saw Körner's actions as part of a conspiracy of German and British financial interests to gain control of the Chilean economy.[13] Finally, it can be argued that Körner assumed that the rebels represented legality and constitutionality, and that his duty was to serve them (Wilhelm II subsequently disagreed and criticized him for his actions, however).

There could have been no Civil War in 1891 without military support and participation. There could, in turn, have been no meaningful military support or participation had not the navy been so strong and cohesive and the army so divided regarding reforms and politics. Naval strength had come about because of wartime triumphs and historical, geopolitical exigencies. The breakdown of army officer-class internal cohesion and ties with the ruling group were likewise the result of historical developments, as well as of social and economic change reflected in the decades after 1851. The demise of the Penquista dynasty, the disruption of the aristocratic-oligarchic-military fusion, and the erosion of the Portalian centralized executive political system that had begun in mid century culminated (with regard to civil-military relationships) only in the 1891 conflict. For as long as the army officer class functioned as an extension of the state—itself an extension of the aristocracy and oligarchy—and as long as the army officer class did not see itself as a distinct interest group, it could not actively oppose the state or an individual at its head.

Civil-military relationships ceased to be based on family ties and on a relatively simple set of common interests (national defense, frontier expansion, internal order) as the century approached its end. The relationship between army and navy also changed, as it began to seem possible that the navy would become the most favored service. This created a tenuous, crisis-based army-navy relationship, but one through which leaders of both services thought their interests would be best realized in 1891.

By 1891 a form of corporate self-interest could be detected in the actions and attitudes of Chilean army and navy leaders. The army in particular manifested such self-interest in the post-1891 period that civil-military relationships were temporarily restructured in abrupt and radical fashion.

PART II: 1891-1931

5

The Army and Political, Social, and Economic Change, 1891–1931: An Overview

The Civil War of 1891 created a new political system in Chile, one in which Congress replaced the chief executive as the principal power. For thirty-five years this Parliamentary Republic resisted all challenges. In 1925, however, it began to crumble, and two years later it collapsed forever with the election of General Carlos Ibáñez del Campo to the presidency. In 1931, forty years after José Manuel Balmaceda took his own life at the close of the Civil War, General Ibáñez fled Santiago for exile in Argentina and the Chilean Army was ridiculed for its support of his four-year authoritarian regime. How and why was the essential civil-military relationship in Chile—military subservience to civilian authority—inverted, and what is the significance of such an inversion with regard to past and future?

Most assuredly this inversion was not the result of "military intervention," an overused term in studies of Latin American civil-military relationships. Where institutions of government are strong, a military organization cannot intervene overtly for the purpose of resolving national problems or taking power. Tradition is no substitute for institutional strength.

Forces at work since the last decades of the nineteenth century weakened civilian institutions and transformed the society and the economy to the point where the military became the only force capable of performing the tasks normally reserved for civilian authority. In short, old relationships disappeared or changed, and new influences led to the collapse of civilian authority and the introduction of military political power. To some this seemed a tragedy, to others an inevitability, to still others a kind of reincarnation, military-style, of the Portalian era.

At no time, significantly, did the Chilean Army officer class cease to be representative of the sector of society from which it drew its membership. Soon after the Civil War of 1891, however, it did cease to reflect the nature of the political system to which it was subservient. The army was undergoing institutional change and modernization, and this made for a dichotomous relationship with the state.

Military Professionalism:
A Continental Phenomenon[1]

During the first quarter of the twentieth century the armies of Latin America's major countries underwent a process of professionalization. In South America military professionalization was seen as a way to alter those aspects of civil-military relations which were aberrant by civilian reckoning, and to tie the military more effectively to the state. In countries where the military had figured prominently as a political force or arbiter, professionalization was supposed to expel the army from politics. In countries that had been defeated in war, professionalism was seen as a method of creating a modern effective military organization.

During the nineteenth century, South American international conflict created interlocking tension zones in which military strength, diplomacy, and economic considerations helped to maintain a type of power balance early in this century. In chapter 1 we noted briefly the existence of three such zones: the Pacific-Andean zone, comprising Peru, Bolivia, and Chile; the heartland zone, which was of interest to Brazil, Argentina, Paraguay, and Bolivia; and the Amazon Basin zone, involving Brazil, Peru, Colombia, Ecuador, and Bolivia. In the twentieth century only two of these zones would be the scene of international conflict: the Amazon Basin zone and the heartland, scene of the Chaco War (1932–36).

Chile did not go to war after 1883 and, except for a brief, poorly conceived and executed mobilization in 1920, martial spirits dissipated. But a martial tradition prevailed. Triumphant twice in the nineteenth century against her Andean neighbors and successful in stifling indigenous resistance to southern frontier expansion, Chile held her army in esteem. The fact that Chile was surrounded on all sides by potentially hostile states helped to perpetuate the national belief in a need for military strength. There were running border disputes with Argentina (technically resolved in 1902) and border problems and treaty grievances with restless, landlocked Bolivia (likewise technically resolved, in 1904). And Chilean troops occupied Tacna-Arica until 1929, when, by mutual agreement, Tacna reverted to Peru and Arica became Chile's northernmost province. Despite her apparent geographic isolation, Chile was involved in all the tension zones of the continent, so the belief that a strong army was indispensable never vanished entirely from Chilean minds.

In Chile military professionalization, or modernization, meant modern education, training, and organization based on Prussian models. It also meant regulation of salary, promotion, and retirement systems, and modern equipment, armaments, technology, and coordinated maneuvers. It was designed to provide for defense, and offense if necessary, to assure Chile's position in the face of foreign hostility. Professionalization was never viewed by its proponents as necessary to maintain the army's apolitical stance or to tie it to the state. The army's loyalty was traditional, its service unquestioned.

By the time professionalism—expertise, corporate self-interest, and responsibility—was achieved, the army's loyalty to the state was questionable and its apolitical tradition was broken. This was not the result of simple disobedience or irresponsibility on the part of military leaders, nor did it result from outright military political adventurism. Military men were loyal to the state, but they were also imbued with a sense of self-interest which led them to think that they belonged to a separate class and to believe that the state had certain responsibilities to them.

Professionalism developed similarly in other South American armies during this period. In Argentina, Brazil, and Peru, the other major powers of the continent, experiments with European military orientation similar to Chile's produced much the same results. German or French training helped to create military institutions that were modern by local standards. Political, social, and economic change resulted not only in a degree of modernization but also in instability and conflict, ferment and disorder, collapse and bankruptcy. Professional officers, convinced that they were the only guarantors of order, took upon themselves the task of setting things right. A good case can be made for military professionalism as a cause of political participation; professionalism certainly did not inhibit political action. By 1931 Argentina, Brazil, and Peru were governed by professional military officers and their civilian supporters, and in 1931 General Ibáñez was driven from power in Chile after having served four years as president.

The Military and the State:
Change and Alienation[2]

The South American political upheavals of 1930 and 1931 were all, of course, related in some degree to the Great Depression. In Argentina, Peru, and Brazil civilian malfeasance, ineptitude, and failure to deal with severe social and economic problems, as well as civilian prodding of the military into action, were also causes of military involvement. These influences and pressures existed in Chile by the end of World War I, a decade before they became apparent in Argentina, Brazil, and Peru.

The history of Chilean civil-military relationships in the late nineteenth and early twentieth centuries is, therefore, an enlightening case study in the alienation of the army from the state. Moreover, the fact that alienation took place where the relationship had been so close makes it clear that there is no foolproof way of ensuring military subservience to civilian authority in Latin America. In order to understand how an army with an enviable record of discipline and obedience can cast off these traditions and seize power, it is necessary to examine the Chilean Army and Navy in an era of change.

In part I we placed much emphasis on the establishment by Diego Portales of military obedience to civilian authority in the 1830s and the maintenance of that relationship between 1831 and 1891. As we have seen, those sixty years were by no means static, but none of the major political, social, or economic changes visibly altered the fundamental civil-military pattern. The factors examined in chapter 1 aided in keeping the army apolitical and the administrations relatively free of conflict. The disappearance of some of those factors and the development of new influences changed civil-military relations so drastically that professional army officers violated the constitutional proscription of political deliberation.

Of the factors that led to civilian control of the military, the nature of the ruling class was probably most important. The Basque-Castilian aristocracy was probably the single most important element of civilian control, for its flexibility, its internal cohesion, and its fusion with military leadership made for civil-military homogeneity.

It is important to remember that by 1891 all the factors upon which civil-military relations had been based during the nineteenth century had altered. The changes in the ruling class were especially noticeable, although the Basque-Castilian group continued to supply most of Chile's political leaders and all her presidents. The addition of numerous non-Iberian families to the aristocracy made it more heterogeneous by the end of the century, leading to intraaristocratic conflict in 1891. This did little to destroy the concept of aristocratic, autocratic rule, but much to change the specific characteristics of government; it did little to change Chile's economic structure, but much to complicate it.

After 1881, the Basque-Castilian extended presidential family was characterized by two extreme variants of oligarchy. First, there were presidents who were not related, or were only distantly related, to their predecessors: Santa María, Balmaceda, Jorge Montt Álvarez (1891–96), Ramón Barros Luco (1910–15), and Juan Luis Sanfuentes Andonaegui (1915–20), whose presidencies covered most of the period between 1881 and 1920. Barros and Sanfuentes were pathetically weak executives; they were tied to the oligarchy only through marriage of siblings or children.

Second, the extended presidential family bore evidence of extreme political incestuousness, seen by some as a remnant of the past. The 1896–1906 decade is illustrative of this. Federico Errázuriz Echaurren (1896–1901) was the son of a former president (Federico Errázuriz Zañartu), and was the brother-in-law of his successor, Germán Riesco Errázuriz (1901–6), who, in turn, was his brother-in-law's cousin! A modicum of normalcy was represented by Pedro Montt Montt (1906–10), merely the son of Manuel Montt. But none of post-1891 presidents were as dynamic or forceful as the pre-1891 chief executives.

The erosion and ultimate alteration of the Portalian state parallels decades of change within the oligarchy, the aristocracy, and the families making up the extended presidential family. By the 1860s, the independence generation (those leaders born before, but reared during, Chile's break with Spain), the generation most familiar with autocratic, centralized, executive government, had grown too old to supply acceptable leaders. Chile's new leaders of the postindependence generation were more issue oriented, more attuned to political opposition and the exercise of legislative authority. By the 1860s the mid-century generation (those born after the structuring of the Portalian state), experienced in legislative-executive struggles, came to the fore. With the exception of Balmaceda and Admiral Montt, these were men who rose to prominence as skillful legislators. (Table 1 indicates dates of birth, death, and presidential terms of the Chilean presidents up to 1920.)

If we continue to examine generation groupings of the extended presidential family, we find that members of the independence generation began what parliamentary experience they had at an average age of thirty-two years, while those of the postindependence and mid-century generations averaged thirty years of age at the time

TABLE 1

The Chilean Presidents, 1817-1920

Pre-Portalian Executives

President	Term of Office
Bernardo O'Higgins y Riquelme, 1778-1842	1817-1823
Ramón Freire y Serrano, 1787-1851*	
Francisco Antonio Pinto Díaz, 1785-1858*	

PENQUISTA-SOUTH CENTRAL VALLEY DYNASTY

Independence Generation

Joaquín Prieto Vial, 1786-1854	1831-1841
Manuel Bulnes Prieto, 1799-1866	1841-1851
Manuel Montt Torres, 1809-1880	1851-1861
José Joaquín Pérez Mascayano, 1800-1889	1861-1871

Postindependence Generation

Federico Errázuriz Zañartu, 1825-1877	1871-1876
Aníbal Pinto Garmendia, 1825-1884	1876-1881
Domingo Santa María González, 1825-1889	1881-1886

Mid-Century Generation

José Manuel Balmaceda, 1840-1891	1886-1891
Jorge Montt Alvarez, 1845-1922	1891-1896
Federico Errázuriz Echaurren, 1850-1901	1896-1901
Germán Riesco Errázuriz, 1854-1916	1901-1906
Pedro Montt Montt, 1848-1910	1906-1910
Ramón Barros Luco, 1835-1919	1910-1915
Juan Luis Sanfuentes Andonaegui, 1858-1930	1915-1920

*Both served more than once between 1823 and 1831. For other chief executives, 1823-31, see Fernando Campos Harriet, *Historia constitucional de Chile* (Santiago: Editorial Jurídica de Chile, 1969), pp. 127-28.

they first entered Congress. Independence generation presidents entered La Moneda at an average age of forty-four years, postindependence generation presidents at an average age of fifty-one, and mid-century generation presidents at an average age of fifty-two. As might be expected, chief executives during the years after 1871 had substantially more years of experience with parliamentary politics before being elected to the presidency than did their pre-1871 predecessors.

Independence generation presidents began administrative duties (cabinet or significant diplomatic appointments) at the early average age of twenty-nine years, for during that period the talent pool was not extensive. Postindependence generation presidents took on such tasks at an average age of forty-one years, and mid-century generation chief executives at thirty-seven. Therefore, the early autocrats (1831–71) had comparatively more and earlier executive-administrative experience than did chief executives from Errázuriz Zañartu forward.

Chilean presidents from 1823 to 1920 entered politics before reaching the age of thirty excepting only Francisco Pinto and Admiral Montt (José Pérez entered politics just after his thirtieth birthday). They usually began their careers by being elected to parliament. The independence generation chief executives (excepting Pérez) reached La Moneda in their forties; postindependence generation presidents in their mid forties to mid fifties; and mid-century generation presidents from their mid forties to late fifties (except Barros Luco, who was elected to the presidency at the age of seventy-five, after nearly a half-century of public life, most of it in parliament. Clearly, executive abilities and experience became less and less necessary for presidential candidacy as Congress rose after mid century. As this trend continued into the twentieth century, respect for the authority of the chief executive declined, gradually if perceptibly. Table 2 represents presidential political experience in graphic form.

It is remarkable that, through all these changes, the executive position remained well within the confines of the Basque-Castilian aristocracy. The political orientation of the great families changed over the ninety years between Lircay and the election of Arturo Alessandri Palma in 1920, but change was not effected by challenges from outside the ruling class. Because of the continued power of the Basque-Castilian aristocrats, there was no question of the army being courted by parties, factions, or individuals, nor was the army

TABLE 2
Major Preexecutive Political Experience of Chile's Presidents, 1831-1920*

Name	Presidential Term(s)	Preexecutive Political Experience	Age Political Career Began	Age Legislative Career Began	Age Became President
Bernardo O'Higgins	1817-23	Alcalde (Chillán) 1804 Military service (to rank of Brigadier) 1810-17	26		39
Ramón Freire	1827-29	Military service 1816	29		36
Francisco Pinto	1827-29	Minister to Argentina 1811 Minister to England 1813 Military service 1816-30 Cabinet service 1824 Vice-President 1827	36		42
Joaquín Prieto	1831-41	Military service 1814-31 Provincial administration 1814- Chamber of Deputies 1823-25, 1828-29	28	37	45
Manuel Bulnes	1841-51	Military service 1825-41	26		42
Manuel Montt	1851-61	Chamber of Deputies 1834- Cabinet service 1837- Supreme Court 1838-	25	25	42
José Joaquín Pérez	1861-71	Minister to Argentina 1830 Chamber of Deputies 1834- Cabinet service 1844- Senate 1852-	30	34	61
Federico Errázuriz Z.	1871-76	Chamber of Deputies 1849- Intendant (Santiago) 1865 Cabinet service 1865- Senate 1867	24	24	46

Name	Dates	Service			
Aníbal Pinto	1876-81	Chamber of Deputies 1852- / Intendant (Concepción) 1862- / Senate 1870 / Cabinet service 1871-	27	27	51
Domingo Santa María	1881-86	Senior ministry official 1846 / Intendant (Colchagua) 1848 / Cabinet service 1863-	21		56
José Manuel Balmaceda	1886-91	Chamber of Deputies 1854- / Presidential secretary 1864 / Minister to Argentina 1878 / Cabinet service 1881-	24	24	51
Jorge Montt A.	1891-96	Naval service 1865-91 / President, Junta of Government 1891	46		46
Federico Errázuriz E.	1896-1901	Chamber of Deputies 1876- / Cabinet service 1890 / Senate 1894	26	26	45
Germán Riesco E.	1901-6	Senior ministry official 1880 / Senate 1900	26	46	55
Pedro Montt M.	1906-10	Chamber of Deputies 1876- / Cabinet service 1886- / Senate 1900-	28	28	58
Ramón Barros Luco	1910-15	Chamber of Deputies 1861 / Cabinet service 1872- / Senate 1891- / Minister to France 1897	26	26	75
Juan Luis Sanfuentes	1915-20	Chamber of Deputies 1888 / Cabinet service 1901 / Senate 1901-	30	30	57

*Unless beginning and ending dates appear, dates of service indicate permanent or intermittent service in parliament or ministries from the given date forward, in certain cases broken by other duties. I have rounded off years of service to the nearest whole, and this does not significantly alter the conclusions. Dates of presidential service for Freire and Pinto indicate periods *during which* they served more than once.

sympathetic to the nonaristocratic sectors and their aspirations prior to the 1920s.

Basque-Castilian dominance ended in 1920 with the election of Alessandri to the presidency. Alessandri, a nonaristocrat by any definition, was of Italo-Chilean descent; he made a strong-minded, heavy-handed leader. It is, of course, significant that the demise of the old ruling class coincided precisely with the new political activity of the military, but the end of Basque-Castilian rule was by no means the single cause of military political activity. By the 1860s, it will be remembered, the struggle that led ultimately to the executive-legislative conflict in the Civil War of 1891 was already under way. A recalcitrant Congress had chipped away at the strength of the executive branch, and after 1891 the legislative branch dominated politics and government.[3]

The Basics of Civilian Authority:
Executive Strength, Civil-Military Homogeneity,
Officer-Class Cohesion

Basic to the tradition of Portalian civil-military relations was executive authority over the military, exerted through the War Ministry. The Constitution of 1833 gave the president the right to select ministers, and they were responsible to him. He was, in addition, the commander in chief of the armed forces. But after 1891, by common agreement among political leaders, ministers were responsible to Congress. As a result, the war minister was subject to censure and no-confidence votes, and protocol forced ministers to resign their posts if other cabinet members were forced out also. Thus Congress exerted more control—always in the name of democracy, and to preclude tyranny—over the executive branch and hence, by extension, the military. Circumscription of executive powers led to a decrease in presidential prestige in the minds of military men, who thus lost respect for executive authority. Things had changed since the days of Prieto, Bulnes, and Montt.

After 1891, furthermore, ministerial responsibility to Parliament, frequent censures, votes of no confidence, and resignations based on political differences meant that there was little continuity in the War Ministry. A number of war ministers between 1891 and 1925 were distinguished men (some were former officers themselves), but their administrative talents were not sufficient to keep them in power for long.

Congress was made up of shifting, squabbling coalitions between 1891 and 1925, and this was not conducive to the resolution of national, let alone military, problems. The army was more responsible to Congress than it was to the executive branch. Therefore it became enmeshed in congressional politics, and more than a few officers owed desirable assignments, foreign travel, and promotion to political connections. As the executive branch lost authority and Congress gained it, the power and prestige of the president as commander in chief of the armed forces inevitably diminished.

A basic element of military subservience to civilian rule in Chile was the connection between the civilian aristocracy and the military. Family ties helped to perpetuate civil-military fusion into the 1880s, and even today the military tradition is strong in some Chilean families.[4] The majority of army and navy leaders through the War of the Pacific belonged to, or were associated with, the Basque-Castilian aristocracy. But from the land and sea battles of Iquique and Angamos, Tacna and Arica, and Chorrillos and Miraflores there emerged a number of self-made officers who owed their position more to expertise, achievement, or heroism than to influence, name, or connections.

The appeal of a military career in an age of military buildup, furthered by Körner's enhanced stature after the rebel victory in 1891, brought many nonaristocratic aspirants to the Escucla Militar.[5] These young men felt little or no kinship with the oligarchs. Large numbers of men born in the 1870s (too young for the 1879–84 or 1891 crises) reached staff and command positions in the 1920s, when the political, social, and economic structures of Chile were strained more than they had been at any time since the days of O'Higgins, Pinto, and Freire. It is not surprising that these were the political officers who took power into their own hands; they were Prussianized professionals who knew nothing of the rigors of campaign or conquest but much of institutional and national frustration.

Because Chile engaged in no wars after 1883, and because there were no civil crises between 1891 and 1920, the Chilean Army was, in a sense, an institution in search of a role. There were no warmongers in the officer class, but there were those who decried the lack of attention paid the army by successive administrations. Army leaders were sensitive to the institution's schism in 1891, to the rise of the navy after 1880, to the latter's solidarity in 1891, and to its prestige in the age of Alfred Thayer Mahan.

When the army did respond to a national emergency in 1920, it did so in an embarrassingly disorderly fashion. Loss of face after Germany's defeat in World War I did not contribute to military self-respect, and political intrigues in 1919 set the army against itself. While the process of professionalization continued between 1885 and 1920, the internal cohesion of the officer class diminished. Professionalization actually furthered the cleavage between junior and senior officers, and in turn the cleavage hampered the growth of universal professional attitudes.

Students of the Latin American military have tended to oversimplify political and social distinctions between junior and senior officers. There is validity in such distinctions, but only if careful qualifications are made for specific circumstances. Chilean junior officers as a group were probably more professionally oriented than their seniors between 1885 and 1925. Junior officers had access, after 1886, to the Academia; their commanders did not. Junior officers had opportunity to travel and study in Germany, France, Switzerland, Italy, and Spain; most senior officers did not. Broadly speaking, junior officers were more technically oriented; knew more modern concepts of warfare; studied the Boer War, the Russo-Japanese War, and Balkan conflicts; and they thought of military service as their only route to prestige. Generally speaking, senior officers were career oriented but lacked the technical skills of the subalterns. But the senior officers were the "blooded heroes" and still commanded respect. Such generalizations hold for the years between 1885 and 1925 but are, at best, conjectural after that.

There were, therefore, grounds for intrainstitutional conflict over purely professional matters between junior and senior officers, as well as between branches of the service, and for conflict among those officers still linked to civilian power groups. Intrainstitutional conflicts did not subside with professionalization but went hand in hand with it. Differences in politics, religion, education, age, specialized training, and rank all contributed to conflict. By 1925 the officer class up to the level of colonel was closer to the middle sectors of civilian society than to the aristocracy; above the rank of colonel, the hierarchy still behaved like an extension of the old ruling class.

The Chilean Navy withstood intrainstitutional conflict until 1927, and its officer class, except for most engineers, was still more closely linked to the civilian aristocracy than the army's. Based in Valparaíso, the navy remained a veritable extension of the *porteño* aristocracy. Army-navy relations were not always cordial, but this was no fault of naval chiefs, nor was it caused by family ties. After 1891 the navy became as popular in Chile as the army—later even surpassing the army's place in the public eye.[6] The navy's popularity was indicated by government appropriations as well as by close ties between political leaders in Congress and the naval leaders who had served them in 1891.

Thus the army's increasing professionalism led it to break with both civilian institutions and the navy, to become less and less closely identified with state, nation, and society. The factors that had led to civilian supremacy in the post-Lircay years proved less and less applicable by the turn of the century. Civil-military fusion strained and broke by 1920; the demographic influences were radically altered; nationalism became a justification for military hostility toward government rather than a binding agent; the ruling class proved politically unresponsive and irresponsible and was challenged by politically ambitious nonaristocrats; the masses were no longer docile; national self-doubt replaced Chile's sense of mission as economic and social problems proved insoluble by a government whose authority was located in neither the executive nor the legislative branch; and antimilitarism competed with traditional reverence for the armed forces. We turn now to a fresh examination of change in order to complete our introduction to the years 1891–1931.

A Changing Chile:
Urbanization and Demographic Shifts

Between approximately 1885 and 1931 Chile became a highly urbanized nation. Large numbers of lower-class families migrated to the desert provinces of northern Chile to work in the nitrate fields. Antofagasta and Iquique were transformed from rustic towns into cities with severe urban problems. Chile had barely 2,000,000 citizens in 1880. Her population had grown to over 3,700,000 in 1920 and to more than 4,200,000 a decade later. Nearly half of all Chileans lived in towns, and in 1930 nearly a quarter of the population lived in the Santiago-Valparaíso area. Santiago spurted from a city of 275,000 in 1900 to one of 700,000 by 1930; Valparaíso gained 50,000 inhabitants during the same period, and in 1930 had just under 200,000 citizens. Concepción-Talcahuano, Antofagasta, and Iquique were, of course, smaller, but they showed similar growth patterns. Predictably, rapid urbanization brought overcrowding, poor living accommodations, and bad health and sanitation conditions. Slums grew in Santiago, Valparaíso, and Concepción-Talcahuano. Crime and drunkenness increased. Conditions deteriorated in the 1920s, when Chile's European nitrate markets dwindled and miners and workers from the North as well as from the rural South swarmed to Santiago and Valparaíso. The government of Arturo Alessandri used funds originally designated for other purposes to finance hostelries for arriving indigents, and there was wholesale corruption in the administration of these monies.

Between 1900 and 1920 another type of demographic shift changed the face of Chile. In search of new opportunities, professionals and members of the middle class began to move to the provinces.[7] By 1930, proportionately more professionals and business people lived in the provinces than had done so in 1900. Social change in urban, rural, Central Valley, and provincial areas was the result.

Chile's urbanized society in the 1920s was far more complex than the Central Valley society of the nineteenth century. The aspirations of workers, students, shopkeepers, professionals, the unemployed, and tradesmen prevented the great landlords and mining barons from having things entirely their own way. Politicians were aware of the changes in Chile but did little about them. The state was virtually without an effective administration until 1920. By then the unresolved social problems that confronted the middle and lower classes encouraged military leaders to rectify the situation by restructuring the state. They would claim they were doing so in the name of all Chileans and for all Chile. Chilean demography, then, was no longer conducive to civilian authority over the military.

A Changing Chile:
Officer Class and Civilian Elite

Social change in Chile between 1891 and 1931 was reflected in the composition of the officer class and its relations with the ruling elite. The military modernization schemes of Körner and his German and

Chilean cohorts so enlarged the army officer class that by 1920 only the top echelons of the army were closely connected with the oligarchy and aristocracy. Even these connections were rather peculiar, based not so much on family ties as on the army schism of 1891.

To what civilian elements could the military hierarchy have been connected? The financial decline of the Basque-Castilian aristocracy accompanied its political decline and the steady decline of executive authority. Few members of the aristocracy, furthermore, foresaw what would happen to Chile's mineral economy. Few correctly understood social problems, and few thought of social reform in terms of social justice. Rather they thought in terms of charity and paternalism. Few objected to a government that largely ignored potential sources of opposition to democratic ideals. In short, the Chilean ruling class ran out of talent. Few of its young members became army officers, for there were opportunities elsewhere. Every young aristocrat who did choose a military life cast his lot with the navy.

By World War I the Chilean aristocracy had been thoroughly diluted—ethnically through German, French, Italian, Slavic, British, and Irish admixtures, and socially through absorption of self-made men. The cohesive political power of the oligarchy began to dwindle as early as 1910, when representatives of the provincial upper-middle classes moved into positions of influence in Congress. The Civil War of 1891 has been cited in more than one source as the true beginning of the aristocratic breakdown; as we know, lines were sharply drawn in that conflict, and political rivalries continued along after the war ended. Political rivalries did not necessarily mean overt conflict in Chile, however, because expediency was often as important as principle in political affairs. This tended to institutionalize political differences.

Civil-military fusion in the postwar decades, therefore, would have been a useless deterrent to military political ventures even if it had been possible. By 1920 some members of the military high command seriously doubted that continued rule by oligarchy in its existing form was in Chile's best interests. Such leaders as General Guillermo Armstrong Rivera and General Manuel Moore Bravo, by no means raving liberals or reformers, understood that continued rule by Chile's impotent ruling class might well lead to violent revolt, loudly being urged by labor leaders. Armstrong and Moore took part in a 1919 plot which, had it been successful, would have restored the strong executive system.

The rise to power of Arturo Alessandri signaled the ultimate collapse of the aristocracy as a ruling class, but not its demise as an influential sociopolitical sector. Alessandri's program appealed to army men who yearned for a strong chief executive, thus involving them in the issue as never before. But soon his demagoguery and his almost intentional exacerbation of existing problems alienated army officers and even some of his civilian supporters from his style of reform politics. Contrary to some theories, the nineteenth-century fusion of civil and military elites was *not* replaced by a fusion between early-twentieth-century political and military elite groups, between business and professional supporters of reform and the professional, Prussianized officers.

A Changing Chile: Military Nationalism

Chilean army officers were highly nationalistic in the early twentieth century. Resolution of frontier disputes with Argentina and Bolivia notwithstanding, the question of Tacna-Arica remained unresolved until 1929, and national defense became more than a purely military concept. It was between 1891 and 1931 that the role of the Chilean army underwent radical change; because it did, members of the army officer class became ultranationalists.

What do we mean by role? In the context of this study so far, two of the four types of role recently described by Samuel P. Huntington have been emphasized: the *political role* and the *instrumental role*.[8] The former refers to the activities of the military as a political interest group, and the second implies the use of the military as a tool of policy, both foreign and domestic. Both of these roles changed after 1891, and we must now use a third of Huntington's role types to assess change: the *ideological role,* referring to the influence of military ideas (and ideals) on society.

By 1920, after ninety years of inactivity, the army was nearing the assumption of a political role. By 1925 it had assumed a political role; two years later that role would be firmly defined by General Ibáñez and others. The army ceased to be an instrument of major importance in foreign affairs—military thinking to the contrary notwithstanding —as naval power was more fully appreciated and as the chance of war diminished. Nevertheless, the instrumental role of the military in domestic affairs increased. It was the army that broke strikes, and broke the heads of strikers, between 1900 and 1925, and it was the army that supported Alessandri when he attempted to assure election of a compatible Congress in 1924. These roles were direct reversals of those the army had fulfilled prior to 1891. And as the instrumental role was directed less toward foreign and more toward domestic affairs, the political role became imminent.

The ideological role of the military was closely connected to nationalism. The military identified with the state and society, but army leaders had lost respect for the state since 1891, and society was in ferment. While the officers were being told that they were the very latest in military organization (or should be), and that they were defenders of national integrity and dignity, they realized that their country was backward. There were plenty of civilians to tell them of this. Particularly aware of these paradoxes were those officers who went abroad for advanced specialized training after completing the regular Academia course.[9] The majority went to Germany, where they saw an autocratic monarchy which nevertheless had adopted pervasive social welfare and labor legislation. Germany, moreover, held its army in the highest esteem. German greatness was based on military prowess. So was much of Chile's, but her government was not as responsive as Germany's, and Chilean professional officers felt shortchanged.

Their nationalism, then, was fraught with discontent and resentment. They blamed politicians, political parties, democracy, capitalism, speculators, foreign investors, and labor agitators for all of Chile's problems in the 1920s; and in the name of Chilean honor, dignity, and integrity they assumed an institutional-political role between 1924 and 1927. This led to their support of General Ibáñez as president between 1927 and 1931.

Chilean officers found fault with education, the Constitution, social and economic policy, the press, the electoral system, and banking and financial practices. The generation of army officers educated at the Escuela between 1894 and 1898, many of whom studied at the Academia during the 1912–14 session, were the spokesmen for such ideas; led by Ibáñez, they formed the nucleus of the political officers' clique of the 1920s. They attended the Escuela when it was staffed by numerous German officers, and the Academia when German influence was at its peak. Intensely proud of their profession, they were ashamed of their country's government and of those who were in charge of it. As we will see, their devotion to duty, their expertise, cooperativeness, and sense of responsibility were elements of their professionalism that led in 1924 to a political action that would impose military ideals and ideas on the rest of society with a vengeance.

A Changing Chile:
Decline of Responsive Government

Because Chile's eroding oligarchy did not respond to the challenges of the new century, neither its political leadership of the country nor the political system constructed after 1891 endured when challenged by army officers in the mid 1920s.

Before 1891, the Chilean political system was characteristically responsible and responsive. Elected and appointed officials established an enviable record among Latin American nations. The judiciary, the diplomatic corps, the civil service, legislators, and chief executives adhered, with some exceptions, to the norms established during the Portalian era. They were responsible in their conduct of national affairs, and they were responsive to the politically articulate society. As a result of two major factors, however, responsibility and responsiveness did not mark the conduct of national affairs during the Parliamentary Republic.

The first factor was the nature of the political system itself. After 1891, the Constitution was interpreted to preclude strong executive leadership. The lack of strong leadership was also the result of the creation and fission of political parties (beginning, really, with the creation of the Radical Party in 1862 and the Democrat Party in 1887), because coalition politics and government by temporary concurrence of coalition components became common. Ministerial responsibility to Parliament, circumscription of executive influence in elections, exclusion of appointive officials from Congress, and congressional control over fiscal affairs reduced the president to figurehead status. By no means should one infer from this that executive leadership would have meant automatic responsibility and responsiveness after 1891, but it would have meant continuity. The new order served the interests of the victors of 1891, but, obviously, it did not help either Balmaceda's supporters or the vast majority of

Chileans who were utterly excluded from political life because they did not vote or were told how to vote.

The Parliamentary Republic, furthermore, was merely oligarchic control in a new guise. It was not designed to be responsive to the masses, who, at best, were tolerated and were never considered political equals by the upper classes. At no time between 1891 and 1931 did over 10 percent of the Chilean population vote in a major election. What, though, would have constituted responsibility or responsiveness to the bulk of the population? For one thing, a meaningful record of social and labor legislation would have made the historical record of Chilean parliamentarism a more glowing one. No political party, save possibly the Democrats, saw social and labor legislation as anything more than institutionalized charity. Social justice and the dignity of the laboring class did not figure prominently in political or social philosophy, and those who sounded warnings of what impended if legislation were not forthcoming were in a distinct minority.

Both these factors would have been unimportant if the Chilean aristocracy and its Basque-Castilian leadership group had not disintegrated. Politically divided in 1891, the aristocracy was also becoming larger and representative of frequently conflicting interest groups. By 1920, as previously stated, the Basque-Castilian aristocracy no longer dominated politics. By 1920, at the very latest, the great landlords of the Central Valley no longer dominated Chilean life. Since the mid nineteenth century, financial power had been shifting to bankers, businessmen, mining barons, and merchants. Although these new aristocratic elements were oligarchic in temperament, they were by no means cohesive. The paternalism of the feudalistic Central Valley land-based society gave way fully after 1891 to a liberal, laissez-faire attitude, by virtue of which workers—increasingly important as an economically productive force—were not considered integral parts of a corporate society.

The social breakdown of aristocratic cohesion and the political decline of the traditional oligarchs and destruction of the strong executive system were, therefore, all responsible for the drawing apart of government and society. The new political system by no means served the masses. Significantly, as Chilean society became less homogeneous, the military—specifically the army—became slightly more homogeneous with respect to the social origins of both the officer class and the troops. As this happened, labor unions—the only type of pressure group available to lower-class Chileans—were being organized.

A Changing Chile: Labor and the Masses[10]

As social change became increasingly apparent, internal change in the polity, beyond oligarchic breakdown, took place. As noted, from 1910 on, upper-middle-class politicians from the Central Valley and from the northern and southern provinces initiated a form of challenge to the crumbling oligarchy by gaining seats in the lower house of Parliament. The fact that these new aspirants to political leadership—primarily Liberals, Radicals, and Democrats—were unable to provide effective leadership or to function as a meaningful opposition was a great disappointment to labor and to many professional army officers after 1920.

There were no strikes in Chile until the late 1880s. Thereafter—except during the Civil War period—a major strike of miners, dock workers, railroad personnel, or laborers occurred on the average of once a year until 1927. Mass violence was serious in the mining and dock strikes of 1903, 1905, 1906, and 1907, and there were 300 strikes, large and small, in the second decade of the century. The years 1917–20 saw the most strikes, the highest rate of unemployment, and the most rapid decline of mining operations in the history of Chile to that time. The collapse of Chile's nitrate markets in Europe meant that the nitrate mines shut down or curtailed operations, leaving thousands unemployed. These were the people who flooded the cities searching for relief and were victimized there by the brutality of rapid urbanization and the corruption of government officials ostensibly assigned to help them.

The Chilean masses were quite free to organize politically, although, to be sure, property qualifications (curtailed in the nineteenth century), literacy qualifications, and apathy militated against true, independent political action; bribery, pressure, and threats influenced workers and peasants to listen to the *patrón* when election time came around. The freedom to organize theoretically allowed the masses to participate in the political processes, but politics in Chile were actually still controlled by a select group, and most individual parties were impotent if they did not represent the aristocracy or a segment of it. Only the Democrats and the tiny

Socialist Party qualified as popular parties. The former grew increasingly distant from the masses after the turn of the century, and the latter was pitifully weak. Legality, then, provided no entrée to power for mass-supported organizations or leaders.

By 1910 probably only a hundred thousand workers belonged to syndicates. A decade later, with twice that number of workers, the major syndicates had joined forces to create the monolithic Federación Obrera Chilena (FOCH), led by one-time typographer and Socialist deputy Luis Emilio Recabarren Serrano, father of Chile's organized labor movement. In the dark days of 1920 when the Chilean economy was reeling, Recabarren led FOCH into the International movement in opposition to capitalism. The "red menace" came to Chile. The IWW had organized and established a branch in Chile in 1919. But the same forces that militated against popular political organizations militated against syndicates; syndicates were freely organized but they had no effective legal status. Strikes, demonstrations, and the like might be tolerated—and they might not. More than once between 1891 and 1925 the army proved the reluctant agent for the government's antipathy to labor. Broken heads, bullet wounds, and deaths were the results in Valparaíso, Iquique, Antofagasta, the Lota coal mines, and elsewhere.

Introspection and Reappraisal: Lack of Civilian Action and Military Decline

In one important sense the masses were part of the political system. In a "laissez-faire" atmosphere where they were perfectly free to organize parties and syndicates and perfectly free to work within the sociopolitical and economic structure, the organized masses were coopted by the parties, party leaders, and the "system"; those who coopted them stood firm until they were forced to yield by the military. When that happened it was due as much to fear on the part of the military leaders that popular violence would destroy Chile as to the military's belief in social justice. No longer docile, the masses were alienated both from the aristocracy and from Chile's embryonic socially climbing middle sector; nevertheless, they were part of the "system." Although no amount of violence, demonstration, or strike activity could topple the Parliamentary Republic as long as it could rely on brute force to blunt labor's thrust and contain mass pressure, the prospect of continual repressive action against the Chilean working man did not please army officers.

Not all Chileans were blind to what was happening to their country. Speeches, pamphlets, editorials, essays, and books criticized foreign economic penetration, conspicuous consumption, political sterility, poor leadership, the lack of awareness of the dignity of labor, and Chile's declining financial position in world trade.[11] One of the great tragedies of this period of Chilean history was the inability of the state to adjust properly to change. It was a tragedy understood by few and considered serious by even fewer. In the nineteenth century there had been a reason for optimism and pride in Chile. But after 1891 and the advent of parliamentarism, there was also reason for introspection. The resulting self-criticism and doubt led in turn to serious questioning of national priorities, but it was too late for civilian institutions to prevail unscathed. After 1891 there were no frontiers to be pacified, no enemies to ward off. Territorial expansion, economic development, immigration, and normal population growth created many new problems, and coping with them was beyond the abilities of the parliamentary state.

Chile's failure to come to grips with her problems caused some intellectuals to examine their country's institutions in order to find out what was wrong. Unfortunately, very few offered any solutions. By the end of the first quarter of the twentieth century, it was widely believed that the country ought to have a modern labor code and some kind of welfare legislation. Few doubted that health and sanitary conditions needed attention or that new sources of revenue would have to be found to continue to finance the government's activities at a reasonable level. But no plan was acceptable to the coalitions, cliques, and coteries that managed the nation's affairs.

Not all Chileans were devoted to the parliamentary system. After 1891, Nationals (remnants of the mid-century Montt-Varista group) and Democratic Liberals (Balmacedistas) still championed the cause of the strong executive. Neither had the power or the leadership to challenge the parliamentary system as a whole, though, as Conservatives, Liberals, and Radicals had challenged the Portalian system after 1851.

As noted, the strongest voices for reform were associated with the Radical and Democrat parties after 1891. These parties, however, endorsed the parliamentary system and the idea that reform had to come out of that system. There was constant talk among reformers about what was wrong with Chile, but those in a position to do so would not or could not produce.

National self-criticism and introspection are symptoms of health if they lead to action; they are symptoms of sickness and no more if they lead to no action or if action cannot be provided owing to economic or political realities. Chile in this sense was ill by 1920, if not before.

Chileans have blamed British investors, the ambitions of neighboring republics, United States diplomatic maneuvers, oligarchic control of political leadership, lack of responsibility and responsiveness, and parliamentarism—both foreign and domestic factors, in other words—for Chile's decline as an economic power and sociopolitical example for South America after the Civil War of 1891. Domestic factors far outweigh foreign influence, however.

A state whose institutions are being questioned and criticized, but which can neither allay popular discontent nor extinguish it, and which cannot maintain the support of the armed forces, will not continue to exist. Nationalistic, patriotic, professional army officers see intervention as their natural role in the defense of the fatherland. They will preserve what others seek to destroy, but in preserving they will restructure, and in restructuring they may indeed be destructive. The lack of confidence in Chilean institutions, lack of pride in the state, and lack of trust in individuals or administrations were strong motivation for Chilean army officers after 1891. In 1924 they proved strong enough to goad officers into action.

The publication of Karl Liebknecht's *Militarismus und Anti-Militarismus* (1907)[12] was a turning point in thought about military organizations. Directly or indirectly, those who espoused antimilitarism in Latin America during the 1920s were being influenced by Liebknecht, as were military men. Armies, to Liebknecht, existed to serve the interests of capitalist-imperialist-industrialist society and its leadership. Years before there was such a term as "military-industrial complex," Liebknecht proclaimed that armies served oligarchies and aristocracies to oppress the masses. Conscripts shot their fellow men when armies were called in to put down labor agitation, and members of the oppressed classes shot their brothers when countries went to war.

In the Chile of the 1920s, where Liebknecht may have been known to a few Marxist labor organizers and a few army officers who had studied in Germany before World War I, the army was busy putting down labor agitation regularly, and conscripts were shooting their fellow men. These activities did not make the army popular among the working class.

Nor did the ruling class continue to single out the army as Chile's pride. Despite the efforts of Körner, the purging of the army in 1891 and 1892, and the remaking of the officer class, the army still identified with the past: with Lircay and Prieto and Portales; with Yungay and Bulnes; with frontier expansion and Montt; with Chorrillos and Miraflores; with Santa María and Balmaceda. Civilians looked upon the army as a menace to proper conduct of parliamentary government rather than as the symbol of national greatness. Chilean greatness was now history; there were no new symbols. As war seemed less and less likely, a large, well-trained army seemed less and less necessary. In modern states, reasoned Chilean leaders, military organizations were quiescent until called to arms. In modern states, reasoned Chilean army professionals, the state made sure that the military could respond to a call. Between 1891 and 1924, army appropriations, internal organization, discipline, opinions, and overt political actions were subjected to such scrutiny and criticism by politicians that military prestige was reduced to an all-time low in Chile. For six years, therefore, beginning in 1925, army leaders did all they could to restore their prestige. We turn now to specific discussions of civil-military relations between 1891 and 1931.

6

Professionalism and Political Interest, 1891–1920

The three decades between the Civil War of 1891 and the heated presidential campaign of 1920, which resulted in the election of Arturo Alessandri, were critical to civil-military relationships. It was during this period that the Chilean Army achieved a high point of professionalism based on the German model, only to see Germany's army suffer defeat in 1918. And it was during the same period that the worst results of parliamentary irresponsibility and governmental impotence manifested themselves in civilian affairs. The interaction of professionalism in the military sphere and parliamentarism in the civil, influenced by social and economic problems, led men in uniform to voice political opinions openly. Their opinions proved to be at odds with most civilian thinking on political issues.

Between the administrations of civilian presidents Balmaceda and Alessandri, the principal military figure was Emil Körner. No one man was as influential in civilian affairs as Körner was in the military. The colonel was more a symbol than he was an event maker; no spokesman for the military on extraprofessional matters, he confined his activities strictly to creating a modern army. It is for these reasons that he is historically significant, and his creation, the professional army, so important politically.

Körner's significance in early-twentieth-century Chile rests on the one political gesture of his career: his participation in the revolt against Balmaceda in 1891. Körner associated himself in this enterprise with military men who defied their commander in chief and with politicians who consorted with military men to achieve political change. No political army officer of the time ever invoked Körner's name in any but a strictly professional context, but Körner's actions in 1891 certainly did not foreshadow the continued existence of an apolitical officer class. The epitome of the military professional, Körner set an early example for officers who acquired political interests.

Chilean officers acquired political interests for several reasons already alluded to in the previous chapter. Most important was the erosion of the Portalian state—the demise of the strong commander in chief, who was replaced by the state. The abstract concept of the state was probably as prestigious as any individual at this stage of Chilean political development, but it was no longer based on the Portalian ideal. Traditions of organizational and administrative efficiency were well established, but as an ideal the state had lost most of its prestige in the eyes of military men by 1920.

The depersonalization of the traditional relationship between the state and the military, already in process in the nineteenth century, rudely confirmed in 1891, and in practice until 1920, did not prevent military involvement in political affairs. Most historical evidence, moreover, leads one to believe that it was not designed to do so.[1] Nor was military professionalization.[2] In point of fact, depersonalization through parliamentarism and the rise of military professionalism motivated men in uniform to take political action. The intent of this chapter is to show that professionalism and parliamentarism mixed no better than oil and water.

The Civil War of 1891:
Destruction of the Portalian System[3]

By mid 1890, Balmaceda was a minority president in deep trouble. His proposals for social and fiscal reforms (such as distribution of southern lands and attempts to control foreign investment and currency speculation) met with little favor either in Congress or in the business community. His anticlericalism lost him support on the right, and his heavy-handed manner denied him support from Radicals. Futhermore, he was considered an enemy of foreign nitrate interests because of his advocacy of greater national control over the industry. Balmaceda had the backing, at this time, of Liberals, but even some of them consorted in Congress with the opposition parties: Conservatives, Nationals, and Radicals. The administration was in trouble in 1890; electoral improprieties, inflation, the increased size of the bureaucracy and its corruption, and Balmaceda's insistence that Enrique Salvador Sanfuentes Andonaegui be designated his successor in 1891 further isolated him from Congress.

Congress closed its 1890 session without approving the 1891 appropriations bill. This situation had occurred several times before but had always been resolved through compromise. On January 1, 1891, Balmaceda announced that in 1891 he would spend an amount equal to 1890 appropriations. The president counted on the upcoming congressional elections to return a sympathetic majority, and his January 1 proclamation was as much an appeal for national backing as it was an official policy announcement.

Within one week Chile was plunged into civil war. On January 7, under the command of Maritime Governor Montt, the Valparaíso squadron steamed north to Iquique to avoid a confrontation with the Valparaíso army garrison. Aboard Montt's flagship were Ramón Barros Luco, president of the Chamber of Deputies, and Waldo Silva Algüe, vice-president of the Senate. Barros and Silva published a manifesto signed by a congressional majority deposing President Balmaceda.

The Balmaceda government struggled against great odds to defeat the rebels. The latter, with control of the seas and access to the nitrate fields, with no need to resort to dictatorial, repressive measures, and with the aid of Körner's knowledge of modern tactics and strategy, broke the resistance of the central government on August 21 at Concón and on August 28 at Placilla, near Valparaíso. The occupation of Santiago followed a few days later. On September 18, the last day of his constitutional term, Balmaceda committed suicide in the Argentine Legation.

When congressional leaders pronounced against Balmaceda, the majority of army officers affirmed their loyalty to their commander in chief, and by mid August they had staffed an army of some forty thousand men—mainly conscripts. As noted in chapter 4, many younger officers and many who had family ties with the opposition political leaders joined the rebels. But the rebel troops never numbered much more than ten thousand men. Unfortunately for the central government, the recalcitrance of conscripts, rivalries among members of the loyalist officer class, and lack of munitions and equipment made it impossible to put more than ten thousand in the field at one time. The central government did enjoy certain advan-

tages, namely internal lines of communications, freedom to act
through martial law, and no transportation or communications
problems. In a short war—where attrition and financial collapse were
not factors—they could have won, and, indeed, the war was a
stalemate until August. The nature and composition of the congressional army made the difference.

Up in Iquique, Körner assumed the responsibility of training the
rebel force. Körner's motives for breaking with his commander in
chief, as we have seen, were several, and we may never know which
was most compelling. Professionally, he certainly believed that a
congressional victory would enable him to proceed freely with his
Prussianization program. A congressional victory, moreover, would
allow him to mold a new army unopposed by conservative commanders who remained loyal to Balmaceda and who were wary of new-
fangled ideas. German economic interests were indeed sympathetic
to Congress and hostile to Balmaceda's plans to reduce the number
of foreign investors. German southern landlords and merchants
sympathized with Radical opposition to autocratic executive rule by
the president. Although Balmaceda was aware of the need for a strong
army, he was known to favor limitation of the size of the standing
army, and Körner had dreams of a 100,000-man standing force!
Finally, Körner simply had a golden opportunity in 1891 to apply
modern tactics and strategy in the field—a strictly professional motive.

The German accepted the position of secretary general of the rebel
general staff and served under its chief, Colonel Adolfo Holley. With
his disciples from the Escuela and the Academia, Körner forged the
nucleus of Chile's early-twentieth-century Prussian-style army on the
dusty drill grounds of Iquique and Antofagasta and sent them into
battle at Concón and Placilla. Körner's open-rank infantry assault
tactics baffled the traditional-minded central government commanders, and Congress emerged triumphant.

Consequences of Victory:
The Search for the Germano-Chilean Military Ideal[4]

Victory allowed Körner a virtually free hand for nearly a decade in
the creation of a new army. By mid September 1891 a series of
courts-martial began the process of cleaning Balmacedistas out of the

officer class. Colonel Estanislao del Canto, a bitter foe of the late president, received instructions as commander of the rebel army to prosecute those holding the rank of captain and higher who had served in the Balmacedista army. Canto proceeded to supervise the courts-martial of four categories of officers: those who had served Balmaceda; those accused of war crimes; those who had committed war crimes but who had acted supposedly under orders; and those who simply failed to appear to hear charges against them. The majority of the captains, majors, lieutenant colonels, colonels, and generals who had served in the loyalist army were retired, jailed, or put under house arrest. Officers who served in the rebel army were allowed to remain in rank if they chose. In this way the composition of the army officer class was dramatically changed within the space of one calendar year.

Meanwhile the nature of the officer class began to change too. In November 1891 Brigadier General Emil Körner became chief of the Chilean General Staff and resumed his duties at the Academia. Körner was now in an enviable position; he was the dominant figure in instruction and administration, and he would soon be much more.

Early in 1894 he traveled to Germany to inspect artillery batteries being completed at the Krupp factory in Essen, and when he returned in 1895 he was accompanied by thirty-six German officers. Most of these served a two-year tour of duty in Chile, and a new contingent of twenty-seven Germans arrived in 1897; some members of each mission remained in Chile for a decade. During the 1890s—and in some cases well into the first decade of this century—Körner and his German missions went about their work uninhibited. After twelve years as an instructor in the Academia, Lieutenant Colonel Wilhelm Ekdahl became its director in 1904. Other Germans taught at the Escuela and the Academia. Germans also served in instructoral, advisory, and administrative capacities in the War Ministry, General Staff, procurement commissions, specialty schools for artillery, infantry, cavalry, and noncommissioned officers, provincial garrisons, and the elite Presidential Palace Guard. German penetration of the Chilean officer class between 1895 and 1910 was more consistent and thorough than European penetration of any Latin American or Asiatic army in the pre–World War I years.[5]

Chilean officers who distinguished themselves in the classes and training organized by their German mentors won study trips to

Europe. Between 1895 and 1910 some fifty Chileans studied in Germany, Austria, Italy, Belgium, France, and Spain—the majority in Germany. By the mid 1920s most administrative, staff and command, and instructoral positions beneath general officer rank were held by Prussianized officers who had studied at the Academia or in Europe, generally both.

In the years immediately prior to World War I one could see many young Chilean officers sporting monocles, trimmed moustaches, cropped hair, and the regulation spiked helmet. Highly trained, often well traveled, imbued with a sense of duty and self-esteem, these officers were almost all of modest middle-class origins. To them military service was a career; ambition, duty, and expertise were paramount. In their training at the Escuela and Academia they learned etiquette and social conduct, and by Chilean standards they were a sophisticated lot.

While the officer class was being renovated, restructured, and Prussianized, the army acquired a new relationship to society. Even before the adoption of obligatory military service in 1900, the army assumed responsibility for educating its share of common Chileans. An illiterate peasant or worker did not make a good soldier in a modern army, and young officers found themselves teaching the basics of reading and writing to lower-class Chileans who—in a country whose government had allegedly devoted much time and many resources to public education—were totally ignorant and illiterate. Along with literacy came hygiene, civics, and a bit of Chilean history (military style). Although military service was not every man's dream of the way to spend six months of a year, it became a vehicle for the diffusion of military ideals, discipline, and patriotism, and brought the rudiments of a basic education to many Chileans.

In 1900 Chile had a well-equipped, modern, trained standing army of 6,000, commanded by a select officer class of 800. By 1902, agreements with Argentina precluded the possibility of war with that nation, which only six years before had seemed imminent. Obligatory military service was in effect, German training was at a high point, and the Chilean Army was the envy of its neighbors. Argentina and Peru had only recently begun to modernize their armies, and Bolivia was still a chaotic nation. Over the next decade, though, the government would not acquiesce automatically to Körner's every demand, and military-state relationships would show some signs of strain.

Civil-Military Relations Strained:
The Realities of Prussianization

Official sources, annual reports, and the like indicate that military ambitions—not just those of the Germans—outran the willingness or capacity of successive civilian administrations to provide for the army.[6] These and other sources also show that the military was unable to live up to its own expectations. Both these factors should be considered in assessing the relationship between professionalism and political interest.

Körner's prestige and popularity—and his boundless arrogance—led him to sound off on certain vitally important matters in a very forceful way. Whereas the annual *Memoria del Ministerio de Guerra* had hitherto been merely a report to Congress on military activities, expectations, and policies, it became more a statement and recommendation of policy between 1895 and World War I. Repeatedly Körner and his cohorts chided the government for allowing low salary schedules to prevail, and urged more training in Europe for officers. He continually demanded administrative reorganization, which also called for additional funds. Early in the century, however, these demands did not meet with much success, nor did the army's criticism of the 1900 Obligatory Service Law.

This law theoretically made all young Chilean males liable for service, but those with social, political, or family connections regularly escaped service, and only those of humble origins were ever drafted. Furthermore, the law prohibited discrimination in public employment against those who had fulfilled their military obligation, but the civil service, bound by tradition, was not open to those of humble origin. Thus tradition, class distinctions, and—to a certain extent—prejudices now tended to separate the military from comparable sectors of civilian society. To Chileans not fortunate enough to be born into a wealthy or influential family, military service provided absolutely no social mobility or advantages. This discrimination frustrated them, and it also frustrated many professional army officers.

Officers saw hypocrisy and failure within the service, too. The 1906 military reform program made the Chilean Army into a paper copy of the German Army—but only a paper copy. The 1906 reforms were supposed to create a streamlined administration with a staff for each branch of the army—artillery, cavalry, infantry, engineers, instruction, health and sanitation, quartermaster corps, and armories—under the direct supervision of the inspector general and the War Ministry. But the effect was just the opposite; decentralization, confusion, and understaffing were the results. There were not enough capable officers to make the staff system function, and Prussianization in administration and organization probably reached its limits in Chile at this point. Coordination of divisions and branches between ministry and field, and even within the ministry, simply could not be attained, and many undertrained junior officers and officers with political connections were hastily shoved into positions for which they had not been prepared. The 1906 reforms constituted an attempt at wholesale Prussianization; selective adaptation of German programs might have succeeded. By 1910, official publications lamented the outright aping of the German model, and even Körner doubted what he had previously championed.

Professional grievances notwithstanding, the Chilean Army had gained an international reputation. Early in the twentieth century Ecuador, El Salvador, and Colombia requested Chilean officers as instructors and advisers. The official military literature of all these countries periodically praised the efforts of Chileans in writing military codes, carrying out instructoral duties, organizing maneuvers, and devising advanced training and specialty courses. The successes of the Germans in Chile were thus transmitted to two friendly nations to the north of Peru and one in Central America. Chileans who served in Ecuador, El Salvador, and Colombia were, to a man, selected from those who had performed well for German instructors in the Escuela and Academia and in garrison duty: Captains Juan Pablo Bennett Argandoña and Francisco Lagreze and Lieutenants Julio Salinas, Armando Llanos Calderón, and Carlos Ibáñez in El Salvador; Captains Estanislao García Huidobro, Ernesto Medina, Luis Bravo, and Julio Franzani, and Lieutenants Arturo Montecinos and Luis Negrete in Ecuador; Captains Arturo Ahumada Bascuñán, Diego Guillén, Pedro Vignola, Manuel Aguirre, and Carlos Sáez Morales, and Colonel Washington Montero in Colombia all served with distinction and established the Chilean Army as South America's military leader between 1902 and 1914.

Superficially, then, the Chilean Army appeared to be a Latin American version of the German Army. Beneath the surface, however, weaknesses and inconsistencies were already apparent to Chilean officers, particularly those below the rank of colonel, who were most immediately affected by Prussianization. Emil Körner retired in 1910, the centennial year of Chilean independence, after a quarter-century of service. He died a Chilean citizen, and Chileans are proud of him to this day. But for some time after his passing his legacy proved a mixed blessing. The great gulf between theory and practice, between appearance and reality, created discontent in the officer class, expressed in the form of professional grievances (some of which have already been noted) and as outright objection to Chile's form of government. In several cases professional grievances were linked to objection to the form of government, and when this happened political interest infected the officer class.

The Beginnings of Military Politics: Discontent, Discussion, Intrigue[7]

As early as 1907, less than a year after the 1906 reforms went into effect and nearly three years before Körner retired, army officers in the Santiago garrison organized the "secret" Liga Militar. Their primary objectives were to function as a lobby and to organize professional support for new salary, promotion, and retirement schedules. Liga members believed that the government was disorganized and that it lacked direction, but they themselves showed little organizational ability or direction at this time. The public knew about the Liga and so did the high command, the War Ministry, and the administration of Pedro Montt. The Liga committed no breach of discipline, however, and no retaliatory action was taken.

In 1910 things warmed up. Montt died in office and was succeeded by the parliamentarist par excellence Ramón Barros Luco. Barros, an instigator of the 1891 congressional revolt, was an incredibly incompetent and lackluster chief executive; significantly, most discussions of his career have emphasized his anecdotes rather than his accomplishments.[8] He was not popular with army officers. Körner's retirement, the opening of the new Club Militar, the centennial celebration, and rumors of an extraordinary number of promotions in commemoration of Chile's one hundredth anniversary were frequent topics of discussion in military circles.

Prior to the festive centennial activities, however, no extraordinary promotions were announced. Only a few navy officers, besides those up for regular advancement in both services, were promoted. Liga leaders therefore planned a public demonstration during the September 18–19 national holidays; they only called it off at the last moment when urged to do so by the high command because of the impression it might give to foreign visitors. By this time the Liga was advocating structural changes in the army as well as salary, promotion, and retirement reforms. Liga members specifically maintained a critical attitude toward the Barros government.

During 1911 Liga members continued to meet in nonconspiratorial circumstances and invited selected civilians to their evening sessions. Two civilians were approached regarding leadership of a golpe: Emilio Rodríguez Mendoza, a diplomat and author, and Gonzalo Bulnes Pinto, historian of the War of the Pacific and son, grandson, and nephew of former presidents. Bulnes was extremely popular with the army officers, and his high pedigree made him an ideal choice as a civilian ally. When Liga members staged a special banquet during the 1911 independence commemoration, Bulnes was the only civilian in their midst, and he knew of their plan for a forthcoming golpe.

The plan called for action in January 1912. With the support of the Liga, Bulnes would inform President Barros that his deposition was imminent unless he named a new cabinet composed of independent leaders acceptable to the Liga and unless the new cabinet were to take action on a number of issues: governmental corruption (blamed on the politicians); public education reforms (to educate the masses); judicial reforms (to put an end to corruption in the courts); national health, sanitation, and alcoholism (all considered disgraceful); crime (a serious problem in the cities); the nagging Tacna-Arica question; economic policy (restriction of luxury imports and encouragement of manufacturing); and the revision of electoral registration procedures to allow more Chileans to vote and to free them from coercion.

The Liga, in fine, struck at the problems that afflicted the parliamentary system and the country it governed. Should Barros be unwilling to accede to the Liga's demands, Bulnes would govern by decree. All this worried Bulnes, who begged off just days before the golpe was to have been staged. His withdrawal left the Liga without a prestigious civilian accomplice. Only someone of his stature could have confronted the administration and only someone with his family background could have depended upon military support at this time. Although there were no recriminations and no purges of Liga officers, this was not due to lack of knowledge of what was going on. The Liga simply was not taken seriously by Barros; but it may have been tacitly allowed to function by the high command, for military men continued to voice opinions about a political system that they considered to be, in the words of an involved contemporary, "the negation of the harmonious and progressive movement of a society."[9]

The Parliamentary Republic:
Lack of Leadership in the Face of Crisis

In his excellent study, *Chile and the United States, 1880–1962*, Fredrick B. Pike titled his chapter on the Parliamentary Republic "The More the Country Changes, The More Its Government Remains the Same." No writer has ever said so much about Chile in the years 1891–1920 in so few words. The politics of national leadership, in which military professionals were beginning to express interest, was characterized by vapidity and vacuous rhetoric, and Chilean parliamentarism was a perversion of its British and French models. Ironically, the breakdown of civil-military fusion in Chile after 1891 was furthered by imitation of foreign models (British parliamentarism and German militarism) as well as by domestic changes.

In any society, military men speak out occasionally on political issues, and they frequently become acerbic in their assessments of what is wrong with the country. Where social, economic, and political issues are acute—or where they are neglected—military men frequently come through with opinions, accusations, and criticisms that appeal to similarly dissident civilians. When this happens civilians can and do look to the "guardians of national honor and dignity" for solutions. This did not happen in Chile until the 1924–27 crises, but it almost happened at the close of 1919, years after the Liga had dissolved.

Had Chile's nineteenth-century chief executives been less powerful or less respected by the military, some of those who served in the early twentieth century might not have looked so bad by comparison. And were it not for the fact that the Basque-Castilian aristocracy had achieved great success through oligarchy in politics, economic development, and social stability, the new parliamentary system might not have looked so bad either. But Jorge Montt, Federico Errázuriz Echaurren, Germán Riesco Errázuriz, Pedro Montt, Ramón Barros, and Juan Luis Sanfuentes did look bad. Among them, only Riesco and Pedro Montt could be classified as executive material by comparison with their predecessors. As we have seen, over the years the incidence of prior administrative experience of Chile's chief executives showed a decline when compared to that of the nineteenth-century presidents.[10] In essence, these new "leaders," with the exception of Admiral Jorge Montt, were products of parliamentarism; they owed their prior positions, candidacies, and elections to the presidency to coalitions, cliques, and coteries to which they remained beholden during their presidencies. The presidency became a reward for being noncontroversial or "dependable," as in the case of Jorge Montt, Riesco, and Barros; for being the scion of one or more great families, as in the case of Errázuriz, Riesco, and Pedro Montt; or for giving years of service to the party or coalition, as in the case of Sanfuentes.

None of these leaders was able—assuming one had been willing—to respond to Chile's problems. When strikes occurred, troops were rushed to the scene. When political struggles broke out, cabinets were dismissed, coalitions altered, and new cabinets assembled. When fiscal and economic crises developed, no bold plans were conceived. Chile suffered from a kind of political stagnation complicated by economic dislocation and social ferment—a most unhealthy combination of ills.

Economically the country was suffering from an inflationary spiral heightened by repeated issues of large quantities of paper money. This did more to wreck the country's international standing than to hurt those who were paid with paper, but the effect on critics was the same. Argentina surpassed Chile as the economic power of the Cono Sur, and Brazil was becoming an important commercial and diplomatic power. The public debt rose steadily; industrialization and agricultural production slowed. Real wages of miners, workers, and peasants declined in the face of inflation. Imports of luxury goods outranked in value imports of machinery and manufacturing equipment.

Alcoholism, poor health standards, illiteracy, low wages, crime, and horrible living conditions pervaded the lower reaches of society, while the upper classes lived in luxury. Labor violence increased in seriousness and frequency. In 1901, 1903, and 1905 Iquique, Antofagasta, Valparaíso, and Santiago were wracked by violence. In December 1907 nearly two thousand workers, including women and children, were shot down in Iquique by army troops called in to break a strike. Earlier the new ship *Blanco Encalada* had shelled workers in Antofagasta. In 1908 there was hardly a day when strikes and violence did not occur. When World War I disrupted the nitrate trade, some fifty thousand unemployed began the trek from the nitrate fields down to central Chile, only to find thousands more unemployed there. After the war, more dislocation occurred, and by this time the ten-year-old Marxist-leaning FOCH could attract one hundred thousand Chileans to a demonstration in the capital. Throughout this period the only official response to socioeconomic disruption was terrorism, bullets, beatings, and imprisonment.

If the state was listening to the people, it did not hear. The rulers of Chile behaved as if they were hermetically sealed from the agonizing country. Change meant a new cabinet; legislation had little meaning; debate became an exercise in phraseology; issues became meaningless. In 1910 the venerable Barros turned the presidential sash over to Juan Luis Sanfuentes, a hard-nosed, irascible Democratic Liberal, brother of Balmaceda's designee for the 1891 presidential election. Sanfuentes won by one electoral vote as the candidate of La Coalición, a coalition of Democratic Liberals, Nationals, some Liberals, and Conservatives. He was opposed by the so-called Liberal Alliance—a branch of the Liberals, Radicals, Democrats, and some Democratic Liberals. A headstrong and ambitious parliamentarist, Sanfuentes governed Chile while the worst of social and economic ills plagued the country.

The Military Response to Crisis:
Military Opinion on National Issues

By the time Sanfuentes came to the presidency, the Liga was no longer active. But already there were signs that army officers were beginning to take an active interest in national issues. Part of the professionalization process was the stimulation of writing in professional journals on military themes—training, maneuvers, special studies, technical subjects, routine matters, foreign policy, and the like. In these writings could be seen the germination of military ideology. This would have been unthinkable in the "old army," but it was very much a part of modern military life in Chile.

In a 1914 monograph, *El problema de nuestra educación militar,* for example, Captain Alberto Muñoz Figueroa minced no words in calling Chilean society anachronistic and regressive. This, he said, was to blame for the laziness and incompetence of many senior officers who owed their commissions and assignments to political friendships and corruption. Chilean society was so stratified, he wrote, that the lower classes were perpetually destined to inferior status —and that made them useless as a source of soldiers. Much of his monograph was devoted to a plea that the army be equipped to educate the masses, to teach them to read and write and to be good citizens, for no one else would take the responsibility.

Major Aníbal Riquelme's article "Relación que debe existir entre la política de un estado i el alto comando del ejército," published in the official *Memorial del Estado Mayor del Ejército de Chile*,[11] openly blamed the country's problems on the parliamentary system and opined that political leaders should consult the military on all issues of national importance. Riquelme also stated that the Constitution should be changed to provide for more executive leadership.

Such grumbling was not limited to subalterns. General Manuel Moore, commandant of Division IV (Valdivia), chided the Sanfuentes administration, in a 1917 essay written for officers of his command,[12] for meddling in the promotion process and for failing to provide effective government for all the people. He was alarmed that political influence and family background—the criteria for success in civilian life—were allowed to infiltrate the army. That same year Captain Domingo Terán, in his award-winning essay for a Club Militar literary competition,[13] accused the government and the political system of indifference to the professional and financial needs of the army and of allowing the obligatory military service law to be circumvented by sons of influential parents.

By the time World War I broke out, the Chilean Army had grown to a force of over seventeen thousand troops and more than eight hundred officers. The officer class had grown little, while the standing army was nearly three times its size at the beginning of the century. The army was divided into four divisions—I in the Far North, II in Santiago, III in the Central Valley, and IV in the Far South—and had twelve infantry batallions, five cavalry regiments, four regiments of artillery, and two companies of engineers. Appropriations for training, barracks, schools, uniforms, equipment, and arms also rose—but not sharply. The legal number of lieutenants remained constant while the number of officers of the rank of captain through general rose; clearly the size of the officer corps was being diminished through reductions in the lower ranks only.

As the criticisms of Muñoz, Riquelme, Moore, and Terán indicate, the government was blamed for failing to provide adequate facilities and funds for maintenance of high military standards. Some army officers—Terán was a notable example—believed that successive antimilitaristic administrations yielded to navy requests for additional funds while shortchanging the army. Many officers were sensitive about the use of the army as a strikebreaking force. Nevertheless, hard antimilitarism and hostility to the army were still confined mainly to the inarticulate masses, and the fact that organized labor became stronger during the war led military men to fear workers and not to side with them in their protests against governmental inactivity.

Military hostility to the parliamentary system, fear of revolution from below, and the burning desire for more forceful executive direction of national affairs were responsible, probably in equal proportions, for the renewal of plotting by military men at the close of hostilities in Europe. Chile's European nitrate markets collapsed at the end of the war after a brief spurt of activity between 1916 and 1918, and workers continued to stream south. Inflation continued unabated, dependent economic enterprises curtailed activities, wholesale and retail sales declined, dock workers were laid off. Chile was in a recession, and FOCH became increasingly radical.

The Complot de 1919:
A Threat to the Civilian Political Tradition[14]

Early in March 1919 four conservative admirals were dismissed suddenly from the navy for alleged participation in a plot against the Sanfuentes administration. Although he represented the aristocracy and parliamentary oligarchy and was supported by Conservatives, by this time Sanfuentes had alienated many of his supporters, and it is quite possible that navy leaders had conspired with rightest politicians to replace him. But whatever its motivation, the purpose of the navy plot is not known. The significance of the four forced navy retirements only became apparent in April 1919 when Sanfuentes ordered Generals Guillermo Armstrong Rivera and Manuel Moore placed under surveillance. The government accused Armstrong and Moore of planning a golpe against Sanfuentes, along with seven colonels and lieutenant colonels.

Armstrong and Moore were known to have Masonic connections and were alleged to be anticlerical. They were consistently opposed within the service by Generals Carlos Hurtado Wilson and Jorge

Boonen, allegedly the proclerical, anti-Masonic conservative leaders. The Church, Masonic connections, and conservative political opinions were merely peripheral issues; so were professional rivalries. The crux of the civil-military crisis of 1919 was the involvement of Armstrong and Moore in an organization known as the Army Society for Regeneration (Sociedad del Ejército de Regeneración, or SER), which planned to offer army support to Sanfuentes should the 1919 May Day workers' celebration result in violence. Apparently SER planned to go so far as to suggest that Sanfuentes assume extraordinary powers and govern through martial law. No firm evidence ever established Armstrong's and Moore's complicity in a real golpe, but they were retired just the same, at Sanfuentes's insistence. They both denied all allegations, pleading that they feared a Communist plot to overthrow the government by violence and turn Chile into a people's republic. The SER revelations made it clear both that members of the high command believed that an executive needed emergency aid to govern and that military men generally feared Marxism and organized labor.

While the government was investigating SER, new developments in the military belied the words of the two generals and further involved the officer class in politics. The Junta Militar was discovered; it supported SER and the generals and planned to demand congressional action on legislation to ameliorate workers' conditions and stop economic collapse. Armstrong and Moore denied any knowledge of the junta, but the government, press, and public all saw SER and the junta as one. Fifty army and navy officers—lieutenants, captains, majors, lieutenant colonels, colonels, and navy captains—had appended their signatures to the junta's constitution, which served also as a manifesto.

The grandiloquently phrased document—written, according to most sources, by Lieutenant Colonel Julio César del Canto Toske, the son of Estanislao del Canto—stressed reinforcement of the chief executive's powers in the face of Marxist threats to democracy. And in public declarations junteros admitted that they would depose Sanfuentes and replace many government officials with military officers if the president refused their support. They said they wanted major legislation in the areas of labor, fiscal, and military reforms, with emphasis on the latter.

During the ensuing trials of SER and junta members, Arturo Alessandri was named more than once as a participant in the junta. Alessandri, a Liberal senator from Tarapacá, briefly minister of the interior in 1918 after the Liberal Alliance had scored victories in the congressional contests, and an ambitious seeker of the presidency himself,[15] would have been named provisional president had the military actually moved against Sanfuentes. Of course, he denied any connection with the army plotters. His congressional immunity freed him from investigation and trial, but he had attended junta meetings, and junta leader Major Bernardo Gómez Solar was his close friend.

It took the government more than a year to clear up the trials of those involved in the 1919 plotting. Never was evidence introduced to prove "clear and present danger" of a golpe, but enough circumstantial evidence—testimony, documents, confessions—existed to convince articulate, literate Chileans and most political leaders that Armstrong and Moore, SER, and the junteros had seriously considered overthrowing the government as a last resort. At the very least, the officers involved in the bifurcated Conspiracy of 1919 had advocated overt military participation in the political process. This in itself was a shock. Military personnel were constitutionally forbidden to deliberate political matters; Sanfuentes sternly refused their proffered services, and the government considered them treasonous. In short, what military men had considered necessary, patriotic measures were considered treason by civilians at a time when the country was, to put it simply, in a real mess. Some sixty officers were found guilty, if only by implication. Of these, twenty-seven were retired, six were acquitted, and the rest were confined or banished ("relegated") for periods ranging from ten months to four years.

As it had in 1891, the officer class underwent a kind of purge, and conservative or apolitical officers remained in control. The Conspiracy of 1919 showed that army—and some navy—officers were divided into two broad categories at that time. First, there were those who objected to the parliamentary system strongly enough to propose its alteration by offering support to their constitutional supreme commander. Of these, the majority were below the rank of general, and their interests ranged far beyond military action to shut off the possibility of mass insurrection during economic distress. This schism precluded effective action by those with political interests.

Second, most of the high command and most provincial garrison commanders either had no political interest whatsoever or sided with the defenders of parliamentarism. Both these groups claimed to represent pure professionalism, but not necessarily for the same reasons. The fact that the Conspiracy of 1919 split the army in these ways made military political action an impossibility, but it indicated political interest for more reasons than simple political grievances.

La Movilización de 1920: A Threat to Military Integrity[16]

As the conspiracy trials drew to a close in 1920, a new crisis developed to draw the army further into Chilean political life. By this time Emil Körner was dead, the German Army had been discredited, and Chilean Germanophiles were a frustrated group. The Conspiracy of 1919 had cast a dark shadow on the integrity, unity, and cohesiveness of the officer class, and the army suffered a loss of prestige. The crisis of 1920 developed after the presidential election, contested by Luis Barros Borgoño of the Conservative–Liberal–National–Democratic Liberal National Union and Arturo Alessandri of the Liberal–Democratic Liberal–Radical–Democrat Liberal Alliance.

The voting was extremely close. Demagogic and energetic, Alessandri had much support from the masses, but most of them could not vote. Barros was a political mediocrity, distinguished only by years of congressional service and by being the son of historian Diego Barros Arana. Questions over electoral votes, credentials of electors, and fraud caused Sanfuentes to create a special tribunal to decide the election. In Santiago, Valparaíso, Concepción, Antofagasta, and Iquique, popular demonstrations in favor of Alessandri were kept under control only with great difficulty, despite Alessandri's acceptance of the tribunal arrangement. The United States ambassador even cabled Washington suggesting that one or two battleships sent into Chilean waters might calm the situation![17]

Suddenly, in mid July, three weeks after election day, War Minister Ladislao Errázuriz mobilized the armed forces. The recent golpe in Bolivia—which had brought to power an aggressive Republican regime bent on reincorporating Bolivia's lost Pacific provinces—as well as masses of Indians supposedly whipped to a frenzy by Protestant missionaries, and Peruvian troops massed along the border north of Tacna-Arica all posed a threat to national security. The government announced that it was sending army and navy forces to the northern desert to meet the threat. This was the first time in fifty years that the Chilean armed forces had been called into service.

The mobilization proved embarrassing both to the government and to the armed forces. While Chilean ladies were volunteering for the Red Cross, while those workers who still had jobs donated wages for military needs, and while patriotic groups harassed Peruvians and Bolivians residing in Chile, the Chilean troops arrived in Arica. Intelligence reports showed no evidence of Peruvians or Bolivians anywhere near the frontier in other than ordinary numbers and in civilian capacity.

Most of the army officers sent north were known to be sympathetic to Alessandri's campaign promises for labor, social, fiscal, and military reforms. Generals Hurtado and Boonen, leaders of the conservative officers' group, had seen to that. Rumors spread that the war minister and his friends were making large sums of money selling provisions to the army at high prices. War materiel was in short supply, communications were poor, and organization was confused at best. Food was bad, the hastily constructed barracks were like slums, and dysentery, lung congestion, and fever spread among the troops. The best that can be said of the Mobilization of 1920 is that it was an unfortunate mistake; the worst, that it was a risky and elaborate hoax to remove reformist elements in the army from populous central Chile at a time when the Parliamentary Republic was being challenged and labor agitation was widespread in the North. Whatever the explanation, the army had been compromised indeed. Officers and men had been dumped in Antofagasta, Iquique, and Tacna for no real reason. A growing number of army officers became alienated from politics and politicians. Their alienation would soon goad them to take matters into their own hands.

Facing pressure from the Liberal Alliance and fearing mass violence, the electoral tribunal gave the presidency to Alessandri. For all his demagoguery, Alessandri proved not to be a radical reformer. To many Chilean politicians, he seemed unfit for national leadership, unscrupulous, shifty, and untrustworthy; he was an Italo-Chilean arrivé, not their kind. But neither his program nor his prior political performance scared the parliamentary oligarchs. Making him president was the lesser of two evils in 1920. Better Alessandri in the presidency, for five years a captive of parliamentary politics, than Alessandri as a disgruntled demagogue when so many miners and workers thirsted for a leader and army professionals sought a strong president by any means.

And so, in the thirty years since the Civil War tore the country apart, the Chilean Army had become both a professional organization and a budding political interest group. The creation of a modern professional army under political conditions characterized by weak national leadership and unresponsive government resulted in an officer class within which professionalism *could* encourage political interest. Political interest, then, was a result of the professionalization process and did not develop despite it.

The failure of the Parliamentary Republic to respond to the critical needs of the majority of Chile's population comprised one broad set of causes for the politicization of the military. For at the same time that the government encouraged the army to become South America's most powerful (1891–1906) and then allowed it to fall into disrepair (1906–20), successive administrations failed to respond to the need for national reform. The army's image of itself alternated between extreme pride and shame, between optimism and frustration. A decline in military respect for civilian politics and for Chile's political system resulted.

Such feelings were by no means inevitable. It is altogether possible that, had the government coddled the army with salaries, promotions, and retirement adjustments (a perpetual source of bitterness to officers since there were no major upward revisions after 1904) and placated officers with new equipment (artillery and aircraft were useless in the 1920 fiasco), few officers would have become critical of Chilean parliamentarism. Spanish military defense juntas of the World War I years, for example, criticized the incompetent Madrid government, but they backed it in the face of Catalan separatism and were concerned far more with the state of the profession than with real social or political reform. The Liga, the junta, and SER were also concerned primarily with internal military matters, but Chilean government and politics proved so weak and corrupt that professional officers saw their profession's problems as inseparable from those of society in general.

Chilean officers did not withdraw their support from the Parliamentary Republic until they felt compelled to act in order to preclude mass violence and upheaval after World War I. The political crumbling of the Basque-Castilian aristocracy and the succession of mediocre, do-nothing presidents created a power vacuum. The state, so omnipotent in the past, was no longer the object of respect and obedience. Patriotism was reexamined in military circles when the

Liga, SER, and the Junta Militar offered military solutions during the second decade of this century.

The gulf between theory and practice, illusion and reality, was a constant source of frustration for ambitious, dedicated army officers, and so was what they considered the preferential treatment shown to the navy. The fact that a few navy officers involved themselves in the Liga and in the 1919 Conspiracy did little to create solidarity among the armed forces, and without navy acquiescence the Chilean Army could not hope to pull off a golpe. The lesson of 1891 still stung the army. Army prestige suffered repeated blows at the worst possible time, in 1919–20. Germany's defeat, the failure of the uncoordinated conspiracy, and the grotesque parody of mobilization in 1920 made the army look absurd. Chile's Latin American military client states still sent their cadets and officers to study in Santiago, and Chilean missions still worked abroad. But Peruvian, Bolivian, Argentine, and even Brazilian counterparts were surging ahead in training, equipment, and expertise.

The state had let the army down, thought some officers; political incompetence was holding Chile's military machine back. More importantly, the state was letting down the majority of its citizens. The political system was moribund, and the Chilean Congress functioned more like the Spanish Cortes than like a parliament. Party politics, figurehead presidents, coalitions, local control of elections, municipal autonomy, and ministerial responsibility to Congress all functioned to maintain a plutocratic Congress which did not appear to be interested in serving the people. Money, family connections, influence, bribery, payoffs, club life, and opulence seemed to be the only desires of politicians, and army officers did not approve. And the government seemed powerless to prevent strikes, poverty, alcoholism, slums, and crime.

In 1920, army officers—and all of Chile—were faced with the rise of Marxism, economic collapse, political chicanery, and military backwardness. Many professional officers—among them a number of militant Germanophiles, trained during the Körner years or soon thereafter—looked to Alessandri's triumph as a harbinger of change for Chile. In the next chapter we will examine the rise to power of these political officers, perhaps the only group capable of political action in post–World War I Chile.

7

The Rise of the Political Officers, 1920–27

On September 5, 1924, a committee of army officers, nominally led by Colonel Arturo Ahumada Bascuñán, commandant of the Escuela Militar, waited on President Alessandri in his offices at La Moneda. These officers bore a petition containing demands for legislation suggested by Alessandri himself, drawn up during the previous night by Major Carlos Ibáñez del Campo, director of the Cavalry School.

Within a week Alessandri left the country, and his new interior minister, Inspector General Luis Altamirano Talavera, formed a Junta of Government that included himself, Admiral Francisco Neff Jara, and General Juan Pablo Bennett Argandoña and appointed a new cabinet.

On January 23, 1925, Lieutenant Colonel Ibáñez, aided by Lieutenant Colonel Marmaduke Grove Vallejo, ousted the Altamirano government and installed a new junta headed by civilian Emilio Bello Codesido, but dominated by military leaders. Less than three months after Altamirano's ouster, Alessandri returned.

On October 1, 1925, after having successfully overseen the promulgation of a new constitution, Alessandri resigned again, this time turning the government over to Interior Minister–Vice-President Luis Barros Borgoño. Two weeks later Emiliano Figueroa Larraín was elected to the presidency; he resigned on May 5, 1927, turning the government over to Interior Minister–Vice-President Ibáñez. On July 21, 1927, Colonel Ibáñez was elected president.

Not since the 1820s had Chile witnessed such a flurry of top-level administrative changes—seven in as many years, six alone between September 1924 and July 1927. The causes, sequence of events, and results of this process have been detailed and analyzed elsewhere, and it is not our purpose here to reproduce these details.[1] Rather, the focus of this chapter is the rise of "political officers" of the Chilean Army, for it was this group that was responsible for the 1920–27 political upheavals and changed Chile's social, political, and economic structures.

On Political Officers:
Chilean Traditions Shattered

In one sense, obviously, a political officer is one whose interests go beyond the mere fulfillment of his assigned duties. But all officers have some interest in politics. Constitutional proscriptions of deliberation by military men cannot preclude the holding of opinions. Such constitutional proscriptions are designed to prohibit—or at least to discourage—overt political deliberation and participation in political processes reserved to the civilian sector. Obviously, not all officers who have political opinions function as political officers. For some, professional interests and duties outweigh any inclination to become involved in political affairs. When, on the other hand, some members of an officer class do overtly deliberate and participate, their peers inevitably become political, for they either stand back and tacitly allow others to involve themselves in political affairs or they oppose military involvement. Even if they oppose involvement on strictly professional grounds—citing the Constitution, military tradition, or codes of conduct—their opposition can benefit civilians who are likewise hostile to military involvement, just as their tacit acceptance will aid their fellows in uniform who become political.

The pronunciamento, the cuartelazo (barracks revolt), or the political involvement of one or two military figures need not lead to politicization of the entire officer class. But when, over a period of years, a nucleus of officers professes political interest, or when events continue to attract military men to national affairs, it becomes increasingly difficult for an officer class to go about routine duties as if nothing else were transpiring.

In the case at hand, a good portion of the Chilean army officer class was political or politicized—the two are not synonymous—by the time Alessandri took his inaugural oath on December 23, 1920. The number of political and politicized officers increased steadily at intervals during the 1920–27 years. Alessandri regularly visited the barracks and exhorted officers to support his program; he reinstated members of the Conspiracy of 1919; he appointed known political officers to high posts; he ordered the army to supervise congressional elections in March 1924; he met with officers on September 5, 1924, and accepted their petition; and between September 5 and 8 he attempted to dominate the armed forces and use them in his valiant, if bumbling, efforts to bring down the parliamentary system.

Other civilians, friendly and unfriendly to his cause, connived with military leaders for political purposes throughout the years between mid 1924 and mid 1927. But the Chilean political officer was not solely a creature of the Alessandri period. If he had been, the armed forces would have functioned politically as they had in 1891, as a mere extension of civilian political alignments. By 1920 the army in particular had a history of professional intrainstitutional conflict, and this developed into political conflict during the 1924–27 period. By 1927 naval intrainstitutional conflict also took on a political tone. The causes of conflict, therefore, were both political and professional.

The activities of the Chilean political officers in the crises of the 1920s can be examined from several viewpoints. How, for example, did officers stand on the executive-legislative struggle for control of government? How did social or family background influence political behavior? Did age, rank, years in service, the time at which an individual began his service, specific service experience or assignments, branch of the service, or kinship influence political behavior? Was German or German-style training, or the lack of it, an influence on political behavior? All these things did have an influence, but they do not lead to an easy compartmentalization of political officers into "young versus old" or "junior versus senior" categories. In this chapter we shall avoid compartmentalization except when solid documentary evidence warrants and supports it.

A professional officer class will not become political on its own or fall under the influence of political officers unless several forces are at work. These forces are social, political, and economic distress unameliorated by a government which may or may not be representative of an unsuitable political system; professional self-consciousness or sense of identity engendered by specialized training and distinguishable status; some kind of recognized leadership group within the officer class; some kind of model, goal, or sense of mission to inspire military political action; and resentment of civilian politics, politicians, and parties to the point of wanting to punish or purge them (this last being quite variable). All these forces were at work in Chile early in the century, at no time more forcefully than during Alessandri's first term in office.

Alessandri:
The Demise of Parliamentarism and the Destruction
of the Civilian Tradition[2]

Arturo Alessandri's 1920–24 administration perpetuated and exacerbated the failings of the parliamentary system. Administrative continuity was nonexistent; Alessandri assembled sixteen cabinets prior to the events of September 1924. This was not as bad as some previous administrations. Pedro Montt and Ramón Barros had each formed eighteen ministries, and Sanfuentes had governed with twenty-eight; since 1900 there had been over one hundred separate cabinets. By 1924, the average tenure for a full cabinet was three months. The composition, tenure, and effectiveness of cabinets continued to depend on congressional support.

At the beginning of his administration Alessandri had a Liberal Alliance majority in the Chamber of Deputies (seventy Aliancistas to forty-eight Unionistas) but confronted a National Union opposition in the Senate (twenty-two Unionistas to fifteen Aliancistas). This obviously inhibited the chances for passage of his legislative programs. Even more damaging was the fact that the president's own coalition did not solidly support his efforts. The Liberal Alliance was divided against itself on the issue of executive supremacy. Alessandri, who had publicly opposed Balmaceda thirty years before, became the advocate of stronger executive powers to enable the government to solve the economic crisis, and he tied executive authority to social and economic reform. But most Radicals and many Liberals continued to support parliamentary supremacy as the correct expression of political democracy. Democratic Liberals supported Balmaceda's ideals but were not known for any commitment to broad reform. The fractious Congress resisted Alessandri, and parties plagued him with demands for patronage, cabinet posts, and diplomatic appointments, while at times refusing him support if rival parties were included in a cabinet.

In the 1924 congressional elections the president obtained a Liberal

Alliance majority in the upper house. But a majority of Liberal Alliance senators proved no more cohesive or supportive than one of Liberal Alliance deputies. The posting of army officers at polls in 1924 did much damage to Alessandri's prestige within his own divided camp and may have been an unnecessary measure. For by September 1924 little important social or economic legislation had been attended to; the few laws that had been passed were not yet widely applied.

The 1924 Congress spent most of its time discussing a parliamentary remuneration bill which, though unconstitutional in essence (legislators in the past had either been men of means or had lucrative jobs, and the Constitution prohibited salaries for legislators), was so worded as to make it technically constitutional. While the government's financial straits prohibited the payment of monthly salaries to civil servants, public school teachers, and military personnel, a Liberal Alliance majority was preparing to pass legislation enabling legislators to receive salaries. The fact that many Aliancista legislators were not men of means mattered little to the soldiers and civil servants who had not been paid for six months or more. They desperately wanted action, but it was not forthcoming, and they had no political pressure group to plead their case.

When Alessandri came into office the government was virtually bankrupt. It is useless to speculate whether any of Alessandri's programs could have cleared up the situation. In fact, his social and economic reforms were not very radical, and Congress never gave him support to put them into effect anyway. Unemployment continued unabated. With nearly one hundred thousand miners and dockers out of work by 1922, uncounted thousands more in subsidiary enterprises were affected by the nitrate collapse. Nitrates sold less and less, and those that were sold were from stockpiles, not fresh production. Chile supplied three-quarters of the world's nitrates in 1895 but only one-quarter in 1925. The government, of course, had no significant sources of revenue apart from mineral imposts and the tariff. Bills calling for urban property taxes (not a land tax), use taxes on government lands, and graduated income taxes with a minimal rate on high incomes were so butchered in Congress that even those that passed between 1924 and 1927 were useless. By the end of 1923 the budget deficit was close to 110 million pesos; three years later it nearly tripled.

Confidence in the constantly warring Liberal Alliance, National

Union, and their constituent parts was at a low ebb by 1924. The vast majority of Chileans were apolitical, but unemployment, nonpayment of salaries to the employed, inefficiency, corruption in government, and inflation made them at least vaguely aware of the failure of their political system. FOCH grew in strength; strikes and demonstrations continued to attract thousands, and labor leaders grew increasingly militant. What made the situation especially unbearable was the fact that Alessandri had promised so much in 1920 and delivered so little. He had pledged such reforms as a modern labor code; low-cost workers' housing; increased government responsibility in health, welfare, and labor; more public schools; and women's rights. These were not rash promises by Parliamentary Republican standards but necessary reforms, given the desperate situation of the country by 1924. By coaxing, wheedling, threatening, and compromising, Alessandri got the Alliance and the Union to begin work on these measures that year; then he got his Senate majority. But instead of concentrating on major legislation, the new Congress spent too much of its time on the salary bill.

Military men expressed considerable hostility toward civilian politics and government between 1920 and 1924. The same tone that characterized the writings of Muñoz, Riquelme, Moore, and Terán prior to the post–World War I economic collapse and the advent of Alessandri continued in the 1920s. Essays, pamphlets, and mono graphs written during this period or about it by Lieutenant René Montero Moreno, Captain Oscar Fenner Marín, Captain David Barl Menezes, Colonel Bartolomé Blanche Espejo, Major Carlos Sáez Morales, Captain Tobías Barros Ortiz, Captain Gaspar Mora Sotomayor, and Colonel Agustín Benedicto allude to the failure of the civilian political system, the poor economic condition of the country, and the neglect of the armed forces.[3] Brazilian Tenentismo of the 1922–24 period; the pronunciamento of Miguel Primo de Rivera, the captain general of Catalonia in 1923; the role of the Spanish military defense juntas; and Mussolini's march on Rome all found their way into Chilean military literature. Seminars were held during the winter months of 1924 on national problems and on Primo's new regime in Spain. Political deliberation assumed major proportions as the political officers emerged into public view. By mid 1927 the officers had achieved political dominance, the culmination of a process that had been going on for some twenty years.

The Chilean Army Officer Class:
Anatomy of a Political Interest Group[4]

In 1924 the Chilean army officer class could be divided into two broad groups: the high command and the subalterns. The high command (division and brigadier generals) was composed mainly of men who had entered the army in 1891. Inspector General Altamirano was the ranking officer in 1924; Division General Luis Felipe Brieba Arán and Brigadier General Mariano Navarrete Ciris, both prominent political figures in the civil military crises of 1924–27, had been in the army since the Civil War of 1891. Brigadier General Pedro Pablo Dartnell Encina and Division Generals Juan Pablo Bennett, Luis Cabrera Negrete, and Luis Contreras Sotomayor had entered the army prior to 1891 and emerged on the side of the victors. Except for Bennett and Cabrera, all these men entered the army well after the War of the Pacific and in the midst of civil conflict.

The average age of members of the high command was fifty-four years; the average number of years in service was thirty-six. Many of the high command had entered the service at a young age, some as common soldiers, and not all were graduates of the Escuela Militar. Some had received commissions as civilians in 1891. Altamirano, the senior officer, fifty-seven years of age in 1924 after thirty-three years of service, was three years older than the average general, and had served three years less than the average.

Altamirano stood out as the most political member of the general officer class. He was the ranking artillery officer and had participated in the battles of Concón and Placilla. Altamirano was related to Alessandri by marriage (his sister was the widow of Senator José Pedro Alessandri, the president's brother, whose death in 1923 left a seat vacant from Ñuble Province and occasioned a bitter electoral struggle in the March 1924 contest). "Don Lucho" had served briefly as war minister in 1923.

As of mid 1924 the high command of the Chilean Army was still composed primarily of nineteenth-century soldiers. Traces of the spirit of 1879–84 were still present, as was the spirit of 1891. Not all the generals were Escuela graduates, and only a handful had been influenced by German training techniques or had a record of service or study abroad. Altamirano, Contreras, and Bennett were artillery officers; Navarrete and Brieba, infantry officers; Dartnell was an engineer; and only Cabrera came from the cavalry. Nevertheless, all had held important administrative and instructoral or staff positions.

None had close family ties with the Basque-Castilian aristocracy. Half had begun their careers in 1891 and half before. Most were unfriendly to Alessandri for either professional or personal reasons. None could be classified as a sociopolitical reformer, though Dartnell and Navarrete would both figure prominently in the reform programs of the 1925–27 and 1927–31 governments. Bennett, something of an anomaly, was a member of the 1924–25 Altamirano government and was very sympathetic to the demands of subalterns for political as well as military reform. It is clear from this information that the political officers of the high command, both from the army and from the navy, were not a monolithic, superannuated, rightist interest group; of course we have no way of knowing the attitudes of the senior officers who did not become involved politically.

During the regular session of the new Congress of 1924, Generals Altamirano, Brieba (war minister at the time of the March 1924 elections), Contreras, and Bennett and the retired Juan de Dios Vial Guzmán began meeting with Admirals Luis Gómez Carreño and Guillermo Soublette and with conservative anti-Alessandri civilians. In these clandestine meetings they formed a secret society called TEA (Tenacidad, Entusiasmo, Abnegación, or Tenacity, Enthusiasm, Abnegation) designed to throw out Alessandri. Members drew up a bill of particulars that read much like the pronunciamento of congressional leaders in 1891! Altamirano, Vial, and Contreras were the military ringleaders. Brieba's bungling of the March 1924 electoral supervision and his own weak defense of the officers involved motivated him to plot against Alessandri out of vengeance. Bennett played only a minor part. Gómez and Soublette represented conservative navy interests. TEA did not depose Alessandri, but the subalterns caused him to leave the presidency later in 1924. At that time Altamirano, Bennett, and Admiral Neff took control.

Examination of the political officers below the rank of brigadier general—members of the Junta Militar y Naval (JMN)—reveals as little political homogeneity as that found in the upper ranks, but clear conclusions can be drawn on some of their attitudes.

The JMN: Agent of Military Politics

The JMN is the group that officially deposed Alessandri by presenting him with a petition. It was originally composed of lieutenants and captains who visited the Senate on September 2 and 3, 1924, to protest the imminent adoption of the parliamentary remuneration bill. When it was formally organized on September 5 in the Club Militar, the JMN included one colonel, three lieutenant colonels, nine majors, six captains, and four lieutenants. Ultimately the group comprised thirty-five army officers, of whom seven composed the Mesa Directiva (Board of Directors). Let us now examine the composition of the group as shown in table 3.[5]

With only a few exceptions, none of the 1924 junteros was closely related to oligarchs. It is true that the incidence of family connections both with the aristocracy and with families of military officers increased slightly in the lower ranks between 1910 and 1930, but we lack data to confirm this tendency or to establish its relationship to political action. This increased incidence of connections to the upper classes may have been responsible for the decrease in political action after 1932, when lieutenants and captains with family ties to the civilian upper classes or to military families became majors and lieutenant colonels and moved into staff and command positions. On the other hand, there is considerable incidence of political action by sons of distinguished officers and relatives of distinguished citizens.

The JMN and its *mesa directiva* functioned for only thirteen weeks in late 1924, but during that time it helped the president get much of his own reform program through a recalcitrant Congress. The September 5 JMN petition called for a veto of parliamentary remuneration; immediate passage of the 1924 budget; an income tax measure; new military salary and promotion laws; and other social reform legislation.

When the junta refused to disband, the furious Alessandri resigned, leaving Vice-President Altamirano as chief executive. At first, the JMN yielded to tradition, discipline, and hierarchy and tacitly supported Altamirano's new Junta of Government. Nevertheless, the JMN fought with the Junta of Government over constitutional reform, new presidential elections, and continued reform legislation. In each case the JMN favored what Alessandri had struggled for: constitutional reform to balance legislative and executive authorities; revised electoral registration procedures; and state assumption of a major role in welfare, health, education, labor, and the economy. These issues divided the high command from the subalterns, but the JMN thought that it had achieved satisfactory compromise and disbanded in December 1924. These same issues helped cause the overthrow of

TABLE 3
Junta Militar y Naval
(September 5-December 13, 1924)

	Birth Date	Entered Army*	Branch
ARMY COLONELS			
Arturo Ahumada Bascuñán	1872	1888	Infantry
Francisco Javier Díaz Valderrama	1877	1890	Engineers
Carlos Fernández Pradel	1872	1891	Cavalry
ARMY LIEUTENANT COLONELS			
Bartolomé Blanche Espejo	1879	1895	Cavalry
Pedro Charpín Rival	1876	1894	Artillery
Matías Díaz Quinteros	1875	1896	Infantry
Alfredo Ewing Acuña	1876	1894	Infantry
Emilio Salinas Manríquez	1877	1895	Engineers
Félix Urcullo López	1878	1896	Infantry
Ambrosio Viaux Aguilar	1876	1896	Artillery
ARMY MAJORS			
David Bari Menezes	1886	1901	Artillery
Roberto Canales Avendaño	1876	1898	Infantry
Carlos Grasset Barros	1879	1895	Artillery
Marmaduke Grove Vallejo	1878	1897	Artillery
Carlos Ibáñez del Campo	1877	1896	Cavalry
Arturo Mújica Valenzuela	1879	1898	Infantry
Rafael Poblete Manterola	1887	1904	Infantry
Guillermo del Pozo Luque	1883	1899	Infantry
Arturo Puga Osorio	1879	1895	Artillery
Carlos Sáez Morales	1881	1897	Artillery
Carlos Vergara Montero	1883	1898	Infantry
ARMY CAPTAINS			
Sócrates Aguirre Bernal	1893	1909	Infantry
César Arroyo	n.a.	n.a.	n.a.
Tobías Barros Ortiz	1894	1909	Artillery
Luis Cabrera Gana	1883	1900	Cavalry
Oscar Fenner Marín	1892	1909	Cavalry
Carlos Millán Iriarte	1887	1909	Artillery
Angel Moreno L. de Guevara	1887	1909	Artillery
Armando Vásquez Rovinet	1892	1912	Artillery
Guillermo Villouta	n.a.	n.a.	Carabineros
ARMY LIEUTENANTS			
Mario Bravo Lavín	1898	1912	Cavalry
Enrique Calvo	n.a.	n.a.	n.a.
Alejandro Lazo Guevara	1895	1913	Cavalry
Silvestre Urízar	n.a.	n.a.	Artillery
Enrique Zúñiga	n.a.	n.a.	n.a.

NAVY CAPTAINS

Julio Dittborn
Benjamín Barros Merino
Carlos Jouanne
Luis Escobar

POLICE OFFICERS

Carlos Dinator Espinola
Diego Ramírez (ret.)

MESA DIRECTIVA

Lieutenant Colonels Blanche and Ewing
Majors Ibáñez and Puga
Lieutenants Bravo, Lazo, and Urízar

*Admission to Escuela Militar is the date used normally to indicate entrance in Chilean army service.

n.a.—data not available

Altamirano by a revivified, smaller subalterns' group in 1925, when it became obvious that the government planned to engineer the election of Ladislao Errázuriz, Conservative aristocrat, champion of parliamentarism, and much-criticized minister of war during the Mobilization of 1920.

The JMN:
A Statistical and Correlative Survey of
Political Motivations and Cohesion

The typical subaltern political officer favored reform and the restoration of presidential powers and was hostile to the parliamentary form of government. Reform did not mean revolution, but hostility to parliamentary rule could (and did) mean hostility to civilian party politics as well. As we know from their writings, strong, progressive, regenerative leadership was what junteros wanted.[6] But why? We can supply some answers by assessing the junteros as political officers through the statistics noted in table 3.

The key members of the JMN were the lieutenant colonels, majors, and captains. Colonel Ahumada resigned as chairman on September 6; Colonels Fernández and Díaz were participants in name only. Of the seven lieutenant colonels in the JMN, all but Matías Díaz would figure politically. Their average age was forty-seven, and they averaged nearly twenty-nine years of service; the relationship between their ages and years of service is roughly the same as that of their superiors. Majors were more numerous than members of any other rank in the JMN. Their average age was forty-three years and average length of service twenty-six. Captains averaged thirty-four years of age and had typically served nearly sixteen years. Because these figures show that the ratio of age to rank to years in service varied so little between the high command and the subalterns of the JMN, we may conclude that ambition to advance in rank quickly was of only minor importance in determining political interest.

The JMN included members of all branches of the army, but infantry (the largest branch) and artillery had the highest representation. JMN members represented all units in the Santiago area and some provincial garrisons; the schools, staff, and police also had representation. A comparison of the average ages in each branch of the service proves revealing. For example, artillery and infantry lieutenant colonels averaged forty-eight years of age and twenty-nine years of service. Blanche, the lone cavalry lieutenant colonel, was only forty-five years old and had served twenty-nine years. The lone engineer was forty-seven and had served twenty-nine years. Because there was only one cavalry officer and one engineer among lieutenant colonels, these comparisons do not offer conclusive evidence of a trend, however. Artillery majors averaged forty-three years of age and twenty-six years of service; infantry majors were on the average a year younger, but they had served two years less. The only cavalry major was forty-seven years old and had been in the army twenty-eight years; he was older by four or five years than the average for majors and had served two to four more years. This man was Carlos Ibáñez del Campo, the director of the Cavalry School. Artillery captains were typically thirty-four years of age and had served fourteen years; the one infantry captain was thirty-one and he had been in the army fifteen years. Two cavalry captains averaged thirty-six years of age and nineteen years of service.

Cavalry and artillery majors and captains, then, were slightly older in 1924 and had put in more years of service in the Chilean Army than their infantry and engineer counterparts. Because these officers would therefore tend to be a relatively frustrated group, one might expect a correspondingly high incidence of political activity among cavalry and artillery men, and that is precisely where it was highest. With the exception of Lieutenant Colonel Ewing—an irregular attendant at JMN meetings—all members of the elected Mesa Directiva were either artillery or cavalry officers.

The most opinionated, vociferous, and radical; the most respected, accomplished, and cunning; in short, the most significant political officers of the JMN were slightly older than the norm: Carlos Ibáñez and Marmaduke Grove were above the average age for majors, as were most of their cohorts, with the exception of Bartolomé Blanche. Juntero officers as a group were slightly older than the average age for other officers of equal rank. But there was no apparent discrepancy between the age/rank/years-in-service ratios of members of the high command and of the subalterns of the JMN. No one could argue that the general officers were superannuated.

If an officer had not achieved the rank of colonel upon attaining the age of fifty, however, or if he had served thirty years without attaining that rank, retirement was virtually automatic. No member of the JMN had been overly long in rank; there were exceptions to the thirty-year rule, but not many, and a good number of lieutenant colonels and majors were anxious. According to law the minimum time between the rank of second lieutenant and the rank of brigadier was twenty years, but in fact many members of the JMN saw their careers waning while they languished in lower ranks.

Other correlations can be made on the basis of friendships from Escuela and Academia days. Lieutenant Colonels Charpín and Blanche and Majors Grove, Ibáñez, Sáez, and Viaux all studied at the Escuela together. Blanche, Grove, Ibáñez, Pozo, Canales, and Urcullo all attended the Academia in the 1912–14 course—the last Prussianized course prior to the Great War. All the lieutenant colonels, in fact, and the majority of majors and captains, were in school together at the Escuela between 1894 and 1898 (lieutenant colonels and majors) or 1909 and 1913 (captains and lieutenants). Thus the core of the JMN was educated after the Civil War—when the Portalian state crumbled—or had reached staff level before World War I—after the Basque-Castilian aristocracy had divided, and precisely when the Parliamentary Republic began to show signs of weakness in the face of labor agitation, corruption, political conflict, and, finally, economic decline.

Alessandri had few friends in the JMN—Ewing, Millán, and Aguirre were close to him—but they and other officers apprised him of what went on until he resigned. Although there was little support for Altamirano in the JMN, the military code of discipline permitted him to run the government, while civilian confusion over the events of September 1924 precluded any alliance between reformist subalterns and civilians until January 1925.

The JMN was by no means a cohesive group. Ewing, Millán, and Aguirre were unhappy with the hardliners, Ibáñez, Blanche, Grove, and Sáez, who allowed Alessandri to resign. Naval delegates supported the Junta of Government. The Alessandristas wanted the president back, but the hardliners did not. Thus military tradition and naval support balanced political differences.

There was only sporadic agreement on what should be done. The Mesa Directiva represented only the hardliners, and other junteros grumbled about that. By December some junteros, dismayed by Radical and Democrat attacks on the army, or finally apathetic where politics was concerned, stopped coming to meetings. When rumors of a Ewing candidacy for the upcoming emergency presidential elections of 1925 began to circulate, the high command stepped in. The

JMN disavowed any support for Ewing and agreed to dissolve, provided the cabinet were reconstituted. They did and it was, but to no avail. The Junta of Government went ahead with plans for devolution of political leadership to civilians without any constitutional reform and were soon faced with reaction.

Some of the political officers of 1924 had been promoted, all had been paid, and Congress had indeed approved new military fringe benefits and higher appropriations. These improvements and the spate of reform legislation in late 1924 satisfied some officers, but others believed their country had to be changed. By mid January 1925, secret meetings were being held by Alessandrista politicians and a revolutionary committee was formed, led by Grove, Ibáñez, Fenner, Aguirre, Lazo, and Bravo. On January 23 they ousted the Junta of Government. Soon Arturo Alessandri was on his way home from Italy.

Ibáñez, Grove, Blanche: Prototypal Officers[7]

In early 1925 the three most politically influential men in the Chilean army were Lieutenant Colonels Ibáñez, Grove, and Blanche. Their careers marked them as epitomes of the Chilean political officer in the 1920s.

Carlos Ibáñez del Campo (1877–1960) was born in Linares, the son of a modest landowner. Ibáñez had one brother, Javier, who was also an army officer briefly, and one sister. He attended a public primary school and then the Liceo de Hombres in Linares. In 1896 he entered the Escuela Militar in Santiago and was commissioned a second lieutenant in 1898. Young Carlos excelled in horsemanship more than in academic studies. He had few close friends during his academy years but knew Pedro Dartnell well and was highly thought of by one of his instructors, Arturo Ahumada. Athletic, handsome, sober, and hardworking, Ibáñez was impressive if not brilliant as a second lieutenant. He was promoted to first lieutenant in 1900.

Three years later, while a student at the Academia, he was selected for the first El Salvador mission directed by Captain Bennett, and there he took charge of the military school and formed the tiny nation's cavalry corps. Ibáñez won acclaim in the Central American country for his horsemanship and for taking part (against orders) in a battle, really little more than a skirmish, involving Salvadoran and

Guatemalan forces in 1906. He held the rank of colonel in El Salvador, made an advantageous marriage to Doña Rosa Quiroz Avila. (Captain Bennett and Lieutenant Llanos also married Salvadoran ladies and Llanos remained in El Salvador.) Ibáñez later enjoyed relating his El Salvador adventures to friends, especially his becoming "El Héroe de Platanar" for his 1906 battlefield exploits. This adventure made him the only Chilean officer to take part in a real war after 1883.

Captain Ibáñez served with the Cazadores cavalry regiment and then returned to the Academia for staff training. In 1914 he was on the staff of Division I, Tacna. He may or may not have done undercover intelligence work in Peru and Bolivia during World War I. If so, he may have been able to see firsthand the foolishness of allegations of Andean military threats in 1920. In 1919 Major Ibáñez was police prefect in Iquique after a brief stint as commandant of the Carabineros School and another with Cazadores. The presidential campaign and the Mobilization of 1920 occurred while Ibáñez was in Iquique.

President Alessandri named Major Ibáñez director of the Cavalry School in 1921, and in that position Ibáñez frequently saw Alessandri professionally and socially. Once in 1923 the president visited the Cavalry School and asked the officers to support his cause. In 1924 Ibáñez was still a major, nearly forty-seven years old, with little chance of promotion, or so he thought. What happened that year changed his life.

Marmaduke Grove (1878–1954) was born in Copiapó, at the northern end of the Central Valley. His father was a Radical leader who opposed Balmaceda in 1891 and was exiled for his beliefs. Like his future friend and foe Ibáñez, don Marmaduke attended public schools and the Liceo de Hombres in Copiapó. He won entrance to the Escuela Naval in 1892 (something of a coup, given his modest antecedents). Impulsive by nature, Grove was a discipline problem in Valparaíso, though a good student. In 1894 he was dismissed from Valparaíso; two years later he was accepted by the Escuela Militar to participate in a special course for aspirants to junior-officer standing because of the threat of war with Argentina. There, under the supervision of Körner's German cohorts, Grove flourished; his previous military training and his wise refusal to divert further energies to student politics served him well. Upon graduation in 1898, Second

Lieutenant Grove entered a mounted artillery group commanded by Lieutenant Colonel Luis Altamirano.

In 1901 Grove became a first lieutenant and was assigned to the staff of the Escuela Militar. Four years later he was selected for duty in Germany and spent time in an artillery regiment. Grove enjoyed himself immensely in Germany. He had calling cards printed up which read "Marma, Duque de Grove" to spoof German nobles who held military rank. He spent much time in Danzig and at the Charlottenburg Artillery Training School, where he received a diploma. Young Grove was a classic example of the Chilean officer who, through travel and observation, realized how backward his supposedly advanced homeland really was.

In 1910 he returned to Chile a captain and became battery commander in the Grupo Maturana. He studied at the Academia from 1912 to 1914 and was assigned to the Tacna garrison in 1914. The next year he married; ironically, his wife, Doña Rebeca Valenzuela, was the daughter of the Escuela Naval commandant who had expelled him years before.

Grove, a sometime participant in the 1907–12 Liga Militar and a fervent Mason, was known for his advanced social and political ideas. In 1918 he was promoted to major, served on the Division I staff, then on the General Staff, and the next year was appointed subdirector of the Escuela Militar. For his outspoken criticism of War Minister Errázuriz in 1920, Grove was transferred to the Miraflores artillery regiment in Traiguén, but moved back to the Escuela in 1921 at Alessandri's insistence. When Chilean politics, economic instability, and social discontent reached an all-time high in 1924, Major Grove was Arturo Ahumada's right-hand man at the Escuela. The events of 1924 changed his life too.

Bartolomé Blanche (1879–1970) was born in La Serena. He is the least discussed political officer of the 1920s because, unlike Ibáñez or Grove, he did not play a political role. But he served in key positions from 1924 through 1927 and maintained iron discipline in the officer corps. He merits consideration as an unusual political officer.

Blanche's father was a teacher of mathematics and later rector of the Liceo de Hombres in La Serena, where young Bartolomé went to classes. He entered the Escuela at the age of sixteen in 1895 and graduated as a second lieutenant in 1896 when the Argentine war threat still loomed. He was assigned to the Presidential Cavalry

Escort and promoted to first lieutenant in 1898. For six years he served as a cavalry officer, consistently ranking as the outstanding horseman in the Chilean Army. He was known as an extremely serious and dedicated officer; like Ibáñez and Grove, he was very fond of military life and a firm believer in the noble character of the profession. In 1904 Lieutenant Blanche went to Germany for cavalry and infantry training in the Hanover Ulans. He excelled in international riding exhibitions in Europe. There, like Grove, he served with young officers from various countries: Argentina, Japan, China, Hungary. He was fond of discussing his experience in Germany and particularly proud of his performance there. He liked to show a well-worn photo of himself in German-style uniform seated with his fellow students (including a young U.S. Army captain).

In 1907 Captain Blanche was on the staff of the Cavalry School in Santiago and helped to shape the curriculum of that young institution. After riding brilliantly in the 1910 Argentine Centennial Equitation Competition, he was a squadron commander from late 1910 until mid 1912 in the Granaderos Regiment in Iquique; he was then sent to the Academia. He married Doña Enriqueta Northcote in 1913.

During 1915 and 1916 Blanche was on the general staff and undertook two reconnaissance expeditions in southern Chile for the purpose of ascertaining the feasibility of government-sponsored agricultural and cattle-raising enterprises. Major Blanche served as subcommandant of the Cazadores regiment in 1917 and was named commandant of Granaderos. He commanded this group during the 1920 mobilization at Tacna. As a lieutenant colonel, he became commandant of Cazadores in 1922 and was stationed in Santiago. This was his assignment when the events of 1924 propelled him into the post of president of the JMN.

Carlos Ibáñez, Marmaduke Grove, and Bartolomé Blanche were all political officers, each in his own manner. The golpe of 1925, four months after the resignation of Alessandri, locked them into political roles. Ibáñez became war minister as the army assumed a watchdog political position. Until Grove fell from grace, he was Ibáñez's assistant. Grove became a bitter foe of Ibáñez in 1926 and was sent to Europe, where he conspired to overthrow his erstwhile compatriot. Blanche, undersecretary of war and JMN president in 1924, was promoted to colonel and then became director general of police in 1925. When Carlos Ibáñez rose to the presidency in 1927, Blanche became a brigadier general and war minister. In this position Blanche had to make sure that the army supported Chile's military president, and he did so very effectively.

Examining the service records of these men prior to 1924, we can see that each was a distinguished officer. Professionally all had excellent reputations. Only highly regarded officers like Blanche and Grove were sent to Germany, and many JMN members did go to Germany. Similarly, highly regarded officers, among them JMN members, were the ones sent to Ecuador, Colombia, and El Salvador. Each of these three political officers filled an important position in 1924; each was a graduate of the Academia, where the three had been colleagues from 1912 through 1914; and each was a staff officer with subcommand or command experience. They represent the combined influences that made certain officers of the Chilean Army political: distinguished service records, service abroad, staff and command training and experience, extensive connections and friendships with officers of the same or higher rank, and important assignments as of September 1924. Yet they were different in many ways.

Carlos Ibáñez was the most calculating and politically astute. He was cognizant of the risks he took in participating in the JMN, in leading the golpe of 1925, and in controlling other political officers from his office in the War Ministry, from 1925 through 1927. It was Ibáñez who, through his control of the army, pressured civilian politicians into reluctant acceptance of the new Constitution of 1925. His actions personified the hard-line professional military position in civilian-military relations of the 1920s. Ibáñez distrusted and scorned the vacuous rhetoric and irresponsible conduct of the politicians and advocated strong progressive national government and regeneration of Chile as an economically stable and socially advanced South American country. He tried to champion these causes as president, from 1927 to 1931.

Marmaduke Grove was easily the most colorful and personally magnetic of the political officers; he was also unpredictable, highly emotional, and at times irrational. Grove was extremely popular, but his colleagues did not look upon him as a leader. He wanted radical reforms to alleviate the human misery he saw in the Atacama and in the slums of Santiago; he believed in true popular sovereignty; and he held advanced ideas about social functions that could be performed by the army in the fields of education, sanitation, and civic action. His heart was in the right place, but his head was that of the *golpista;* the golpe de estado was his preferred way to set things right. He was impatient with Alessandri, with Congress, with the Altamirano government, and with Ibáñez. He was cashiered in 1928 while in England.

Bartolomé Blanche clearly saw the need for change in the 1920s, but he did not want the profession to destroy itself by assuming a political role. He was extremely critical of the officers who protested congressional inactivity in September 1924. Although he did not forbid those under his command to attend Senate sessions in order to protest parliamentary remuneration, he did forbid them to attend in uniform. He took a dim view of the September 5 petition and likened those who carried it to La Moneda to "railroad workers carrying their grievances to management." When the army took a stand, Bartolomé Blanche was determined that politics interfere as little as possible with military life. He sympathized with the lower classes and was extremely critical of politicians, including Alessandri, but, as a devoted professional, he believed that the discipline of the army must not be subverted by continual plotting, deliberation, and golpes.

Ambition and resoluteness, appeal and daring, discipline and dedication, then, were the outstanding respective characteristics of these three men. If these qualities had been combined in one man, Chilean civil-military relationships between 1924 and 1927 and after would have been different. Still, had there been no crisis in 1924, would there have been protest in the Senate galleries, a JMN, a presidential resignation, a Junta of Government, a golpe in 1925, and a second chance for Alessandri? The answer is probably no, for nothing in the behavior of any of the political officers indicates that they would or could have become political officers under other circumstances. Even the potential of TEA was limited; too many people knew about it. Events made political officers in Chile; only after they became political did these officers even begin to make events.

Political Officers as Representatives of Their Class: The Military as Interest Group[8]

Earlier we pointed out that military subservience to civilian authority was partly due to military connections with the Basque-Castilian aristocracy and with the oligarchy. There is a correlation between the schism in the aristocracy and decline of the oligarchy at the turn of the century and the development of the army as a potential political interest group. It is not surprising that the presidency of Alessandri and the introduction of new elements into Congress in 1924 (the list of retiring senators in the lame-duck session after March 1924 constituted another society blue book) led to the flowering of the army as a political interest group. National problems were too great to be resolved by a new civilian government. The army, which had included nonaristocratic elements for some forty years, was no longer an extension of any civilian ruling class. Most officers were of modest provincial origins and no longer respected, feared, or felt obliged to civilian members of their own socioeconomic group, the ever-amorphous upper middle class. It is a long way from the crisis of 1891 to that of 1927 by way of the crises of 1912, 1919 and 1920, and 1924–25, but the path is discernible.

It should be obvious by now that there is no simple explanation for the assumption of a political stance by Chilean army officers in 1924–25. One pattern that seems important, though, is that of military education, training, and elite status in an elitist sociopolitical milieu. Surely correlations of age, rank, and years of service are not conclusive indicators of political motivation or action unless they are carefully qualified by observations on education and training, promotion schedules, government support for officer training, and the like. Conflicts between young and old or junior and senior officers cannot be taken at face value. The army's loss of prestige in 1919–20 and after Germany's defeat in World War I must also be considered. The JMN was predominantly German-trained and looked to the pre–World War I German civil-military relationship as ideal. Members of the JMN believed that the German state was responsible and responsive to the needs of both its citizens and its armed forces.

Above all it is certain that the political officers could not have emerged in Chile had it not been for the army's widespread willingness to support the protest movement of September 1924. Officers were united in their support partly because the civilian leaders did not prove responsible or responsive in conducting affairs of state. The government "listened" to the military but it did not hear; politicians attempted to use the army for their own purposes but did not reward the army in any way. The army officer class listened to the politicians and the government but was not convinced of goodwill. Also responsible for military support of the protest movement was the fact that the army officer class, at least from lieutenant colonel down to the rank of lieutenant, was as close-knit and ingrown in the mid 1920s as the Basque-Castilian aristocratic ruling group had been in the nineteenth century. Escuela and Academia training and garrison and mission duty made for numerous friendships, connections, and loyalties. Contemporary writings by military men indicate these close ties, which led to a strong sense of corporate self-interest in the Chilean army officer class.

Between the ouster of Altamirano, Bennett, and Neff and Alessandri's return two months later, Carlos Ibáñez gained control of the army and began to make it into a political entity to be recognized and dealt with as a partner by civilian parties and leaders. This was not done without difficulty; a putsch attempt by conservative political leaders (including some former members of the TEA), some retired generals, and members of the Valdivia infantry regiment was thwarted, and naval opposition to the rude treatment of Neff and to Alessandri's recall almost resulted in a replay of 1891. The stern Blanche literally faced down recalcitrant army leaders and mutineers; then naval engineers, subalterns, and civilian employees threatened a bona fide mutiny if the January 23 golpe did not ultimately restore Alessandri.

Soon Alessandri and Ibáñez were feuding as if Chile were not big enough for the two of them. Alessandri suspected Blanche, Grove, Navarrete, Inspector General Juan Emilio Ortiz Vega, and Ibáñez of plotting—in concert and separately—during the winter months of 1925. It was General Navarrete, hardly a political activist but a convenient figurehead, who conveyed the army line to the consultative commission holding hearings on constitutional reform in July 1925. He told the commission members in no uncertain terms to approve what they had before them. They did so, and Chile's new charter was approved in August, albeit by less than half the electorate.

Had the Constitution, with its restoration of executive-legislative equilibrium, bill of rights, increased state responsibilities for health, labor, and welfare, and separation of Church and state really functioned upon its adoption in 1925, army officers might not have felt compelled to continue their political actions. The manifestos and proclamations of the JMN and of the golpistas of January 1925 were explicit, however; army officers expected the country to change through constitutional reform.

But it did not. Political parties could not even agree on candidates for the regular presidential election of 1925! A naval mutiny against the high command was stifled. Because Ibáñez opposed Alessandri's choice for president—Liberal Armando Jaramillo—the infantry grumbled. Politicians sounded out Ibáñez on his availability for a unity candidacy. He agreed, and when Alessandri called on him to resign his cabinet position, he declined. Alessandri gruffly resigned again on October 1, hoping to topple Ibáñez in doing so; his friend Captain Aguirre tried to raise the infantry to defend Alessandri and failed. But Ibáñez gave up his candidacy; his control of the army did not extend beyond professional bounds at this point.

During October 1925 Ibáñez, the Alessandristas, the infantry, the navy, and the civilian parties were in a frenzy. Finally Emiliano Figueroa Larraín became the unity candidate of the major parties and defeated his opponent, José Santos Salas, former army surgeon and ex–minister of health and welfare, the candidate of an ad hoc labor and employee group.

The Figueroa presidency was a tragedy cut short mercifully by Ibáñez. Figueroa was a Democratic Liberal—a Balmacedista. But he was of the old school and made no move to use his new executive powers. The new Congress showed a similar lack of inclination to adhere to new prescriptions regarding ministerial responsibility and presidential prerogatives. Had all that had transpired since September 1924 been in vain?

As Ibáñez solidified his grip on the army it became apparent that the answer to that question was no. The new high command was of his making. Gone were Altamirano, Dartnell, and Navarrete; the benign Bennett also retired. In their place were Generals Charpín, Ortiz Vega, Indalicio Téllez Cárcamo, and Ahumada, who soon retired, and Colonels (soon to be generals) Blanche, Puga, and Viaux, as well as Ibáñez himself. The old JMN and its allies now controlled the high command, staff and command posts, and all the military educational institutions. With few exceptions, the army was Ibáñez's to use as he saw fit. In another sense, however, Ibáñez served only because the army allowed him to serve.

By the end of 1926 military discipline was solid. Promotions had quelled those officers whose politics were designed solely to advance their careers, and military reforms obtained from Congress in 1924 (and later by decree) were put into effect. Retirement, cashiering, and assignments abroad silenced Alessandristas and other dissidents.

Politically, though, Chile slumbered on; the economy remained in a depressed condition; social reforms were not put into effect. The peso had stabilized, unemployment was down, and some of the nitrate *oficinas* were functioning again, but nothing was being done by the government to stimulate economic growth, and the state had not assumed its assigned responsibilities for social improvement. The government was so disorganized that foreign observers remarked on the continual possibility of impending military action. Cabinets rose and fell; only Ibáñez remained a permanent fixture. Only he, of all the members of Figueroa's government, publicly and repeatedly chastised the Congress and the politicians for disobeying or circumventing the new Constitution. On November 13, 1926, Ibáñez declared that all the cabinet members should resign; he claimed that the cabinet was incompetent, that Chile was heading toward communism, and that the executive branch needed emergency powers. His statements sounded like those of Armstrong and Moore seven years before.

There was no objection from the army or the navy, for Ibáñez controlled the former, and forces at work in the latter soon rendered it into a seagoing Ibañista support group. Ibáñez determined that the state should fulfill the promises made in 1920 by Alessandri, in 1924 by the JMN, and in 1925 in the new Constitution; methodical and ruthless, he assumed the responsibility for making these promises come true.

In the following chapter we will examine another facet of Chilean civil-military relations: the coming to political power of Ibáñez and the exercise of that power by his government from 1927 to 1931. The 1927–31 period is unique in Chilean history because it was the first time in over a century that a military man had actually occupied the presidential palace legitimately as constitutional chief executive. The Ibáñez administration was the closest thing to a military dictatorship Chileans experienced until 1973, and it was the first authoritarian, problem-oriented military regime in modern Latin American history.

8

1927–31: Inversion of Civil-Military Relations

Between 1927 and 1931 Carlos Ibáñez del Campo was the most powerful man in Chile. Because of his military background, his government was considered a military dictatorship until recent scholarship demonstrated otherwise. Until the overthrow of Salvador Allende, Chile never had a functioning military dictatorship, not even in the immediate postindependence period. Until 1973 the Ibáñez regime was the only Chilean government in which the military assumed a political role equal to, or more important than, that of civilians. This chapter is concerned with the degree to which the military dominated and changed Chilean government and politics between 1927 and 1931, and the degree to which civil-military relations were temporarily inverted and, to a certain extent, permanently changed.

Our discussion will concentrate on several themes: the elimination of civilian resistance during and after the assumption of authority by Ibáñez and his allies, both civilian and military; the establishment of equilibrium between the army and navy, which allowed a controversial military figure to hold the reins of power; the utilization by Chile's new leaders of historical antecedents and examples to justify their government and reform policies; and the introduction into government and administration of civilian elements that supported the cause of reform and modernization.

Aspects of Civil-Military Inversion:
Traditional Techniques, Military Style[1]

The techniques of Ibáñez were consistent with those of earlier Chilean leaders. The elimination of civilian resistance to Ibáñez's assumption of authority, while crudely done and perhaps not wholly within the law, was no cruder than measures taken by previous Chilean governments to handle dissidents in and out of uniform. Diego Portales brooked no interference in dealing with dissidents in the post-Lircay purges, and he cleaned all Liberals out of the army. His restructuring of the national government was far more arbitrary than anything that the Ibañistas would do a century later. In 1891 opponents were eliminated again in the restructuring of the national government and purging of the army officer corps. The retirement or confinement of army and navy officers involved in the Conspiracy of 1919 and the retirement of numerous officers in 1924 at the insistence of the JMN were also instances of the elimination of dissenters. Both civilians and military personnel, then, had experienced rough treatment from governments or agents of reform throughout Chilean history. Elimination of opposition, if not universally popular, was surely consistent with Chilean history.

The establishment of an intramilitary equilibrium was related to the elimination of opposing forces or individuals. Since the events of 1879 and 1891 had demonstrated the importance of naval power to Chileans, the army, while achieving professional status and becoming South America's best and most modern land fighting force, had not been esteemed as highly as the navy. Therefore naval support was necessary for the success of any political adventure by the military; this, in turn, required the purging of the naval high command. Once progressive-thinking captains (whose situation was similar to that of JMN lieutenant colonels and majors in 1924) moved into the Admiralty and began to apply new ideas and obtain new equipment, the navy could be counted on for tacit support of any political officers in the government. Captain (later Admiral) Carlos Frödden and Admiral Hipólito Marchant were the leaders of the new navy.

Cohesion within the army officer class, lacking as early as the appearance of the Liga Militar in 1907, was obvious in 1919 and again in 1924–25. Rivalries and jealousies based on rank, age, branch, training, and the like had to be eliminated if army officers were again to become apolitical. Through purge and reestablishment of firm discipline they were largely eliminated between 1927 and 1931. This is perhaps the most critical and difficult hurdle for a military group involved in Latin American political life. Ibáñez and Blanche, Frödden and Marchant set a standard of equilibrium and discipline that was not exceeded until the 1960s and the advent of what are called "institutional golpes."

Chilean history is so rich in content that any successful political movement must be historically oriented in some way. The steady offensive by politicians and military leaders against parliamentarism and do-nothing governments was two decades old by 1927. The prestige of government, once so great, had been slipping since before World War I. Civilians—reformers, the authoritarian minded, many staunch Catholics—yearned for a revival of strong government. So did military leaders. They had historical precedents and, they thought, many other good reasons for associating Chilean greatness—economic, diplomatic, and military—and political and social stability with strong government.

Finally, the introduction of new elements into leadership positions also had historical precedent in Chile. Portales in 1831, Montt at mid century, and the rebels in 1891 all had introduced new personnel into high positions. The aristocracy had embraced new members. Alessandri had carried on his coattails numerous new forces to the government. Within the military, Chileans of modest and humble origins could rise to positions of responsibility. However, it took concentrated effort to change the political system as well as its personnel, and despite the new charter of 1925, the system did not change until 1927 and after.

Chilean civil-military relations between 1927 and 1931 fit into no definitive mold. We cannot simply classify Ibañismo as reform-leftist or reaction-rightist, but it is even worse folly to attempt to classify it as moderate. Similarly, it is impossible to show that Ibáñez's government was supported and staffed by members of any single social, political, or economic interest group, for right, center, and left lent support to this regime and opposed it. This diversity became at once the strength and the weakness of Chile's government from 1927 to 1931.

Likewise no blanket statement can convey the situation within the armed forces or the attitudes of military leaders. The fact that Carlos Ibáñez wore a uniform did not guarantee him military support; then again, it did not preclude it. Personality, political sympathies, intraservice rivalries, and other factors motivated military men either to support Ibáñez, tacitly or actively, or to oppose him. This was as true of the navy as of the army.

What was Ibañismo? The most informative discussions generally refer to it as personalist, authoritarian, reformist, modernizing, vigorous, efficient, regenerative government. Such definitions could refer to anything. To many, indeed, Ibañismo is really a development of the 1950s, when Carlos Ibáñez returned to the presidency.[2] Between 1927 and 1931 Ibañismo was never fully exploited and no true cult of personality developed. Ibáñez's cold and aloof demeanor, his rectitude, and his businesslike manner, however, helped to create a cult of government similar to that introduced by the leaders of the Portalian era. Ibáñez was compared to O'Higgins, Portales, Montt, and Balmaceda. Like O'Higgins, he was a reformer; like Portales, he was a creator and solidifier; like Montt, he was a strong authoritarian executive; and like Balmaceda, he was all of these. Significantly, Ibáñez enjoyed being compared to these Chilean statesmen; he also enjoyed being likened to Benito Mussolini and Miguel Primo de Rivera. The parallels between Ibáñez and Primo and their governments are most illuminating and would make a stimulating study in comparative political systems.

The wholesale introduction of new elements into politics and government between 1927 and 1931 was perhaps the most notable achievement of the Ibáñez regime. Despite Chile's incredible record of constitutional observance, the middle sectors had achieved little by themselves and in fact had been coopted by the ruling class. Ibañismo and military participation in politics, not democracy and constitutionality, gave them their first real taste of power as well as initiating the social and economic modernization characteristic of the rise of the middle sectors in Latin America.

These are the bases for examination of civil-military relations between 1927 and 1931. They may best be understood by examining first their presence and then their relationships to the circumstances which allowed Ibáñez to come to power.

The Establishment of Equilibrium:
Ibáñez the Manipulator[3]

When Ibáñez called for the organization of a new cabinet in November 1926, he knew his hand was a strong one. By this time most of the prestigious and senior army officers who might challange him had been removed, and his own men were in key positions. The public and the press were clearly weary of Figueroa, so Ibáñez knew he had some popular support. Still, there is no evidence that the colonel had fixed his sights on La Moneda. The defunct JMN had promised two years earlier that the armed forces would tolerate no caudillo. All the evidence leads one to believe that Ibáñez was simply determined at the end of 1926 to see that military-sponsored reforms and constitutional changes were enacted. His strong position in the army made him the leader of military and civilian supporters of these goals.

The navy still posed a threat to military participation in the reform of politics. With some difficulty naval leaders had maintained an equilibrium in the officer corps since 1924. Naval members of the JMN were reliable captains who had listened to the high command. Neff's presence in the Altamirano government had balanced off the naval archconservatives led by Admiral Luis Gómez Carreño, and the conservatives had maintained control of the Navy Ministry during 1925 and 1926. The naval high command was still hostile to Ibáñez, to military involvement in civilian affairs, and to too much political change. But these attitudes altered in early 1927.

In January some dissident navy captains came to Santiago to talk with Ibáñez. They were impressed with concessions he had won for the army—promotions, salary increases, and the like—and they wanted to modernize the navy. They wanted the same things for the navy that the events of 1924 and 1925 had produced for the army. The major roadblock, they thought, was the navy minister, Admiral Arturo Swett Otaegui. Ibáñez suggested to Manuel Rivas Vicuña, the interior minister, that Swett be eased out of the cabinet, but Rivas refused to discuss the matter.

Then Ibáñez discussed naval affairs with Colonel Aníbal Parada, a cavalry commander stationed near Valparaíso. Their discussion centered on the possibilities of a naval mutiny. Parada lost his notes on the meeting, and they were found by a very thorough chambermaid in the Viña del Mar hotel where Ibáñez and he had met. The notes—detailing army measures and troop displacement in the event of a mutiny and listing high-ranking naval officers "close to retirement"—ended up in Rivas's office at the Interior Ministry. Thus was created a major confrontation. On February 6 Rivas demanded that Ibáñez reveal the meaning of the notes. Ibáñez refused, seized the notes from Rivas, and stormed out of the Interior Ministry. Three days later Rivas resigned, and the press went wild with speculation.

Ibáñez became interior minister on February 9. Earlier that day he had issued a statement blaming Chile's ills on political parties, Congress, Communists, and, for good measure, incompetent, superannuated politicians. He promised to eradicate these evils with vigor. Ibáñez remained interior minister until April 7, when President Figueroa took a leave of absence. A month later the president resigned. Ibáñez, as vice-president, had no trouble getting the presidency for himself.

Elimination of Resistance:
Ibáñez the Disciplinarian[4]

The elimination of civilian resistance to Ibáñez and to military participation in political affairs began in February 1927, but it had to be maintained for four years. This period was very painful for civilians and caused many to distrust the military in the years after 1931. It is therefore an important episode in Chilean civil-military relations.

Civilian resistance was purged, obviously, so that there could be no challenge to the policies of Ibáñez and his cohorts. Purges took several forms, but they were always directed toward providing Chile's new leaders with an unobstructed path to the implementation of the 1925 Constitution and social and economic reform. Between February and May 1927, for example, a strong interior minister, a president, a Supreme Court justice, and numerous political leaders were purged, all of them unwilling to yield to the concept of strong executive authority.

Rivas Vicuña was goaded into resignation in February 1927 when Ibáñez unabashedly and rudely gathered up his notes, thus challenging the interior minister's authority. President Figueroa, a miserably weak executive, was pressured into leaving the presidency. He had no alternative but to name Ibáñez as interior minister on February 9, for who would have been willing to take Rivas's place and risk Ibáñez's rudeness and open contempt? Ibáñez's designated minister of justice, Aquiles Vergara Vicuña, proceeded to demand the firing of the chief justice, Javier Angel Figueroa, the president's own brother! The president could not conceivably dismiss his brother, so he chose to leave public life. Ibáñez then became vice-president, and the new interior minister, navy captain Carlos Frödden, promptly dismissed the chief justice. The Ibáñez clique then proceeded to renovate the high court and lesser tribunals. Predictably, the resignation of Rivas, the purging of the courts, and even the resignation of the president met with little popular opposition.

Concurrently, during early 1927, political leaders who were hostile to Ibáñez, to the military, and to the new cabinet received notices of deportation. Banking on fears of communism, Interior Minister Ibáñez decreed that military courts had jurisdiction over political offenders and those considered dangerous to the state. Again public response was favorable. The names of those deported, relegated, or confined read like the latest edition of the Chilean political blue book, giving the new government an apparent leftist tinge. Rightists and defenders of the parliamentary system packed their bags; Rafael Luis Gumucio, editor of *El Diario Ilustrado*, Chile's conservative newspaper, and president of the Chamber of Deputies; Gustavo Ross Santa María, conservative politician and financier; Ladislao Errázuriz; Agustín Edwards MacClure, one of the last of the Nationals; Communist leaders Elías Lafferte of the Stalinists and Manuel Hidalgo of the Trotskyites; alleged Marxists Daniel Schweitzer and Carlos Contreras; and numerous staunch Alessandristas and advocates of parliamentary rule all left Santiago for lengthy journeys. By the time President Figueroa resigned his mandate there were few left who had the courage, prestige, or respect to challenge either Ibáñez or the policies he championed.

When all the Rivas cabinet but Ibáñez resigned in early February, Ibáñez, as interior minister, appointed Captain Frödden to the Navy Ministry, replacing Admiral Swett, and soon moved naval headquarters to Santiago. The new war minister in 1927 was General Ortiz Vega, a respected member of the engineers, the least politically motivated branch of the army. For the duration of the 1920s army-navy rivalries ceased to exist; for a time Ortiz's presence in the War Ministry kept intraarmy conflicts to a minimum. Solid military support, gained through these appointments and through promotions, and increased expenditures allowed Interior Minister Ibáñez to concentrate on other matters. There was no military-based opposition to him or to the new cabinet's actions between February and July 1927, when he became president of Chile.

Historical Antecedents:
Ibáñez the Savior[5]

On April 8, 1927, just one week after he became vice-president, Carlos Ibáñez received a large delegation of military well-wishers at his home. In an almost gross display of adulation, army and navy leaders let it be known that they supported the one-time cavalry officer who had made good in recent months. Accompanied by military music and popular tunes played by bands from the Santiago garrison, Ministers Frödden and Ortiz made lengthy toasts to the new vice-president and General Orozimbo Barboza Urrutia, an artillery officer, brother of General Quintiliano Barboza (both of them sons of the nineteenth-century military leader), delivered an "extemporaneous" speech praising Ibáñez. Barboza extolled the army as creator and symbol of Chilean greatness and hailed Ibáñez as a national savior. Barboza's salute to militarism received hearty applause. Ibáñez replied modestly that Chile—and he—owed much to the armed forces and that his government would assure fulfillment of all guarantees made by the military in 1924. After 400 officers had paid their respects, the bands played the national anthem and the reception ended.

Two months later Ibáñez was inaugurated as president. Figueroa's resignation on May 5 propelled Ibáñez into the candidacy he had originally toyed with in 1925. He won the election easily with some support from all parties. Democrats, Radicals, Liberals, and Independents believed he would reform and modernize the government; Church leaders and some Conservatives believed he would halt the rise of communism (an easy task given the state of the left at this time) and trusted that as an authoritarian he would not give the masses complete freedom. Right, center, and left all had something to gain; agriculture, business, manufacturing, the professions, and the white collar class also yearned for resolution of political, social, and economic problems. In the election of May 22, 1927, Carlos Ibáñez received 98 percent of the vote. Typically, less than 10 percent of the population was eligible, and less than half of those eligible voted. Decision making continued to be the province of only a few Chileans.

A dramatic feature of Chilean presidential inaugurations is the presentation of the presidential sash by the outgoing chief executive to his successor. In recent times there has been no more dramatic presentation than when Christian Democrat Eduardo Frei performed the honors for Socialist Salvador Allende in 1970. Prior to that the most dramatic inauguration was that of July 2, 1927. Circumstances dictated that Emiliano Figueroa not be present, for his sash of office was tainted by politics and his tortured term of office.

President Ibáñez received the sash worn originally by José Manuel Balmaceda from Enrique Balmaceda Toro, Chile's new interior minister. History, drama, and nostalgia unfolded before the eyes of those present. Enrique Balmaceda delivered an impassioned speech claiming that his father, just before his suicide, had charged him with placing the sash over the heart of someone who was worthy of Balmaceda's grand design for Chile, which included strong government, nationalism, progress, and modernization. Ibáñez, said the son of the martyred autocrat, was the "perfect incarnation" of Balmacedismo.[6]

Ibáñez replied modestly but emphatically that he accepted the sash as a sacred trust, praised President Balmaceda for his vision, and said that, had Balmaceda been successful, Chile would never have suffered the political, social, and economic crises of recent years. A new cult of government was born, and Ibáñez would soon be compared with the great autocrats—O'Higgins, Portales, Montt, and, especially, Balmaceda—in speeches, the press, literature, and official sources.[7] Chile had regained control of her destiny.

Introduction of New Elements: Ibáñez the Innovator

As soon as Ibáñez rose to power it became obvious that he would not govern with traditional methods, tactics, or personnel. Emergency powers granted early in 1927 allowed the Interior Ministry to dismiss superfluous personnel in the name of economy and efficiency. The deportations and confinements and the attack on the judiciary cleared out objectionable civilian leaders, many of whom had resisted the changes and reforms in effect since late 1924 and those incorporated in the 1925 Constitution. Many were deemed objectionable simply because they opposed military deliberation and political action.

In no way was the introduction of new, civilian elements into the government more obvious than in the composition of the cabinet led by Interior Minister Ibáñez, which began its work in February 1927. This change in the leadership of Chile outlasted the Ibáñez government.

Charged by Figueroa with the formation of a new cabinet after his showdown with Rivas Vicuña, Ibáñez chose his ministers without consulting party leaders; his was the first cabinet to be formed this way in thirty-five years. The new foreign minister was Conrado Ríos Gallardo. Ríos, only thirty-one years old, was a journalist, editor of *La Nación,* the Santiago daily owned by Eliodoro Yáñez Ponce, the Liberal politician who had opposed Alessandri's candidacy in 1920. Not known for any reformist policies, Ríos was a strident nationalist and a polemicist; he proved able in reorganizing the Foreign Ministry. He was a fervent Ibañista, an advocate of strong executive government, and after the ouster of Ibáñez founded the magazine *Hoy* to defend the 1927–31 regime. Ríos was instrumental in arranging the 1929 Tacna-Arica settlement that ended nearly forty years of negotiations with Peru.

The new minister of justice and education was Aquiles Vergara Vicuña. Thirty-five years old, Vergara was a former army officer who had studied briefly at the Spanish General Staff School in Madrid in 1918 and had retired as a captain to practice law. It was Vergara who initiated the attack on the courts in 1927. Subsequently he quarreled with Ibáñez and left Chile, first to escape confinement, later to fight in the Chaco War as an officer of the Bolivian Army.

Pablo Ramírez Rodríguez became finance minister. Ramírez, who was forty-one years of age in 1927, was Chile's economic czar for over three years. He was a prominent dissenter, an anti-Alessandri Radical, a technocrat, and a believer in firm executive leadership. Ramírez organized the Compañía de Salitre de Chile, COSACH, the ill-fated nitrate trust through which, it was hoped, production and marketing of Chile's major export would be coordinated and enlarged. Ramírez was the closest civilian to Ibáñez during his presidency, with the possible exception of the president's son-in-law Osvaldo Koch.

General Ortiz and Captain Frödden filled the positions of war and navy ministers respectively. They were close to Ibáñez and owed their positions to him. The three remaining members of the February Cabinet were holdovers from the Rivas Vicuña cabinet organized in November 1926. Arturo Alemparte continued as agriculture minister; Isaac Hevia remained minister of health and welfare; and Julio Velasco stayed in Public Works. None of these men had previous cabinet-level experience of any length; all were sympathetic to Ibáñez and were capable administrators.

But Ramírez, Ríos, and Vergara were the principal advisers to

Ibáñez. Their youth, energy, honesty, and ability set the tone for the entire cabinet and established ability as the most important criterion for the selection of top-level administrators. The faces changed between February 1927 and July 1931, but until the very end of the Ibáñez regime there was a greater incidence of new, energetic, young upper-middle-class administrators than ever before in Chilean political history. What Alessandri had, in a sense, begun (his presidency had been criticized for the introduction of loyal unknowns with little talent), Ibáñez refined and accomplished with greater success. The composition of government would be changed; the aristocracy could no longer dominate Chilean politics.

Beginning in 1927, then, nearly five months before a military man actually became president, military domination of Chilean government and politics through inversion of civil-military relations was dependent upon and characterized by each of the four themes we have been discussing. We now turn to the Ibáñez presidency itself to see how three of these themes—elimination of opposition, equilibrium in the armed forces, and introduction of new faces—fared until July 26, 1931. Here we will begin to glimpse the reasons for the destruction of Ibáñez and military participation in politics and for the reestablishment of traditional civil-military relationships under a new form of government after 1931.

1927–31: The Opposition[8]

At no time between 1927 and 1931 did Ibáñez have solid support from a single political organization. Although Chile's long tradition of party fission and coalition politics precluded this, it did enable Ibáñez to obtain support from portions of all parties. The aborted military movements of 1907–11, 1919, and 1924 had not resulted in well-distributed civilian support.

Military participation in politics set Conservative against Conservative, Liberal against Liberal, Radical against Radical. It led to reassessment of priorities by political leaders. The prospect of material progress, firm government, discipline for the workers, and stabilization of the economy made many former foes of political activity by men in uniform accept, even praise, Carlos Ibáñez. But others clung to principle, doctrine, or particularistic views and connived continually to get rid of Ibáñez and send the army and navy back to barracks and base. The government, in turn, engaged in continual repression. Much of the plotting involved military men and menaced discipline and equilibrium. Repression did not meet with great disfavor, however, and did not always come as a result of plotting.

During the second half of 1927 politicians who represented the old regime followed the deportees of early 1927 into exile. Eliodoro Yáñez, supposedly a backer of the new government, left the country after being accused of plotting with infantry officers. His newspaper, *La Nación*, became government property. Former president Alessandri received a deportation order in October after being accused of plotting. He left for Argentina accompanied by Conservative senator Luis Alberto Cariola, who had only recently been named editor of *El Diario Ilustrado*. Several politicians who accused the new government of selling out to Peru in Tacna-Arica negotiations followed them. At the end of 1927 prominent leaders of all political parties, several prominent press figures, Liberal Alliance Alessandristas, and leading rightists were residing in Europe and Buenos Aires. In their company were Major Millán, Captain Aguirre, Colonel Grove, and General Enrique Bravo Ortiz; Millán and Aguirre were staunch supporters of Alessandri, Grove had fallen from grace, and Bravo was the only senior officer who had opposed Ibáñez's continuation in the cabinet late in 1926.

An examination of the names and political connections of those deported or confined during 1927 and 1928 reveals that deportation and elimination were directed against no single group, though Alessandristas did suffer the most. Opposition to the new government, as mentioned above, made strange bedfellows. Examination of names and political connections of those deported and confined also shows an impartiality in the anticivilian and antipolitical activities of the new military-civilian leadership.

Table 4 gives pertinent information on roughly 10 percent of the politically significant persons purged by the Ibañistas in the first two years of the regime.[9] These were the most widely known and influential Chileans deported and confined by the Ibáñez government in its early stages. The proportions of Liberal Alliance members, National Union members, and Communists to the overall total for the entire 1927–31 period are almost exactly the same as for the period examined here. Clearly, all the groups suffered, the Liberal Alliance

TABLE 4

Deportations and Confinements, 1927-28

Name	Political Affiliation (Party/Coalition)	Charge
Arturo Allesandri (and various family members)	Liberal/Alliance	Plotting & corruption
Luis Alberto Cariola	Conservative/Union	Antigovernment writing
Agustín Edwards MacClure	National/Union	Plotting & corruption
Rafael Luis Gumucio	Conservative/Union	Antigovernment writing
Ernesto Barros Jarpa	Liberal/Alliance	Criticism of Ibáñez
Jorge Matte Gormaz	Liberal/Alliance	Criticism of Ibáñez
Galvarino Gallardo Nieto	Liberal/Alliance	Criticism of Ibáñez
Gustavo Lira	Liberal/Alliance	Criticism of Ibáñez
José Santos Salas	Independent (leftist)	Alleged Marxism
Santiago Labarca	Radical	Criticism of Ibáñez
Ladislao Errázuriz Lazcano	Conservative/Union	Plotting & corruption
Eliodoro Yáñez	Liberal/Alliance	Plotting
Arturo Olavarría Bravo	Liberal/Alliance	Criticism of Ibáñez
Manuel Hidalgo	Communist (Trotskyite)	Plotting
Elías Lafferte	Communist (Stalinist)	Plotting
Daniel Schweitzer	Marxist	Plotting
Carlos Contreras	Marxist	Plotting
Eulogio Rojas Mery	Liberal/Alliance	Criticism of Ibáñez
Elías Mitchell	Radical	Criticism of Ibáñez
Luis Izquierdo	Liberal/Alliance	Plotting
Luis Salas Romo	Radical/Alliance	Plotting
Gaspar Mora Sotomayor	Alessandrista	Plotting
Enrique Bravo Ortiz	Army dissident	Criticism of Ibáñez

most of all, for it was the coalition blamed for Chile's decline after World War I. In addition, Liberal Alliance Alessandristas were those immediately affected by the ouster of Alessandri, the closure of Congress, the election of Figueroa as a compromise candidate, and the political rise of the military. Regardless of their specific political affiliation, all Alessandristas decried militarism or authoritarianism or both in Chile.

By the end of 1928 there was little civilian opposition to the Ibáñez government inside the country. Those civilians who had wished vocally for the regime's hasty demise were in emigré colonies in Paris and Buenos Aires. There they worked with the military exiles, most of whom were close to Alessandri and who also wanted Ibáñez out. The two groups collaborated in several attempts to oust Ibáñez. The presence of a military authoritarian in La Moneda was no cure for civil-military political conniving, which had been going on for years in Chile and now continued outside the country.

Decision making in a democratic, even a pseudodemocratic, system, like Chile's in the early twentieth century, is an agonizing process. The intricacies of debate, compromise, amendment, and parliamentary procedure did not appeal to Chile's political officers. As the primary agency of parliamentarism, Congress was blamed for most of Chile's problems, and Ibáñez's modern version of the Portalian state set about to discipline legislators. Long sessions, absenteeism, and speechifying ceased, and in many cases legislation was too hastily passed. Senators and deputies who were absent too much or who spoke too long found themselves encouraged to "take a long rest," resign, or even leave the country.

The Constitution was amended in 1929 to assure that Congress would function as the executive branch wanted it to (these amendments were later scrapped), and in late 1929 Ibáñez even pressured party leaders to eschew open campaigns for upcoming congressional elections in favor of an arranged slate to preclude electoral disputes. By this time party leaders were either pro-Ibáñez—like Juan Antonio Ríos Morales, president of the Radical Party—or were unwilling to oppose his wishes. The arranged slate was accepted and the chosen candidates duly elected. Congress became a docile civilian partner, both houses dominated by Ibañista Liberals, Radicals, and Democrats. The Ibañista Republican Confederation of Civic Action (Confederación Republicana de Acción Cívica, or CRAC) represented the president's interests in the legislature.

Elimination of civilian opposition from 1927 to 1931, then, took several forms: deportation and confinement; purging of the courts; and arrangement of congressional composition to "cleanse the country" —"cauterization," Ibáñez called it—and to make the branches of government function as the new leaders wanted them to. It was the new leaders, of course, who made this new form of government work, once civilian opposition was eliminated and military equilibrium established.

1927–31: New Leadership, New Programs[10]

Carlos Ibáñez, never a man of ideas, was only a man of action when he was assured of success. His schemes for Chilean regeneration were either developed from the military movements of 1924–25 or suggested to him by advisers. All too often military-political leaders in Latin America are given credit for originating programs and policies, when in fact they deserve credit only for supervising, permitting, endorsing, and promoting. Yet the programs and policies of the Ibáñez years did lead to the creation of a modern, somewhat diversified economy and to the modernization of society. Although promulgated by fiat in many instances, the programs and actions of the 1927–31 government deserve credit—and criticism.

Apparently the nature and composition of the Chilean polity early in this century was not conducive either to change or to modernization. Therefore the polity underwent change only in conjunction with alteration and then inversion of the essential civil-military relationship. Military influence definitely led to constitutional change after the spate of reform legislation in 1924. Continued military influence, exercised during the 1925–27 period by War Minister Ibáñez, resulted in acceptance of new constitutional norms and in a large-scale infusion of reformist and authoritarian civilian supporters into government service. Continued military-reformist influence also resulted in the assumption by the state of new responsibilities in the fields of health, labor, welfare, education, and economic development. Because increased state responsibility, authority, and action in these spheres were anathema to the traditional national leaders, it was only natural that new talent was recruited for new jobs at the national and local level. The Chilean middle sectors moved into government—that is, into political leadership—but without gaining economic influence.

One way to indicate the infusion of a new socioeconomic group into Chile's traditional ruling class is simply to indicate the surnames of those active during the 1920s. From the first of Alessandri's many cabinets until his final fall in 1925, one can discern a trend toward proportionately more (1) nonaristocrats, (2) political independents, and (3) individuals representative of the "democratic left." Between 1927 and mid 1931 this trend continued, with the addition of a definite admixture of individuals who tolerated, even advocated, authoritarianism, though generally in the name of vindication of Balmaceda. In this sense the civil-military relationship of the later 1920s promoted not only the idea of a strong, active government but that of sociopolitical leveling.

The February 1927 Ibáñez–Ríos Gallardo cabinet provides a convenient example. Three of its members, Ríos, Ramírez, and Vergara, were strong advocates of Balmacedismo and tacitly condoned Ibáñez's authoritarian manner, though Vergara became disenchanted before the year was out. All three made it a point to bring young, able—if inexperienced—men into their ministries and to give them a measure of responsibility. Enrique Balmaceda, who replaced Ibáñez in the Interior Ministry, had been involved in politics for some years but was by no means a member of the inner circle of government during the heyday of parliamentarism. José Santos Salas, who accepted the Health, Labor, and Welfare portfolio when Ibáñez became president, was of humble origins and had very advanced social ideas. Eduardo Barrios Hudtwalcker, the celebrated novelist, who served briefly as education minister, and Osvaldo Koch, Ibáñez's son-in-law, who filled both the Justice and Interior posts, were not members of the aristocracy by any means. Alejandro Lazo, Ibáñez's confrere at the Cavalry School in 1924, served in ministerial capacities before he too fell from grace in 1928; his origins were decidedly humble, and his ideas, according to most contemporaries, bordered on socialism.

In May 1928, when Ibáñez was ill, Enrique Balmaceda became alcalde (chief administrator) of Santiago, the most prestigious municipal official in Chile. His replacement for a month in Interior was Koch; then Guillermo Edwards Matte, an aristocrat with authoritarian leanings, filled the post. Edwards Matte openly admired Mussolini and Primo, and his proto-Fascist ideas alarmed many.

Administrative reorganization in the ministries and expansion of government activities necessitated a search for manpower. There were two primary sources for this manpower: the middle sectors and the military, the latter, as noted, populated by men of humble origin. The Civil Service Administration was modernized and expanded, the social security system was put into effect, the Civil Registry expanded its activities. The national airline (forebear of the present-day LAN, Línea Aérea Nacional, one of the continent's best) began modestly but gave work to hitherto unemployable technicians and administrators in addition to numerous army officers and pilots. An expanded Commerce Subsecretariat of the Foreign Ministry went to work on trade problems. Municipal governments were reorganized and staffed with Ibañistas. Independent figures like Moisés Poblete Troncoso and Luis Galdames worked on educational reforms. The retired General Navarrete, as education minister, planned and supervised the foundation of the National Bacteriological Institute in 1929.

The strong suit of the Ibáñez regime was the massive public works program put together by Finance Minister Ramírez. Chilean prosperity thus was based on putting the unemployed back to work. The revival of the nitrate industry (which had begun quite coincidentally in 1926 before Ibáñez came to power) and foreign investment and loans provided the fiscal wherewithal. Chilean prosperity—based on employment, trade balance figures, growth of export-import activity, stabilization of the peso, and growth in gross and real per capita income—can be said to have existed only between March 1928 and the end of 1929. But no major reverberations of the worldwide economic crash were felt until late 1930. During this brief 1928–29 period the budget was balanced, but only superficially, for there was an extraordinary budget for loans and public works projects; as late as 1926 there had been an overall government deficit.

Public works prosperity meant money in the pockets of Chileans. Stonemasons, bricklayers, carpenters, tile layers, ditchdiggers, painters, electricians, plumbers, craftsmen of all kinds, miners, dock workers, factory and shop workers, drivers, maintenance personnel, farmers, peasants, merchants, shopkeepers, clerks, railroad employees, teachers, nurses, and droves of white-collar bureaucrats found work aplenty in the late 1920s. Road, railroad, school, dock, and warehouse construction and irrigation and conservation projects went on at a pace never before contemplated in Chile. Into the ranks of supervisory agencies came middle- and lower-class Chileans. Government posts multiplied and bureaucratization became a reality in Chile. Over $250 million (about 2 billion pesos) was pumped into the economy. Labor unions fell under government control and their leadership was reorganized, but materially the Chilean workingman benefited. So did his union boss, who had a new legitimate status.

The sociopolitical composition of labor, education, the bureaucracy, and high-level political leadership changed dramatically during the 1920s and even more between 1927 and 1931. Business, finance, manufacturing, mining, and land still remained the domain of the great families and their allies, but the professions—medicine and dentistry, law, architecture, and engineering, as well as labor, education, administration, and politics—experienced a social transformation quite similar to that undergone by the army officer class earlier in the century. This helped to establish a civil-military equilibrium, a static condition between 1927 and 1931 under authoritarianism, but one which could and would prevail when "democracy" was restored in the 1930s.

1927–31: Military Equilibrium[11]

Military equilibrium was maintained by elimination of civilian opposition, by introduction of new elements into government and administration, and by material modernization, a kind of public-works pork barrel for men in uniform.

Basic to widespread military participation in Latin American politics and government—as distinguished from the participation of one or a few military figures—is the restructuring of staff, command, and ministry levels. The extent to which military influence on or dominance of politics and government politicizes the military depends on many variables. The political officer who tells his subordinates that they cannot participate in political action or deliberation will probably be challenged. Discipline cannot endure in the lower ranks in the face of continual political action by superiors.

Similarly, until the 1960s it was rare for the army and navy (and since World War II the air force) of any Latin American nation to be in accord politically or to remain in accord once involved in politics and government. Until the time of the so-called institutional golpes such as those in Brazil in 1964, Argentina in 1966, Peru in 1968 (the best example), and Chile in 1973, interservice rivalries precluded unified action.

The army-navy rivalry in Chile was one of the most critical problems facing Ibáñez, his fellow political officers, and their civilian political friends between September 1924 and February 1927. The demands of the JMN; relations respectively with Alessandri, Altamirano and his Junta of Government, Alessandri again, and Figueroa; and the circumstances surrounding Ibáñez's ascendancy were all affected by the navy's position. When finally, in early 1927, Ibáñez's power —and hence that of the political officers—increased to the point of virtual control of the government, the navy could be handled. The appointment of Captain Frödden to the Navy Ministry in 1927 was a gauntlet dropped at the feet of the Admiralty, and it resulted in the resignation (promptly accepted) of Admirals Swett, Soublette, Braulio Bahamondes Montaña, Carlos Ward, Alfredo Searle, Juan Schroeder, Ismael Huerta, Bracy Wilson, and Olegario Reyes del Río. This cleared the high command of naval conservatism and allowed men like Frödden and Alejandro García Castelblanco, Calixto Rogers, Abel Campos, Edgardo Von Schroeders, Arístides del Solar—all captains or recently promoted admirals—to rise. Not all these officers were Ibáñistas, for the navy maintained its distance from politics, but they did not challenge the Ibáñez government.

Furthermore, the navy, like the army, enjoyed the largesse of the government. As Carlos López Urrutia, author of the recent, solid history of the Chilean Navy, has told us, this was a period of great growth and modernization for that institution. The Ibáñez government saw to it that six destroyers were ordered from the British Thornycroft Yards. These new ships were heavily armed, equipped for placing mines and launching torpedoes. Delivered in 1929, the *Aldea*, *Hyatt*, *Orella*, *Riquelme*, *Serrano*, and *Videla* were the latest word in speed, maneuverability, armament, and comfort. The navy also received new patrol boats, torpedo boats, tankers, and transports, three submarines, and a sub tender. Bases and facilities in Valparaíso and Talcahuano were modernized at great expense. The modernization of equipment, facilities, and new ships kept the navy in its traditional conservative apolitical stance. Naval headquarters, in Santiago since 1927, posed no threat to the army's influence in national government.

Because the army was so involved in the politics of social, economic, and political change, it was more difficult to make sure that opposition would not come from that quarter. Since the discovery of the Conspiracy of 1919, both civilian and military leaders had been aware of the potential conflicts within the army officer class. Disagreements based on age, rank, training, branch, and the like could be smoothed over, if not permanently settled, but the sociopolitical variations in the composition of the officer class were always a potential source of conflict. Discipline was usually maintained by means of retirements, promotions, and reassignments. Above the rank of captain, promotion was by selection, and selection was not always an objective process. Such methods were used by the Hurtado-Boonen army conservatives against the Armstrong-Moore SER cabal and the Junta Militar of 1919. They served to maintain a shaky, temporary balance between the events of September 1924 and January 1925 in relationships between the JMN and the Altamirano-Bennett-Neff Junta of Government. After 1925, Ibáñez used the same methods. By mid 1927 the army high command, like the navy's, was made up primarily of recently promoted general officers who were close to or trusted by Ibáñez.

General Blanche became war minister on June 21, 1927, succeeding Frödden, who had held both the navy and the war posts in a short-lived experiment with a ministry of national defense in the Ibáñez-Ríos cabinet. The next day General Blanche published a circular to be posted prominently in all military installations. Blanche pulled no punches; disobedience, poor discipline, political meddling, or political deliberation would be dealt with harshly and quickly. The Blanche circular made the point that civilian-military squabbling and civilian interference in military affairs—ranging from intervention in routine policy matters such as promotions to attempts to coopt the military for partisan political purposes—had corrupted the officer class. The movements of 1924 and 1925 had been incomplete, and the vested interests among the military had not yet been displaced. No longer would the army allow itself to be corrupted and coopted; once again it would become an apolitical, patriotic organization. In short, the day of deliberation was past; a military man was in the presidential palace, and he would brook no opposition. As war minister until 1931, Blanche established an enviable record for keeping an army steeped in politics out of the political limelight. Until the Ibáñez regime began to fall apart in mid 1931, only six officers held high-level government office: Ibáñez himself, Blanche, Ortiz, Navarrete, Lazo, and Frödden. Clearly this was not a military dictatorship.

The best way to keep a military organization out of politics when a military leader is involved in politics is to rid the organization of the most blatantly political officers whose motivations and allegiances differ from those of the leader, or who have minds of their own. Blanche saw to it that these types did not threaten Ibáñez—or himself. Dissident political officers were frequently posted to Punta Arenas; military Alessandristas were sent to Europe or jailed; the worst offenders, like the outspoken Grove, were cashiered. In the most serious cases, like that of Grove in 1928, there was always adequate proof or circumstantial evidence of corruption or crimes against the state.

Erstwhile junteros like Aguirre and Millán (Alessandristas); dissidents like General Bravo or Colonel Carlos Vergara Montero, an infantry officer close to Eliodoro Yáñez; officers popular in their own right like Alejandro Lazo; and radicals like Grove were not tolerated. There were no assassinations or executions, but they were forced to change their life style, to say the least, as well as their place of residence. With the exception of Vergara, all these officers involved themselves in conspiracies to unseat Ibáñez in 1928, 1929, and 1930.

The most famous of these was the bizarre Dover Conspiracy and Avión Rojo escapade of 1930, in which Grove, Bravo Ortiz, and several politicians flew across the Andes from Argentina in an attempt to raise the southern garrison at Concepción. The plotters were seized and tried; they ended up on Easter Island for their efforts. Alessandri and Conservative leaders were implicated.

Barring wholesale restructuring of a military organization—a method historically used by civilians to preclude military involvement in politics—the next best way to preserve military subservience to political officers is to modernize the organization. Strict professionals —those with no interest in military political action or who only tacitly support it—characteristically desire the constant improvement of their profession. In addition to ridding the army of undesirables, the Ibáñez regime gave the army a generous dose of the same thing it gave the navy and the civilian sector: material benefits.

As of 1928 the Chilean Army consisted of 25,000 men and just over 1,200 officers. But it was not the sole land force. Carabineros de Chile, a paramilitary force created by the amalgamation of all police forces under the Interior Ministry, was composed of over 750 officers and 19,000 men. Commanded by Ibañista General Aníbal Parada, the force was Ibáñez's counterpoise to the army. Well equipped and trained, efficient, commanded by graduates of the Escuela, it became South America's finest national police force. To this day, with its own schools, it is independent of the army and responsible for the maintenance of internal order. But the army received major attention from the Ibáñez government nevertheless. By law the president was (and is) the supreme commander in chief. Hitherto command functions had been delegated to the inspector general. The inspector general was now a loyal Ibañista, and General (as of 1927) Ibáñez commanded through Blanche, the war minister.

Despite the government's natural interest in military moderniza- tion, it certainly did not waste money on extravagant equipment for the army between 1927 and 1931. Nearly 20 percent of the rifles in use in 1928 were obsolete Manlichers of pre-1891 vintage; the rest were 1895 Mausers, classified as "modernized." There were over 1,300 automatic Colt and Browning rifles of 1923–25 vintage and nearly 80,000 pistols of varying quality. The army had 20 new machine guns and 600 obsolete 1916 Japanese copies of Hotchkiss 7 millimeter models. There were 900 artillery pieces in 1929, over half in poor condition or obsolete. All artillery came from Krupp or

Schneider. Purchases raised the number of modern firearms, but much Chilean firepower remained pre–World War I vintage. By 1929 the air force had 75 planes, Junkers, Wieboldt, Curtis, Sopwith, Vickers, Avro, "fairly serviceable" according to a U.S. military observer. The situation in the air force improved little by 1931.

Thus, although the Ibáñez government attempted to modernize the army, the fact that long years of neglect had made it a paper tiger hindered attempts to recapture the glories of the Körner years (when most of the equipment was purchased). New arms, equipment, barracks, salary raises amounting to a doubling of 1924 figures by 1928, promotions, and a better pension plan simply did not amount to wholesale dedication of national resources to the benefit of the army. The government was unwilling to establish military equilibrium at the expense of the civilian sector. By 1931 the army was no more up to date than it had been before World War I.

In this chapter we have stressed four themes—elimination of civilian opposition, establishment of military equilibrium, the use of historical justification, and the introduction of new personnel—as those most important for any assessment of civil-military relations between 1927 and 1931. It should be obvious that they were all interrelated and that all are basic to a comprehensive assessment of Chilean civil-military relations. All had historic precedent, and all were peculiarly Chilean themes. In the final part of this study we shall see how these themes and those factors mentioned earlier have either continued to be significant in Chilean civil-military relations or been significantly altered with time, thus affecting the nature of civil-military relations in recent years.

PART III: 1931-73

9

Civil-Military Relations, 1931–70:
An Overview

So far we have assessed and interpreted Chilean civil-military relations from the standpoint of certain factors that molded relations in the nineteenth century and whose alteration, continuity, or disappearance likewise affected relations between 1891 and 1931. We have seen that by 1931 Chile had experienced a significant inversion of civil-military relations, brought about during the presidency of Carlos Ibáñez. This inversion was partially the result of the alteration and disappearance of nineteenth-century factors and was accompanied by the four themes discussed in chapter 8. The question before us now is, How many of the themes we have been discussing continue to be useful for the study of Chilean civil-military relations?

No matter how much continuity appears on the surface of a country's history, it is not wise to cling steadfastly to any set of influences or characteristics as indicative of continuity. How long, for example, does the German Army retain its archetypal Prussian character? An attempt to prove that the Chilean Army's "return to the barracks" in 1932 was simply the result of the reestablishment of traditional civilian politics is really an attempt more to describe (and poorly) what happened between 1932 and 1938 than to explain, interpret, or analyze it. Actually the Ibañistas had achieved much of their program by 1932, and military interest in politics dropped off of its own accord. In short, we need not lock ourselves into the position of continuing to depend on ideas that apply to the past. Instead we must learn what new events and ideas may have replaced those that were important in the past. As general concepts, though, the factors discussed originally in chapter 1 do bear reexamination here to

175

ascertain the effect of continuity and change between 1891 and 1931
on events between 1931 and 1970.

A Flexible Elite:
The Party System and Civil-Military Concurrence[1]

The Basque-Castilian group that had dominated society, politics,
government, and finance between 1830 and 1920 was replaced after
1932 by a revived political party system so flexible that a Marxist was
constitutionally elected president in 1970. This nonexclusive party
system was remarkably successful in maintaining widespread support
for civilian control of government. Such support can be construed as
both cause and result of military noninvolvement in politics. Certainly it helped keep civilians in power until 1973.

The fusion of civil and military aristocratic leadership, so pronounced in the early and middle nineteenth century, is not nearly so
obvious after 1932. Probably a necessary ingredient in the nineteenth
century, it was not necessary again until recent times, for between
1932 and 1973, there existed no great dichotomy of goals or interests
between civil and military leadership groups. (The presence of such a
dichotomy after 1973, however, will make continued examination of
the lack of fusion as either cause or effect imperative.)

Because the reservoir of administrative and military talent in Chile
had grown a great deal since the time of Portales, the size of the
leadership group no longer bore any relationship to military subservience. The interests, both common and separate, of political and
military leaders must now be examined if we are to arrive at an
understanding of recent civil-military relations. We need to reexamine the political system, but not as an extended family monopoly,
and the military profession, but not merely as a uniformed subgroup
of that monopoly.

Geopolitics: No Longer Significant

Demography, ethnic composition, and South American geopolitics
are not very useful for this part of our study. Phenomena that were
unusual if not unique by South American standards of the mid
nineteenth century were no longer significant as determinants of

Chilean civil-military relations by 1931. In the twentieth century, Chile's good communications and readily available transportation were no longer barriers to militarism.

Of course these factors were important in some ways. Chile is more an integrated nation-state than is either Brazil or Peru, where the military also functions politically. Conversely, Argentina, a well-integrated state like Chile, has experienced frequent military-political participation akin to that in Brazil and Peru. What is probably important about the infrastructure of Chilean society in determining civil-military relations is the way it functions and the people who make it function.[2]

Social change, then, becomes more significant than demography and ethnic composition in assessing civil-military relations in recent times. We can no longer rely on expansionism or on matters of race and topography as explanations for Chile's recent development or the nature of its civil-military relations.

Nationalism: A Matured Phenomenon[3]

Chile is no longer xenophobically nationalistic. Peru and Bolivia are still considered "old enemies," but few seriously believe that they are constantly plotting to recoup their 1879–83 losses. Argentina's existence is no longer viewed as a threat to Chile's. The administration of Salvador Allende, of course, fanned the flames of nationalism frequently by accusing Argentina of being a militaristic pawn of the United States in the latter's alleged campaign to destroy Chile's experiment in Marxism. But the nationalism discussed in part I is no longer a determinant of civil-military relations.

Nationalism has matured as a civilian phenomenon in Chile, identifiable with the ongoing political process, economic policy, and social reform rather than with military policy. During the decades before 1973 the military had no need to play a nation-saving, problem-solving, crisis-averting, nationalist role. The military in other Latin American countries, in contrast, has often acted as an agent of nationalism. In Peru before 1968, for example, the military emerged as the champion of economic nationalism, and in Argentina the nationalist economic schemes and labor policy of Peronism prove too extreme even for many nationalistic army leaders. It is significant, nevertheless, that the military junta which replaced the Allende

regime on September 11, 1973, immediately emphasized its nationalist character.

Responsibility and Responsiveness: Modern Variables in a Complex Society

One cannot say that the civilian ruling class in Chile was totally
competent, responsible, and responsive and that therefore the military had no grounds for political action based on collective civilian
malfeasance. It would be equally invalid to claim that Chilean
government and politics remained in the hands of civilians because
civilians in Chile had proven competent, responsible, and responsive
whereas civilians in Peru, Bolivia, Argentina, and Brazil had not. On
the whole, recent Chilean political leaders are not that superior to
their neighboring counterparts, and Chile's democratic system did not
perform that much more successfully than the civilian systems of
other Latin American countries in the resolution of chronic social and
economic problems.[4] Loyal adherence to democratic norms is no
substitute for action. Nevertheless, in Chile the state did devote
proportionately more effort, whether successful or not, to such
problems.

One hundred years ago—before a serious economic recession and
inflationary monetary policy began to trouble the nation—Chile's
leaders faced no problems more serious than price fluctuations in export commodities and agricultural and mineral goods. The restricted
distribution of income confined the impact of economic policy to
oligarchic circles. With the penetration of British, German, and then
United States capital; with the nitrate collapse after World War I;
with the *política prestamista* of the Ibáñez era, and then the Great
Depression, economic problems became far more complex and their
impact far more widespread. Modest gains in income redistribution
during the interwar years and after 1945 have added to the
complexities of capitalist economics and have not resulted in the
dramatic solution of economic problems. Interwoven are complex
social problems arising from the steadily widening area of state
responsibility, urbanization, economic diversification, industrialization, politicization of the poorer classes, and the like.

Thus, while sophisticated and generally beneficial progress has been made toward the resolution of socioeconomic difficulties in the last four decades, Chile can by no means boast that civilian-directed government and politics is equivalent to economic strength or social harmony. The government may have been competent, responsible, and responsive, but it did not produce real success nor did it satisfy the comparatively larger number of politically articulate Chileans.

It would be fair to say that since 1931 a smaller percentage of the politically articulate population of Chile has been satisfied with what its government is doing for the country than was the case a century ago. If Chilean politics had remained in the hands of a small group, this could conceivably have resulted in action by the military on several occasions. But the conduct of Chilean national affairs was affected by a larger proportion of the population, representing a wider ideological spectrum, than ever before, and the system's failures, consequently, had not only more critics but more defenders.

This means that, despite its failures, civilianism in Chile had more organized adherents, administrations and parties had a broader base and a "loyal opposition," and fewer Chileans were available to fill the ranks of the apathetic or of those who find salvation in a uniformed regime. Obviously this by no means indicates that a wider political spectrum and a proportionately larger number of political participants in themselves preclude military political action.[5]

We can conclude, however, that—despite the decided alteration or eradication of the principal factors conducive to the establishment of civilian political hegemony in nineteenth-century Chile—that hegemony was indeed reestablished and restructured in the 1930s, and held firm for four decades. Not until 1973 did such problems as traditional party fission and fusion, economic woes, the rise of extremist political parties, and the increasing incidence of strikes, violence, and left-wing labor militancy—problems that directly contributed to military participation in politics and government in Chile between 1924 and 1931 and elsewhere on the South American continent since 1930—lead to military involvement in Chilean politics! One reason this is so was the widespread belief in Chile that civilians could govern better than military men. A brief examination of Chile in 1931 and 1932 will help us understand why.

But before addressing the 1931–32 equivalents of the final factor emphasized in chapter 1 and discussed in chapter 2—a distaste for military meddling in civilian affairs—we need to reexamine the four

themes important during the 1927–31 inversion of civilian-military
relations to see how significant they were with regard to reestablishment of the traditional Chilean pattern.

The four themes forming the basis for our discussion of the
civil-military inversion peculiar to Chile between 1924 and 1931 were
the elimination of resistance to the regime; the establishment of an
interservice equilibrium allowing a controversial figure to take and
hold power; the utilization of historical antecedents and examples to
justify purposes and goals; and the introduction of new elements
supportive of modernization. Are such themes applicable to the
"inversion of the inversion"?

Elimination of Resistance: "Neo-Portalianism"

It is consistent with Chilean political tradition that, in crisis
situations, resistance to a new order be eliminated or neutralized. So
it was in the 1830s and 1890s and in 1919 when military (and some
civilian) leaders hostile to the new order or distrusted by the existing
order were retired or purged, and when some civilians were also
purged. The pattern was repeated during the intramilitary struggles
between 1924 and 1927 and during the Ibáñez regime that followed.

After Ibáñez's fall, and during and after the horrendous sequence of
events between mid 1931 and late 1932, Chilean administrations
relentlessly purged military opposition. The reelection of Alessandri
to the presidency in 1932 marked a continuation of the elimination of
resistance, and by the end of 1933 few vestiges of military Ibañismo
were present. Similarly, the reconstituted civilian order did not
permit extreme opposition from civilians. True to Chilean form, then,
strong measures proved "painful but necessary."[6] True to Chilean
tradition, a majority of the politically articulate supported and
permitted such measures. With regard to civil-military relations, all
but a few post-1932 administrations have dealt severely with disciplinary problems and suspected intrigue in the military.

Interservice Equilibrium: "National Defense"

Interservice equilibrium does not just serve to pacify the navy and
air force when army leaders function politically as in Chile between

1924 and 1931. We have witnessed so many military political balancing acts in recent years—the military functioning as referee between contending civilian political groups or internally regulating purely military political squabbles in Argentina, Peru, and Brazil, for example—that it is almost automatic to see military rule as an equilibrating as well as a governing device.

In Chile, interservice equilibrium as established and maintained through the Ministry of National Defense after 1933 was a device allowing the government to deal with the military through one spokesman, a spokesman for both the government and the armed forces. The ministry also epitomizes the concept of joint administration of the various branches of the military. This concept, of course, has been extremely important in military science ever since World War II. Originally designed to break the political power of the army, the combined ministry became a cherished institution to the Chilean military.

Historical Justification: "Veneration"

In Chile civilian control of the military has been the rule more than the exception, at least until 1973. For every comparison of Ibáñcz to O'Higgins, Portales, or Balmaceda, there are dozens of references to "civilian conduct of governmental affairs" and "military responsibility to the government and attention to national defense."

It was military pressure that led to the framing of the 1925 Constitution, and that charter excludes the military from politics! Chile's great national holidays, May 21 and September 18–19, commemorate strictly military events: independence in September, the naval battle of Iquique in May. Congress, political functionaries, the chief executive, judges, labor leaders, employees, and workers turn out for these occasions. No one celebrates the military movements of September 5, 1924, or January 23, 1925; July 26 is famous in Chile not because Ibáñez resigned on that winter's day in 1931, but because Fidel Castro assaulted the Moncada barracks in Santiago, Cuba on that date in 1955. In short, Chileans have been proud of their armed forces as defenders against external threats, but they have historically been equally proud of the fact that, for better or worse, civilians ran the country after 1831 with the sole exception of the 1924–32 years. Pride in civilian capabilities was, of course, severely shaken in 1973.

Introduction of New Elements: Political Change

Each successive Chilean administration between 1931 and 1973 introduced new elements supportive of at least a modicum of modernization and change. The polity has not been guilty of exclusivism but, like the nineteenth-century aristocracy and oligarchy, has proved expansive. Real change became more rapid after 1927, and several pronounced infusions of new talent have resulted from the changing political groups that have influenced politics and government. Nevertheless, the major breakthroughs of the 1910–31 period should not be neglected, for during those two decades nonaristocrats made the first steps toward influential presence in politics and government. (Here we use "nonaristocrats" in place of the more widely used but vaguer term "middle sectors.") Alessandri and Ibáñez introduced, however ineffectively or crudely, middle-sector leaders, professionals, and technicians into national circles.

After 1932 the introduction of new elements took the form of an evolutionary process in which national politics moved from right to center to extreme left depending on who controlled administrative and organizational services. So, in a sense, there was a continual renewal rather than a grudging recalcitrant policy of warding off change by the politically influential. There was no need for a "middle-class military coup" between 1932 and 1973 to "help out" the middle class.[7] Responsible Chileans who favored maintenance of the status quo in the key election years of 1938, 1952, 1964, and 1970 were not able to maintain it through the ballot box, but they were loath to use the military as a political tool. This last point has either been misunderstood or neglected by observers of Chilean politics, although it has been a distinct possibility at least twice, in 1938 and in 1970.

The points made above lead to the conclusion that themes historically important in Chilean civil-military relations are either inapplicable to the last forty years or are still so basic to Chilean politics that they continue to apply to recent variations of civil-military relations. In the following pages we shall, therefore, examine this conclusion more specifically and introduce modern factors that were conducive to Chilean civilianism until the 1970s. Paramount among these are the revived organizational solidarity of the civilian sector, the rejection of the idea that uniformed men had any business in politics and government, and the army's acceptance of and preference for an apolitical stance. Each of these points warrants a concentrated examination.

These three factors are really outgrowths of the events of 1931 and 1932, one of the most bitter and tumultuous periods in Chile's history—indeed in the history of Latin America. The bitterness and tumult began the day Carlos Ibáñez left office and did not subside until Arturo Alessandri took office for the second time in December 1932. During those sixteen months Chileans relived the years 1823–31. Every conceivable woe descended upon their political system as well as their economy; the armed forces were guilty of the grossest political misbehavior—misbehavior which made the plotting of 1919, 1920, and 1924–25 look like healthy child's play.

Civil Solidarity, Military Politics, and Antimilitarism: The Holocaust of 1931–32[8]

Some years ago it was fashionable to speculate on what would happen when the great strong men of modern times left the scene: "When Stalin, Adenauer, Salazar, and De Gaulle pass away," people asked, "what will befall the USSR, Germany, Portugal, and France? Could India survive without Nehru, Egypt without Nasser, Indonesia without Sukarno?" We have often read speculative appraisals of Spain without Franco and Cuba without Castro.

In polities where institutionalization and political tradition are strong, the demise or ouster of a dynamic, charismatic, or long-term personalistic leader does not bring about collapse—trauma and power struggles yes, but not collapse. But where the demise of the leader is accompanied by economic upheaval and compounded by a lack of institutionalization and tradition, it is difficult for the system to survive the transition. Such was the case in Chile after the fall of Ibáñez, and the collapse of the system there, exacerbated as it was by continual military presence in politics, destroyed the credibility of military leaders and those civilians who had sided with them.

Therefore in the festering sore of Depression-era Chilean politics, society, and economics, the military appeared as gangrene. Only a few years before, Ibáñez himself had described the military mission as one of healing and compared his job to that of a surgeon. Now, in

1931–32, that same military appeared to be a cure worse than the disease.

Four years had not been long enough to institutionalize Ibañismo. There was no organized political backing for the regime, nor was there a trained successor waiting in the wings. Traditional party-based support was widespread, but not deep. Reform programs had taken hold, but not firmly, and no program was so radical as to provoke reaction in the ensuing years. Far more serious for the authoritarian-minded was the absence of a program of internal capitalization to protect Chile from the drying up of foreign capital sources for the Ibáñez regime's economic schemes.

In 1931, Chile's economic slump, the failure of COSACH, growing unemployment, and inflation were blamed on Ibáñez and his cohorts and on the military and civilian authoritarians who had supported them. Accusations of malfeasance and violation of the Constitution did not cease when Ibáñez left for exile in Argentina. Accusations against the military also continued, for even without Ibáñez the military continued as a political force, directly responsible for the making and breaking of each administration for the duration of the 1931–32 holocaust. After the military authoritarianism of the Ibáñez regime, then, there was no individual and no group able (far too many were willing) to provide continuity, to keep the system going. Continuity would have meant prolonging military authoritarianism, and many Chileans felt that authoritarianism was precisely what had caused all the problems.

In late July 1931, there was no sign of civilian political organizational strength, rejection of military-backed solutions for political problems, or military eschewal of a political role. The traditional Conservative, Liberal, and Radical parties were atrophied. Their legislative cadres had functioned as Ibáñez's lackeys. Those parties that were not led by Ibañistas had no leadership to speak of. The nontraditional parties of the extreme left were either emerging from dormancy (the Communists) or yet to be conceived (the Socialists). Despite this situation, there would be proportionately more party than military organizational strength by the end of 1933.

But weaknesses, divisions, and uncertainties, plus the desire for internal order, forced politicians to deal with military leaders in order to hold power in 1931 and 1932. Leaders of the right, center, and left all connived with men in uniform between the fall of Ibáñez and

Alessandri's "second coming." Military men, in turn, consorted of their own accord with Alessandri the Liberal; with the self-styled Socialist Carlos Dávila, Ibáñez's former ambassador to Washington; and with Radicals, Conservatives, and even Communists. A revolt rocked the navy. Air force planes buzzed La Moneda. Barracks were assaulted. Betrayals were frequent. Forced retirements were prevalent. Marmaduke Grove made another forced trip to Easter Island. In less than two years, ten distinct administrations governed the country as Ibañistas, Grovistas, Alessandristas, and others jockeyed for power.

The most ludicrous episode of this period (yet most significant for the future) was the Socialist Republic of Chile (June 4–October 1, 1932), which was conceived, maintained, and destroyed by the military. The Socialist Republic of 1932, like the military movement of 1924, was a first for Latin America, and the Socialist Republic was a military-fostered experiment as well.

Created on June 4, 1932, the Socialist Republic was first led by General Arturo Puga Osorio (nominally an Ibañista), Carlos Dávila (a civilian Ibañista), and Eugenio Matte Hurtado, a leader of the Socialist faction, New Popular Action (Nueva Acción Popular, or NAP). Marmaduke Grove, the former Ibañista, coconspirator with Alessandri in Dover, Calais, Paris, and Buenos Aires, commodore of the air in 1932, and NAP fellow traveler, was defense minister. No more heterogeneous group could have been assembled. The army soon fell to pieces as Dávila rose during the winter months to become sole leader of the government.

In every phase of its development and collapse, the Socialist Republic was the military's creature. Its shortcomings were also the military's, Chileans would ultimately say. And so military involvement became synonymous not only with authoritarianism and depression, but with golpe, countergolpe, extremism, continual depression, and government without directions. Military prestige did not revive when the Socialist Republic collapsed in October 1932 and General Blanche reluctantly took the reins of power as provisional head of state. A military-supported *civilista* group demanded his resignation and got it.

As we shall see in the following chapter, what prestige the military had gained as progenitor of reform and progress between 1924 and 1931 was lost quickly after the fall of Ibáñez. It took decades to regain fully. Those painful months in 1931 and 1932 are as responsible as any other factor for the acceptance by professional officers of an apolitical role until the 1970s.

The New Professionalism: Noninvolvement

Nothing is worse for military professional development than political involvement, if the ultimate criterion of professionalism is noninvolvement. In Chile, where professionalism has been equivalent to noninvolvement longer and more strongly than in, say, Argentina, Brazil, or Peru, the experiences of 1931 and 1932 were a bitter lesson. The lofty ideas of the military essayists between 1910 and 1930 helped lead to the army's assumption of power as "the national institution," "the school of democracy," and "the guarantor of good government," but that assumption of power led ultimately to disgrace. After 1932 Chileans blamed officers for the very things they had praised them for only a few years earlier.

When their superiors were supporting Ibáñez, then abandoning him, then involving themselves in the struggles of 1932, new generations of cadets and junior officers were being taught that discipline, obedience, loyalty, and professionalism meant no political involvement! The army's (and the navy's and the air force's) corporate integrity depended on discipline and obedience. Politics destroyed discipline, compromised obedience, and made conditions in the Escuela, Academia, and specialty schools unconducive to education and the gaining of expertise.

Chilean cadets and officers traditionally wear their uniforms with pride when off duty. During 1931 and 1932, however, and for several years after the restoration of civilian control of government, a soldier wearing his uniform in public was likely to find himself scurrying to home or barracks, his blouse, cap, or pants stained with spittle, garbage, or worse. A man in uniform who endures these forms of disgrace reacts in one of two ways: by becoming a political creature or by withdrawing to the safety of the barracks. By 1933 it was impossible to react politically.

With course work often interrupted—literally so that cadets and officers might take part in a golpe—and shifts of personnel so frequent, the career became a liability. Better to restrict the definition and circumscribe the responsibilities and attitudes of the career than to see it destroyed. By the end of the Socialist Republic there were officers of all ranks who were perfectly happy to return to the simple pleasures of routine garrison duty or administrative chores.

Systemic Flexibility: Accommodation to Change and Constitutionality, 1932–70[9]

With the restoration of Chilean normalcy—that is, uncontested civilian control of national affairs—the political system showed evidence of accommodating dissent. This is not to say that all constitutional guarantees were fulfilled, for they were not. Nor does it mean that dissidents easily made themselves heard. What it does mean is that without the threat of probable military involvement, Chilean politics became more representative of more Chileans than it had ever been before, to a point where recourse was not made to military support. The fact that the military had not consistently sided with any party or distinguishable socioeconomic interest group between 1927 and 1932 actually diminished its appeal as a political ally until 1970.

In successive elections after 1932 the majority (really plurality) candidate succeeded to the presidency. The fact that congressional and municipal elections took place separately gave the opposition a chance to balance off the administration. The incidence of blatant fraud and corruption may not have declined in recent times, but there were more opportunities for redress and more faith in judicial and legislative checks on executive abuse than had existed before 1932. Party politics since 1932 have reflected socioeconomic differences, something they did only occasionally and superficially before that time.

Alessandri and his supporters yielded constitutionally, if grudgingly, to the Popular Front–supported candidacy of Radical Pedro Aguirre Cerda in 1938. Upon Aguirre's untimely death in 1941, a special election resulted in the presidency of another ill-fated Radical, Juan Antonio Ríos Morales (1942–46). A third Radical, Gabriel González Videla, served from 1946 to 1952. At this crisis point, Ibáñez was reelected president by a large majority. Six years later the tired, ill old general passed the presidential sash to a man he had once persecuted, Jorge Alessandri Rodríguez, the son of don Arturo. Alessandri in turn passed the sash to Christian Democrat Eduardo

Frei Montalva in 1964. And Frei turned his presidential responsibilities over to Socialist Salvador Allende Gossens in 1970.

During all this time the military abstained from political activity.
Only on occasion, as we will see in the pages to follow, have military
leaders spoken, written, or organized for political reasons. Not once
until 1970 did such activities pose a serious threat to normal
constitutional processes. On only one occasion between 1932 and 1972
did a military "movement" endure for more than a few weeks. In
those forty years national administration passed from the hands of
extreme Conservatives to Marxists, and on the way it was influenced
by Liberals, Radicals, Christian Democrats, various types of Socialists,
and even some neo-Fascists.

Although the Chilean political system could not solve every
problem that came up, its wide representation of society did preclude
the need for unilateral political action by the armed forces. In this
sense Chile between 1932 and 1970 demonstrated a form of systemic
continuity with the pre-1920 era.

The restoration of civilian normalcy might conceivably have been
as short lived as the Socialist Republic were it not for the fact that a
modicum of economic and social progress was fostered within the
revived political party system. Each time conflict and crisis appeared
between 1932 and 1970, governments either responded or were
changed by the interest group most affected. The system, at least
superficially, continued to respond electorally to the plurality of
politically articulate Chileans who represented chiefly the middle-
and lower-income brackets.

Chilean Political Configurations, 1932–70:
A Brief Interpretation

Clearly Chileans who went to the polls in 1932 expressed the desire
to return to moderate political principles. Their votes for Alessandri
were votes for the Constitution of 1925 as well as votes for the
candidate who astutely proclaimed himself "the same man as in
1920."[10]

It was Alessandri who had been turned out by the military and not
allowed to finish his term. It was Alessandri who still appealed to
middle- and lower-income voters, for he had originally—if only
vaguely—championed several of their causes. It is significant that his

supporters neglected his scandalous political activities in 1931 and early 1932. Just as significant was the low voter turnout in 1932. Six years later, weary of Alessandri's moderation on social reform, alarmed by his close ties with Conservatives, Liberals, and the fascistic White Guard militia, and stunned by his praise for the austerity policies of his finance minister, the archetypal oligarch and financial prestidigitator Gustavo Ross Santa María, the opposition barely elected Aguirre. White-collar, professional, and labor voters proved victorious: the Popular Front was born.

Radicals (Chile's largest party), Socialists, Communists, National Socialists (Nacis) joined forces democratically to support Aguirre's statist policies. Chilean Radicalism, with its emphasis on state-supported economic diversification, industrialization, and increased social benefits to employees and workers, lasted fourteen years; the Front itself was a memory by 1946. In the hotly contested elections of 1938, 1942, and 1946, the popular will prevailed against the supporters of traditional laissez-faire capitalism and liberal democracy. It prevailed again in 1952 in one of Chile's most controversial campaigns. Vowing to get the country moving ahead in the midst of inflation and recession, Ibáñez marched back on the scene. Radical bureaucratization, featherbedding, and administrative incompetence in state-supported medical insurance, pensions, and economic planning were attacked by the new Ibañistas. Supported by the Agrarian Labor Party and other groups, Ibáñez won the presidency, but for numerous reasons he provided few solutions. It was during his term that Chile's most serious brush with military-political plotting between 1932 and the fall of Allende developed. This episode, to be discussed in chapter 11, served to reinforce civilianism and strengthen antimilitarism at a critical stage for Chile.

Jorge Alessandri fared no better than his father's old enemy in stabilizing the economy or providing answers to increasing social problems—in health, education, housing, unemployment, and the like—between 1958 and 1964. Yet his presidency, noted for its hostility toward heavy military expenditures, did not cause overt discontent in the military. The civilian political system held strong through the decline of the Radicals from 1952 onward. Overt military interest in politics reached a low point for the post-1932 era between 1958 and 1964.

It did not revive until 1970. The Christian Democratic landslides of 1964 and 1965 gave Chile a government backed by one of the largest majorities in its history. The early years of Frei's presidency generated much hope. Agrarian reform, the Chileanization of copper and of ITT and American and Foreign Power subsidiaries, and crash programs for housing, economic diversification, and education won the praise of civilians and military men alike. But inflation continued, hard currency reserves dropped, and labor rumbled; the Christian Democrats caught a serious case of Chile's endemic political disease, and the party began to split. Through all these changes, failures, and incertitudes, Chile's military remained outside the political arena. And then came Marxism and with it the assassination of the army commander in chief, the two most serious crises for the military in recent times.

Needless to say, the fact that until 1970 extremism was not an issue in recent Chilean politics militated against military-political participation. Marxists functioned within the legal system except for the decade 1948–58, when the Communist Party was outlawed. Just as in the days of the Parliamentary Republic, the coopting of extremists tended to soften their attack and blunt their ability. To put this point another way, until 1972 the Chilean military was not forced to consider the possibility that a group like Peru's Alianza Popular Revolucionaria Americana (APRA), Argentina's Peronists, or Brazil's Partido Trabalhista Brasileiro (PTB) might dominate the government. The Chilean military did not have a "traditional rival" in the sense that the Argentine, Brazilian, and Peruvian military have had.

No case could ever be made that social or economic change, demographic shifts, or population growth—important factors in civil-military relations elsewhere—slowed down in post-1932 Chile, thereby reducing the potential for civil-military crisis. Chile endured the same kinds of growth and change patterns as those prevalent in countries where for some time it has been more accurate to speak of "military-civilian relations."

By 1930, as we have seen, Chile's population totalled over 4,200,000. Ten years later Chile had over 5 million citizens, almost half of whom lived in urban areas. Over 20 percent lived in the Santiago–Valparaíso–Viña del Mar and Concepción-Talcahuano complexes—the centers of administration, manufacturing, and commerce. The concentration of population in the major urban areas, including the northern nitrate ports, was roughly the same in 1940 as it had been in 1920. But by 1940 that population was better served by the political system than it had been in 1920. The capital city itself had a

1940 population of 830,000, over 130,000 more than in 1930. And, until 1940 at least, internal migration to the cities, with its ensuing difficulties, did not cause problems for which the political system could not provide palliatives (or controls).

Northern Chile was no longer a scene of devastation as it had been when the nitrate markets collapsed after World War I. Modern technology in copper mining made the Atacama newly productive. Antofagasta, 700 miles up the coast from Santiago, had a population of 50,000 in 1940. Iquique, 250 miles farther north, had over 30,000 inhabitants. The complex of Coquimbo–La Serena, important for copper shipping as well as agricultural exports, boasted a combined population of over 40,000. In Chile's cities and copper installations, Radical, Socialist, and Communist strength was evident and important in the key election year of 1938.

The Chilean population continued to grow rapidly during and after World War II, and there has certainly been no lessening of pressures on administrations to "do something" about housing, public social services, medicine, education, unemployment, working conditions —the panoply of problems of the urban working classes. In attending to urban problems, however, the government tended to neglect the rural labor force. Agrarian reform did not become a major political issue until the 1950s; it did not become a critical problem—one for which peasants and parties truly mobilized until the 1960s. Neither agrarian reform nor the plight of labor was an area of prime interest to the military. For better or for worse, politicians reserved these areas of activity for themselves.

Internal Security: Carabineros de Chile

Until the 1970s, when political conflict did occur Chile's military did not have to meet it. Strikes, riots, street violence, demonstrations, and the like did not normally constitute grounds for calling out the army. Only when an extremely serious menace to public order—such as the total disruption of a city's activities—developed, did the army have to act. The Carabineros de Chile paid great dividends in Chilean civil-military relations until the collapse of the Allende administration. It is the carabineros who perform police duties in Chile. Unlike the police in neighboring Argentina or Peru, the Chilean national police is a real paramilitary organization, as professionally trained and equipped (for their own needs) as the army. Therefore it is the carabineros whom the citizens know best.

The familiarity of the force has been a double-edged sword, of course. Peace keeping, riot breaking, and truncheon wielding gain both praise and curses. The Interior Ministry, under whose authority Ibáñez placed the carabineros, was a part of the civilian administration like the Defense Ministry. But the responsibility for internal order and security was also a civilian matter. If heads were bloody, the administration was blamed or praised.

Since the military had little to do with police action, it was seldom attacked for brutality in putting down a riot or for disregard of the right to protest and demonstrate. Therefore lower-class hostility toward the army (as much a myth as a reality in Latin America) or popular belief that the army was a bastion of conservatism (an absurdity in recent times) were rare in Chile. In 1973, on the other hand, when the military did become involved in internal order, and security became a military matter, the army's lack of experience was obvious, and popular hostility to the military resulted!

Likewise, middle- or upper-class support for the army as bastion against extremism, defender of private property, and guarantor of order at all costs (again as much myth as reality) was not widely in evidence. Thus a politically ambitious Chilean military leader or group of political officers was really in a neutral position. After 1932 the military was removed from social questions.

Military leaders preferred things that way (at least until 1972), because since 1932 they had been only marginally concerned with social questions. That such questions increased in number and magnitude goes without saying, but civilian groups sought to cope with them in a constitutional fashion. As we have stated earlier, the success of their efforts was limited, but, until the seventies, the existence of civilian efforts and the belief that they should take place within constitutional, democratic norms outweighed lack of success or belief that success would be achieved by circumventing the Constitution.

Official Military Thought on National Issues: A Comparison and Interpretation[11]

Comparative history has its uses as well as its shortcomings. Here it may be useful to compare army thought on socioeconomic questions in Chile with the thought of other armies in Latin America. Such a comparison must be made strictly on the basis of the armies involved, not of any similarities in the polities or societies. As varied as they may appear, the roles and functions of armies in different nations are more similar than are the roles and functions of parties, syndicates, or political systems.

In Argentina, Brazil, and Peru military thought on socioeconomic issues was plentiful and openly expressed in the 1930s. It was not in Chile. In Argentina, Brazil, and Peru less civilian strength was exerted on the military to remain quiescent, but there were also more urgent issues unresolved prior to 1932. The military in Argentina, Peru, and Brazil did not have a tarnished record like the military in Chile, but antimilitarism in Argentina, Brazil, and Peru was much stronger and military political participation more common. Finally, a case can be made that Argentine, Brazilian, and Peruvian military thought was more advanced and refined on some socioeconomic questions than Chilean military thought; by 1930 many such questions had already received a military answer (whether correct or not) in Chile.

The *Memorial del Ejército de Chile (MECH)*, the official journal of the Chilean General Staff (the army's house organ), for the years 1930 to 1940 shows a lower incidence of articles on socioeconomic issues than do the army journals of Argentina, Brazil, and Peru. While Argentines were urging industrialization, Chileans had nothing to say on the subject. While Brazilians were supporting centralization of government and economic diversification, the Chileans had no case. While Peruvians were discussing the use of the army as a means of integrating the Indian and the *cholo serrano* into the mainstream of society, Chileans had no case either.

Whatever the reason—whether ministers were warning the Publications Section to avoid socioeconomic issues, whether chastened military editors were not accepting articles, or whether a new generation of uniformed essayists had other interests—the fact remains that the official military journal simply did not indicate interest in social and economic themes. In comparison with most official journals of the major military powers of South America (Argentina, Brazil, Peru, and Colombia), during the last four decades Chile's *Memorial* has ranked lowest in proportion of socioeconomic materials to purely professional content. Moreover, Chileans do not express continual interest in any one issue, whereas industrialization, a viable political system, and national integration have continued to inspire military men in Argentina, Peru, and Brazil. Industrialization, a viable political system, and national integration; economic nationalism, internal development, and antiimperialism; education, vocational training, and social reform all have many civilian spokesmen in Chile. We shall hear more of *MECH* in chapter 12.

In sum, short of a national crisis of real magnitude, the armed forces were not motivated to participate in politics. In thought and action, with only a few exceptions, military leaders supported civilian government, the political system, and social and economic change. It is significant that change was moderate and, until recently, free of extremism in the executive branch. After 1932 Chile maintained a civil-military relationship that was the envy of Latin Americans who saw the military as inhibitive to democracy, and this relationship had the support of Chile's military leaders. It was a continuation of the general pattern established in the late nineteenth century, but modernized with new components and balancing factors. In the following chapters we shall see how these new elements were born in the dark days of 1931–32, how they developed between 1933 and 1970, and then how in the crisis situation of 1970 civilianism held firm in Chile, only to collapse in 1973.

10

The Repudiation of the Military, 1931–32

The months between the resignation of Carlos Ibáñez and the second election of Arturo Alessandri comprise one of the great protracted crises of Chilean history. This modern crisis ranks with the break from Spain and the Civil War of 1891 in importance; it is comparable to the early Portalian years and the presidential election of 1920 as a watershed epoch.

During the seventeen months between the departure of the general and the second inauguration of the Lion of Tarapacá, the Chilean armed forces steadily dissipated the support given them by civilians between 1924 and 1931 and ultimately lost the respect of the civilian sector. This crisis period is the only instance of true military caudillismo that Chileans have endured since the tumultuous decade following the downfall of O'Higgins in 1823. The 1931–32 experience also affected more Chileans than any other crisis. It produced such bizarre results that we can effectively argue that this experience is one of the primary reasons why the military refrained from political participation for four decades since.

These years were a time more of political adventurism than of institutional participation, more of personalistic caudillismo than of group action. Whereas the opportunistic Ibáñez had been the only figure capable of filling a vacuum in the 1924–27 crisis stage, there were several claimants to power by 1931. Ibáñez displaced no other military political chieftain; his successors took turns displacing each other. Ibáñez was able to unite the military, if only tenuously; his successors were unable to do so and succeeded in dividing the army, navy, and air force against one another. Earlier than other Latin

American countries, Chile endured the disastrous effects of a professional military organization fallen prey to frenetic, individualistic ambitions, rivalries, and jealousies, and the outcome convinced civilians and military men alike that the armed forces should indeed remain "essentially obedient," as the Constitution dictated. Ibáñez's heirs were victims, not masters, of the situation during those terrible months. In order to demonstrate this, an account and an interpretation of the events of 1931–32 is in order.

July–September 1931: The Aftermath of Ibáñez[1]

When Ibáñez left office on July 26, 1931, he turned over the reins of government to Pedro Opazo Letelier, the Senate president. Under normal circumstances leadership would have fallen to the senior cabinet minister, but there was no cabinet, for all ministers turned in their resignations along with Ibáñez. Opazo reluctantly accepted the duties and officially announced that Ibáñez had left the country via the Trans-Andean Railway to Argentina.

Chileans greeted this news with unmitigated joy. People thronged to the center of Santiago. With carabineros and army personnel withdrawn to barracks, students directed traffic. The celebration was active but orderly. Opazo quickly appointed new ministers; significantly, he named General Carlos Sáez Morales to the War portfolio. Sáez was a prestigious professional, a friend of the ex-president, but no Ibañista in the political sense. General Blanche, the inspector general, retained his position because he was known primarily as a stern disciplinarian. Ostensibly, then, there was no purge in the offing at this time. Opazo relied on military relief that the controversial Ibáñez had been replaced and an apparent acceptance of the situation by army leaders.

This reliance proved well founded until army leaders became convinced that, in the wake of the Ibáñez regime, Chile looked forward to a renewal of oligarchic power and a renaissance of weak executive government and ineffective parliamentary politics. Civilian political leaders reinforced these convictions when they began a purge of the officer class in an effort to eradicate all traces of Ibañismo. To an extent, then, adventurism and caudillismo—the momentary expressions of professional militarism—did reflect political convictions, just as the 1924 and 1925 movements and the rise of political officers had done.

As soon as demonstrations ceased in the capital, Opazo resigned his duties (officially he was serving as vice-president), naming Juan Esteban Montero Rodríguez to replace him. The Radical Montero had served as interior minister for five days prior to Ibáñez's fall and had made a name for himself, along with his cohort, Treasury Minister Pedro Blanquier, by permitting total civil liberties and publishing the government's true financial situation. No friend of the military, Montero was a symbol of the old political order.

Montero proceeded to name a new, predominantly civilian cabinet, retaining for himself the Interior portfolio, and very carefully keeping General Sáez and Admiral Calixto Rogers in War and Navy, respectively. He announced that elections for a new president would take place in October, but this did nothing to ease the problems of his provisional administration. From right, center, and left came demands to retire Ibañista officers forcibly, to dissolve the carabineros, to break up the Ibáñez nitrate combine COSACH, to repudiate all debts contracted by the Ibáñez government and Pablo Ramírez, and to close the so-called Thermal Congress, filled with Ibañista puppets.[2]

Politicians looked ahead to October's elections as the panacea, and electioneering resumed the hypnotic effect it had had before 1925. Old names crept back onto the front pages. Alessandri had first refused to run, using an Ibáñez ploy. "A unity candidate would be best," he declared, for this would preclude the possibility of a vicious campaign. But party leaders did not throng to his door immediately.

Montero was now the man of the hour. On August 18, he "yielded" to professional associations and to Conservative, Radical, and Liberal leaders, who were revitalized after the departure of Ibáñez and jubilant with their electoral importance. He announced his candidacy, resigned the vice-presidency, and turned the government over to Manuel Trucco Franzani. One month later Alessandri became the Democrat candidate.

With politicking resurgent, the military leadership began to face the facts. Blanquier, back in Finance, sought to cut government expenses by shutting down the official newspaper, *La Nación*, lowering army officers' salaries, reducing the size of the civil service, and cutting the salaries of those who kept their positions. Sáez and Rogers were hard pressed to keep order in the army and navy. Before the end of August, the new Trucco government ordered the retirement of army officers as an economy measure. Not surprisingly, the majority of those slated for early retirement were known Ibañistas. The purge had begun, and it was met with grumbling.

When Montero ordered Sáez to replace several garrison and division commanders, the grumbling increased. Used to privileges for four years, the army was reluctant to suffer humiliation. Purge and punishment, used previously to curb the Chilean military, would not be successful weapons in 1931 and 1932, for the purgers and punishers were simply not powerful enough. Nevertheless, Sáez continually assured the government that the army was quiescent.

He was either misinformed or too self-confident. Sáez resigned on August 14, disgusted by demands for further retirements, replacements, reassignments, and salary cuts. His own replacement was the controversial general Enrique Bravo Ortiz, an old Ibáñez-hater, confrere of the Grove-Alessandri opposition group, and a passenger on the Avión Rojo. By the second half of August, then, the Trucco government was essentially neutralist vis-à-vis the military; Trucco was neither distrusted nor feared. The army under Bravo was ostensibly free from Ibañismo. Was this the return to normalcy?

No, it was not, for it was much too soon to speak of such a condition as normalcy, given the mounting depression. Civilianism was only an illusion; actually there was little to stop a politically motivated military at this time, except residual effects of the trauma of Ibáñez's political demise and a fear of public opinion. The military, however, was not yet capable of action. Purges continued, as Bravo, unlike Sáez, did not hesitate to purge Ibañistas and reincorporate anti-Ibañistas.

Horacio Hevia, Trucco's interior minister, extended the purge of Ibañistas to the civilian sector. Hevia and Bravo announced that officers' salaries would be cut and that Ibáñez would be retired without pay. But the army did not react. Still shaken and publicly despised, the officer class sullenly bent to the will of the provisional government. Nevertheless, there would come a point at which ambitious officers motivated by the desire to reestablish the military's privileged position would fall prey to political influence of another sort: insinuation that the government was "out to get them" and that they should "do something about it." Once they became convinced of civilian institutional weakness, the saviors on horseback would be easy to find in barracks, schools, and offices.

In September 1931 Chilean military saviors could also be found in engine rooms, galleys, and crews' quarters as sailors revolted against the economic austerity policies of the government and what they thought was a revival of the old political order.

The Navy Mutiny of 1931: A Chilean *Potemkin*[3]

On the last day of August, officers at the Coquimbo Naval Base announced to their crews that the government proposed to restore fiscal soundness to the republic by slashing the salaries of all government employees. No mention was made of army or navy reductions, but the crewmen reacted negatively nonetheless. On the night of August 31, delegations from all Coquimbo squadron ships were assembled, supposedly to arrange an athletic tournament.

Next morning, ships' officers were taken prisoner. Discussion of the tournament had given way the previous night to a discussion of the government's austerity policy directed against middle- and low-income citizens and its benign attitude toward those with high incomes. This, reasoned mutiny leaders, was chicanery directed against those who had no means to object, and indicated favoritism toward the privileged few. The ideas of Karl Marx were echoed that night in Coquimbo. A telegram sent to naval headquarters in Santiago explained the mutiny and also alluded to the inability of the existing government to survive without doing injury to the lower classes. The mutineers proposed that the government forcibly extract loans from wealthy Chileans, cease its quest for finances from foreign bankers, and widen access to credit so that small businesses could survive the economic pinch. The mutineers also demanded an end to press attacks on the armed forces. In this mutiny, the first instance in Latin America of a socioeconomically oriented revolt by the military rank and file, we can see the concern of uniformed men outside the officer class for the common citizen. Seven years earlier, to be sure, army and navy officers had shown political concern, though not for the masses. But in Coquimbo, clearly, and then down south in Talcahuano, the crews were more radical in their thinking.

That Marxist thought, socialism, and extremist solutions should have found their way into the navy should not seem strange. Unlike officers, who were career professionals removed from many civilian realities, crewmen were recruited from the lower sectors of society, and they did not lose touch with the civilian lower classes. Their lot while on duty was by no means luxurious. Significantly, there was no comparable movement from the army rank and file at this time. This is because the gap between officers and members of the rank and file was not as pronounced in the army as it was in the navy. Too, there was probably more cohesion in the army—cohesion born of a mutual hesitancy in late 1931 to act politically.

On September 1, attempting to resolve the mutiny situation, the cabinet decided to send a mediator to Coquimbo, but the question was, Who should it be? Navy leaders were unwilling for a "neutral" party (that is, an army or air force officer) to act on their behalf, and they did not want a civilian mediator. The cabinet collectively distrusted the army and realized that the air force could not enforce any policy on its own. For these reasons the Admiralty's request that the navy be allowed to attempt to suppress the mutiny by itself was granted. Interservice rivalries, the tenuous nature of civilian-military relations, and institutional pride were the prime considerations in deliberations on this matter.

Late that same day another telegram was received in Santiago. The rebels now demanded suspension of foreign debt payments, subdivision of large landholdings, and improvement of the crews' living and work conditions. This convinced the cabinet that the crews were under the spell of communism. The cruiser *Latorre,* after all, had recently returned from England, where, the admirals assured the politicians, Communists had twice attempted to inspire naval mutinies.

The next day Admiral Edgardo von Schroeders agreed to undertake mediation of the navy's problem. Schroeders proposed to demand freedom for the captured officers, meet with mutiny leaders, and persuade them to voice their complaints through the proper channels. This was folly, for by this time crews in Talcahuano also had mutinied upon receiving orders to move up the coast to blockade the Coquimbo mutineers. Commanded by petty officers, eleven ships steamed north from Talcahuano to join, not blockade, their sisters.

Meanwhile, Schroeders was in Coquimbo. There he went aboard the *Latorre* convinced there was no "red menace" in the navy. He based his conclusions on official Communist Party disavowal of the movement. He was apparently correct in minimizing Communist influence in Coquimbo, but he later correctly stated that the Talcahuano mutineers *were* Communist influenced.[4] While he was in

Coquimbo, meeting with little success, he learned that the cabinet had resigned and that a new one had been selected.

The cycle of new cabinet—new crisis—new cabinet which had been so devastating to Chilean civilian politics in the early 1920s began to plague the country anew, contributing to deterioration of the very shaky reestablished civilian leadership. General Carlos Vergara Montero (essentially anti-Ibáñez but not as vociferous as Bravo) was now war minister; Admiral Enrique Spoerer was navy minister. The new cabinet reversed the Hevia austerity program, declaring there would be no salary cuts.

With the army superficially mollified, the salary earners placated, and the popular (if stuffy) Spoerer in the Navy Ministry, Schroeders renewed his efforts at mediation. He became more resistant to the mutineers, telling them that there was no hope of army support; that, given the new cabinet's decisions, lower-income groups would not feel the weight of reduced income; that other reforms were unfeasible; that Navy Minister Spoerer would "study the situation."

A compromise resulted. The mutineers would release their prisoners, there would be no reprisals, and Spoerer, as promised, would "study the situation." But on September 4, perhaps fearing that the Talcahuano mutineers were still steaming north to rendezvous at Valparaíso for joint signing of the compromise agreement, the government recalled Schroeders. There would be no compromise; only force would reestablish discipline. Buttressed by War Minister Vergara's mastery over the army, the Trucco government resolved to fight if necessary. Vergara assumed active command of all army forces and on September 5—ironically the seventh anniversary of the army petition of 1924—ordered an air assault on the navy mutineers.

Vergara was obliged to move in force, for rumors circulated of a revolt by the coastal artillery (confirmed in Talcahuano, but not Valparaíso), a revolt at the Quinteros Air Base, and revolts in nearly all the barracks. It was even rumored that the Talcahuano-Coquimbo mutineers were steaming north to occupy Iquique and Antofagasta: shades of 1891—with class warfare!

By nightfall on September 6, shore installations at Coquimbo, Concepción, Talcahuano, and Valparaíso were under government control. But at sea the squadrons had indeed joined forces in the Coquimbo roadstead. This made land action unnecessary and prepared for the entrance of a heretofore purely ornamental air force onto the political stage. Lieutenant Colonel Ramón Vergara, the war minister's younger brother, serving as air undersecretary, took command of a World War I–vintage fighter squadron and proceeded to strafe the mutinous squadrons. Though little damage was done to either vessels or planes, the mutineers did surrender on September 9.

The Chilean *"Potemkin"* revolt of September 1–9, 1931, was certainly not a Communist-inspired mutiny.[5] It was a protest movement by hard-pressed sailors desperate to improve their own situation and anxious to gain civilian support by advocating easy access to credit, agrarian reform, and a kind of redistribution of income. It was only incidentally a protest against antimilitarism. Army and air force action did restore civilian confidence in those institutions, but the whole affair served primarily to renew distrust of the military.

October 1931–June 1932: The Failure of Civilianism[6]

In the second half of 1931 it was obvious that discontent within the political system centered in two camps: the armed forces and the lower classes. The military, smarting from loss of prestige, was only conditionally loyal. The lower classes were increasingly falling under the spell of extremist political philosophies, as restored civilian government showed itself unable—or unwilling—to adopt radical measures to deal with unsolvable problems. As the saying goes, politics makes strange bedfellows; the military and the far left would soon bed down together politically.

With an illusory calm restored following the naval revolt, the presidential campaign went into high gear—to the neglect, needless to say, of more pressing problems. Montero defeated Alessandri handily on October 4 in what must be interpreted as a victory for the political right. Alessandri did not generate enthusiasm on the left in 1931, and too many Chileans recalled his involvement with the military between 1919 and 1925, which had resulted in his loss of power. Many also recalled Alessandri's actions against Ibáñez between 1928 and 1931. The few Chileans eligible to vote—only 9 percent of the population in 1931—evidently wanted to minimize civilian involvement with the military.

Montero faced a future more dismal than the one Alessandri had faced back in 1920. The economy was in a shambles. Party politics was renascent; unemployment, inflation, poverty, and hunger went unchecked. The military was, to put it mildly, restless. The recent reestablishment of political freedom permitted extremism to grow in popularity. As desultory as Montero's performance was, it is hard to believe that anyone could have done more. Opposition to Montero and his Conservative-Liberal-Radical administration soon coalesced into three groups.

Alessandri still had a following, and he knew how to use it. By the time he regained his old Senate seat in April 1932, he had support from Democrats and from some Liberals and Radicals. Ibañismo was not dead; the ad hoc Socialist Carlos Dávila became leader of a heterogeneous group of leftist Ibañista officers, many recently retired, and civilian Ibañistas. NAP, led by Eugenio Matte, later with the connivance of Marmaduke Grove, soon entered the lists.

Montero's was by no means a happy presidency. His troubles began in late 1931, and with them came a resurgence of military political activity. In 1924, political officers met frequently simply to exchange ideas, but military political activism took on a more sinister tone in late 1931. The Trucco government's indecisive treatment of the mutineers of September established a pattern of incertitude toward the military which did not diminish under Montero. Furthermore, the frequent reassignments of garrison commanders, the ministerial changes, and the purges aided in perpetuating a climate of tension within military circles. The same lack of continuity and consistency that had characterized both civilian affairs and War Ministry administration during the Parliamentary Republic did not bode well for reestablishment of "normalcy" in civil-military relations in 1931.

Just days before Montero's election, in fact, the holdover Congress took up a thorny political issue: constitutional violations allegedly committed by Ibáñez and members of his government. Only the staunchest of anti-Ibañista officers could stomach the harsh language directed against military men who had served in government positions between 1927 and 1931. Only with difficulty were some civilians able to prove that what appeared as collaboration with Ibáñez was really service to the fatherland. Because the congressional offensive did not originate from a solid organizational base, it was blunted by fierce military resistance. Even in its chastened state the military had not abandoned its cherished corporate self-interest.[7]

No one in Congress (the Senate was most active in all this) raised the question of the constitutionality of the Congress itself, selected as it had been by Ibáñez himself. The crude attacks on army and navy officers did nothing to improve civil-military relations. By the end of November, Ibañistas responded to charges against them in the pages of *Hoy*, Carlos Dávila's Ibañista-Socialist journal. Most of their responses fell on deaf ears.

What happened in Chile in late 1931 was quite comparable to the blistering attacks on followers of both the fallen Augusto B. Leguía (president of Peru, 1919–30) by the Sanchecerrista military clique and the ousted Hipólito Irigoyen (1916–22, 1928–30) by the military in Argentina. In many ways the events in Chile during this entire seventeen-month period can be compared to the bitter struggle among civilian, military, Aprista, and oligarchic interests in Peru. In Chile, of course, a revived civilian political system was reacting to four years of military rule before the desirability and strength of the civilian system had been reestablished.

As the purges continued, Ibañistas began to gather around Dávila, and the labor–left wing Socialist movement built up steam. Demonstrations and violence occurred in Santiago and Valparaíso in November and December. Unemployed workers attacked the army barracks at Copiapó on Christmas Eve. A general strike took place on January 11. Opposition to Montero—albeit divided in origin—was quite open. Poor Montero struggled on, his government powerless to do anything constructive, his policies and methods based on laissez-faire principles, anachronistic in depression-mired Chile.

By March 1932, the factionalized opposition was better organized than the government. Military Ibañistas, led by Generals Ambrosio Viaux Aguilar and Pedro Charpín Rival, Colonel Arturo Merino Benítez (the former air commodore who had been retired, reincorporated, dismissed, and denied his pension by Congress), and Alejandro Lazo, conspired against Montero with Dávila and disgruntled active officers in Santiago and Valparaíso. The new air commodore, Marmaduke Grove, conspired with Eugenio Matte and his NAP friends. Grove and Matte disagreed with the Ibañistas on almost everything except the unacceptability of the do-nothing Montero regime.

Illustrative of the extremely fragile nature of civil-military relations was Grove's presence in the air force directorship. The flamboyant Grove, an inveterate plotter, was a staunch enemy of Ibáñez, and when he returned from confinement on Rapa Nui, Montero reluctantly appointed him air commodore to the great disappointment of the Vergara brothers. Montero's commander in chief of the army, General Indalicio Téllez Cárcamo, did not trust Grove, but, curiously, General Sáez vouched for his ability and desire to abstain from politics. Grove's presence was detrimental, in the final analysis, to Montero's government, for he alone spurred Ibañistas to action.

Leftist opposition to Montero was based on several key points. In their demonstrations and strikes, workers demanded nationalization and communization of the nitrate installations, dissolution of Congress and COSACH, and forced loans from banks for government expenses. Montero was unwilling to allow any of these measures. The Alessandristas also attacked the government. Their leader, who had returned to his old Senate seat and almost immediately began attacking the government's fiscal policies, accused Montero of doing absolutely nothing to bring Chile out of its depressed state. He directly blamed Montero for allowing the value of the peso to fall to an all-time low ($0.0403). He claimed (inaccurately) to speak for Democrats, Doctrinaire Liberals, and Social Republicans. By May he also claimed ties with disaffected Radical Party leaders.

By mid-1932 Montero no longer seemed like the man who could guide Chile back along the path to civilian democratic government ("normalcy") and economic recovery. (It may well be that there was still no consensus that the two routes were at all the same.) Montero's brand of government was that of the past; his methods, those of his 1891–1923 predecessors; his policies, those of laissez-faire. He might be called the Herbert Hoover of Chile.

Civilian government, to the dismay of many Chileans, was not solving the country's problems. It was not reducing the problem of military political action, nor was it helping to restore continuity in "normal" military affairs. It did not respond to the situation of the unemployed. The barely democratically conceived Thermal Congress continued to function; so did the unsuccessful COSACH. Civilian government, administered on a day-to-day basis, barely functioned, with Montero doggedly assuring everyone that economic recovery would be forthcoming through traditional policies.

The inefficacy of Montero, democracy, civilian government, laissez-faire economics—in short, traditional social and economic values and policies—led would-be national leaders to search for panaceas. Army officers contemplated an Ibañista restoration. Could Ibáñez provide order, discipline, and economic stability? Others considered military rule without Ibáñez himself. Leftists pondered the merits of Marxism, realizing that Montero's policies were not innovative or successful. And so the left and the military produced rumblings of revolt, hazy ideas of social, economic, and political alternatives. The creation of the Ministry of National Defense on March 4, 1932, combining the navy and army ministries, and the replacement of the war minister, General Vergara, with Miguel Urrutia, a civilian and an intimate of Montero, did not meet with army approval. No civilian had served as war minister since the time of Alessandri. This alone alienated army officers who might otherwise have welcomed a respite from political action.

Thus for a number of reasons the position of the Montero administration became untenable by mid 1932. Because no other civilian power group was capable as yet of taking power or formulating any kind of governmental plan of action, the opposition looked reluctantly to the army for the means to their varied ends. Montero's opponents seemed untroubled by the fact that Montero had been elected, that overthrowing him would violate the Constitution, that extremism was the alternative, and that the military would no doubt play a major role in any alternative regime.

In the Santiago, Concepción, and Valparaíso garrisons, in the National Defense Ministry corridors and offices, in the Club Militar, and in the army schools there was much talk of plots, golpes, even civil war. In April, Montero declared a state of siege, reshuffled the cabinet, and named a new defense minister. The new minister made more reassignments, thereby merely reshuffling the conspirators. A cast of characters assembled for what became the most bizarre golpe in Chile's history: the revolt of June 4, 1932.

Leading roles in the June 4 episode would be played by Montero, Grove, the Vergara brothers, and Lieutenant Colonel Pedro Lagos Lagos. Supporting members of the cast were Alessandri, Dávila, and Merino Benítez. The coup would be a civil-military tragedy—tragic for civilians because it proved their inability to control the situation, and tragic for the military because it destroyed discipline. The golpe of June 4, 1932, and the ensuing Socialist experiment are directly responsible for the ultimate demise of the Chilean military as a politically deliberative group, and for the resultant reestablishment of true civilian political hegemony.

June 4, 1932:
The Collapse of Post-Ibáñez Civilianism[8]

The action began, as always, in Santiago, just after Montero's declaration of siege in April. The new defense minister, Ignacio Urrutia Manzano, instructed army commanders to make a thorough investigation of suspected plots and plotters, both retired and on active duty. His instructions were acknowledged, but no one made haste to fulfill them. General Carlos Vergara, head of Division II (Santiago), was particularly reluctant to comply. His was a difficult position; he was a former war minister and was not happy at having been replaced in the confusing game of "musical portfolios." Vergara balked at the minister's order to transfer Lieutenant Colonel Lagos, commandant of the Infantry School. It is not known whether he voiced his disapproval at Air Commodore Grove's apparent immunity from investigation, but several of his colleagues did. Lagos, son of one of Chile's War of the Pacific heroes, continued to hold his post, to the chagrin of Montero and Urrutia Manzano.

Under siege, army and civilian conspirators met clandestinely in private homes. Grove moved freely. Dávila, Merino, and Lazo were ordered apprehended but remained free throughout April and May. The exhortations of Montero and Urrutia went unheeded; clearly their authority over the military was illusory. By late May, Lagos was known to have met with Dávila and his cohorts. Civil control of the military was nonexistent!

Late on the evening of June 2, unbeknownst to Montero and Urrutia Manzano, Dávila, Matte, Grove, and Lagos met at Lagos's home. Lagos, who emerged as a key conspirator, would claim later that the meeting took place to "exchange ideas with respect to the situation of the armed forces and the political, social, and economic atmosphere of the country." This was outrageously euphemistic, for what the participants really discussed was how many officers could be counted upon to remain loyal, declare neutrality, or support a military movement to depose Montero. The conclusions reached that night go without saying: more officers would remain neutral or support a golpe than would defend the government. This meeting might have resulted in a firm conspiracy had not Grove refused to discuss details of the matter with Dávila. Grove would have nothing to do with Ibañistas and left the meeting in a huff.

Act II of Chile's 1932 civil-military tragedy began the next day when Urrutia ordered Grove's dismissal, accusing him of plotting a golpe. Grove resisted, stating that he was in no way involved in any plot. That afternoon he was relieved of his command of the Air Force School (El Bosque) and placed at the disposition of the defense minister. At last a key conspiratorial figure had a pretext for action.

Grove was not without his defenders. At least two officers refused to accept his El Bosque post on professional and ethical grounds. In fine, they would not replace a man unjustly dismissed. This, of course, was as much insubordination as it was professional ethics! On the afternoon of June 3, Lieutenant Colonel Vegara officially relieved Grove at El Bosque. Grove left angrily for his home, but later that evening he returned to find Vergara absent, and when the new air commodore returned himself, Grove and other officers loyal to him took the younger Vergara brother prisoner. Grove announced he had decided to overthrow the Montero government because he had been dismissed without just cause.

Though it is inconceivable the government had not expected some kind of military movement, Grove took Montero by surprise, and the president did not cope strategically with the situation. By this time, though, he could probably have done nothing, so unpopular was his government and so weak his authority over the military.

By 2:00 A.M. June 4, General Vergara had posted troops around La Moneda. He also ordered Lagos to proceed to El Bosque for a sunrise attack and alerted the Admiralty to be on the lookout for a naval mutiny. When Lagos arrived at Grove's headquarters he entered into talks with Grove. Lagos was now acting on behalf of Dávila and the military Ibañista cabal. He told Grove in no uncertain terms that his barracks revolt was doomed, that he was outnumbered ten to one, but admitted that he himself was no friend of Montero. Grove replied that he wanted Montero out and a Socialist regime installed. Lagos countered by stating that any new government must include Dávila and General Arturo Puga Osorio, an ally of former president Ibáñez. As distasteful as this was to Grove, he gave in.

Lagos appeared in downtown Santiago shortly after sunrise. He informed General Vergara and Defense Minister Urrutia that he would not order his soldiers to fire on comrades in uniform. The government's position was hopeless, for no element of the Santiago garrison would move on El Bosque. The army collectively refused to defend the government. The government responded by pressing the prestigious General Sáez into action. Sáez met with Grove in the late morning of June 4 and tried to dissuade him from his course of action. But Grove refused, sounding more like a Marxist than an army officer (assuming that the two were still antonymous in Chile). He spent little time complaining about his dismissal but told Sáez that the Montero regime was a tool of the plutocracy and foreign interests, and that the people deserved better.

Just after noon, planes from El Bosque buzzed downtown Santiago, and elements of the capital garrison flocked to Grove's headquarters. Infantry, cavalry, engineers, carabineros, and Lagos's command went over to the rebels. Meanwhile Montero and Urrutia tried desperately to maintain the government. They refused to return a telephone call from Ibáñez in Mendoza, Argentina but did ask Arturo Alessandri to treat with Grove. Lagos had betrayed the government, Sáez had failed, and now a civilian, a former president, would try his hand.

Alessandri visited El Bosque twice that afternoon; his position in his talks with Grove has remained controversial to this day. Did he offer support to Grove, as was later suggested by Chilean Socialists, or did he merely fulfill his obligations as mediator? Did he indeed advise Grove not to let up? Did Grove offer him the vice-presidency in a provisional regime—after earlier telling Lagos he would accept Ibañistas, sworn enemies of Alessandri? Whatever happened at El Bosque on that day—and we have several garbled, conflicting versions—it benefited Grove as well as all anti-Montero forces in the short run, benefited Alessandri in the long run, and did even more damage to the army in the eyes of civilian leaders.[9]

At approximately 6:00 P.M. Montero notified Grove of his resignation. One hour and fifteen minutes later, Grove, Matte, Dávila, Merino, and Puga entered La Moneda. Chile's first military golpe in six and one-half years was a success. Dávila, Matte, and Puga proclaimed themselves a junta of government.

One cycle of plotting ended, and another was just beginning. One untenable regime was demolished; another came into existence. Constitutional democracy was scrapped; socialism was (temporarily) the new order. Through it all the military remained politically involved, creating and then reinforcing its image as a destructive, predatory political force.

What really brought about the downfall of Montero and his administration was their inability to cure Chile's woes and the inability of the war and defense ministers to curb military political deliberation. Furthermore, the civilian political system was absolutely bereft of organization at a time when uncontrollable economic forces were buffeting the country. Without organization there could be no government action of any type; without civilian control of the military, governmental action would have done little good anyway.

Traditional leaders, parties, and political ideas were caught in a socioeconomic maelstrom. Political institutions had to be reconstructed as the maelstrom increased in intensity. At the same time, many Chileans were losing faith in traditional modes of politics, and extremist solutions appeared as attractive as traditional ones. Yet when extremist solutions proved unsatisfactory and political traditionalism was again restored, extremism would lose much of its allure.

Throughout the crisis the military tenaciously tried to cling to its identity, but its institutional solidarity was as weak as that of parties, the Constitution, and civilian politics. There were no examples to follow and no consensus to respond to except the example of intrigue and the public consensus that somehow the military could provide order.

In the army a kind of winnowing process was already under way. Ultimately it would remove from the officer corps almost everyone remotely connected with the Ibáñez era of 1924–31, the anti-Montero movements of 1931–32, and finally the Socialist Republic of 1932. Purge, voluntary retirement, and disgrace through association were already clearing out the officer corps by the time planes from El Bosque buzzed the presidential palace on June 4, 1932. These processes eventually produced an apolitical officer corps. Our next chapter will examine the inability or unwillingness of the officer corps to act in a political manner from 1933 forward and the forces that militated against such acts. But first it is appropriate to survey Chile's last brush with civil-military authoritarianism: the Socialist Republic of 1932.

The Socialist Republic: Phase I, June 4–16, 1932

Since his days as a naval and army cadet, Air Commodore Grove had been known as a perennial dissenter. He loved the military life, yet he reacted so strongly against social injustices that he was constantly a discipline problem. Incapable of maintaining a fixed opinion, Grove was mercurial in his political loyalties. He was an incurable romantic born a century too late. Some believed him mad;

most believed him a charlatan. Yet he is still remembered for his genuine devotion to social justice for the lower classes. Hence it was only natural that Marmaduke Grove be the central figure in the Socialist Republic.

Once conceived, the Socialist Republic began its operations inauspiciously. Dávila and Matte, the two leading civilians in the movement, did not agree on just what socialism meant. Matte, like Grove, leaned toward Marxism. Dávila leaned toward statism, and his Ibañista background led many to link him to Italian fascism. With Grove (defense minister), Merino Benítez (the new air commodore), and Puga involved in the government, the military became enmeshed in this quarrel from the beginning. It was hoped that Puga, as interior minister and junta chairman, would mediate, but he soon saw the futility of that.

The new junta outlined its program in a statement to the public soon after taking office. In considering the program of the Socialist Republic, we must remember that official junta statements are not to be confused with NAP positions such as those expressed in the famous *Los 30 puntos* (1932). The government proposed expedient programs; NAP and allied organizations expressed ideals in *Los 30 puntos*. This distinction is especially important from the standpoint of civil-military relations because the army, through its relationship with the government, appeared to be closely linked to NAP, Dávila-Ibañismo, *Los 30 puntos*, and all facets of socialism, Marxist or otherwise!

The June 4 junta statement called for control of interest rates, greater access to credit, price controls on domestic and imported goods, and higher tax rates for the wealthy. It placed responsibility for the feeding, clothing, and housing of the indigent in government hands for as long as the economy continued in its depressed state.

Within a week NAP appeared to have the upper hand in political affairs. Street demonstrations, the singing of the "Internationale," the closure of Congress—long a NAP demand—and Puga's resignation gave the government a definite Socialist cast. On June 12 Dávila too resigned from the junta. The names being spoken and chanted by Santiago crowds were Grove and Matte. Communist (not Socialist) demonstrations were daily occurrences; on June 10 Grove felt it necessary to denounce communism publicly and to broadcast a warning to Communist leaders against further demonstrations.

Military support for the Socialist Republic eroded steadily during the first week of the regime. On June 12, just after Dávila's resignation was announced and immediately following a Grovista workers' rally, Grove confronted the high command at the Defense Ministry. Generals Vergara, Sáez, Fernando Sepúlveda, and Luis Otero tendered their resignations. Generals Agustín Moreno and Guillermo Novoa, Colonel Aníbal Godoy, and Lieutenant Colonels Lagos and Merino demanded a full and categorical denunciation of the Communist Party and a greater voice for military men in the government.

The lines were clearly drawn. The high command would disassociate itself from the government unless the government listened to military men. Actually the army's position was stronger at this time than it had been under Montero but, just as important, the army feared a violent confrontation with Marxist-inspired and manipulated workers and citizens. As defense minister, Grove was theoretically responsible for communicating the army's position to the junta on behalf of the high command. But he was too intimately tied to the junta and to NAP to be effective as defense minister at this time.

In the civilian sector Socialists, Communists, Democrats, the syndicates, and the Teachers' Federation supported the government. Professional associations, Radicals, Liberals, and Conservatives, as would be expected, did not. The balance of power lay with the army, just as it had in the Chilean political impasse of 1924.

The Socialist Republic:
Phase II, June 16–September 13, 1932

On June 16, the army made its move in an involved golpe characteristic of the civil-military movements of 1931 and 1932. Ibañista Captain Mario Bravo Lavín occupied the Defense Ministry with the Buin infantry regiment.[10] Grove fled his office. Admiral Carlos Jouanne, the navy director general, angry that Grove had pledged his support to the mutineers of September 1931, confronted Grove at the presidential palace and demanded that Grove and Matte resign. Unable to muster military or popular support, Grove and Matte resigned and were unceremoniously arrested and shipped off to Easter Island. NAP, Grovismo, and communism had proved too much for either the army or the navy to swallow. But what about socialism of the Dávila variety? For it was Dávila who emerged as socialism's new prophet on June 16, 1932.

That the military still controlled the balance of power was made

clear when, on June 16, civilian political leaders called on General
Sáez to reenter active service for the purpose of convincing men like
Bravo, Lagos, and Merino that the army should refrain from further
political action. Sáez was indeed able to convince the military
conspirators of June 16 to allow Dávila and other civilians to run the
government by hinting that promotions were in the offing for
cooperative officers! La Moneda ceased to be what Sáez himself
described as "a barracks, the gallery full of soldiers with bayonets
fixed," and Dávila was allowed to take power, along with Alberto
Cabero and Nolasco Cárdenas. Radical Juan Antonio Ríos Morales
became interior minister, and General Puga became defense minister.

The new government had definite Radical, technocratic, and
Ibañista tinges, but it did not have the support of the right or the far
left, of Conservatives, Liberals, or syndicate leaders.

Ríos met the threat of civil disorder by declaring martial law—and,
not surprisingly, thereby placated army officers fearful of confrontation. He specifically prohibited the sale of firearms and alcoholic
beverages after 6:00 P.M., late-night theater performances, and
assemblages of more than three persons, and he established a 10:00
P.M. street curfew and censorship of press and radio. Santiago and the
provinces were orderly by June 30.

This was a blessing, for on July 6 Carlos Ibáñez came home to assess
his chances for a return to power. Ibáñez soon found, however, that
except for cavalry officers he had no military support; nor did
syndicates or parties see him as the answer to their particular
problems. Always a reasonable man, Ibáñez returned to Argentina on
July 24, this time as Chilean ambassador to the Buenos Aires
government. Before he left he persuaded Dávila to dissolve the junta
and assume the presidency. He also convinced his old comrades in the
high command that this was a much more efficient way to run the
country. Weary of juntas, power struggles, and personality conflicts,
the army high command consented.

Because the balance of power remained in military hands, army
and navy leaders were able to exert enough pressure on Dávila to
keep his cabinet appointments more moderate than those of the
previous regime. For example, the new minister of justice was
Guillermo Bañados, an Alessandrista. Enrique Zañartu, Dávila's
finance minister, was a political moderate and a respected, progressive economic thinker. Even more revealing of the military's influence
was the reestablishment of the War and Navy ministries under

Colonel Lagos and Admiral Francisco Nieto respectively. Both services thus regained a semblance of professional autonomy. For the time being, both were glad to have it.

Dávila's socialism, whose goals were no more realistic than those of Matte and NAP, was only slightly less extreme. Dávila eschewed fiery denunciations of capitalists, latifundistas, bankers, speculators, and foreign interests, but his corrective measures were nonetheless dramatic. In the late 1931 and early 1932 issues of *Hoy*, Provisional President Dávila promised state control of means of production, utilities, and transportation, stringent import controls, expansion of copper and nitrate markets through negotiation, restructuring of the tax system, subdivision and collectivization of some large landholdings, tight controls on profits of foreign investments, price controls, and a technical education campaign for rural Chile. In short, Dávila's program was a sort of economic nationalism that became popular—in some cases respectable—decades later in Latin America. Dávila and Chilean Socialists, whatever their specific loyalties, were years ahead of their time.

By the end of August, Dávila was pressing ahead with plans to renegotiate the public and foreign debt, nationalize all mining activities, form a government-capitalized industrial complex, and create a "General Secretariat of Production and Prices."[11] The secretariat—had it ever come into being—would have given the government power to control prices of articles of prime necessity (food, clothing, medicine, power, and transportation), to expropriate any enterprise, and to stipulate that producers had to supply items of prime necessity, regardless of the price or profit margin, under pain of expropriation without compensation. The secretariat scheme proved to be too "Communistic" for army and civilian leaders who had bided their time hoping for the best. It gave too much unrestricted power to the government, even at a time when vigorous action was desperately needed. It was economic dictatorship. There were no markets to expand; Chilean industry could not supply import substitution items; government appeals failed to stabilize the currency; and Dávila's issue of paper money (to get currency into circulation) had only continued the inflation. The value of the peso fluctuated from market to market between fifty-eight and seventy to the U.S. dollar during the third quarter of 1932. Agrarian reform (promised but only barely implemented) alienated rightist support for Dávila as a preferable alternative to Matte, NAP, and Grove.

Carlos Dávila, never popular with the unemployed, debt-ridden, inflation-burdened middle and lower sectors, could not hope for support in the traditional parties. Chileans who feared Marxism, who yearned for democratic government, and who had had enough of authoritarianism would not support his economic rehabilitation schemes. Clearly he owed his support to his respectability (in contrast with the likes of Matte), his ties with the military, and to his nondemagogic manner; these were not the components of a solid power base by any stretch of the imagination, even Dávila's.

By late August 1932, Chileans were remembering his conspiratorial role in the fall of Montero and his Ibañista background, and stories began to circulate concerning the rough treatment of Grove and Matte en route to Easter Island. During the last quarter of 1932, there were many grounds for opposing Dávila, socialism, authoritarianism, and, last but not least, military involvement in politics.

When Dávila announced in September that a constituent assembly would draw up a new Constitution, divide itself into a bicameral Congress, and fix the date for presidential elections, public opposition mounted. Memories of the rigged Thermal Congress and the irregular promulgation of the 1925 Constitution were still fresh, and it was known that Dávila intended to be a presidential candidate. On September 12, the army high command vetoed his presidential ambitions, aware that civilian opposition to Dávila's program was widespread, and that junior and middle-grade officers were meeting and talking about a golpe. The high command's desire to preclude further disruption of discipline became the major consideration in the army's political role.

On September 13, Dávila met with the high command—Sáez; Otero; Novoa; General Humberto Arriagada, the carabineros' commandant; and Admiral Jouanne, the naval spokesman. Dávila reluctantly agreed not to seek the presidency; moreover, he agreed to step down rather than see the capital torn by violence and suffer the indignity of a golpe. Once again the military had dictated terms to government; once again a chief executive had resigned rather than provoke violence.

Constitutionally, Supreme Court Justice Abraham Oyanedel should have succeeded to the presidency, for Dávila's cabinet ministers had also tendered their resignations, and there were no parliamentary officials. But Oyanedel refused, so the high command persuaded the retired General Blanche to become provisional president. With extreme reluctance, Blanche acquiesced; mindful of his past associations with Ibáñez, the distinguished general promised to step down just as soon as a civilian successor could be found. Blanche and the high command were bone weary of conspiracies, bayonets rattling in the presidential palace, scuffling in ministry corridors, and rampant indiscipline in schools and barracks. They moved quickly when Colonel Merino greeted Blanche's presence in La Moneda by pronouncing against the government; Merino's attempted golpe fell flat.

Within a week it was plain that Blanche, the high command, and most garrison commanders wanted to step down. It was equally plain that civilian political leaders would not support Blanche or any other uniformed politician, and that they would by no means stand in Blanche's way if he chose to walk out the front door of La Moneda. Socialism had died with Dávila's resignation; the military presence died with Blanche. To many Chileans the two—socialism and military presence—had become, if not synonymous, equally obnoxious. Neither had rehabilitated Chile, and both had become associated with economic decline, political instability, and social discontent verging on class warfare. Most politically articulate Chileans—less than 10 percent of the population—believed (as they would later indicate in elections) that neither the military nor socialism was preferable to reestablishment of traditional constitutional normalcy. After all, this was virtually the only untested alternative left by October 1932!

On September 27 General Ricardo Ludwig, the recently appointed commander in chief of the army, received a telegram from General Pedro Vignola (Division I commandant in Antofagasta) that put the army's position into clearer focus.[12] In the telegram Vignola bluntly asked how long Blanche planned to stay in power; whether, as rumored, Ibáñez was coming back; whether Blanche would guarantee elections. Vignola further stated that he believed Blanche was laying the groundwork for an Ibañista restoration, and that he, for one, was disgusted with the ministry, staff, and Division II leadership in Santiago for giving the army a bad name.

Several years before, Vignola's voice would have been one crying in the wilderness (geographically as well as figuratively) but in 1932 it spoke for the emerging apolitical professionalism of army officers. In fact, Vignola and his counterpart in Concepción had already pleaded for restoration of constitutional normalcy a full two months earlier.

The same day that Vignola sent his telegram to Ludwig, a citizen's committee took over the municipal government in Antofagasta and warned Vignola not to move his command out of the barracks for any reason. Civilians did the same in Concepción, and a civilian committee, with navy and air force support in Santiago, demanded that Blanche resign. He did so on October 1; the Chilean armed forces were out of politics for the first time in eight years. In a sense the military had repudiated its own position. Civilianism was renascent, for the time being without military-induced complications.

11

Civil-Military Relations, 1932–70

From 1932 to 1970—from the repudiation of socialism and military political activity to the election and inauguration of the Marxist-Socialist Salvador Allende—the Chilean armed forces refrained from the type of political activity that is common among Chile's neighbors, Argentina, Brazil, Peru, Bolivia, and Paraguay. Most attempts to explain this fact amount to description rather than explanation.

In this chapter we will try to do both. We will attempt to describe the political conditions that precluded participation by a politically ambitious military and obviated the necessity for such participation. We will also try to explain why political conditions in Chile until the 1970s were not propitious to military political participation, whereas similar—though never identical—conditions or developments have been conducive to the assumption of a political role by men in uniform in other Latin American countries. We will focus on several themes in attempting this.

Civil-Military Relations, 1932–70:
An Interpretation[1]

In the first place, political conditions in Chile that affect civil-military relations only partially resemble those in the nearby states. Disruption of party politics and civilian government along with collapse of the economic system are phenomena Chile shared with other countries in 1931 and 1932, but in Chile the surrounding conditions were not the same. The rise of a labor left, the develop-

218

ment of ambitious middle-sector parties and movements, and the tenacity of the right wing are not uniquely Chilean. But their development and experience in Chile differed from their growth in Argentina, for example.

All of Latin America, with the possible exception of Mexico, felt the impact of the Cold War in the years after 1945, but the political climate of Chile during the late forties and the fifties was not at all like that of, say, Brazil, Guatemala, or Cuba. Similarly, the export of the Cuban brand of Marxism did not affect civil-military relations in Chile as it did civil-military relations in Bolivia, Honduras, or Venezuela. In Chile, finally, the coming to power of extremists was accompanied initially not by planes buzzing the presidential palace or by insurgents operating in the provinces, but by election—democratic and constitutional.

The ability of civilian government to function in Chile was not diminished by any of the above-mentioned political conditions. The repudiation of military political activity in 1932, following close on the heels of the repudiation of leftist authoritarianism, restored a belief in what we have called normalcy, that is, civilian, constitutional, essentially democratic government, which was accepted as preferable to what had preceded between 1924 and 1932.

The restoration of the electoral process allowed the electorate, however small, to make decisions. The restoration of constitutional democracy allowed an opposition to function legally, as long as its members abided by the law. Finally, action against leftist extremism taken during the 1930s and 1940s could be rationalized as action taken to preserve and protect a constitutional government and a democratically inclined society against unconstitutional and antidemocratic behavior.

Second, political change in Chile (as differentiated from a change in the conduct of politics) occurred repeatedly under the Constitution, and by Latin American standards a sense of fair play prevailed until the 1970s. New parties organized, grew, or diminished, were represented or lost their representation, and each had every chance of becoming the official party. Radicals, Christian Democrats, and the Socialist–Communist–non-Marxian coalition Unidad Popular (Popular Unity) all shared in this experience. In each case after 1938 a plurality, and in one a majority, took power and held it, subject to the popular will, and all agreed that such opportunity was preferable to military involvement. Most considered it preferable to leftist or right-wing authoritarianism. Chileans experienced militarism and leftist or right-wing authoritarianism thirty to forty years before most other Latin Americans did. "Constitutional Marxism," of course, did not fall into any of these categories. This alone may have doomed it and changed the preferences of many!

Third, for reasons mentioned in earlier chapters, the armed forces showed little evidence of political ambition after 1932. As we shall see, this does not mean that men in uniform refrained entirely from expressing opinions or exerting pressure. But it does mean that they were not able to speak for the institution. In Peru, there is a definite military ideology, but the Chilean military did not seem to have a single point of view on socioeconomic questions until 1973. Surely the experiences of 1931–32 help to explain military reluctance to interfere, but they do not entirely explain forty-three years of subservience. The definition of the military's role, however, may. The role of the armed services was redefined with difficulty in the years after 1932, and we will deal with it in this chapter and again in chapter 12.

The role definition of a Latin American military organization depends greatly on its professional orientation, the duties assigned to it by the government, the ancillary tasks growing from such duties, and the military's own vision of how duties and tasks might better be carried out, especially if they go unattended by civilians. The usual source of expression of the military point of view is the army.

Such was the case, as we have seen, in early-twentieth-century Chile. Army officers spoke and wrote about education, illiteracy, the shortcomings of parliamentary democracy, and economic stagnation. Their opinions were shared by some civilians, and many of those civilians collaborated with the military Ibañistas in the 1920s. By Latin American standards, their goals were modest. There were no Indians to integrate, no vast hinterland to open up and develop, no rigid resistance to expansion of educational facilities or economic modernization. Transportation, communications, and power sources had not been ignored by civilians. Chile's international position, as expressed through diplomacy, was not severely endangered by civilian malfeasance.

Furthermore, the goals established in 1924 and 1925 for social reform, expansion of government areas of responsibility, and the laying of groundwork for economic development were acceptable to many civilian leaders. Therefore, in the post-Ibáñez and post–Social-

ist Republic days, the army did not retain a developmental role as it
did in Peru during the 1930s, or in Brazil and Argentina at about the
same time. It did not become involved with world ideological
questions and the labor left wing during World War II, as the
Argentine Army did, and it did not view Chile as ungovernable by
civilians or unmanageable owing to a lack of civilian technological
expertise, as the Brazilian Army did. In other words, the belief that
"military men can do the job better," held by the Argentine,
Brazilian, and Peruvian military ideologues, did not develop, nor did
opportunities for military men to express themselves at length
develop until 1970–73. The forces that motivated Argentine, Brazilian, and Peruvian officers to act politically were present in Chile, but
the Chilean officer's perception of them was not the same, for his
professional milieu was different, at least until 1970.

Finally, we must realize that after 1932 civilians utilized a number
of techniques to hold the military in its place so skillfully that it was
extremely difficult for a politically oriented movement within the
army to get started. These techniques had a cumulative effect so great
that the probability of a golpe diminished from 1932 to 1970. From
1970 forward we are forced to reconsider this trend, and we will do so
in the concluding chapter.

Techniques that civilians used to hold the military in its place
include administrative maneuvers, expansion of the police functions
of the carabineros, exercise of presidential prerogatives, appointments
and retirements, the brief unofficial sponsoring of a civilian militia
during the early 1930s, antimilitary press campaigns, coddling the
military with equipment, yielding to modest demands—in short, a
wide range of measures. From the civilian point of view these
measures proved most successful in the reestablishment and maintenance of the army as essentially obedient. Let us now turn to that
reestablishment, and then to its maintenance.

Resurgent Civilianism:
The Reelection of Arturo Alessandri[2]

On October 1, 1932, when Bartolomé Blanche resigned the provisional presidency, Supreme Court Chief Justice Oyanedel appointed
Javier Angel Figueroa Larraín to the Interior Ministry and charged
him with forming a government. Figueroa's task was easier than his

predecessors' of 1931–32, for the traditional parties had begun to regroup, the left was in decay, and the military no longer exerted pressure. The newly appointed War Minister Sáez and Navy Minister Admiral Arturo Swett (reincorporated after he retired in protest against Ibáñez's power play in 1927) held their subordinates in check, whereas a year earlier they would have been unable to do so. Sáez made reassignments stick and formed a military tribunal to judge all involved in insubordination during the previous year.

As electioneering began, the pressure on the military declined slightly. So did most of the effects of the depression. The peso edged upward in value. Several new trade agreements were reached for copper and nitrates. The Trans-Andean Railway, out of service in late 1931 and during the winter months of 1932, began operating, putting disgruntled laborers back to work and moving trade goods once again. Unemployment dropped only slightly, but the slight turns for the better, coming as they did after socialism had been discarded and the military repudiated, were associated with civilian political revival. Both the left, albeit in disarray, and the right, albeit regrouping, offered candidates.

The Communist Party nominated Elías Lafferte, the Stalinist once exiled by Ibáñez. The Socialists nominated Grove. Both parties, though involved with the Socialist Republic, extremism, and authoritarianism, were willing to abide by the election rules. Thus the Marxist left moved into the legitimate political system for the first time in eight years. Representing the right were Conservative Party president Héctor Rodríguez de la Sotta and Liberal Enrique Zañartu, also supported by the Agrarian Party, composed of southern landlords. Both Rodríguez and Zañartu were members of the aristocracy, which was anxious to regain the power it had lost in 1920.

But neither the new left nor the old right was to triumph in the first Chilean presidential election clearly drawn between political extremes. The center prevailed, thereby establishing something of a pattern for the next thirty-eight years. In the frenzy of electioneering in October 1932, Radicals, Democrats, and many Liberals agreed that the choice between right and left was unacceptable. They therefore rekindled the flame of the Liberal Alliance and nominated Arturo Alessandri Palma.

Alessandri's candidacy syphoned off support from both extremes. Conservatives and Liberals feared Grove and Lafferte, socialism and communism. The far left feared a Conservative and Liberal renaissance, a return to the pre-1920 past. This all benefited Alessandri. Some saw him as the least of several evils; to only a few was he still the roaring lion of 1920. Alessandri, a Liberal, represented a centrist plurality and still retained something of the aura of a people's candidate. He had struggled for reforms and against military authoritarianism. He had worked hard on the Constitution of 1925 and had suffered for his principles. He could justify each of his past actions by saying he thought only of Chile. Enough people believed him to vote for him. And it helped that the extremes were divided. Alessandri took office on December 23.

Twice before in Chilean history war heroes had assumed control of the country after a period of military political involvement, the Portales-Prieto clique in 1830 and the leaders of parliament after the Civil War of 1891. Alessandri, still a hero of political wars, followed their lead. He knew as they had that the reestablishment of normalcy depended on the maintenance of military discipline and obedience. To achieve this Alessandri called on Emilio Bello Codesido.

The Mechanics of Civil-Military Relations: The Ministry of National Defense[3]

Bello had credentials that impressed military men. He had been one of the few trusted civilians during the rise of Carlos Ibáñez, not because he favored military political activity, but because he was a Balmacedista (Balmaceda's son-in-law, in fact). Thus he was associated with forceful government, and he had great prestige as an able, just administrator. Certainly Alessandri could have picked no better man for the job of minister of national defense. The Defense Ministry had existed briefly before, but with Bello in office, structure, procedure, and rules were established for the first joint army-navy ministry (the air force was later included).

The Defense Ministry can be viewed from several angles as a basic component of military responsibility to civilian government in post-1932 Chile. The combining of service ministries allows a single figure to serve as chief administrative official. One way to gauge the degree of civilian control or the amount of military influence is to see whether that minister is a civilian or a military man. If the minister is a civilian, military influence is probably not heavy or well organized. If he is an officer, even a retired officer, chances are the military's influence, or the need for military support in a particular situation, is considerable. The majority of defense ministers in Chile since 1932 have been civilians.[4] My conversations with about fifty Chilean military figures have made it clear that for several reasons Chilean military opinion was favorable to civilian defense ministers, at least until 1973.

Civilian ministers represented the political plurality in that they were appointed by the president and served as his pleasure. They may not have been from the president's own party but they represented parties or coalitions that supported the administration, or they may have been independent minded enough to put partisan views aside in ministerial service.[5] The 1925 constitutional changeover revived cabinet responsibility to the chief executive, whereas from 1891 to 1925 the cabinet had been responsible to Congress. Responsibility to the president meant that the military was normally independent of parliamentary power struggles. The link to the president was the stronger link; in Chile the president was the elected representative of a plurality of voters, so the military was more closely connected to the populace. Here again we must consider the cumulative effects of this phenomenon, or at least the belief in it, over four decades.

Some civilian ministers have been uncontroversial figures chosen for their administrative ability, some have been political lightweights chosen to emphasize the military's subservient position,[6] some have been distinguished figures appointed to accentuate respect for the military,[7] and some have been civilians who were popular with military men.[8] Emilio Bello exemplified the last two types. So did Juan de Dios Carmona, Eduardo Frei's first defense minister. Salvador Allende's first defense minister was a well-liked, elderly former military-school instructor. In the 1940s and during the 1958–64 term of Jorge Alessandri, defense ministers were less distinguished. Carlos Ibáñez (1952–58) clearly used political confidants, officers, and retired officers to gain military support for his wobbly administration. This tactic did not work for Ibáñez.

From the military standpoint civilian ministers were preferable primarily because they were not officers. Simplistic as this principle may seem, it was a significant ingredient in the maintenance of civilian hegemony. Between 1924 and 1932 the ministers of war were military men. This was precisely the period in which the military was politically involved and during which there were numerous purges and disciplinary actions. A civilian minister might lack expertise or be overly involved in partisan politics, but he still appeared preferable to survivors of the professional holocaust of 1931–32.

Interservice rivalries play a part in the preference for civilian ministers. Navy officers have indicated unanimously that they have not wanted an army officer as defense minister. As the air force developed and became independent of army control, air officers have been of like mind. Army officers might be insulted if an admiral were appointed defense minister. Even within the army, branch rivalries preclude cabinet appointments; a cavalry officer, for example, would not be popular with infantry, artillery, or engineers officers.

So, except under crisis conditions, officers state, they prefer that a civilian be in charge of the Defense Ministry. At the same time, the "prestige profile" of most civilian defense ministers has been low; even their offices are less impressive than those of general staff officers. They do not have internal authority over the army. Their own appointments are based on recommendations made by the general staff. The officer corps retains a certain insulation that effectively buffers civilian administrative control.

The relatively low prestige of defense ministers—compared, say, with their counterparts in Interior or Foreign Relations—served two purposes between 1932 and 1970. It assured the high command that a civilian with clout would not wield widespread powers, and it indicated to the high command (at certain times when an administration felt it necessary) that the military was not an administration's prime concern. The latter attitude, of course, could be a source of disgruntlement to the military but was mitigated by the lack of internal authority of civilians over professional affairs. In short, the military was to a large degree left alone to manage professional affairs within the civilian-dominated polity.

Civilian authority over the armed forces was buttressed further by the military's acceptance of the joint command principle. This principle—that effective administration and application of modern military science, tactics, strategy, and logistics is best realized through joint operations and administration—was transposed to the classical administrative sphere. In the early 1930s, without realizing its significance, Chile adopted a ministerial apparatus that would theoretically foster the principle of joint command and joint operations. The high commands are physically together in one building. The main center for naval operations is, of course, at Valparaíso, and air headquarters is more closely associated with airfields than with downtown Santiago, but ministerial level operations go on in the capital. The fact that the infighting, rivalries, and instability of 1931 and 1932 forced the combined ministry issue cannot be overemphasized. That civilian authority over the military was sometimes only a balancing act goes without saying, but that authority is nonetheless based heavily on the existence of the Defense Ministry and the variables within and around it.

The Mechanics of Civil-Military Relations: The Army Commander in Chief[9]

It is the constitutional prerogative of the Chilean president to appoint the commander in chief of each service. He may theoretically select any senior officer for this position. Normally he selects the senior general or admiral, but if he chooses another officer those officers senior to the man he chooses tender their resignations. Thus the choice of commander in chief can be an effective method of cleaning house, moving a political ally up to the top spot, or placating dissidents without resorting to blatant interference. In the high ranks a general's connection with troop commanders is based on personality as well as chain of command. Division generals in the ministry have well-earned prestige, but they are also vulnerable because they are cut off from garrisons.

The army's commander in chief is therefore the key man. He is selected on the basis of ability, personality, seniority, and reliability. He must be a senior officer, and he must be able to maintain discipline. Prior to 1973 he had to be committed to civilian control, such as it was. In recent times the greatest controversies regarding who should be commander in chief came after the reelection of the old war-horse, Carlos Ibáñez, in 1952. Ibáñez's meddling with army officers did not gain him the support of the whole officer class but only that of a small number of politically ambitious officers.

In the 1930s Alessandri chose his commanders on the basis of reliability and ability. His first commander in chief was General Vignola, the civilista from the northern desert. General Oscar Novoa Fuentes succeeded Vignola in 1933. Between them Alessandri, Bello, and Novoa established the formal and informal guidelines for Chilean civil-military relations after 1932.

Oscar Novoa was forty-seven years old in 1933, young for a

commander in chief. A member of the Escuela class of 1904, he had toiled nearly thirty years as a competent, uncontroversial artillery officer. He was far down the roster of artillery officers during most of his career and rose partially because of retirements and purges in 1931 and 1932. He was a dedicated soldier with a very strict sense of discipline and obedience.

Novoa considered the military episodes of the 1920s and early 1930s detrimental to the institution and ultimately to Chile. He did not protest against the political affairs of 1924 and 1925 or later, because to do so would have been undisciplined. His garrison duties came first. In this sense, then, he was one of those professionals whose tacit approval of the conduct of political officialdom was based on a very narrow concept of professionalism and an institutionally oriented concept of self-protection and perpetuation. Novoa was in no way politically ambitious, and he viewed the military as an agent of defense and foreign policy. He was a stern (though personally warm) career officer, untainted by any association with the political officers of 1924–32, dedicated to military subservience to civilian authority for the benefit of the institution and likewise to military insulation from civilian influence over internal professional affairs. Like Bello, Novoa was in ideal man for the job, able, reliable, and uncontroversial.

He was promised by Alessandri and Bello before he accepted the job of commander in chief that civilians would not interfere in professional matters and that he would be given a free hand to deal with political officers, insubordinates, and breakers of discipline, whatever their political leanings, if any. In return he personally guaranteed that anyone involved in plots or conspiracies or who appeared to have inordinate political connections would be punished or dismissed from the officer corps. Gone were the days of reassignments. Circulars went out from Novoa's office informing all officers of the new order of things.

No army is ever entirely free of political officers, but there were remarkably few of them in the Chilean army of early 1934. Indeed, by the end of 1932 not one name connected with the 1924–32 period appeared on the army list for 1933.[10] Normal retirements of officers who had not achieved a certain rank by a certain age or after a stipulated number of years in service allowed younger officers to move up. This meant that, precisely when civilians were reestablishing their hegemony, the higher levels of the officer corps were being populated by men with more future years at high rank facing them. Generals and colonels were comparatively younger between 1933 and 1938 than they were between 1920 and 1927 or 1927 and 1932. The average age for generals between 1933 and 1938 was nearly that for majors and lieutenant colonels between 1920 and 1927 and for colonels between 1927 and 1932. Novoa's age, forty-seven, was the average age for generals.

Thus another of the political motivations of the 1920s was removed. Novoa assured the officer class that political connections would not earn promotions but that dedication, special studies, seniority, and fiscal realities would. The fact that Alessandri kept his word, that Bello proved a skillful administrator and Novoa a reliable disciplinarian, made Chile's financial situation more bearable for the officer class, for it did become necessary to reduce expeditures for armaments, equipment, and military construction, as well as to maintain low salary levels during the 1930s.

The restoration of military subservience by Alessandri, Bello, and Novoa was of long-range importance, but it might not have been accomplished without the use of a counterpoise: the Milicia Republicana (Republican Militia or White Guard). Just as Chile had had a citizen's militia ostensibly ready to act if the military continued its political activity one hundred years earlier, so did Chile in the 1930s have a civilian group ready to act against a resurgence of military political interest. But the Republican Militia reflected the temper of the early 1930s just as socioeconomic issues and political decisions did. The militia was a decidedly rightist group, determined to fight Marxism as well as militarism.

Civilianism with a Vengeance: The Republican Militia, 1932–36[11]

The Republican Militia had been established as a shock-troop organization during the early days of the Socialist Republic by Julio Schwartzenberg and Eulogio Sánchez Errázuriz for the purpose of restoring civilian constitutional government and preventing a Communist take-over. Militia members trained in small cadres on private property outside the capital and had attempted to maintain secrecy. But the military and Socialist Republic leaders knew of its existence;

hence the army's continual fear of civil disorder during the winter of 1932. Blanche ordered an investigation of the militia's activity in September, but after his resignation the inquiry was dropped and the militia surfaced as a semisecret organization, known to exist but not to what extent.

Nearly two thousand men participated in maneuvers on October 9, 1932,[12] which caused consternation in the army and among leftists, for despite public statements to the contrary, the militia did not appear at all to be a nonpartisan group. Landowners, businessmen, professionals, and students belonged, but there were few workers in the militia ranks. Men such as Alessandri's nephew Gustavo; Luis Altamirano, son of the junta chief of 1924–25; and Domingo Durán, justice and education minister in 1933 were militia leaders. Gustavo Ross, Alessandri's finance minister, was a major financial contributor and helped in organization. Alessandri openly supported the militia and allowed surplus army equipment to be channeled to its members. Conservative and Liberal legislators publicly praised it as a patriotic citizens' group devoted to the defense of the Constitution.

Others, however, saw it as a Fascist-leaning goon squad; many of its members wore Hitler-style mustaches and approximately 85 percent of its marching members in a May 7, 1933, display were fair-haired. The Partido Nacista of Jorge González von Marees, formed in late 1932, ultimately ordered its members to withdraw from the militia, but the stigma of fascism did not leave the White Guard.[13] Nacis, Socialists, and Communists denounced the militia, Conservatives, Liberals, and Radicals supported it. Obviously, those in favor of change feared the militia, while defenders of the civilian status quo in the early 1930s supported it.

The army firmly opposed its existence, but to no avail.[15] It was demobilized only in July 1936, after four years of controversial existence. Whatever its real purposes, the militia did serve as a counterpoise to the military for the four years immediately following the deep involvements of 1932. Until 1936 it served as a threat to the left; probably fortunately for Chile, it was no longer in existence when Radicals, Socialists, Communists, and Nacis coalesced in the Popular Front for the 1938 presidential elections.

The dissolution of the militia was fortunate for the reestablishment and maintenance of military subservience to civilian authority. The best thing that Novoa could say about the militia was that it was a "necessary evil." Rumors constantly circulated in Santiago and the provincial towns from 1933 to 1936 that the army was preparing a golpe, a petition, or a power play because of its opposition to and fear of the militia. Bello, Vignola, and Novoa held the line, however, and squelched all possibilities of army memoranda, petitions, open letters, or manifestos. They also took preventive action against conspiracies, both during and after the existence of the militia. For example, a plot led by retired captain Alejandro Lazo in 1936 to kidnap Alessandri, Bello, and Novoa never got off the ground.[16] Lazo supposedly represented non-Marxist leftists but probably represented only Ibañistas.

The navy's attitude toward the militia differed from the army's. In a statement of May 19, 1933, the navy described the militia as a worthy citizen's group dedicated "to the conservation of the nation's institutions"; thus the navy established itself as a supporter of civilian government.[17] The situation of the conservative navy would have been quite different if, for example, the left had won the elections of 1932 with a Grove or a Lafferte, or if Socialists and Communists had gained control of Congress in the parliamentary elections of 1932. A citizens' militia supporting that kind of regime would not have been looked upon by the Admiralty or by the traditional parties as being dedicated "to the conservation of the nation's institutions." Furthermore, army anticommunism might have led the high command to reassert itself politically. (We can only wonder what Novoa's position would have been.)

In fact, the army was not only insulated but isolated. Few army leaders welcomed the drift to the right under Alessandri in the 1930s; by 1936 Alessandri governed with support from Conservatives and Liberals, not Radicals. Most military writers agree that oligarchy had made a comeback. But even fewer officers favored Marxism after 1932. The Radical middle ground was not politically fertile, and most Radicals were antimilitary, but ideologically the Liberal-Radical-Democrat programs were attractive to progressive and moderate military men. The Chilean Army was not tied politically to the aristocracy, the left, or even the middle-sector parties. The rightist Republican Militia alienated the army, and the army had nowhere to go for civilian support in the event of a political power play. Until 1973 civil-military relations were administrative and formal in one sense, social in another (based on family kinship and social origins), but they were not political.

Opposition to Alessandri:
Political Renaissance for Ibáñez and Grove[18]

The Socialists and Communists were in the opposition from the outset of Alessandri's second term. Emergency powers granted to the presidency in April 1933 were used for a year to jail agitators, suspend constitutional guarantees, censor the press, and restrict public political meetings. Alessandri used them primarily against Socialists and Communists in the name of defense of the Constitution and "the nation's institutions," order, and stability. He had the Republican Militia to rely on if emergency powers were not enough.

Significantly, the omnipresent but hardly dangerous Grove won a Senate seat while serving a deportation term in southern Chile, dramatically illustrating Alessandri's use of emergency powers without obvious justification; the ability of the political system to function, allowing a confined "enemy of the state" to stand for parliament, win, and take the seat; and the extent to which constitutional government was restored. Grove was freed the minute his election became official.

The Alessandri government's economic policies from 1933 to 1937 are comparable to those of the Justo and Ortiz administrations in Argentina from 1932 to 1940: economic recovery through a return to former trade patterns, austerity, renegotiation of debts, new loans, and fiscal conservatism in the area of government activities. These policies and measures helped to restore the fiscal integrity of the state but did but little for the financial betterment and security of the majority of Chileans.[19] By 1937 Chile's credit was again established because the budget was nearly balanced, but the currency continued to slip in value. Inflation had not been curbed, and the economy was not expanding dramatically. Fewer people were unemployed than in 1932, but there were still more mouths to feed. Radicals and some Democrats (now Democráticos) broke with Alessandri in 1934, making it plain that his was a Liberal-Conservative administration.

By late 1937 Radicals, Democráticos, Socialists, Communists, and the major syndicates agreed to unite in opposition to the obvious candidacy of Gustavo Ross, autocrat, currency speculator, and Alessandri's finance minister and close confidant. The Popular Front was born, and it would have the sympathy of the army high command, not necessarily for ideological reasons, but because it would represent the will of the majority (and because the high command would object heatedly to Alessandri's use of troops to quell labor disputes in 1936, 1937, and early 1938). Furthermore, Alessandri and the groups he represented (or who supported him) were by no means popular with the army, owing to the militia and the budget slashes.

Another basic component of post-1932 Chilean civil-military relations was about to be tested: the army's respect for the democratically expressed will of the majority. We need not dwell here on the history of the Popular Front, except for one aspect: the army's commitment to respect for the Constitution and for the aforementioned will of Chilean voters. This commitment, forged by Bello and Novoa, was reinforced in 1938 when the army unwillingly became involved in political conflict. What in some Latin American countries would surely have resulted in military resentment and perhaps a golpe, in Chile served in 1938 to convince military leaders that they had no true political friends in the civilian sector and that noninvolvement was better than political action.

The same men who had fostered involvement in the 1920s bore the responsibility for committing the army to noninvolvement in 1938. This time the cast of characters for a near civil-military tragedy included Alessandri, Grove, and Ibáñez. Ibáñez was back in Chile in early 1938, the darling of the Chilean Naci Party and affiliated groups. His champion was the recently forcibly retired inspector general of artillery and railroads, Colonel Tobías Barros Ortiz.

Barros had always been close to Ibáñez but had not been intimately enough involved in 1924–32 affairs to be purged or considered politically dangerous. But by 1937, his political activities in promoting the candidacy of the "General of Victory" were too much for the high command.[20] Barros's forced retirement in December 1937 angered many professional officers. They blamed Alessandri, for they considered the move a political one, yet they grew wary of Ibáñez for causing such a move. Barros simply continued his campaign as a civilian, and Ibáñez was not without influential support from workers, intellectuals, retired military personnel, and political independents of an authoritarian mind.

Former air commodore Grove had few links left with the military but nevertheless presented the military with a dilemma. If his Socialists should gain power in 1938, what would happen? Another Socialist Republic, military involvement, disorder, conspiracies, and more buzzing of the presidential palace, or another "Creole *Potem-*

kin"? Few officers thought well of their former colleague, his Marxist rhetoric, or his civilian supporters. But they did not look with disfavor on the promises and hopes of Socialists per se.

Alessandri, through Bello and Novoa, had restored civilian hegemony in civil-military relations, but he had not done it without causing army men to grumble. Cuts in expenditures, "professional stagnation," the militia, strike-breaking activities, and the forced retirement of Barros and a few other officers all contributed to army discontent in the 1930s. The obvious political turn to the right, Alessandri's attempts to justify his actions toward Barros (he violated his own promise not to meddle with the army by repeatedly speaking directly to officers, and in effect asking them to support him, the Constitution, and democracy in 1938), and fears that the army high command would help Ross in the election turned many officers against Alessandri. Alessandri's meddling by any other name was still meddling. During the first eight months of 1938, life was by no means easy for Chilean army officers.

The 1938 Putsch:
A Tragic Boost for the Popular Front
and Civilianism[21]

On Sunday, September 4, 1938, Chilean Nacis and other Ibáñez supporters staged a victory march commemorating the fourteenth anniversary of the 1924 military movement. The march was orderly; participation was enthusiastic but controlled. The next day, however, Chileans witnessed still another of the bizarre episodes connected with the Alessandri-Ibáñez-Grove civil-military triangle, the struggle between authoritarianism and democracy. Just after midday gunfire broke out in downtown Santiago. Naci youths had occupied the University of Chile complex—two and a half blocks from La Moneda, one long block from the Defense Ministry—and the Social Security Building, just across the central plaza from La Moneda. A Creole putsch had begun.

The General of Victory surrendered to the Infantry School commandant, requesting protective custody; he said he knew nothing of what was transpiring in downtown Santiago, and he was probably right. Government forces now surrounded the Nacis in the university. The rebels surrendered and were induced to march to the Social

Security Building. Used as shields by their carabinero captors, they were forced to assemble inside the building.

"*¡Mátenlos a todos! ¡Que no quede ningún vivo!*" (Kill them all! Let there be no survivors!), was the command given by carabineros commandant General Humberto Arriagada to his subordinates. Who gave the initial order? Later testimony by Arriagada placed the blame on Alessandri, but also indicated that Arriagada thought the putsch was to be accompanied by an army golpe![22] Sixty-two youths died that day, no matter who gave the order or what was the involvement of Carlos Ibáñez and the Chilean military.

The September 5 putsch had several effects. First, it made the Naci-Ibáñez candidacy (until that time a serious candidacy and a real threat to Popular Front possibilities) untenable. The General of Victory and all those associated with him became political pariahs. Ibáñez and Naci leader González told their followers to vote for Pedro Aguirre Cerda, the Popular Front leader. Second, the military —in particular, the army—was severely jolted. We still do not know just what would have happened had troop commanders pronounced on September 5; although they did not do so, they may have been involved in the affair. Investigations indicated that a number of retired officers backed out along with Ibáñez and that there were strong rumors of some kind of political action in the major garrisons throughout Chile. Finally, Alessandri and Ross came out worst of all, given their efforts to gain the presidency for the latter and the stake Liberals and Conservatives had in winning this presidential election. As objectionable as were the Nacis, the summary execution of sixty-two young citizens turned opinion against the Alessandri administration. Never before had Santiago seen such a bloodbath or such a bitter campaign.

On October 25 the Front candidate, Aguirre, won the popular vote, 222,720 (50.3 percent) to 218,609 (49.4 percent) for Ross. Aguirre's greatest margins of victory were in the desert North and in Santiago. Ross carried most of the populous Central Valley. Had Ross carried Santiago (a distinct possibility, were it not for the September 5 executions) or had he done better in the capital city itself, he would have won, and the Chilean right would have carried on. Congress confirms presidential elections in Chile and is not technically bound to observe slim margins, so Aguirre's victory was no sure thing.[23]

On the day following the election rumors began to circulate. Would the army step into the tense situation? Would Alessandri use the army to force a vote for Ross in Congress? Would Alessandri convince General Novoa and General Arriagada to use the army and carabineros to maintain presidential extraordinary powers granted by Congress after September 5? Or would the president himself, given the situation, seek to remain in La Moneda and continue to govern through extraordinary measures past his mandate?

The army was the key to the presidency in 1938. Six years after Alessandri had begun his work to restore military subservience to civilian control, the military was still important; the civilian leaders of the Chilean political system were still unable to agree on the succession to legitimate authority! Ross appealed to the high command (through friends, for Ross would have never soiled his hands by dealing with army officers himself) to declare the election void, supervise a recount, or, at the very least, investigate electoral irregularities. He was willing to try anything. Alessandri did discuss the merits of continuing in La Moneda until new elections could be held. He too was willing to try anything. But Aguirre's was the greatest pressure. He had labor, the unemployed, the Radicals, the Socialists, the Communists, and the Fascists. He had won the election. His advisers convinced General Arriagada that if Alessandri or Ross were in the presidential palace, the carabineros would be blamed for the September 5 massacre, that if the army and carabineros participated in an attempt to subvert the popular will there would be real trouble, and that if they did not support the majority candidate they would be punished severely when and if Aguirre took office. They made Arriagada "an offer he could not refuse." They "offered him nothing less than his life," in the words of Ismael Edwards Matte, the man who made the offer.[24]

Arriagada wisely accepted, thus getting himself and other high military leaders off the hook. On November 11, he sent a letter to Julio Bustamante, the intendant of Santiago Province, in which he bluntly told Bustamante that he repudiated any complicity and all plans to use force to impose Ross or suppress demonstrations for Aguirre. The votes had been tallied, he said, and Aguirre was the winner; only Ross's partisans and Alessandri's had failed to recognize this. "Triumph," he went on, "belongs legitimately to Pedro Aguirre Cerda. Not to recognize this would not only be trampling on the popular will . . . but would plunge the country into a bloody revolution which the carabineros would not be able to contain, owing to the magnitude of popular involvement and because repression would be unjust."[25] General Novoa published a concurring letter, and the next day Ross renounced all claims to the presidency. On December 14 Congress declared Aguirre president of Chile. Ten days later he took office.

Chilean Civilianism 1938–70:
An Interpretation[26]

With the inauguration of Pedro Aguirre Cerda, the Chilean Army withdrew again from any overt connection with politics. The withdrawal of 1938 was in a sense the culmination of a series of advances and withdrawals that had begun in the 1920s. These actions had resulted in many changes of leadership and ultimately in a firm tradition of civilian acceptance of access to legitimate executive authority via popular vote, free from manipulation of that popular vote in Congress and free from military subservience to or favoritism toward any specific Chilean political group. Repudiation of any military political involvement between 1932 and 1938 was no longer an issue. Circumstances in 1938, as well as means adopted in the previous six years, made this so. And for the next three decades the strength and flexibility of civilian institutions kept it so.

Between 1938 and 1970 civil-military relations in Chile were primarily relations between a sociopolitical system and a professional institution within that system. The lack of a military presence in the national decision-making process is unique by Latin American standards. Nowhere else in Latin America—save Mexico, Uruguay, and, to an extent, Colombia and Costa Rica—has the military been so conspicuous in recent times by its absence from overt political deliberation. The strength of the party system and governmental institutions and the ability of socioeconomic interest groups—syndicates, for example—to work with and within the system precluded an institutional stance by the armed forces on issues of national import.

Much of the credit for the Chilean military's comparatively apolitical position is due to civilian leaders. Even the much-maligned Alessandri and Ross deserve some credit here, for they did refrain from a desperate appeal to arms in their final hour of defeat. Aguirre and his wobbly Popular Front (shattered by the Moscow-Berlin Pact and only patched together during World War II) initiated fourteen years of center-left national administrations which weathered social, economic, and political storms that might have sunk other Latin American ships of state. The rush of military interventions of the 1940s (Argentina, 1943; Brazil, 1945; Peru, 1948; Venezuela, 1945 and 1948; El Salvador, 1944; Guatemala, 1945) did not spread to Chile, and the Radical-led center-left held tenaciously to power until 1952. Their efforts in expansion and diversification of the economy, in social welfare and labor legislation, while barely radical, proved sufficient to maintain the tradition of civilianism so desired after 1932.

In 1952, when the popular will was again expressed as a threat to the incumbents, there was no fear that the administration would use military involvement in order to stay in office. The Radicals under Gabriel González Videla (1946–52) no longer dominated the center-left. Their policies were shopworn and shortsighted. Heavy government financial obligations for pensions, investment, welfare, education, and economic diversification could not be fulfilled. González's break with Marxists and outlawing of the Communist Party during 1947 and 1948 deprived the Radicals of much labor-left support in 1952. Ibáñez, now the "General of Hope," swept into office promising to restore the "good old days." He failed, of course, and at his lowest point even he could not entice the military to support him.

While Ibáñez was trying to get aid from men in uniform to intimidate his opposition, generals were toppling elsewhere in Latin America—Perón in Argentina, Odría in Peru, Rojas Pinilla in Colombia, and Pérez Jiménez in Venezuela, as well as the authoritarian civilian populist Getúlio Vargas in Brazil. Indeed, there are parallels between Ibáñez and Vargas. Ibañista populism proved no more successful in Chile than did Vargas's in Brazil. Ibáñez could no more function in a strictly constitutional framework than could Vargas. By 1958 Ibáñez, like Vargas before him, seemed an authoritarian anachronism. To the military, Ibáñez was more an embarrassment than a sympathetic friend in the presidential palace.

The career of Ibáñez, his authoritarian populism, and a brief resurgence of military political activity came to an end in 1958. Needless to say, his successor, Jorge Alessandri Rodríguez, was no comfort to the military. He had learned his lessons well from his father, but he did not become involved in military affairs. Military thought concerning Alessandri was mixed between 1958 and 1964: "He is a dignified but narrow-minded man." "He is no friend of the military, but he leaves us alone." "He will do nothing for the masses, but they and we respect him." "He has always hated us, but we bear him no ill will, despite his name." "He is a father image to Chileans." "He could never have been elected if his name were not Alessandri." "He represents stability, moderation, dignity, decency, and disarmament."

Alessandri promised less than Ibáñez, and although he accomplished few dramatic projects—a weak agrarian reform, Chile's first effective income tax legislation, and other fiscal measures—he did prove an able administrator. A Liberal, he was probably the last president of Chile to come from the traditional parties of the right.

Jorge Alessandri's successor, Eduardo Frei, was the first Christian Democrat to be elected president. His grand schemes for agrarian reform, public housing, Chileanization of industry, utilities, and mining, internal capitalization, and restructuring of the economy and the state were promising, but his administration was hard pressed to show their results after six years. The value of the Chilean peso had continued to drop after World War II. By the time Alessandri left office it had been renamed the escudo (1,000 pesos = 1 escudo), and had tumbled again so that 1 escudo was worth only one-quarter of an American dollar.

Chile's immense mineral wealth had produced little in the way of real progress despite the efforts of the Radicals, Ibáñez, Jorge Alessandri, Frei, and the Christian Democrats (PDC). Yet through all this political change and continued economic difficulty, the military did not intervene. In an extremely divided and fragile political milieu no one needed to lean on military support. Despite the fact that only once after 1938 did a presidential candidate win an outright majority of the popular vote, there was no necessity for the military to protect Chilean democratic procedure. In 1938, 1952, 1958, 1964, and 1970 the incumbent party or parties were defeated; the fact that only between 1965 and 1969 did an administration have the support of an outright majority in *one* house of Congress makes Chilean democratic procedure even more noteworthy.

As just noted, of the past four presidential elections the only one that resulted in a clear-cut majority victory was that of Eduardo Frei in 1964.

Tables 5–8 illustrate the extremely tenuous yet civilian-controlled election pattern:[27]

Carlos Ibáñez won a clear plurality but no majority in 1952, yet some of his admirers and military supporters believed that Radicals in Congress would secure the election of Matte, Arturo Alessandri's

TABLE 5
Presidential Election Returns, 1952

Candidate	Vote	Percent of Total
Carlos Ibáñez del Campo (Agrarian Labor, National Ibañista Movement)	446,439	46.8
Arturo Matte Larraín (Liberal, Conservative)	265,357	27.8
Pedro Enrique Alfonso Barrios (Radical, administration)	190,360	19.9
Salvador Allende Gossens (Socialist, Marxist)	51,975	5.5

son-in-law, by throwing their votes to him in return for control of the cabinet. This did not occur, however, and Ibáñez was inaugurated. There was no military involvement at this time. The largest single bloc of the electorate was not defrauded, and regular succession was maintained.

In 1958 Jorge Alessandri won a plurality, but less of a plurality in number and percent than had Ibáñez six years earlier. He was confirmed only with congressional votes by Radicals and others. Allende, the FRAP (Frente de Acción Popular) candidate, showed a remarkable gain in six years, but was set back by the independent Marxist Zamorano. Had Allende been the sole Marxist candidate he could have received nearly 400,000 votes! (But in that event Alessandri would probably have won numerous Radical and Christian Democrat votes.) It is conceivable that Allende could have won. Nevertheless, Alessandri, with merely 31.6 percent of the vote, was a

TABLE 6
Presidential Election Returns, 1958

Candidate	Vote	Percent of Total
Jorge Alessandri Rodríguez (Liberal, Conservative)	389,909	31.6
Salvador Allende Gossens (FRAP, Socialist, Communist, with left support)	356,493	28.9
Eduardo Frei Montalva (Christian Democrat)	255,769	20.7
Luis Bossay (Radical)	192,077	15.6
Antonio Zamorano (independent, Marxist)	41,304	3.3

minority president, able to govern only with the support from other parties than those that had supported his candidacy.

Frei won an outright majority in 1964, the first candidate to do so since Pedro Aguirre Cerda. His total vote was the largest ever received in the election with the greatest voter turnout in Chilean history. He was supported also by Conservatives and Liberals who had little faith in the Radical Durán. Confirmation by Congress was truly a mere formality. Allende nonetheless increased his total vote dramatically and his percentage of the vote significantly. There was no question here of the need for military involvement in assuring victory.

TABLE 7

Presidential Election Returns, 1964

Candidate	Vote	Percent of Total
Eduardo Frei Montalva (Christian Democrat)	1,409,012	56.0
Salvador Allende Gossens (FRAP, with leftist support)	977,902	38.9
Julio Durán Neumann (Radical, Liberal, Conservative)	125,233	5.0

Though nearly two-thirds of the electorate voted for some form of radical change, Allende's percentage of the vote in 1970 actually decreased slightly. Tomic was a talkative but unsatisfactory candidate who, unlike Frei, did not attract votes from the right. Alessandri was the undoing of the PDC. He still represented much to Chileans; he pulled votes from Tomic but not enough to win. Allende's confirmation was not a foregone conclusion, and, as we shall see, despite Allende's promises to govern within the Constitution and to respect the integrity of the armed forces, military involvement became a

TABLE 8

Presidential Election Returns, 1970

Candidate	Vote	Percent of Total
Salvador Allende Gossens (Unidad Popular, Marxist, and non-Marxist left)	1,075,616	36.2
Jorge Alessandri Rodríguez (National Party: Conservatives and Liberals)	1,036,278	34.9
Radomiro Tomic Romero (Christian Democrat)	824,849	27.8

much-discussed possibility. The fact that the army did not step in to preclude a minority Marxist from becoming president is proof of the military's desire to remain aloof from regular constitutional procedures. Nevertheless, the minority qualities of the Allende administration would figure significantly in civil-military elections, 1970–73. The 1970 electoral contest was the closest Chile has come to military participation at election time since 1938, and similar circumstances in virtually all other Latin American countries would have provoked such participation.

Much of the foregoing has described conditions and attitudes, and some of it has been explanatory in nature. What do the conditions tell us beyond the obvious fact that in Chilean crisis situations, some as serious and dramatic as those elsewhere (at election time, for example), the military did not menace civilian control of politics? We have already stated that until 1970–73 those tendencies that other Latin American armies have moved to thwart (or promote) were either absent from Chile, contained by the civilian system, or thwarted or promoted by it. The likes of organized labor, Marxism, unwillingness to accept defeat by incumbents, uncontrollable violence, and abuse of power were already contained by the system; Marxism was accepted as the legitimate expression of socioeconomic opinion, the executive-legislative balance was a jealously guarded tradition, syndicates were politicized and coopted, and violence was contained. Other tendencies conversely were alien to the system. Incumbents did not rely on military support to stay in power or risk thwarting the plurality; they doggedly observed normal procedures. All this tended to mitigate the disastrous effects of economic failure, corruption, malfeasance, and other significant causes of military involvement in Latin American politics.

The fact that politically articulate Chileans are more heavily politicized and patronage-wise than other Latin Americans also led them to eschew the resort to military support. Ultimately, however, these conditions and attitudes indicate that the military, especially the army, had no desire or reason to involve itself in civilian affairs or to have civilians meddle with its corporate integrity. But this was true only as long as the institution was guaranteed its autonomy and a reasonable share of the budget, as long as it was not drawn into extraprofessional matters, and as long as the Constitution was observed by all Chileans. Let us now examine military noninvolvement during the last three decades in preparation for an appraisal of civil-military relations as of 1970–73 and the coming to power of a Marxist administration in Chile.

Military Interest in Politics, 1938–52
Minimal but Present[28]

There are certainly instances of military political involvement (as opposed to action) after 1938. In none of these instances, however, did anything resembling an institutional stance develop, uniting enough of the officer corps to make it function as an overt pressure group. The Popular Front, though an expression of the popular majority, came under the close scrutiny of anti-Communist military men during its early months. The new Aguirre government struggled, like most of its predecessors, with a hostile Congress; Communist leaders began making demands on Aguirre before he was inaugurated. This political infighting placed the administration between extremes, an unenviable position, as Alessandri could testify after his experiences of the 1920s. Prior to Communist withdrawal from the Front following the Moscow-Berlin Pact of 1939, some army leaders became alarmed by the Communists' demands, and memories of 1931–32 began to stir. Military Fascists plotted against the Aguirre administration, seeing it as a weak Weimar-type government unwittingly paving the way for a "red takeover."

One such military Fascist was General Ariosto Herrera Ramírez, scion of one of Chile's old, traditional military families. Herrera had made a name for himself participating in the government offensive against naval mutineers in Talcahuano in 1931. He was an outspoken anti-Communist. He had spent time in Italy as a military attaché in the 1930s, and there, reputedly, he fell under Mussolini's spell. In 1939 he was commandant of Division II in Santiago. With a group of anti-Communist junior officers, Herrera organized a golpe for June 9, 1939, just before the Communists finally withdrew from the Popular Front government. The plot was uncovered, the junior officers dismissed from the army, and Herrera, professing his innocence all the while, damning the government actions as political meddling, and appealing to all patriots to stand firm against the red menace, found himself a retired general. The communism issue received much play in the press for the duration of the affair.

The new Front government had not yet gained the strength

necessary to dominate the military without some effort. Herrera was a popular, able, prestigious and patriotic officer, and some officers of the Tacna infantry regiment (Division II, Santiago) protested his retirement on the grounds that no golpe attempt had occurred. They did not know that Herrera had treated with Conservative politicians and Ibañista-Fascist leaders.

Late in August Herrera talked with Tacna officers, and they told him they wanted him reinstated. Thereupon he sent for Ibáñez, who came to the Tacna barracks. Herrera foolishly talked of a golpe, but the Tacna officers demurred; they wanted him reinstated, to be sure, but they did not want to overthrow a constitutional regime—especially since by August the Communists were no longer associated with it! Herrera was apprehended; Ibáñez was advised to leave the barracks and the country, and did both. The Ariostazo, as this incident has been called, disintegrated.[29] World War II dimmed military support for Ibañista fascism, especially when Ibáñez became the rightist presidential candidate in the emergency presidential election in 1942.

The new president, Juan Antonio Ríos, relied on Commander in Chief Carlos Fuentes and a "group of selected officers" (Grupo de Oficiales Seleccionados, GOS) in high staff and command positions to keep the army neutral.[30] During the war Ríos pushed ahead with the industrialization and diversification schemes of his predecessor, thus allaying any possibility of military advocacy of economic modernization, so widespread in Argentina and Brazil. Steel, petroleum, public housing, communications, government involvement in industry, and utilities projects all got under way without military pressure.

But by 1946, copper stockpiles were sizable, prices were falling, agricultural production was still insufficient, and inflation was still rampant. Communist agitation began anew in the early campaigns of the Cold War. The new González Videla administration faced the Communist threat squarely, but also faced a revival of military fascism—now with Peronism east of the Andes as an example of the alternative to democracy.

In September 1948 President González got wind of a military golpe planned by retired general Ramón Vergara, another of the anti-Communist "winners of spurs" from 1931. Vergara, active and retired officers, and civilians (according to some, the Masons and their leaders!) belonging to Chilean Anticommunist Action (Accíon Chilena Anticomunista, ACHA) laid plans to force González to appoint a military cabinet, to suppress communism with brute force, and to stabilize the country through decree legislation and authoritarian rule. In the event that González refused to comply, he would be replaced with Ibáñez (shades of 1919!).

"The Pig's Feet Plot" (Complot de las Patitas de Chancho), so named because the plotters met frequently for drinks and food, was suppressed,[31] but, like the Ariostazo of 1939, it indicated the continued attraction of the military to fascism, a potential for civil-military accord on the issue of communism, the lasting power of Carlos Ibáñez, and a skeptical attitude on the part of army officers concerning the ability of liberal democracy to cope with some of Chile's socioeconomic realities. In addition, the example of Peronism was still omnipresent in the Cono Sur.

The fact remains, of course, that militarism, fascism, authoritarianism, and *línea dura* (hard-line) anticommunism did not appeal to great numbers of Chileans. Political leaders, labor leaders, businessmen, professionals, and the vast majority of the electorate stood with the Constitution, and for democracy. Neither the right nor the left would unite in support of a golpe. The outlawing of the Communist Party by virtue of the Law for Defense of Democracy in 1948 did not eliminate the Communists but effectively reduced their potential for legal political action. It was as much a response to civilian demands for the defense of democracy as to military pressure for anticommunist action.

Militarism Resurgent:
Ibáñez, PUMA, and La Línea Recta[32]

Still, military leaders were not unconscious of political issues. In 1952, Carlos Ibáñez, a respectable senator, became president. Supported by independents in the National Ibañista Movement and by the Agrarian Labor, National Christian, Popular Socialist, Doctrinaire Radical, and Women's parties, and (unofficially) the Communists, he handily defeated the Liberal Matte (Alessandri's son-in-law), the Radical Alfonso, and the Socialist Allende. Despite Ibáñez's victory at the polls, some military leaders feared that Congress would not confirm his election, and that a Radical-Liberal deal would be made, cheating independent voters and Ibáñez out of their victory.

Ibáñez's cry for an end to *politiquería* (low politics), corruption, waste, and featherbedding had to be assured. Order, discipline, patriotism, progress, and development could only come about with the restoration of Ibáñez, the man who had "done it all" between 1927 and 1931. Between his election and his confirmation and inauguration, a group of Santiago-based officers formed a lodge, PUMA (Por Un Mañana Auspicioso, For An Auspicious Future). The PUMAs vowed to secure the presidency for Ibáñez in the event of congressional chicanery. As events showed, they need not have worried; no one needed to emulate the 1938 positions of Arriagada and Novoa. Ibáñez's victory should have ended the affair, but it did not.

President Ibáñez selected a PUMA leader, Colonel Abdón Parra Urzúa as his minister of national defense (and later named him interior minister). By appointing Parra, Ibáñez embroiled himself in the worst complication of civil-military affairs in post-1932 Chile. He was correct in selecting his own military candidate for the ministry post; Alessandri had selected Novoa, Ríos had selected Fuentes. But Novoa and Fuentes had been generals. Parra was only a colonel; he was also a notorious conspirator and a critic of Chile's political system.

Officers senior to Parra resigned in protest at his appointment, and PUMAs moved into key positions. This, too, had happened before, but not with Ibáñez—the authoritarian, the plotter, the Fascist favorite son, the retired general—in office. When Parra was dismissed from the cabinet in 1954 at the insistence of Interior and Justice Minister Osvaldo Koch (Ibáñez's son-in-law), some army officers breathed a sigh of relief. Others saw the dismissal as evidence of civilian, congressional, and political party pressure on the chief executive and the army itself. The army was confused by Ibáñez's policies and by his vacillation. His antipolitical party line and appeal for order, discipline, stability, progress, development, and patriotism appealed to many officers. So did his promises of budget increases, pay raises, and fringe benefits. But other professionals saw him as a meddling anachronism, dangerous to discipline and military hierarchy. His acknowledged opponents saw him as a threat to the institution.

On February 28, 1955, President Ibáñez took tea with fifty-eight army officers at his home on Calle Dublé Almeyda. So began the brief but sensational history of La Línea Recta (The Straight Line). Straight Line officers proposed two things to their constitutional commander in chief: immediate retirement of all officers who would not swear loyalty to him, and, if necessary, army support for unconstitutional or emergency measures by Ibáñez to restore economic stability and social discipline. Just prior to the "Té Dublé Almeyda," four known Ibañista officers had retired—two colonels, two majors—as part of the annual retirement of officers passed over for promotion—not an alarming number considering fifteen colonels, eleven lieutenant colonels, and twenty majors in all were cut by the military qualification board. Just the same, the Ibañistas saw this as political interference. Ibáñez responded to his aggrieved guests' entreaties by personally intervening to retire several officers known to be critical of him and to reinstate his four uniformed supporters.

Chileans generally connect the Línea Recta with the PUMAs and even with the 1941–42 GOS—the Ramón Alvarez Goldsack and Escuela Militar–led group formed, as later investigation showed, to "study and analyze civil-military concomitances"—but these pre-1952 connections are based more on innuendo than on evidence. The Línea Recta set the army against itself in much the same way that the Altamirano-Alessandri-Ibáñez conflicts of 1924 and 1925 had politicized the institution. Ibáñez desperately wanted to control and use the movement, but he knew well the inherent dangers of meddling with the officer class. He tried to control Línea Recta through the high command, staff, and instructional officers. But some officers strenuously objected to pressure to join Línea Recta and to (1) swear an oath of loyalty to Ibáñez, (2) solemnly promise to serve Línea Recta unswervingly for six months, and (3) agree that "he who withdraws will be punished or liquidated."

Denunciations met with renunciations, retirements, and reassignments. A court martial resulted in the dismissal of several Línea Recta leaders from the army, and Ibáñez hesitated to intervene when the struggle became public knowledge. He washed his hands of the affair and in so doing lost the respect of Línea Recta and non–Línea Recta officers alike. He had meddled, manipulated, pulled strings, and betrayed. Even if he was a former general, an authoritarian, and a man of action, he was a politician in 1955 and hence, the officers believed, could not be trusted.

The Línea Recta was a significant phenomenon, for it indicated that some officers in the Chilean Army still harbored political ambitions. Its obvious philosophical linkages with GOS and PUMA ideas on military influence, socioeconomic questions, and implied support for civil-military political cooperation indicated continued military support for authoritarianism, or at least more vigorous national government, and military distrust of civilian politics. The Línea Recta is a fine example of the dangers faced by politicians in dealing with a "military support group," in interfering with military autonomy, and in playing politics through retirements and promotions.

Similarly, it presents an example of what an officer can expect if he openly favors a candidate or a particular chief executive, or if he seeks to exert military pressure through purging of the officer class and binding it to a civilian leader who is struggling for his political life. From the standpoint of civil-military relations, Ibáñez struggled for his political life after the scandal of Línea Recta and the violent antigovernment demonstrations of April 1957, in which the army had to be called in to quell the violence.

The Línea Recta did much to damage the army not only for the reasons just mentioned, but also because it was thought by many Chileans to be a latent manifestation of Peronism (military-style authoritarianism, not labor-left populism) at precisely the time Perón was losing his grip across the Andes. In the *Plan Línea Recta* (Santiago, 1955),[33] the influence of Peronism became sufficiently clear that the movement appeared to be more than just Chilean "military nationalism." References to austerity; progress; public welfare; the nonpartisan nature of the movement; social justice; economic development; the need to halt national political, social, and economic decay; dirty politics; the parasitic oligarchy and its corrupt policies; the plight of the working class; fiscal chicanery; international communism; abuses of power; and inflation (pp. 1–2) made it clear that Línea Recta was patriotic and progressive, but those references were framed in Justicialista rhetoric.

No one could complain of Línea Recta's motto, "A better Chile, forged by the best of Chileans, so that all Chileans live better," but a majority of both civilian and military leaders dissented from the idea that Línea Recta–Ibáñez authoritarianism was synonymous with "the best of Chileans." The Línea Recta plan of action called for more power for the executive branch; a version of the corporate state; outlawing of small political parties; suppression of legislative remuneration and its replacement by a per diem; censorship of publications; anticommunist legislation; wholesale reform of civil service job requirements; incorporation of more technicians into the civil service; reductions in size and fringe benefits of the bureaucracy and diplomatic corps; administrative reforms; no new small-business licenses for immigrants; coordination of fiscal, agricultural, mining, and labor policy in a ministry of economics; a national planning and research council; wholesale tax reform; price stabilization for consumer items; foreign exchange controls; currency reform; a minimum salary law; revised salary scales for public employees and laborers; more controls over foreign investment; maximum and minimum interest laws; decentralization of industry; suppression of private monopolies; agrarian reform; a massive highway construction program; subsidies for the national airline and merchant marine; reorganization of labor into "vertical syndicates of owners and workers by economic activity"; improved social security and medical services; low-cost public housing; rent controls; paid workers' vacations in government-financed resorts; suppression of the right to strike of utility and prime necessity item–producing workers; establishment of mandatory arbitration by the state; widening of obligatory military service to include compulsory labor on community improvement programs; civic and patriotic education in free public schools; more technical schools; military instruction in secondary schools; and a government-sponsored physical education program (pp. 2–5).

The *Plan Línea Recta* incorporated nearly all the professional military social, political, and economic attitudes applicable to Chile that have been present in recent South American military writings. The *Plan* reads very much like the *planes,* pronunciamentos, and *programas de gobierno* of military regimes from the time of Perón to the late 1960s in Argentina, Brazil, and Peru. The *Plan* smacked of authoritarianism, anticapitalism, and antidemocracy precisely when these were proving disastrous in Argentina and when Chileans were congratulating themselves on being democratic and lucky enough not to be ruled by an Odría, a Rojas Pinilla, a Stroessner, or, until 1954, a Vargas; it was thus an immediate conversation piece but never became more than that.

The *Plan* served primarily to reaffirm the views of most politicians and of most Chileans, political or not, that the military should be kept out of politics. For the *Plan* made it quite obvious that what Chilean military political thought did exist was directed against the political system. By the end of the Ibáñez administration, few Línea Recta officers remained in service, but many Línea Recta fellow travelers still served and still grumbled. Not until 1970, however, would anything so serious as Línea Recta develop in the army, despite the headlines, rumors, and hints of *"¡Golpe de estado inminente!"* appearing ad nauseam in Chilean tabloids.

A Brief Note on Budgetary Matters: Comparative Statistics[34]

We should determine at this point just how well or poorly the Chilean military has fared with regard to budget matters in recent years in comparison to the three most comparable South American countries. Leaving aside U.S. military technical advice and aid, which amounted to nearly 10 percent of total military expenditures, was consistently welcome (whereas other forms of advice seem to have made only limited impact), and resulted in new, modern equipment, the forces as a whole have not done badly by Latin American standards.

In 1940 military expenditures amounted to 2.5 percent of the Chilean Gross Domestic Product (GDP); in 1970, they constituted 3.3 percent of the GDP. Argentine military expenditures amounted to 2.3 percent in 1940 and 2.0 percent in 1970; Brazil's were 2.8 percent in 1947 and 2.0 percent in 1970. Peru devoted 2.2 percent of its GDP to military expenditures in 1942 and 3.3 percent by 1970. Colombia and Venezuela both failed to exceed 1.6 percent during this period.

Chile devoted 25.5 percent of total government expenditures to the armed forces in 1940, 13.0 percent in 1970. For Brazil the figures are 24.0 percent and 17.2 percent respectively; for Peru 21.2 percent and 17.2 percent respectively. Neither Colombia nor Venezuela exceeded 11.3 percent during these years. In U.S. dollar amounts—perhaps more immediately indicative than percentages of GDP or government expenditures—Chile spent $49 million in 1940 on the armed forces and $203 million in 1970 (the biggest increases coming under Ibáñez, 1952–58). Table 9 indicates armed forces expenditures for Argentina, Brazil, Peru, and Chile by percentage of budget and value in U.S. dollar equivalents for 1940, 1950, 1960, and 1970.

From these figures we can see that Chile has devoted a greater percentage of a modest GDP than Argentina and Brazil have of their larger GDPs to military expenditures in the years noted. Neither in 1940 nor in 1950 was Chile in last place in this category. In 1940 Chile devoted one-quarter of the budget to the armed forces, more than Argentina, Brazil, or Peru; a decade later only 17.9 percent of

TABLE 9

Comparative Military Expenditures in Argentina, Brazil, Chile, and Peru, 1940, 1950, 1960, and 1970

Country	% of GDP	% of Government Expenditure	$U.S. (millions)
1940			
Argentina	2.3	23.2	131
Brazil (1947)	2.8	24.0	171
Chile	2.5	25.2	49
Peru (1942)	2.2	21.2	18
1950			
Argentina	3.0	24.6	272
Brazil	2.3	26.8	233
Chile	2.4	17.9	64
Peru	2.6	20.0	43
1960			
Argentina	2.9	20.9	356
Brazil	2.0	20.7	381
Chile	3.4	15.6	135
Peru	2.1	14.7	58
1970			
Argentina	2.0	16.1	388
Brazil	2.0	17.2	792
Chile	3.3	13.0	203
Peru	3.3	17.2	145

Chile's budget went to the military, making it fourth on the list. By 1970 Chile used only 13 percent of the budget on the armed forces, less than Argentina, Brazil, or Peru. But in dollar expenditures Chile still held third place, still spending more money on the military than Peru.

It should be obvious that Argentina and Brazil, with greater GDPs and budgets, may use a smaller percentage of these on their armed forces but end up spending more in terms of cash outlay. In terms of percentage of its GDP and fiscal expenditures, Chile has by no means shortchanged the armed forces, or, specifically, the army, which, of course, receives a fluctuating lion's share of the defense budgetary appropriation—61.8 percent in 1940, 47.6 percent in 1950, 50.7 percent in 1960, and 43.3 percent in 1970.

Since 1950 the Chilean military has consistently received more financial support than the South American or Latin American average; only twice (in 1954 and 1962–65) has Chile been below these averages. In the last two decades, nevertheless, Chile has spent less of its fiscal budget on the military than the average South American or Latin American nation. Which indicator is more significant?

Percentage of fiscal expenditures is probably more significant, for this indicates what portion of a government's revenues is marked for defense, that is, where defense stands in relation to other priorities. On this basis, of the comparable South American powers—Argentina, Brazil, and Peru (and Colombia and Venezuela, as other major continental countries)—Chile ranks fourth in the postwar years. Argentina, Brazil, and Peru all consistently spent a greater percentage of their revenue on the military than Chile; Colombia and Venezuela spent less than Chile. Since 1955 the percentage of the budget spent for defense compared to percentages spent for education and social security shows steady decline; at the same time, nevertheless, the dollar value of Chilean defense has increased steadily. So, while more of the gross domestic product is devoted to defense and more dollars are spent on the armed forces, we must recognize that a steadily diminishing portion of the national budget goes for defense.

Only with respect to the latter indicator can the armed forces of Chile complain. Of course they can also complain about how the defense budget is divided and allotted, for while equipment prices rise, salaries did not keep pace with inflation until adjustments were made by the Allende government in 1971 and 1972. Further figures indicate other comparisons and contrasts with South American and Latin American armed forces. On a cost-per-man basis, Chile spent more than either Argentina, Brazil, or Peru during the period 1955–65 to maintain a 45,000 man army, and far less than Colombia or Venezuela to maintain their fighting forces. During the same years Chile had the fifth largest army, behind Argentina, Brazil, Peru, and Mexico. Between 1955 and 1965 the size of the Chilean Army remained more stable than those of Argentina (reduced between 1955 and 1965), Brazil (increased by over 100 percent), Colombia (increased more than three times, 1955–65), Peru (quadrupled 1955–65), and Venezuela (doubled 1955–65).

All of these figures are relative; they indicate much, but alone they prove nothing. The amount of U.S. aid, percentages of gross domestic product and budget expenditures, amount in U.S. dollars expended, cost per man, comparative size, and the like in no way serve as hard indicators of attitudes and opinions, of ideological stance, or of professionalism and its meanings. Moreover, sources vary widely on statistics, making conclusions based on statistics very risky indeed. Lack of financial support or too much money do not necessarily indicate subservience to civilian interest groups or propensity for political action—though U.S. aid has increased regularly before Chilean presidential elections (to keep the army happy?), and Ibáñez did increase military expenditures to gain army support. No, the fact that "Chilean colonels make only slightly more monthly than Venezuelan lieutenants," is not grounds for a golpe in Santiago. U.S. aid at election time does not "keep the army happy and out of politics." No numerical indicator or set of indicators is solely responsible for the contours of Chilean civil-military relations.

We must turn our attention now to the Chilean military's confrontation with that force which it temporarily tolerated in various forms in 1932 and 1938, began to react against in 1939, 1948, and 1955, and then allowed to take power constitutionally in 1970: Marxism. In the concluding chapter we will attempt to outline the military's sociopolitical situation and its ideology or official political stance in order to interpret its relations with the Popular Unity regime of Salvador Allende Gossens. We will conclude with a description of those factors directly involved in the deterioration of civil-military relations to the point of confrontation and golpe de estado, and with an analysis of just what the golpe of September 11, 1973, means to those relations.

12

Marxism and the Military, 1970–73

In October 1972 Chile was paralyzed by a truckers' strike when the government of Salvador Allende Gossens made moves to nationalize the trucking industry. Military men, including General Carlos Prats González, commander in chief of the army, accepted cabinet positions in an attempt to avert crisis. Prats, as interior minister, helped settle the strike, pacified the opposition, and then stepped down after supervising parliamentary elections in March 1973. A new strike of truckers broke out in July 1973, and taxi drivers and bus drivers also struck. Then, when workers seized pharmaceutical companies and laboratories, Chilean doctors struck, rendering emergency service only. Soon shop owners, airline pilots, and some professional associations went out on strike. By late August, 5 percent of the working population had participated, or was participating, in the wave of strikes or walkouts.

Between the two critical trucking strikes, copper miners walked off the job in April 1973. They returned only in July, reducing production of copper by nearly 10 percent compared with April–July 1972. On June 29, 1973, a golpe attempt led by Colonel Roberto Souper, commander of the Second Armored Regiment, sputtered when Prats, who only days before had been involved in an ugly public incident with a conservative civilian woman, assured army loyalty to the regime. Soon after the golpe attempt, Captain Arturo Araya Peters, Allende's naval aide, was gunned down on the balcony of his Santiago home.

Strikes, labor violence, assassinations, a golpe attempt, military men in cabinet posts, property and factory seizures, impeachment of

253

Allendista cabinet members, urban guerrilla activities—events like these can lead to military intervention.

The essential Chilean civil-military relationship—strict military obedience of the constitutional proscription of deliberation—deteriorated in mid 1973. Deterioration was so serious that even if normalcy had been restored, military obedience in a traditional sense would never have been the same. Normalcy was not restored, for on September 11, 1973, Allende's government was overthrown, and Allende lost his life in the process.

Allende knew his position was deteriorating in July when he asked military men to join a new cabinet after Souper's golpe failed. But army, navy, and air force chiefs demanded too much executive authority. Finally, on August 9, 1973, Allende successfully brought military chiefs into his cabinet again, but Air Force General César Ruiz Danyau quit as minister of transportation and public works after ten days, stating that Allende would not allow him to proceed with vigor in resolving the current truckers' strike. When he resigned as air force commander in chief as well, many of his subordinates demanded that the government reinstate him. Soon rumors spread that the armed forces and the carabineros were on alert and that high-ranking officers would use Ruiz's resignation as evidence that Allende was not dealing fairly with the military and was not really effective as chief executive. Then, on August 22, General Prats resigned as defense minister and as army commander in chief. Prats had yielded to pressure from junior and staff officers, indicating an institutional wish to disassociate the army from the regime.

Meanwhile Allende's principal backers were criticizing his handling of the copper strike. Socialists and Communists officially stated that the miners were in league with capitalists and foreign interests —enemies of the state—and were unwitting tools of opposition parties controlling Congress. Politically and economically, Allende was in deep trouble. For the first time since 1932 the Chilean government was unable to administer national affairs.

Through all these events, from October 1972 to late August 1973, the armed forces, principally the army, superficially stood firm in their constitutional obligations, but it was apparent that the military demand for executive authority as a condition for joining the July cabinet, the Ruiz resignation, the state of alert, and the Prats resignation were not normal ingredients of Chilean civil-military relations. Some observers believe that by mid 1973 it was only the military's neutrality and acceptance of the Constitution that kept the beleaguered Allende in power. The situation was most unusual for the Republic of Chile. Just how unusual it was became tragically obvious on September 11, when the armed forces took over the government.

Chile will never be the same, no matter what Allende's accomplishments or failures, no matter what the record of the September 11 junta. The fabric of state woven since 1932 has been rent in such a way as to make the military wary of any involvement in politics short of total control, for the military did not escape unscathed from its association with Allende, Unidad Popular (UP), and the administration. Praise by the lower classes for the military had turned to criticism when workers occupying factories realized that a loyalist army might force them out at the behest of the man they had elected. Right-wing politicians had criticized the army for siding with Marxists. Until the golpe of September 11, 1973, military men saw their situation as a series of frustrations.

Concomitantly, the middle and upper sectors of Chilean society became less hostile to military participation in politics. Former friends began to oppose the armed forces; former rivals for influence became advocates of military measures to rid the country of Allende, UP, and Marxism.

At this point we must consider Chilean civil-military relations in a new context, a context of relations between the professional military and a society and polity under the leadership of a minority Marxist-dominated administration. Looking back from 1970, when Allende was elected and when army commander in chief René Schneider Chereau was assassinated, we can see that Chilean civil-military relations were unusual by Latin American standards. That is, since the 1830s the military had been kept in its place by civilian authorities and generally had accepted that place except for the events of 1924–32. Only sporadically did military leaders seek to invert the essential relationship; only rarely did they have much of a following, whether civil or military.

But before the golpe of September 11, 1973, civil-military relations appear to have reached a crisis stage roughly similar to the crisis stages of 1920–24 and 1932 that resulted in the toppling of the elected regimes of Alessandri and Montero. Economic distress, social pressures, political intrigue, ministerial instability, internal violence, civil disobedience, and difficulty in the maintenance of law and order were problems for Alessandri and Montero and later for Salvador Allende.

These factors are as influential on military organizations in the early 1970s as they were a half-century ago.

To conclude this study we will focus on 1970 as a turning point and attempt to indicate the ideological stance of the armed forces at that time, illustrate how and why Allende and his UP advisers shaped their policy toward the military, and show what forces were at work that precluded a military stand against Chilean Marxism until 1973. We will then turn to the years after 1970 and attempt to answer some pressing questions: Why did the military remain docile for three years in the face of mounting pressures to intervene? Why did the military initially see UP as a middle ground acceptable to political extremes? How did the Allende administration carry out its policy vis-à-vis the military, thus binding it to the state as closely as it has ever been bound in this century, at least until the golpe of September 11, 1973?

In examining the early 1970s we will have to bear in mind that prediction of the future is out of the question. Events will prove none of what has been written in these pages invalid, but events often do call for new analysis and new interpretations. Possible alternative analyses and interpretations will either be provided or, I hope, be obvious to the reader.

Chile in 1970: Allende's Inheritance[1]

By 1970 the population trends discussed earlier in this study had produced a nation whose population was over 75 percent urban. Of nearly 10 million Chileans, 65 percent were younger than forty-five years of age, and 77 percent lived in central Chile (18 percent of the national domain), the area bounded by Copiapó on the north and Concepción-Talcahuano on the south. Nearly half the population lived in the three central provinces of Santiago, Valparaíso, and O'Higgins. Nearly a half-million people lived in the Valparaíso–Viña del Mar and Concepción-Talcahuano complexes, almost 150,000 in the Coquimbo–La Serena complex, and over 3 million in Santiago. The northern desert cities had burgeoned; Arica had a population of 80,000, Iquique 65,000, and Antofagasta nearly 60,000. Chileans, then, were youthful, urban, and crowded.

Most Chileans began to feel the effects of political change and economic vicissitudes soon after the 1970 presidential election. Inflation became more pronounced than ever before as the escudo plummeted and black-market currency operations spread. United States dollars bought three, four, and five times the official exchange rate by 1972, nearly ten times the official rate in 1973. Politics became more provocative, to say the least, as Allende took office.

The demographic patterns we described as having aided civilians in dominating the military in the nineteenth century, and that contributed to civil-military political interest between 1900 and 1930, appear in the second half of the twentieth century to be potential contributors to military-state friction. Socioeconomic conditions arising out of these demographic patterns can be determinants of military-state friction in Chile if they accompany extreme shifts in other relationships within the political system.

We saw earlier that the demise of the Basque-Castilian aristocracy and its oligarchic rule coincided with the rise of military political interest. Exacerbating both the demise and the rise was the political, social, and economic situation between 1920 and 1924.

The Basque-Castilian aristocracy was replaced as the main ingredient of the political system by a revived political party system whose flexibility and organizational strength between 1932 and 1970 provided for moderate but notable change. It was this flexibility that resulted in the narrow election of Allende in 1970, and it was organizational strength in the political system that held the civil-military balance. Soon after 1970, however, it became obvious that the Chilean political system was geared only to "gradualism," slow, temperate change. Careful though he was, Allende soon found himself at odds with his own followers as well as the opposition. He found himself in a situation analogous to that of Alessandri a half-century before, struggling against insurmountable odds within a system incapable of providing him with the means to achieve his ends. Because of Allende's experience, the Chilean political system can no longer be considered an effective deterrent to military participation in politics.

Whereas only a minority of Chileans voiced political opinions in the nineteenth century, the number of politicized Chileans has increased steadily during this century. Thousands of nonvoters were mobilized by Alessandri in 1920. The political battles of the thirties, forties, and fifties enlarged the electorate. Chile's lower classes are no longer docile, no longer mere participants in the political process. As of 1970 the Chilean lower classes were finally brought totally within the system, presumably to enjoy its benefits as well as suffer from its shortcomings. Their ultimate response to the golpe of September 11, 1973, was naturally a major source of concern for Chile's new government.

As of 1970 the Chilean political system functioned within an ambience of accelerated, but still controlled, change and nationalist fervor. Urbanized by 1970, the Chilean polity was also larger than ever before. Within three years this urbanized, enlarged polity appeared to be out of control. Allende's road to socialism (*la vía chilena*) within a constitutional framework was strewn with debris. The consummate mobilization of the masses in 1970 provided the Allende regime with an unmanageably large support group, for peasants, miners, the unemployed, dockers, factory workers, laborers, and others were promised much. But the democratic way is always a slow way, and well before September 11, 1973, Allende's appeal to the masses was weakening.

Built into the Chilean political system were the concepts of loyal opposition and yielding incumbency. These may be relics of the past. While by 1973 the steadfast loyalty of the opposition to the political system was severely in question, the idea that Allende's regime would yield power through elections was also in question.

In short, the events of 1932–70 may be likened to the situation between 1891 and 1920. Chile had a unique ability to allow diversity in the political system and contain it. As long as diversity was within the bounds of gradualism, Chile's political system functioned well. But with the advent of Marxism as an official policy in 1970, the system was sorely tested.

So were the responsibility and the responsiveness of the ruling class. Civilian leaders of the nineteenth-century oligarchy and the revived party system after 1932 saw military participation in politics as odious. Affairs of state, by Latin American standards, were conducted within the bounds of gradualism, and palliatives appeared to suffice. Expansion of the political system in this century led to an expansion of the political ruling class and, indeed, to a more superficially democratic form of government, but not, lamentably, to an increase in responsibility and responsiveness.

Bureaucratization of the Chilean state, for example, did not lead to better government or even to more active government; more government responsibilities did not necessarily lead to greater effectiveness. By 1970 the bureaucracy (popularly termed *la cuna*, the cradle) amounted to approximately 10 percent of the labor force, a

400 percent growth since 1940![2] But it did not function in a proportionately more efficient or effective way.

An increasing number of Chileans, then, were dependent on the government and hence on its continuance. Family connections, compadrazgo, and friendships helped to perpetuate a monopolistic grip on affairs of state by an extended bureaucratic class. Ties extended from the bureaucracy to the political party system, business, and the military, thus increasing the interrelationships of those with a stake in the government. By the middle of this century it was not uncommon to see an extended family with bureaucratic, military, business, and political party ties; many Chileans, both civilian and military, can tick off the names of relatives active in politics ranging from right to left. This hyperextended family was a weakness as well as a source of strength to the political system and to military discipline, for power groups became far less homogeneous, far less cohesive. It neutralized military political interest yet exposed it to politiquería.

Suddenly the system met with a challenge. It was inconceivable that the extended bureaucracy and the traditionally truculent legislative branch would adapt to Allende's plans. It was inconceivable that the opposition majority would remain truly loyal in Congress when confronted with the UP program. It was equally inconceivable that labor, peasants, and the poor would all respond in the same way, or that they would be willing to accept gradual solutions, so politicized had they become by 1970. It cannot be said that the Allende administration represented "the people" as a bloc. And it appeared very unlikely that the military would remain quiescent long, given the rupture of the civil-military balance established after 1932.

How can we best assess the military's position vis-à-vis the state? We have already noted the dangers of dependence on statistics. How much does it really matter if of all Latin American countries Chile has the second highest percentage of its population in uniform?[3] It matters little if traditional balances are maintained. What does it mean if the military is budgeted for a low or high percent of the GDP? Again, it means little if civilian authority can be maintained.

As long as the Chilean political system functioned in its traditional sense and as long as the state exercised authority, the armed forces could be coddled or shortchanged without fear of a golpe. In 1970 the political system and the state began to have trouble maintaining continuity, and strains in civil-military relations were the result. The government's own figures indicate that Allende's policy between 1970 and 1973 was to coddle the military and attempt to win its obedience and loyalty. Military expenditures rose slightly between 1970 and 1972 as the president ordered new equipment and salary increases.[4] A full year before the 1970 elections Allende's own Socialist Party publicly sympathized with a demonstration for higher salaries and better equipment (as well as changes in the high command) staged by the officers and men of the Tacna and Yungay regiments.

Led by the controversial retired general Roberto Viaux, the regiments barricaded themselves in their headquarters and took control of the main arsenal, the noncommissioned officer's school, and the main recruiting center on October 21, 1969. Viaux claimed that he had the support of most of the army and that he was loyal to President Frei, but demanded the resignation of Defense Minister Tulio Marambio, another retired general. Marambio resigned, giving Frei a free hand, and the "Tacnazo" sputtered, but there were reverberations for the rest of the year.

Socialists praised the army for its loyalty to the government and lamented the need for protest. The Socialists thereby gained a certain degree of sympathy from army officers who did not find supporters for their cause (better pay, new equipment) in other political parties.

Again statistics would tell us various stories. According to one source, Tacnazo officers had no case, for military salaries had increased more rapidly than those of public employees in the previous four years, and defense expenditures had quadrupled over the same period. The army was paid well and had good equipment, concluded the writer.[5] Nevertheless President Frei and Marambio's temporary replacement in Defense reluctantly acknowledged a need to raise military salaries in 1969. This blatant example of melodramatic, old-fashioned military insubordination gave Chilean Marxists a safe opportunity to show army officers that Marxists could be their friends.

Army Attitudes as of 1970:
A Survey of Military Literature, 1930–70

A better method of assessing the military's stance toward the state as of 1970 is to examine military opinion as expressed in the army's "house organ," *Memorial del Ejército de Chile* (*MECH*). These opinions are not just those of individual writers, but have been passed on by a board of editors. As often as not they are addresses or term papers written in staff or specialty schools. Usually the board of editors contains members of the general staff. These addresses or term papers indicate what is being taught, assigned, and written about in postgraduate military training. Although their readership may not be large, the fact that certain types of articles appear in print does signify what is considered important and worthy of dissemination to members of the military profession.

In the Chilean journal, as has been noted, there is a lower incidence in recent years of articles devoted to social, political, and economic subjects than in the military journals of Argentina, Brazil, or Peru. We may rightly conclude that as of 1970, Chilean army officers had relatively little interest in extraprofessional matters.

Between 1924 and 1933 *MECH* was an intellectual desert. During this period of high-level political involvement, officers put little into print besides ideas on the need for reforms in military instruction, a better promotion system, better physical education training, and Chile's educational reforms. One article in 1931 did deal with industrial mobilization and advocated a stronger stand by the state to integrate industry.[6] Another article that year advocated state-directed efforts in the exploitation of petroleum deposits in Magallanes.[7] While articles published in 1931 and 1932 did chide the government for lax application of obligatory military service laws, they admitted that the economic situation prohibited full-scale training.[8] Montero Moreno's previously mentioned anticommunist essay of January 1932 was a blatant departure from the norm.[9] It was fascistic and militaristic, but it caused no stir in civilian circles because of its hostility to the then-renascent Communists. Ramón Cañas, later army commander in chief, briefly apologized for military political transgressions in an October 1932 piece.[10]

MECH fell on hard times in 1933, the victim of budget cuts. In 1934 book-length essays devoted to technical and historical questions began to appear as one or two of *MECH*'s issues. Politics, economics, national problems, and the like received scant mention. By 1935, perhaps to make the journal more attractive, the cheap paper used in *MECH* was occasionally tinted (so was the paper of the Peruvian *Revista Militar del Perú*, *RMP*). Insurance company and utilities advertisements appeared, presumably to subsidize printing costs. It was in the

March–April 1935 issue that General Barceló's seminal article on the evolution of the Chilean Army appeared, as if to remind readers that the army had been of value to Chile once upon a time.[11]

In the 1930s one subject that could be considered an extraprofessional interest found its way into *MECH,* namely education and public health. Captain Angel Varela went so far as to state that "the army has a preponderant role in the intellectual and social development of the citizen." He called the barracks "the temple of civic virtues."[12] Articles of this type had appeared twenty years earlier in Chile, Argentina, Brazil, and Peru; during the 1930s such articles appeared more frequently in the last three than in Chile.

In 1936 the Ford Motor Company, Standard Oil of New Jersey, and Shell Oil bought advertising in *MECH,* which began to look like a popular review. French rather than German sources were quoted, French technical essays were translated, and there was more foreign coverage. Mobilization was still being treated in 1936, always with the suggestion (not insistence) that the state, industry, and the military should work closer together.[13] In a 1937 article the controversial Tobías Barros Ortiz referred to the army as the "armed citizenry" (*ciudadanía armada*), following by over fifty years Goltz's *Das Volk in Waffen,* and lauded the officer's role as a leader in Chilean society.[14] In another 1937 article Lieutenant Germán Reinhardt praised the army's role in developing the Chilean Far South.[15]

Industrial mobilization and the necessity of social discipline for its successful accomplishment was the subject of another 1937 essay, as *MECH* turned to a wider range of international subjects by the end of the year.[16] A two-part translation of Maxime Weygand's study of the education of youth was featured in 1938; it discussed moral discipline, patriotism, hero worship, early military training, and the idea that youth composed a nation's future. The fact that Weygand relied heavily on Hubert Lyautey's forty-seven-year-old "Du rôle social de l'officier" was apparently ignored by both French and Chilean editors, however, and Weygand did not see fit to cite Lyautey.[17] For the remainder of the 1930s European and Asiatic developments took precedence over Chilean matters except for purely technical articles.

By the advent of World War II, then, the army officer class expressing itself through *MECH* was not criticizing state or society, or civilian conduct of national affairs. The idea that "the army can do it better" was not being championed, though the army's virtues and potential contributions were often pointed out, as were shortcomings in Chile's ability to mobilize industry and manpower. The Popular Front regime elected in 1938 doubtless allayed military fears that civilians were not interested in internal development. Surely there was nothing in *MECH* that could be considered the germ of a military ideology.

During World War II Chilean military literature was highly nationalistic. The national development schemes of the Front, President Aguirre's "Chilenidad," Chile's neutrality, and German successes of 1939–42 revived a strident attitude on the part of military writers. Colonel Guillermo Aldona blamed democracy for intellectual mediocrity, mistaken concepts of social equality, and moral laxness. He argued for state action to improve morals and virtues and suggested in a 1941 article that the army would be a good vehicle for a state interested in improving society on all fronts.[18] An editorial in the July–August 1941 issue of *MECH* praised President Aguirre for supporting a heavy infusion of Chilean civics into primary schools.[19] That the barracks was a school at the service of the country was the thesis of Lieutenant Colonel Guillermo Toro Concha's brief essay of 1942.[20] Other wartime articles dealt with military training in secondary school, national economic mobilization, political events in Argentina, geopolitics, and the development of the steel industry.[21] By 1944 the tone stressed the need for more inter-American cooperation.

At the end of World War II *MECH* stopped publishing material dealing with the French and German armies or taken from French or German sources. The journal still published occasional pieces relating to Europe, but generally from the standpoint of United States efforts in the recent war. The strident nationalism of the 1938–44 years disappeared; *anexos*, volumes devoted to pure military history, began to appear regularly. Geopolitics, economic and industrial development, the military's role in the education of young Chilean males, southern territorial development, and atomic energy were themes of the better essays.[22] In the early stages of the Cold War, then, *MECH* was asserting that the army did have a vital role to play in a number of areas, but little was being written on civilian failings or the political system per se. German military influence was noticeably played down. Presidents Aguirre, Ríos, and González were praised for their attention to national development.

In the late 1940s, inspired, no doubt, by economic expansion and the development of the steel and petroleum industries, *MECH* published several articles dealing with industrialization. Geopolitical theories were applied to Chile's position in relation to Antarctica.[23] One officer did advocate military supervision of public works projects,[24] but it may be that the army's preoccupation with Chile's Antarctic territory claim occupied time and thought which might otherwise have been devoted to sociopolitical issues arising out of the Cold War. Between World War II and the Korean War, technical articles took definite precedence.

As Chile's wartime economic growth tailed off in the 1950s, more articles on ways to further economic development appeared. In 1953 a significant article questioned the constitutional proscription of military deliberation on political matters. This was the important "Ningún cuerpo armado puede deliberar," by Fernando Montaldo Bustos, written in the wake of Ibáñez's election and the formation of PUMA. Montaldo's was one of the very few extraprofessional pieces *MECH* published during the 1950s.[25] It was only two years later, of course, that Línea Recta and its *Plan* were revealed to the public.

After 1958 these general trends continued. There were few inconsequential pieces on geopolitics (mainly derivative and not revealing any significant new Chilean adaptations) and economic development of forest products, fishing, agriculture, and the need for economic planning. None of these was as distinguished or innovative as material being published simultaneously in Peru, where the army was rapidly developing its own ideology.

For example, General Ramón Canas Montalva's "El ejército y la república," published in 1964, was merely a reprint of his prologue to one of the volumes of the *Archivo de don Bernardo O'Higgins*.[26] It was written in praise of the army and military virtues—subjects that were not particularly controversial in Chile. Another essay published in 1964 stated bluntly that the army served the public and that public opinion was the expression of the national will; the army did not act, it reacted. Nevertheless, the author believed, it was necessary for the army to maintain good public relations so that its importance and abilities in peace and war could not be neglected.[27] For the remainder of the 1960s *MECH* focused exclusively on geopolitical theory, purely professional matters, international relations, space exploration, and routine military history. One article appeared on economic development (1967); none was published on social or political topics.[28] After an appraisal of themes prevalent in forty years of military writing—bearing in mind that it is the writing and publishing that are important, not necessarily the readership—we must conclude that as of 1970 the official Chilean army journal had become more technically orientated each decade from 1930 on. Strident nationalism, blatant extolling of military virtues as opposed to civilian virtues (or lack of them), and praise of the army's superior capabilities in development or public works were not at all characteristic.

Residual influences of Línea Recta notwithstanding, the Chilean Army had no professional sense of mission beyond a narrowly conceived professionalism related solely to national defense in the strictest sense. The problems of the 1930s, the euphoria of the 1940s, and the political involvements of the 1950s had given way to the interests of an ostensibly apolitical, professional army. The army, like the navy and the air force, did not diverge in any apparent way from its constitutional mandate. The armed forces had no ideology, unlike the armed forces of Argentina, Brazil, and Peru. What happened in 1970, traumatic as it was, did not immediately thrust an ideology or sense of mission on the army, or on the armed forces as a whole, though what happened between 1970 and 1973 obviously did.[29] This is significant, for it may indicate that in Chile external influences were far more important in the formation of a military political stance or a military ideology than they have been in Argentina, Brazil, or Peru. That these external influences, when blended with Chilean military professionalism, seem to have created a sense of mission within three years is all the more significant. That the sense of mission resulted in a very efficient but bloody golpe de estado and in a harsh and repressive atmosphere after the golpe should not be surprising.

Although Chile experienced the first problem-oriented professional military movement in Latin America, the Chilean military is, to put it as simply as possible, the least politically sophisticated or experienced in a major South American country in the four decades since 1930. Professional training has not inclined the Chilean armed forces toward a sense of mission, beyond a set of militaristic values. Chilean officers, for example, have nothing comparable to the Peruvian CAEM (Centro de Altos Estudios Militares) or the Brazilian ESG (Escola Superior de Guerra). Neither the Academia de Guerra nor the Academia Politécnica Militar (primarily for engineers), both of which offer an entrée to high rank, is extraprofessionally oriented. Nor is the high command course, the Academia de Defensa Nacional, which is virtually a prerequisite for promotion to the highest ranks.[30]

Denied any ideological stance by Chile's political system as well as by its professional interest, the army—and by extension the armed forces—played an observer's role in 1970. Despite a wariness about Marxism, Socialist sympathy for the Tacnazo led some officers to believe they had nothing to fear from "a people's government."

When Chileans narrowly elected Allende, the army was actually denied potential support from the only civilian group showing any favor toward potential military political interest: the lower classes. Sociological research carried out in the mid 1960s has indicated that at that time the lower classes would have been relatively amenable to military intervention, alternative forms of government, and the creation of a new political system. Lower-class sentiment was far more favorable to the army than to the carabineros, owing to the police's role in maintenance of internal order, and definitely favorable to military action to forestall violations of the Constitution.[31] That these lower-class views changed in 1970, thus briefly stripping the armed forces of a potential civilian support group, goes without saying, for that year the lower classes helped elect their champion.

Thus the Chilean military was by no means in a situation analogous to that of its Argentine, Brazilian, or Peruvian counterparts when faced with a set of circumstances at least superficially conducive to dramatic change. Publicly assured by Allende that he would respect their autonomy and the Constitution, Chile's military leaders staunchly upheld their end of the thirty-eight-year-old civil-military "bargain." At the same time the armed forces doubtless understood that the grandiose schemes Allende and his allies had for internal development and restructuring might call for the technological expertise of the military. It may be that the campaign promises and plans of 1970 did more to spur military interest in internal development than any movement from within the military itself.

Military Political Involvement in 1970:
The Assassination of Schneider
and the ITT Embroglio[32]

The army's stand in 1970 was voiced by the commander in chief, Division General René Schneider Chereau, who repeatedly asserted the apolitical nature of the military and who had helped to dissolve a plot against the Frei administration in April 1970. The so-called

Schneider Doctrine was quite simple. The army would guarantee honest elections, constitutional access to power for the winner, and support for the new regime. Schneider had no objection to Marxism provided the UP government operated within constitutional bounds. The first few days after Allende's September 4, 1970, electoral victory, rumors flew about Chile: a deal would be made between Christian Democrats and Nationals to allow Jorge Alessandri the presidency; Alessandri would then resign and elections would bring Frei back to La Moneda; the army would intervene to protect democracy. None of these rumors had much substance. Schneider held his ground and spurned rightists who wanted to see Allende's inauguration blocked. The Constitution would be upheld, and the army would not involve itself.

Schneider could not, of course, prevent external influences from affecting the army. Early on Thursday morning, October 22, an attempted kidnapping of General Schneider failed. Eight cars filled with plotters forced Schneider's limousine off the street as he was going from his home in Santiago's Barrio Alto to his office. Six men approached the vehicle and began breaking its windows to get at the distinguished officer. Schneider drew his pistol, to no avail. In the panic one of the kidnappers fired, and the shots hit home. The army's commander in chief died three days later in a military hospital. Not since the murder of Diego Portales in 1837 had such an important Chilean died for political reasons. Santiago was declared an emergency zone and placed under martial law. Within days after the shooting, informers told of a rightist lodge, "Fatherland and Liberty" (Patria y Libertad, PL), which had developed the kidnapping plot. Tacnazo leaders, including General Viaux, and numerous civilians of conservative leanings were arrested and charged. Communists, Socialists, and members of the Leftist Revolutionary Movement (Movimiento Izquierdista Revolucionario, MIR) cooperated with police and army investigators, leading the army once again to the conclusion that its real enemies were on the right. Though all the details may never be known, it was clear enough that PL and its affiliates (both domestic and foreign) wanted to kidnap Schneider to provoke a golpe, but the golpe never occurred. Thirty-two other army and navy officers, as well as civilians, were implicated ultimately.

Shocking though it was, the Schneider affair was not the only external influence brought to bear on the army in 1970. Though documentation was not available until months later, we know that

maneuvering by officials of the International Telephone and Tele-
graph Company to block Allende's inauguration involved gross
miscalculations of the army's position toward a Marxist government
in 1970. Apparently ITT assumed that, since the Tacnazo, General
Viaux's influence had spread in the army. Somehow ITT officials got
the idea that Frei and Schneider were acting in collusion to keep
Allende from taking office, that the army was solidly opposed to
Marxism, that there were contingency plans for a golpe and a military
cabinet, and that the Ejército de Chile could be easily manipulated.
These ideas continued to circulate in ITT memos until the very day of
Schneider's assassination. Despite U.S. ambassador Edward Korry's
allegation that the army was a "bunch of toy soldiers,"[33] desperate
hopes were pinned on military action in Chile. The ITT operation
was riddled with poor appraisals of the corporation's clout, the
flexibility of the Chilean political system, and the nature of civil-
military relations in 1970.

Doubtless there were contacts between representatives of U.S.
interests in Chile and the army high command. The army was
reckoned to be "close to the U.S." and "dependent" on the U.S.
mission for advice.[34] But the Chilean armed forces were nationalistic
above all at this juncture, proud of their history and their constitutional role. Shortly after Schneider was shot, Prats and his air force
and navy counterparts, General Carlos Guerraty Villalobos and
Admiral Hugo Tirado Barros, reaffirmed that the armed forces would
observe the Constitution. As institutions they had no real civilian
political allies on the right. Indeed, rightist groups like PL were
flagrant in their attempts to involve the military in political affairs.
The armed forces, to all intents and purposes, had no enemies on the
left. Many of the mistakes made in assessing the position of the
Peruvian military in 1967 and 1968 were made again in Chile in 1969
and 1970. The United States made no military friends in Chile, owing
to rumors of involvement in assassination and golpe plots.

Allende and the Military: 1971[35]

September 19, 1971, was warm in Santiago. Crowds gathered early
at the Parque Cousiño for the fifty-ninth annual military review and
parade, commemorating the struggle for Chilean independence and
Chile's nineteenth-century military glories. By midday three hundred
thousand citizens were on hand. Never before had a Marxist chief

executive participated in such an event. It was barely a year since Allende's victory at the polls, not yet a full year since the Schneider affair, the ITT embroglio, the hectic maneuvering for congressional confirmation and, ultimately, inauguration. Yet there was Allende in the reviewing stand with ministers of state, parliamentary officials, church officials, and distinguished foreign guests. Allende, his Marxist cohorts, leading opposition politicians, and army commander in chief General Carlos Prats González with his air, naval, and police counterparts: Chileans were adhering to tradition. The various crises of the previous year notwithstanding, the armed forces would pay homage and have homage paid to them. Just prior to commencement of the festivities, at 3:00 P.M., President Allende quaffed the traditional *cacho de chicha* (a horn filled with hard cider) proffered by mounted and resplendent *huasos*, Chilean cowboys. *"Don Chicho* [Allende's nickname] *toma chicha del cacho,"* went the saying. General Augusto Pinochet Ugarte, commandant of the Santiago garrison, approached the stand, dressed in combat uniform and riding in a Toyota jeep field vehicle, to request formal permission to begin the review. Allende nodded, extended his hand, and announced, "The spectacle which is about to begin is visible proof that the armed forces of Chile maintain our traditions." (Two years later Allende and Pinochet would exchange other words in other circumstances when those traditions were shattered.) Then it began. The Escuela band, whose drum major always performs a hyperbolic goose step, swung onto the field, followed by Pinochet and the Escuela commandant on horseback, numerous aides, goose-stepping marchers of the presidential escort, and the Escuela cadet corps. The Escuela Naval band and officials of the Escuela followed, with marching naval cadets behind. The air force band, with Air School officials, came next, as Hawker Hunter jets and helicopters swooped low. Then came the Division II band from Santiago, the noncommissioned officers' band, troops and officers from the Infantry and Engineers schools, Mountain School troops with their skis at shoulder arms, Parachute School troops, Special Forces, Motorized Infantry with commandant Brigadier General Enrique Garín Cea and his staff in shiny new field vehicles, the Buin and Tacna regiments, Signal Corps School, armored regiments, a delegation of nurses, motorized medical teams, quartermaster corps, and maintenance and transportation battalions.

It was a study in contrasts, the Marxist president downing chicha with his congressional foes, the armed forces displaying some turn-of-the-century Mauser rifles along with glittering, motorized equipment, jet fighters, and helicopters. Yet this was, after all, parade day in Chile, when political foes traditionally sat side by side and where new military equipment was displayed along with the remnants of a bygone era. The time had not yet come for traditions to weaken.

This year, 1971, had been a calm one for civil-military relations. General Prats was upholding the Schneider Doctrine, and soon it would be termed the Schneider-Prats Doctrine. United States advisers had not been asked to leave Chile as they had been asked to leave Peru three years before, and U.S. military aid had been increased (while, of course, other forms of U.S. aid had been cut off).[36] The September–October 1971 issue of *MECH* was devoted to military history and to the memory of Schneider, whose words had been echoed by numerous military figures: "We can have a clear conscience and present ourselves to the people for judgment, having carried out our duties in line with the mission and assignments imposed on us by law, and honoring a 150-year-old tradition."[37]

The Allende policy toward the armed forces was in effect. Although the masses were politicized more than ever before and the new managers of national affairs committed to change as never before, the administration still saw fit to regard military support as a prerequisite to political success. Even considering the tenuous nature of his administration and fragile nature of his popular support, Allende probably showed more concern for military support than any president in recent times (save possibly Carlos Ibáñez). Allende practically bent over backward to assure the armed forces of the constitutionality of his administration and to guarantee the military its autonomy and continued goodwill at the hands of a Marxist-led regime.[38]

Before he had been five months in office he had praised the military in a speech delivered in Temuco on March 2, 1971. The military was to be an integral part of national development; specifically, it should participate in future development of copper and steel industries, atomic energy, and scientific research. Integration was not politicization but cooperation, said Allende. "The army is on or near our frontiers, and the barracks are undisputably a factor in the preparation of citizens with a national consciousness, not chauvinistic or superpatriotic, but profoundly . . . national. We must remember that those who go to the barracks are the sons of farmers and workers."[39]

He would tolerate no peoples' militia, he asserted, for with the armed forces and carabineros Chileans needed no militia to guarantee constitutional procedures. He cleverly appealed to the armed forces by saying that there was no such thing as a modern, well-trained, well-equipped army, navy, or air force in an underdeveloped country. The army's and navy's shops and shipyards could not function without high-quality Chilean steel. The armed forces could not be technologically advanced if the country were backward; the country could not be developed, advanced, or rich as long as the people were undernourished and marginally employed. More to the point, if the military were to function properly, so must the government.

Scarcely a week later, he proclaimed:

> We are proud of the professional role of our armed forces. The main characteristic of the armed forces of Chile has been obedience to civilian power, total adherence to the popular will expressed in elections, to the laws of Chile, to the Chilean Constitution. . . . The armed forces of Chile are armed forces of the country. They are not armed forces at the service of a man or an administration. They are of the country, and this, I think, is one of the essential factors that characterize Chile and make it different from other countries.[40]

Clearly, Allende saw the armed forces as a power group in the society, polity, and economy. He wanted the army, navy, air force, and carabineros with him and involved in Chilean development. His messages in the fall of 1971 contained the kind of reasoning (for obviously different motives) found in the pages of Argentine, Brazilian, and Peruvian military journals, which was only rarely found in the pages of *MECH* until his administration.[41] In short, a Chilean civilian was infusing a developmentalist attitude into the armed forces (particularly the army) for his own purposes, thinking he could control that spirit.

Allende's policy in this respect had historical precedent. It was a modern version of the Portales-Prieto-Bulnes policy, as nationalistic and hopeful as the plans of Balmaceda and as clearly cognizant of military goals and of a cooperative military role in national development as the first Ibáñez administration. Historically, Chilean national leadership was most vigorous under Balmaceda and Ibáñez, as well as during the early years of the Popular Front–Radical administrations. Would Marxism and the military forge an alliance analogous to those forged by the Basque-Castilian oligarchs and the Ibañista technocrats with impartial military leaders? For a while it seemed that they would, for Allende's zeal, nationalism, mass support, and constitutionality blended well with the Schneider-Prats position. Nevertheless, Allende's policy, formulated and executed as it was, carried with it the seeds of civil-military discord. Those seeds would take root, grow, and flower in 1973, as steps were taken first to "integrate" and "incorporate" the armed forces, then to rely on their support, and finally to interfere unwittingly in internal military affairs. In this sense Allende's policy could be likened to that of Pinto and Freire in the 1830s, Arturo Alessandri in the 1920s and 1930s, and Carlos Ibáñez in the 1950s.

During 1971, while Allende was praising the armed forces in speeches and press conferences, he and his aides worked quietly to attach the military to their cause. The president began to refer to himself as "Generalissimo" and wore medals at numerous ceremonies involving the military. This conduct was "unusual compared to the attitude of [recent] presidents," noted one critic. He gave talks to troops and officers and lectured to noncommissioned officers and the high command on several occasions. Cristián Zegers equated Allende's methods of communication during 1971 with those of the infelicitous Té Dublé Almeyda some sixteen years before.[42] Allende's first two defense ministers, his crony José Tohá and the former Escuela instructor Alejandro Ríos Valdivia, were far more representative of Allende's wishes than they were of the government's, which bound the armed forces more closely to Allende's position.[43]

While Allende sought to strengthen his ties to the military, opinions within the army began to divide with regard to constitutional obligations to the popular will—Allende, UP, Marxism—versus institutional loyalties (including fears of destruction, anti-Marxism, and the traditional preference for gradualism in national affairs).[44] We can assume that similar divisions were developing within air force, navy, and carabineros. Prats, and Schneider before him, were army "constitutionalists" first and foremost, although they never failed to champion the cause of the institution. Therefore they held that the army had to remain committed to the Constitution, if only for the sake of survival. More significantly, they believed that the army must commit itself to the Constitution because this was the tradition. It is probable, moreover, that Prats had political ambitions of his own and sought to further them by demonstrating his abilities in a cooperative way.

Emerging only gradually were the "institutionalists," who, while not sneering at the Constitution by any means, were concerned for their survival in the face of increasing association with leftist politics. They feared being coopted. They disliked the turmoil which increased month by month, and they were disgusted with constitutional infractions being committed by peasants and workers, MIR, and zealous Allendista cabinet members. Both the constitutionalists and institutionalists can be compared and contrasted equally well to the groups involved in the debacle of 1924–27.

The institutionalists had no publicly known leaders during the 1971–72 period, but it is generally assumed that an institutionalist position—namely, that Allende and UP were destructive forces and had to be eliminated—was expressed most blatantly by the likes of General Viaux, Colonel Alberto Labbé Troncoso, commandant of the Escuela, and General Alfredo Canales Márquez.

Viaux, of course, had been retired. Labbé and Canales were similarly neutralized, the former in January 1971, after he refused to discipline a subaltern for accusing the government of violating the Constitution and venerating Marxist leaders and Castro over Chilean heroes, the latter after ten months of hard investigation in September 1972.[45] Early in 1971 Allende had pushed for the retirement of Rear Admiral Víctor Búnster del Solar, naval attaché in Washington, D.C., Chile's representative on the Inter-American Defense Board (and allegedly a CIA contact!). Another officer who might be considered an institutionalist was retired general Alberto Green, also jailed briefly in March 1972, for allegedly plotting against the government.

These military positions were developing while the administration was showering the army with praise, salary raises, and money for equipment purchases. Therefore, while the constitutionalists could crow, the institutionalists could but mutter. The former could point to the possible consequences of integration and cooperation, and the latter could warn of being coopted. No clear-cut opposition to the regime could develop, and it was to Allende's credit that his policy in 1971 was sophisticated and carefully applied in order to preclude opposition and promote cooperation.

For example, he did not make the mistake that had undone Ibáñez between 1952 and 1958 of seeking to weld the armed forces to him

immediately. Ríos and Tohá represented him more than his administration, to be sure, but they, like their president, operated very
judiciously. Allende was especially careful with appointments at the
high-command level. During his 1952–58 presidency the fumbling
Ibáñez had jumped colonels to high-command and ministerial-level
posts to get "his men" into key roles, but Allende did not fall into this
trap. Upon the death of Schneider, President Frei had appointed
Prats. Upon his inauguration Allende could have asked for Prats's
resignation and replaced him with someone more to his liking.
Actually he could have selected any senior officer to be commander in
chief. Wisely, he did not, thus early allaying fears of army officers that
he would immediately meddle with the institution. He appointed
Vice-Admiral Raúl Montero Canejo (second in line) and General
César Ruiz (third in line) to head the navy and air force respectively.
These designations, well within traditional bounds, were wise, given
the fact that congressional ratification is necessary for such appointments. So were the ordered retirements of Labbé, Canales, and
Búnster, for that matter, for although in Chile the president can order
any officer's retirement without cause, Allende refrained from any
large-scale purge of the officer corps.

Making it even more difficult to mount any organized military
opposition was the fact that the leftist press and radio constantly
extolled the military's constitutional stance. From the time of the
Tacnazo, media representatives sympathetic to UP and Allende
publicly sympathized with the army, praised the military for remaining obedient, and lauded Schneider and Prats. The Marxist line, as
expressed in official sources and the media, was definitely soft toward
the military. But here too problems were abuilding.

Just as the constitutionalist position tended to associate the armed
forces, especially the army, with a controversial regime, the institutionalist position tended to associate the military with the forces of
reaction. Wariness of Allende within the officer corps led some officers
to seek support from, or to sympathize with, the civilian political
opposition. Not all officers were overjoyed at the praise heaped upon
them by *El Siglo*, the official Communist daily, and by *Puro Chile*, the
unofficial Marxist tabloid. Others were disgruntled by *El Siglo*'s and
Puro Chile's criticism of the institutionalist position.

Nor were officers pleased when *El Mercurio*, the independent
conservative Santiago daily, pointed out that Socialists and Communists were attempting to infiltrate the ranks in order to sway troops to

the Marxist cause and investigate various officers and their political sympathies.[46] Unofficial though this campaign was, it did cause some officers to demand that UP, the ministry, and the president call off the "consciousness-raising" campaign. The fact that these same tactics had been used by Peruvian Apristas for decades and by leftist supporters of João Goulart in Brazil in the early 1960s was cause for consternation in the officer corps. Socialist leader Raúl Ampuero's 1971 advocacy of a "people in arms"[47] was a stark contrast to Allende's disavowal of the people's militia. Needless to say, Ampuero's concept of a people in arms was not that of Tobías Barros as expressed in *Vigilia de armas,* or Colmar von der Goltz as advocated in *Das Volk in Waffen!*

When MIR began operating with the remnants of Chile's indigenous population in 1971, goading them to seize farmland and timber stands, both the government and the army were upset. MIR was becoming an embarrassment to Allende. The guerrillalike MIR campaign puzzled army leaders. Was it their problem or the carabineros'? If the administration, using the national police, did not put a stop to the illegal activities of people who nominally (but not really) supported the administration, would the army have to take charge? Were the carabineros being held out of this budding conflict to force the army in? Had the carabineros been compromised or coopted? Would Allende order the army to take the field against Chileans? If so, would the troops obey orders?

The army's position as of early 1972 became clearer with the circulation of an essay by Robinson Rojas, a Marxist writer disaffected with Allende's relative gradualism.[48] At this point, if not before, it became apparent that with specific regard to civil-military relations, UP was hardly a cohesive power group—a fact which should provide Marxists with food for thought for some time to come! If the regime's own support groups were not in agreement on the military question, it is certain that they also disagreed on other matters. Further, if the minority regime's support groups were this divided, the majority opposition was probably in a position to blunt official programs, thereby frustrating the administration and further affecting the institutional cohesion of the loyal and obedient armed forces. Chile has had minority regimes, but none so controversial and troubled as that of Allende and UP, committed to the construction of a socialist state.

The Rojas essay, originally rejected for publication, was eventually printed and is available in English. In it Rojas boldly stated that if the UP government was truly revolutionary, the military would have to intervene. He thereby locked the military into a bourgeois, reactionary position, attacking the institution as representing the imperialist bourgeoisie and as being incompatible with social revolution. He asserted that the only reason the Chilean armed forces had allowed Allende to be inaugurated was their assumption that General Schneider's assassination had been a right-wing accomplishment. Therefore, he reasoned, the Allende regime must be essentially bourgeois itself because the military did not oppose it. Allende's promises and assurances, his coddling of the military, his use of military men in developmental schemes—especially in southern Malleco, Cautín, Valdivia, Osorno, and Llanquihue provinces—constituted a sellout, a conspiracy to weld the bourgeois military to the regime and create an imperialist victory (the USSR was also accused of imperialism here). The army's ties with the U.S. capitalist bourgeois imperialists meant that Allende was tied to the same influences. Reformism was not revolution, and official UP nationalism was not real nationalism. In a captivating turn of phrase, Rojas termed the still-quiescent armed forces an "armed bourgeois referee." Rojas's Marxist logic did attract support from the left for his position, but it did not appeal to the government or the armed forces!

Allende and the Military: 1972[49]

At the beginning of 1972, the Chilean armed forces were in a state of political limbo. They were not yet so closely associated with the regime that they would suffer from its excesses or shortcomings. They were being harangued from the unofficial left by "consciousness raising," infiltration, and the likes of Robinson Rojas. They had already rejected any overt alliance with the right and refused (without ever having been formally asked, one suspects) to treat with PL, ITT, or the CIA to block Allende or topple him. The armed forces now had enemies on the left as well as on the right. This drove the military to support and seek support from the center, such as it was. During 1972 the Chilean armed forces therefore associated themselves more closely with the Allende regime.

This had both positive and negative consequences. We have already seen the effects on the military of interest in politics, close association

with government, or participation in political affairs. We have also
seen what attempts to attach the professional military to an adminis
tration have done to the civilian political system. Such activities have
invariably led to problems in the political system, geared as it has
traditionally been to separation of politics and the military. Such
problems developed during 1972.

By September 1972, Allende had moved beyond praising the armed
forces for their achievements and obedience to calling directly on the
military to aid in the process of social, political, and economic
transformation. Back in March 1971 the president had stated, "The
armed forces' job is to defend the physical and economic frontiers of
the country." This was a clear extension of the concept of national
integrity and sovereignty, akin to that expressed in 1968 by Peru's
military leaders.[50] Then, eighteen months later, on Independence
Day, September 18, 1972, Allende announced over a national radio
network that his government would utilize the armed forces and their
technological expertise to help transform Chile into a modern nation.

Officers were already serving Chile in this capacity. During 1971
and 1972, in numbers larger than ever before (although even more
officers in Brazil and Peru had such jobs), active and retired army,
navy, and air force officers assumed jobs in the mining enterprises
formerly owned by Anaconda and Kennecott, the Pacific Steel
Company (Compañía de Acero del Pacífico), the explosives industry,
the Chilean Development Corporation (CORFO), nuclear research
facilities, agrarian reform and engineering projects, planning and
organizing for the United Nations Conference on Trade and Development (UNCTAD) held in Santiago in April and May 1972, state-run
foundries, telecommunications, and shipping enterprises.[51] By
January 1973, General Alfredo Bachelet Martínez would be put in
charge of the National Secretariat of Commerce and Distribution, an
agency of the Ministry of Economy, at the time headed by Communist Orlando Millas. Serving with Bachelet would be two army
colonels, one admiral, an air force general, and a carabineros general.
The secretariat was charged with resolving food shortages arising
from distribution problems, hoarding, price speculation, and black-
market activities, and handling the distribution and sale of oil, sugar,
rice, coffee, meat, and wheat. It reminded some Chileans of Carlos
Dávila's allegedly communistic "General Secretariat of Production
and Prices."

In January 1973, General Prats in his capacity as interior minister would state publicly that Chile's "difficulties" were caused by reactionary resistance to legal constitutional activities of the Allende administration.[52] A Chilean general, the army commander in chief no less, was serving as interior minister in a Marxist regime and soundly criticizing the political opposition. Such things had happened before only during the second Ibáñez administration, the Socialist Republic, or the 1920s, times when the military's political influence was extremely high.

When Prats was called in on November 3, 1972, to serve as interior minister, he agreed to serve in the cabinet, along with Rear Admiral Ismael Huerta in Public Works and Transporation, and Air Force General Claudio Sepúlveda as minister of mines. The truckers' strike, called to protest the government's decision to nationalize the means of commodity distribution, was paralyzing the country. Prats, Huerta, and Sepúlveda were appointed to convince the opposition of the administration's good faith and to convince truckers that Allende meant business. Prats was replaced as army commander in chief by General Pinochet. The energetic Prats temporarily resolved the strike by guaranteeing that the government would not use force, and then he scuttled plans for nationalization. He was lauded for his efforts by truckers, truck owners, and the rightist opposition. It was at this juncture that Carlos Prats became a political figure to be reckoned with and thus began to involve the army increasingly in affairs of state. At this time, too, a photo of the assassinated Schneider was prominently hung in Socialist Party headquarters along with pictures of Chilean historical figures and internationally known Marxist heroes. It was generally assumed that the Schneider-Prats Doctrine now had a corollary: obedience, discipline, and constitutionality did not preclude participation.

The new fifty-seven-year-old interior minister, first in the Escuela class of 1934, soon proved himself a politician as well as a political figure. On November 30, 1972, he assumed the vice-presidency when Allende left the country for a two-week trip to Peru, Mexico, Cuba, the United Nations, the USSR, Algeria, and Venezuela. Chile's president was warmly received everywhere he went. To the dismay of some, General Prats did not take over the government while Allende was abroad; to the dismay of others, he began to act like a UP partisan (and the opposition press in Chile and numerous foreign papers began to call him the "Red General"). To the great consternation of many rightists, he defended the Allende administration vigorously when the

Bolivian government on December 21 accused Allende of allowing a Bolivian guerrilla group to train in Chile for operations in the altiplano!

Repeatedly during his two-week vice-presidency, Prats called for unity, sacrifice, and an end to partisan politics. In words that at times echoed those of Ibáñez in the 1920s, he asked students, party leaders, labor and management, and the press to shelve their differences with the regime and come together for the good of the country. He was critical of Congress, not for its traditional role as a separate branch of government, but for the bitterness with which even pro-Allende legislators maintained their independence. Prats became quite popular in December 1972; his image was good. He was an impartial nationalist, a patriotic public servant. On December 3 he spoke to his fellow officers, concluding, "I ask my companions in arms to be confident that at no time will I forget the institution I represent and [that] if I make mistakes those mistakes will not compromise the army; on the other hand, the accomplishments of my efforts will contribute to heightening its well-earned prestige."[53]

It would be fair to say that at this point Prats had the army situation well in hand. Only infrequently were there disciplinary problems after the retirement of Canales. Prats's replacement, Pinochet, followed the Schneider-Prats line. Likewise we can see that Prats had at least partially satisfied both the constitutionalists and the institutionalists. He had been called to serve his government and he had obeyed. He had defended his government, but claimed to be a living guarantee that the army would not suffer because of anything he did. His role was quite close to that of a caudillo at this time. He was the army's voice. When Allende returned on December 15 Prats dutifully handed over his duties as chief executive and returned to his still-new post in the Interior Ministry. The truckers' strike settled, his trip completed, the military included in the cabinet, and Prats established nationally, Allende needed the general for yet another important task: supervision of the congressional elections of March 1973. Here again the similarities to Arturo Alessandri's use of the army just forty-nine years before are unnerving.

The 1973 Elections and the Aftermath: Stalemate and Exacerbation[54]

The March 4, 1973, parliamentary elections were a major test of

Allende's power. UP had done well in the municipal elections of 1971 but fared poorly in several special congressional elections in early 1972. In 1973 the entire Chamber (150 seats) and one-half of the Senate (25 seats) would be up for grabs, presenting a real opportunity for UP to increase its control and halt executive-legislative bitterness. The campaigns were particularly violent; at least six Chileans died and over seventy-five were injured during the two months of pre-election frenzy. The cost of living continued to rise, and nothing the government could do stopped inflation from heading for a 300 percent figure by midyear. Prats and his colleagues, General Sepúlveda in Mines and Admiral Huerta in Public Works and Transportation, did their jobs well enough. Copper miners protested against rising prices but less belligerently than usual, the public works program functioned as well as could be expected given the economic conditions, and Prats carried off the elections neatly, with army troops prominently posted, along with carabineros, at polling places.

Not surprisingly for Chilean parliamentary elections, nobody really won, and this fact may have been primarily responsible for much of what was to occur during July and August. In short, UP increased its representation but remained a minority; the opposition Democratic Confederation (Confederación Democrática, CODE), composed of Christian Democrats and Nationals, lost some seats but remained an opposition with a certain degree of unity. The opposition could not muster the two-thirds Senate majority needed to override a veto, and it seemed that executive-legislative relations would continue to be bitter, with all Chileans the ultimate victims. Nevertheless, the press in Chile and other countries interpreted the election as it pleased. "Allende wins!" cried the left. "A victory for democracy!" cried right and center. In the long run, both won and both lost, for the Chilean political system will never again be what it was before September 11, 1973. Table 10 gives the results of the March 4, 1973, election compared with those of recent electoral contests.

While UP did increase its share of the vote (admittedly uncommon for incumbents in parliamentary elections held midway or late in an administration) over 1970, it is obvious that Allendistas received a lower combined percentage of the vote in 1973 than two years previously or four years previously. The vote percentages of CODE (only formally organized in late 1972) must be examined with great care. The 1973 percentage, 55.74, was a substantial increase over that received by individual candidates of CODE component parties two

TABLE 10
Results of March 1973 Elections Compared with
Results of Other Recent Elections

A. MAJOR PARTY VOTE PERCENTAGES, 1971 AND 1973
(rounded off to the nearest whole)

Party	1971 Municipal	1973 Parliamentary
Christian Democrat	26	29
(CODE*)		
National	18	21
Radical Democracy	4	2
(UP)		
Socialist	23	19
Communist	17	16
Radical	8	4
Popular Socialist Union	1	0

B. PERCENTAGE OF VOTE BY COALITION, 1969-73

	1969 Parliamentary	1970 Presidential	1971 Municipal	1973 Parliamentary
CODE*	51.7	62.7	48.2	55.74
UP	44.2	36.2	49.6	43.98

C. COMPOSITION OF CONGRESS, 1970 AND 1973

UP

As of 1970	Senate	As of 1973 Elections
5	Socialists	7
6	Communists	9
3	Radicals	2
2	Christian Left	1
	(Izquierda Cristiana)	
0	Movement of United Popular	0
	Action (Movimiento de Acción	
	Popular Unitaria, MAPU)	
0	Independent Popular Action	0
	(Acción Popular Independiente,	
	API)	
0	Independents	1
16	Total	20

1970	Chamber of Deputies	1973
14	Socialists	27
22	Communists	26
12	Radicals	5
9	Christian Left	1
0	MAPU	2
0	API	2
57	Total	63

CODE*

1970	Senate	1973
20	Christian Democrats	19
5	Nationals	8
5	Radical Left	3
	(Partido de la Izquierda	
	Radical, PIR)	
2	Radical Democracy	0
32	Total	30

1970	Chamber of Deputies	1973
47	Christian Democrats	50
33	Nationals	34
7	PIR	1
6	Radical Democracy	2
93	Total	87

*CODE was not functional until the 1973 parliamentary campaign.

Coalition totals for 1969, 1970, and 1971 represent combined opposition totals.

years earlier, or two years before that. But the CODE vote total was indeed a reduction compared with opposition totals in the 1970 presidential elections.

Succinctly put, what happened on March 4, 1973, was this: Allende supporters received a lower percentage of the vote than they had in 1969 before Allende and the UP were in office. Unidad Popular did better at the parliamentary level in 1973 than in the presidential race of 1970, but worse than at the municipal level in 1971; it remained a minority regime. Confederación Democrática did surprisingly well as an opposition coalition in 1973. There is a danger in comparing vote percentages in different types of elections, or in the same type of election held under different conditions and different times between different candidates. There is also a danger in speculating about future developments in Chile or anywhere else, especially after September 11, 1973, but we must face the possibility that this recent experience may lead to something akin to a two-party system in Chile, divided roughly along lines established between 1970 and 1973. In any case, it is clear that what happened in March 1973 was inconclusive for the entire country; it merely perpetuated and exacerbated executive-legislative conflict (always a point of departure for military-political activists in Chilean history) and it gave both UP and CODE reason to believe that each represented the will of Chileans. And so the struggle went on.

Two weeks after the elections, Prats and his military colleagues resigned from the cabinet, a customary gesture to allow the president to compose a new one after elections. But the officer-ministers did voice their disapproval of lax application of firearms control laws and of Allende's resort to executive orders and decrees to circumvent the recessed Congress. In so doing, the generals and the admiral behaved much like disgruntled politicians. Their political experience had not been altogether pleasant or rewarding.

The new cabinet was dominated by Socialists and Communists, as had been most cabinets since 1970. Socialists held the Interior, Foreign Relations, Defense, and Agricultural portfolios (Tohá returned as minister of national defense). Communists controlled Economy, Justice, and Labor; MAPU held Finance; Radicals were named to Public Works and Transportation and to Lands. Clearly the key decision-making posts were held by Communists and Socialists.

During April and May violence increased. The PIR pulled out of CODE on April 7, causing some difficulties to the right and center.

On April 28 an attack on PDC headquarters resulted in the death of a Communist Party stalwart. Miners went back out on strike on April 19. On May 4 PL leader Mario Aguilar was assassinated and his aide Ernesto Miller severely wounded in a shoot-out with Allende's bodyguards, members of the notorious "Group of Personal Friends" (Grupo de Amigos Personales, GAP).

The administration declared Santiago an emergency zone. As Chile lapsed into near anarchy, General Prats was visiting the United States, Great Britain, France, Spain, Italy, Yugoslavia, and the USSR. Was he preparing to enter politics on his retirement, asked some? Had he been sent out of the country, asked others? Just what was the "Red General" up to? No one knew. His absence from the Interior Ministry (or the absence of someone in uniform) seemed to coincide with inordinate violence and disorder. By May 10, O'Higgins Province, south of Santiago, was also an emergency zone. Miners at El Teniente, in their third week of strike, demanded higher wages. They battled with carabineros and were only subdued by brute force. At the end of May the miners rejected government wage offers and demanded wage increases of over 40 percent! (This would ultimately cost Chile $60 million in revenue.) On May 22, private bus drivers had gone out on strike for a week, crippling transportation in Santiago. Just for good measure, on May 25 former president Frei (now a senator again) received a death threat from the Organized People's Vanguard (Vanguardia Organizada del Pueblo, VOP), the same group that one year earlier had assassinated Edmundo Pérez Zújovic, one-time interior minister and vice-president under Frei.

The new Congress convened as per tradition on May 21, anniversary of the Battle of Iquique. National Party senators and deputies absented themselves as an insult to the chief executive. Allende's third "state of the nation" address to legislators (broadcast to all Chileans) was not at all like his aggressive speeches of May 21, 1971, and May 21, 1972.[55] He spoke bitterly rather than confidently; he was pugnacious rather than reassuring. He catalogued the events and difficulties of his administration. He said he was resolute in his program and his convictions, but whereas in 1971 and 1972 when he had offered nationalization of foreign concerns and restructuring of society and economy as solutions, he had no solutions to offer in 1973. He reminded some observers of Balmaceda and Arturo Alessandri by standing firm on his position in the executive-legislative struggle, attacking the legislative branch as "stagnant," and blaming it for hobbling his regime's programs. He stated that only the executive could call for a plebiscite and that only a two-thirds vote could override his veto of Congress's nationalization schemes (at odds with his own). In short, he brazenly challenged Congress, and in so doing brought to the surface residual military feelings about civilian politics, politicians, and their incessant squabbles at the expense of order and progress. He attacked the far right (but only chided such far-left groups as VOP and MIR) and warned of civil war. It was not the violent seizure of land by peasants that would cause civil conflict, he claimed, but "the violence of those who take nothing because they have everything" (in other words, PL). His plea for public order—"[It] has ceased being the servant of the capitalist system, and it is today a contributing factor to the advancement of the revolutionary process"—would not influence the far left for a minute. He claimed that 1971 had seen the demise of imperialist control of Chile's resources and that 1972 had seen great structural changes, but he made no claims for 1973.

Five weeks after Congress convened it became more obvious than ever that all was not well in Chilean civil-military relations. While motoring to his office on June 27, Commander in Chief Prats was involved in what he thought might be a kidnap or assassination attempt when a Santiago matron stuck out her tongue at him. He had the lady's car run off the street, held her at gunpoint, and demanded her arrest. The government proclaimed a state of emergency. Prats presented his resignation to Allende, who declined to accept it. Then the president harangued a crowd (estimated at 700,000!) and rumors of golpe, civil war, and mass violence spread. Armed workers occupied several large factories. Two days later Colonel Roberto Souper led 100 men of his Second Armored Regiment against La Moneda and the Defense Ministry in the first putsch in thirty-five years. As we know, the putsch failed, for Prats held the army with the government, but the government proclaimed several days of curfew from 11:00 P.M. to 6:30 A.M., and then ordered press, radio, and television censorship.[56]

In order to allow Allende to confront the crisis, his cabinet resigned collectively. The president implored service chiefs to serve again in ministries, but they unanimously demanded a free hand against strikers and those occupying factories as well as heavy cabinet representation, numerous undersecretarial posts, and several governorships. In effect, they demanded military control of the UP regime.

Allende refused and on July 5 succeeded in appointing an all-civilian cabinet with eight holdovers from the March group. The same week two former UP ministers and two UP provincial governors were impeached and convicted of malfeasance and constitutional violations. It did help that the El Teniente strike ended at this time, but the calm was only temporary and illusory. Eight days later *El Mercurio* published extracts of an alleged UP document instructing Allendista leaders to spread rumors that the CIA, the National Party, and PL were conspiring against the government, and instructing Allendistas to be prepared for action.[57] At about the same time *El Mercurio* began publishing material on fraud in the March elections (to the chagrin of the military) and stories of UP paramilitary groups.[58] On July 26, truckers struck again, protesting government-required low cargo rates and lack of spare parts (owing to curbs on imports and government controls exerted over the manufacturing of parts in Chile). The next day Allende's naval aide, Captain Araya, was assassinated. PL denied any connection and blamed the left; VOP and MIR accused the right. If the putsch of June 29 had indicated overt military insubordination, the new truckers' strike of July 26 demonstrated abject weakness on the part of the government. Once military insubordination was proportionately equal to governmental weakness, Allende was doomed.

The truckers' strike of 1973 may have been the most violent in Chile's history. There was no early solution, and Allende's July cabinet resigned after nearly two weeks of the strike had gone by. On August 9 the new cabinet was sworn in. The cabinet included Admiral Montero in Finance, Air Force General Ruiz in Transportation and Public Works, and General Prats in Defense. Prats's appointment as defense minister clearly indicated that Allende was tottering, for only in perilous times, or when in desperate need of placating or disciplining the armed forces, do Chileans turn to active officers for the Defense post. The most obvious comparison at this point would be the Alessandri dilemma of 1924.

General Ruiz, aided by Prats and PDC and National Party leaders, persuaded truckers near Santiago to turn over fifteen hundred idle trucks on August 16. Truckers were equipped with firearms and explosives, but both sides wanted to avoid a bloodbath, especially with retailers shutting shops and workers continuing to occupy factories. The military and Allende's opposition took credit for this partial (and temporary) solution to the strike. But less than a week later the opposition in the Chamber of Deputies passed a vote (81 to 47) condemning Allende for condoning violations of the Constitution and calling on the armed forces to make sure no future violations took place, despite a fatuous appeal by Communists and Socialists that a Bolivian invasion of northern Chile was imminent. The Marxist attempt to unite Chileans against Bolivia's "back to the Pacific" aspirations did not have the desired effect.

The Fall of Allende: Coalescence of
Military Opposition and the Golpe of September 11[59]

By August 22 Allende knew he could no longer count on the armed forces. Even the neophyte observer of civil-military relations in Latin America could foresee the end of the *vía chilena*. That day Prats resigned as defense minister. He resigned because his staff and command subalterns demanded that he do so after a stormy evening meeting at the Escuela. A loud demonstration by the wives of officers in front of his home also affected his thinking. One version had it that Prats wanted to tear gas the ladies and that their husbands would have none of it! Prats said he was resigning so that the army's unity would not be shattered. In short, he no longer had the necessary influence to control the army, and his association with the government in his role as a cabinet minister was seen by the high command as a menace to the institution. Furthermore, the rumor that Prats had obtained Communist backing for the 1976 elections must have frightened some army officers. Army institutionalism won out over Prats's army constitutionalism.

General Ruiz had already left the cabinet, on August 18, because of disagreements over handling the truckers' strike, and on August 23 Admiral Montero also stepped down. Like Prats, both Ruiz and Montero yielded to pressure by their colleagues, Ruiz because of a contrived technicality (he was not commander in chief and therefore was not equal to Prats, even though he was a cabinet member), and Montero because of naval high-command hostility to Allende. General José Sepúlveda stayed on as minister of lands, Air Force General Humberto Magliochetti took over in Transportation and Public Works. Admiral Daniel Arellano accepted the Finance portfolio, and General Orlando González became minister of mines. Former ambassador to the United States Orlando Letelier was

appointed defense minister. Significantly, none of the service commanders in chief were now in the cabinet, Allende's twenty fourth
since 1970. Augusto Pinochet moved up to army commander in chief,
General Gustavo Leigh Guzmán was confirmed as air force head, and
Admiral José Toribio Merino Castro assumed executive control of the
navy. We know now that, owing to politicking within and among the
armed forces, a junta was in formation, for the new commanders in
chief, Pinochet, Leigh, and Merino may already have been involved
in a golpe plot. According to various sources, plotting had been going
on since early 1972. Meanwhile, outside the walls of the Ministry of
National Defense Chilean normalcy was falling apart in the same way
it had in 1924, 1931, and 1932.

On August 24 secondary school students demonstrated in downtown
Santiago against the extension of their winter break (to keep them out
of school so that they could not assemble). Miners at El Teniente were
threatening another walkout, the truckers' problem still was not
resolved, soldiers and sailors were being pressured by leftists to revolt
against their commanders, and some soldiers and sailors had been
confined. Doctors had struck on August 18 "in sympathy with
truckers," and numerous shops were closed. During and after the
military cabinet resignations of August 18–23, engineers, airplane
pilots, chemists, dentists, mining technicians, nurses, and lawyers
joined shopkeepers and truckers. Provincial leaders of the PDC voted
to urge their national leadership to demand Allende's resignation via
Senate president Frei. There were more bombings, looting, and
armed clashes. Even General Viaux got into the act in a well-
publicized motor trip to exile in Argentina at the government's
expense on September 4.

Allende's position was no longer tenable. With the military
prominently represented in his cabinet, but with new military
commanders outside it, he was flanked. With party and congressional
opposition more vociferous than ever, he was at bay. With the
country economically paralyzed and his regime powerless to do
anything, he was a pathetic shadow of his former self. And with
society stumbling into violence, he became a target.

During July and August, according to reliable sources, a cadre of
ten to thirty high-ranking army, navy, and air force officers planned
the overthrow of Salvador Allende and the dismantling of most of
what he and the UP had accomplished since 1970. These plans may
have been "Operación Cochayuya" (a type of Chilean seaweed), the

name given to an air force–navy scheme that the army finally joined. Whatever the specific sequence, the plotters devised an efficient system of communications through messages, and even allegedly had all calls monitored from La Moneda to members of the secret group in order to keep the president from breaking the ring. Plotters knew that they were under surveillance by GAP and civilian investigations police. The golpe, as carried out on September 11, 1973, was the product of their planning. It was designed to be rapid, ruthless, and decisive. Bloodshed was to be expected, and violence was not to be scorned. Except for the brutality and violence of September 11 and the following weeks, this was very much the pattern of the golpes of January 23, 1925, and June 4, 1932. Interests outside the armed forces and beyond Chilean frontiers knew of the plot and hoped it would succeed, but the golpe was definitely a Chilean operation.

On the morning of September 11, President Allende arrived at La Moneda at about 7:45. He knew that a naval revolt was in progress but did not know much about it. At about 8:30 A.M., according to Chilean and foreign media, he received by telephone an offer of safe conduct out of the country. He stalled, still ignorant of the extent of the golpe. He spoke to Chileans via radio from the presidential palace and addressed a throng gathered in the plaza below his office, telling them of an armed forces revolt. He advised workers to occupy all factories. He spurned the offer of safe conduct and was quoted by various sources as stating, "Only dead will they take me out of La Moneda."

By midday, troops had moved into the center of Santiago. With air, artillery, and automatic weapons soldiers and carabineros attacked the presidential palace and other buildings occupied by Allende partisans. Before the air attack began the president was given several more chances to leave his office safely, but he valiantly refused. Hawker Hunter jets strafed, rocketed, and precision bombed La Moneda and other buildings. Sherman tanks released fusillade upon fusillade. Helicopters hovered in the sky. Allende's home, the Cuban Embassy, Socialist, Communist, and other leftist political headquarters and labor offices were under attack. Newspapers, radio and television stations, telecommunications and transportation facilities were occupied. Ministries were taken over. Guests in the Carrera Sheraton crouched on the floor and could only peek over their windowsills to see what was going on across the plaza at the risk of being greeted by a burst of gunfire.

At 1:45 P.M. army troops entered the nearly gutted La Moneda. Amidst the fire and smoke and rubble they made their way to the room where Allende had made his stand. He may well have committed suicide, but more likely he died shooting at the insurgents. It was stated in various sources that he used an automatic weapon given him by Fidel Castro when the Cuban leader visited Chile in 1971. Whatever the circumstances, the president of the Republic of Chile was most certainly dead by 2:30 P.M., September 11, 1973. Chile was under military rule for the first time in over four decades. A tradition had been shattered and so had a Marxist dream. It was well-nigh impossible to believe that civil-military relations that had prevailed between 1932 and 1970 would be restored.

In the wake of Allende, UP, Marxism, and the vía chilena, the plot leaders formed a four-man junta. Generals Pinochet and Leigh, Admiral Merino, and Carabinero General César Mendoza Durán named a military-led cabinet and began to cleanse their country of Marxist influence. Their cabinet comprised:

Interior	General Oscar Bonilla Bradanovic
Foreign Affairs	Vice-Admiral Ismael Huerta Díaz
Defense	Vice-Admiral Patricio Carvajal Prado
Treasury	Rear Admiral Lorenzo Gotuzzo Borlando
Agriculture	Air Force Colonel (r) Sergio Crespo Montero
Public Works and Transportation	Air Force Brigadier General Sergio Figueroa Gutiérrez
Lands and Colonization	Carabinero General (r) Diego Barba Valdés
Justice	Gonzalo Prieto Gandara (lawyer)
Labor	Carabinero General (r) Mario MacKay Jaraquemada
Housing	Brigadier General Arturo Viveros Avila
Mines	Carabinero General Arturo Jovaney Zúñiga
Public Health	Air Force Medical Corps Colonel Alberto Spoerer Covarrubias
Education	José Navarro Tobar
Economy	General Rolando González Acevedo

In one of its first official communiqués the junta stated that the military had taken power in the face of the extremely grave "economic, social, and moral crisis that was destroying the country," and that it would continue "fighting for the liberation of the country from the Marxist yoke." In a fourteen-point declaration the junta declared that it had taken power because:

1. The Government of Allende has lost its legitimacy by denying fundamental rights: freedom of expression, education, association; the right to strike, and present petitions; the right of property and in general the right to live in a secure and dignified manner.

2. The same Government broke national unity by artificially encouraging a sterile—and often bloody—class struggle, thereby wasting the valuable contribution each Chilean can make for the benefit of the country, and leading Chileans to a blind war between brothers, in pursuit of ideas alien to our nature which have been proven false and have failed in the past.

3. The same Government has proven unable to maintain the coexistence of Chileans by neither abiding by nor imposing the Law, thereby seriously damaging a rule of Law on many occasions.

4. Furthermore, it has violated the Constitution in numerous instances by using dubious, ill-intentioned, and biased interpretations of it, as well as other violations which, for various reasons, have gone unpunished.

5. It made use of subterfuges which they themselves have called "legal loopholes"; other laws were not enforced, some were violated, all creating situations that were illegitimate from the start.

6. The mutual respect among branches of the Government has been repeatedly broken by the annulling of decisions of the National Congress, the Judicial Power, and the Comptroller of the Republic, with unacceptable excuses or with no explanation whatsoever.

7. The Executive Branch exceeded its powers in a deliberate and evident manner, trying to hold political and economic power exclusively, to the detriment of vital national activities, thus endangering the rights and liberties of the people.

8. The President of the Republic has shown to the country that his personal authority is subordinated to decisions of

committees and to the leadership of Political Parties which were supporting him, thus losing the authority bestowed upon him by the Constitution, and therefore, the presidential nature of the Government.

9. The agricultural, commercial, and industrial economy of the country is paralyzed or in recession and inflation has increased at an accelerated rate. The Government does not show the slightest concern for these problems, but leaves the people to their own devices and appears as a mere onlooker.

10. The country is suffering from anarchy, suppression of freedom, moral and economic decay, and, in the Government, absolute irresponsibility and total incompetence, which have deteriorated the Chilean situation, preventing the country from occupying its proper place among the first nations of the Continent.

11. All the aforementioned facts are sufficient reason to conclude that the internal and external security of the country is imperiled, that we are jeopardizing the survival of our Independent State, and that support of the Government is unsuitable to the high interests of the Republic and its sovereign people.

12. These same facts, from the viewpoint of the classical doctrine which characterizes our historical concepts, are sufficient to justify our intervention to oust the illegitimate and immoral government, which does not represent the country's majority, thus avoiding greater evils that the present vacuum of power may create, since there are no other reasonably successful means to achieve this same result. It is our purpose to reestablish the economic and social normality of the country, restoring peace, security, and tranquillity which are lost at the present time.

13. For all these reasons, briefly stated here, the Armed Forces have taken upon themselves the duty assigned to them by the country to oust the Government, which, even though it was initially legitimate, has fallen into flagrant illegitimacy. The Armed Forces will hold power only during the lapse of time that circumstances may require, supported by the evidence of what are the feelings of the great national majority, which by itself justifies its actions before God and History, and therefore all resolutions, norms, and instructions

issued for the performance of such a highly patriotic task, which the Armed Forces are prepared to carry out for the common good.

14. Therefore, the legitimacy of these norms and regulations makes them binding on all citizens and they must be complied with by the whole country, especially by the authorities.[60]

The Aftermath:
First Steps toward Cleansing

This remarkable document, published in the Santiago press, once the press was allowed to function after the golpe, smacks of viewpoints expressed at various times during the past four decades in the military literature of Argentina, Brazil, and Peru and in explanations given for military political action in these countries. Only once in recent times have remotely similar ideas appeared in Chilean military thought: in the *Plan Línea Recta.* The public statements issued by Chilean military leaders between 1924 and 1927 contain references to the same values and object on similar grounds to a civilian-led government. It appears that the absence of a fervent military viewpoint on social, political, and economic issues between 1932 and 1970 by no means precluded the existence of the underlying values that coalesced into a publicly expressed justification in a crisis situation. One might also infer that there is much to the theory that military professionalism comprises a number of constant elements that manifest themselves on occasion over the years.

The purge of Marxism and all that it stood for in Chile began as soon as the revolt broke out. Even before La Moneda was attacked and Allende lay dead, the rebel leaders ordered house-to-house searches for leftist leaders and foreigners (leftist refugees from other Latin American countries as well as numerous Cubans). The lists of those wanted had been made up in advance. The number of Chileans and foreigners killed, imprisoned, wounded, temporarily detained, or beaten will not be known for some time, but it is certain that the purge of September 11 was the most brutal episode of its kind in Chilean political history.

The sequence of events on September 11 and in the days following is generally known; therefore, we shall only summarize the critical operations of the junta against Chilean Marxism before offering conclusions on Allende and the military and on Chilean civil-military relations. It is significant that the military executed the September 11 golpe in a united fashion; it was an institutional golpe in which all three services and the carabineros exhibited equal propensities for violence. Military unity, however, may have been temporary, superficial, or both, for postgolpe reports, press coverage of the April–June 1974 trials, and allegations of summary executions in the army, navy, and air force make it apparent that there was considerable dissension within the military both before and after September 11. The army and air force in the attack on La Moneda and naval action in Chile's seaports were, nevertheless, ruthless at every stage. The military functioned efficiently at all times and appeared truly to be acting on its own, not at anyone's behest.

Leftists went into hiding to escape being beaten, jailed, or worse. Allende's wife, Hortensia Bussi de Allende, fled to the Mexican Embassy and later flew to Mexico, then Cuba. Carlos Prats was exiled to Argentina and then assassinated. The junta declared martial law, announced an evening curfew, and told all Chileans to stay off the streets until further notice. On September 12, Pinochet announced that the junta would eradicate Marxism, and many Chileans feared "the knock on the door." Workers were advised to leave factories they had occupied and, along with strikers, to return peaceably to work at a set time. Homes of Marxist leaders, leftist newspapers, and some factories were subjected to air and artillery barrages. A large number of snipers (many of whom did not know of Allende's death and burial on September 12) were shot.

On September 13 the Nationals and Christian Democrats announced support for the junta, and the next day Chile's new government lifted the curfew. Shops opened, rubberneckers crowded into downtown Santiago to look at the damage, Pudahuel International Airport opened, the trains began to run again, and skiers showed up at nearby Portillo for some late winter fun. It was as if things were normal again.

Things may have appeared normal for a brief spell to skiers, travelers, and shopkeepers, but things were very tough for Allendistas. Army and air force barracks and navy ships were full of political prisoners. National Stadium in Santiago was jammed with prisoners, including some North Americans.[61] Dawson Island in the Far South and the Juan Fernández Islands were used as temporary penal colonies. There were reports of 300 people in the Mexican Embassy seeking refuge. All day long troops were seen throughout Santiago, Valparaíso, and other cities, rounding up those whose names were on a list and some who just looked suspicious. At night, patrols, aided by searchlights, toured the streets. General Oscar Bonilla, the new interior minister, announced a list of 10,000 foreigners (later increased to 13,000) who would be "questioned," but also informed Chileans that the banks would be opened on Monday, September 17 (with a freeze on the issue of new currency).

Less than a week after the golpe, Foreign Minister General Rolando González Acevedo announced that Chile would break relations with Cuba, North Korea, and any Marxist country found to be involved closely with Chilean affairs. He announced that private foreign capital would again be welcomed in Chile's copper industry. Admiral Merino announced the preparation of a "White Book" detailing the corruption and scandals of the Allende regime. As an added bonus, Chileans were told that La Moneda and Allende's residence were stocked with weapons made in Marxist countries, that Allende's home was well supplied with luxury food items unavailable to the public, and that the army had discovered an Allende "love nest" filled with pornographic literature and sex devices. Not only the eradication of Marxism but the discrediting and assassination of character were the junta's goals.

In the streets of Santiago teams of soldiers commanded by junior officers began to burn Marxist literature and anything else they considered offensive (including works by Mark Twain, Truman Capote, and Graham Greene, according to CBS News, September 23).[62] The junta dissolved Chile's huge labor federation, CUT, and jailed its Marxist leadership. All mayors and aldermen were fired. A retired colonel was appointed alcalde of Santiago, and other trusted retirees and a few civilians assumed local office elsewhere. When asked why civilian political figures were being replaced by officers regardless of their politics, one general was reported to have replied, facetiously, "The politicians have already done enough; now it is only just that they take a rest." The year could have been 1927 and the speaker could have been Carlos Ibáñez, but this was 1973, and Chile's new military leaders were going far beyond what Chileans had ever experienced before.

Conclusions

Categorization and Some Speculation on the Chilean Political System

We categorize military golpes in Latin America almost automatically. The Brazilian golpe of 1964 was "rightist," as was the Argentine golpe of 1966. A "leftist" golpe took place in Peru in 1968. Since the Chilean golpe of 1973 toppled a Marxist government it must have been a "rightist" movement. Such thinking is simplistic. Categorizing should be avoided, or at least attempted by more sophisticated techniques.

There is no such thing as a rightist or a leftist golpe or regime if the military is professionalized to the degree that the armed forces in Argentina, Brazil, Peru, and Chile have been. In such cases, as fatuous as it may sound, a military golpe is a military golpe and the ensuing regime is a military regime, particularly if uniformed men do indeed make and carry out policy, as they do in Peru. The policies of a military regime are those based on a professional ethos. Order and progress will be paramount. Anyone who interferes or objects will be dealt with, excluded, outlawed, purged; the degree of interference or objection will dictate how dissenters are dealt with. Those who clearly pose no threat to military policies—because of political leanings or ideological acceptability—will be tolerated, utilized, favored.

In Chile the September 1973 junta promised to maintain social reforms, while hedging on the economic policies advanced by Allende. Private property, the junta stated, would be protected, but some large enterprises would remain in the hands of the state, and legally expropriated and divided lands would remain in the hands of those who tilled the soil. The new regime, in other words, was promising to hold to state ownership (but not necessarily operation) of large copper mines, a policy supported by right, center, and left, and it promised to uphold the legal aspects of the agrarian reform, a program favored by the left.

Although the Marxist left will suffer the most from purge, trials, and executions (with or without trial), those on the right who voice objections too loudly and those of any party who demand a quick return to civilian control will not find themselves welcomed to the junta offices with open arms. While relieved that the vía chilena has been halted, neither the Nationals or the Christian Democrats will be entirely satisfied until political power is restored to civilians. Here the right and the center must face the fact that the golpe did not entirely serve their purposes.[63]

From an ideological standpoint the golpe may have served the purposes of the United States. Accusations of CIA, Department of State, and Pentagon interference make the demise of the Allende regime something of an embarrassment to the United States.[64] Had Allende and UP allowed the 1976 presidential elections to be held, could the incumbent coalition have prevailed? Or—much more satisfactory from the United States' standpoint—would Marxism have been repudiated? If indeed the United States controls all that goes on in Latin America, would it not have been better just to wait and see? If there was a "game plan" for the golpe, it was a Chilean game plan based on past experience. Nevertheless, the United States did not express shock that Allende had fallen victim to the military.

Barely a year after the golpe one possible explanation for this lack of shock was made public. Testimony by William Colby, director of the Central Intelligence Agency, given in April 1974 to closed hearings of the House Armed Services Subcommittee on Intelligence was leaked four months later. This testimony made it clear that there was a covert CIA operation between 1970 and 1973 to create difficulties for Allende and UP. The United States government through the "40 Committee," the State Department and the CIA, had authorized the spending of at least $8 million to shore up such sources of opposition to the Allende regime as the opposition media, partisan political activities, labor groups—and specifically the truckers.

All the while, officials in Washington had been saying that the United States was in no way directly involved in the golpe. Rarely have artful dodgers dodged so artfully. The leaking of Colby's testimony and the subsequent admissions by President Gerald Ford and Secretary of State Henry Kissinger that millions of dollars had indeed been channeled to opposition forces in Chile added to the embarrassment.

It would be incorrect, however, to assume that economic sanctions, cutbacks in aid, grants and loans, and the expenditure of millions for harassment of the Chilean government, *caused* that government's demise. Such measures perpetuated certain difficulties and problems, but did not directly cause them. The golpe of September 11, 1973, was more a result of internal pressures than of external forces brought to bear through intrigue. All propaganda and rhetoric aside, this was the prevailing view (in a spirit of détente?) of theoreticians and intelligence gatherers in places like Moscow and Havana.

In no conceivable way did the golpe justify intrigue, and it is ironically significant that very soon after the Colby-Ford-Kissinger "revelations" attention shifted from the question of whether the United States caused the golpe and became more concerned with the proper role of the intelligence agencies and the candor of public officials. Revelations in 1975 of CIA involvement in Schneider's death merely reinforced this shift.

Economically the golpe may serve the interest of United States investors. The junta has no foreign scapegoat like the International Petroleum Company in Peru; foreign capital was welcomed back to Chile immediately. Investment guarantees and compensation for expropriated operations, however, would seem to serve Chilean interests too, given the hard lessons of 1970–73.[65]

In sum, this was a military golpe, neither rightist or leftist, and one which served the interests of Chile *as interpreted by the armed forces.* Other interests are ancillary.

Military definitions of Chile's interests are summarized in the fourteen-point declaration quoted and discussed above. The opinions of the military were based not so much on long-held professional attitudes as on external, nonmilitary factors influencing such attitudes. In chapters 9 and 11 we examined the gradualism inherent in the post-1932 Chilean political situation. Allende's dilemma reflected a serious structural weakness in the system. As we have seen, by mid 1973 the Allende regime was not in control of Chile; its inability to govern or administer effectively was anathema to the armed forces. Like Acción Democrática in Venezuela and the Democratic Front–APRA coalition in Peru just after World War II, the Allende-UP combine found itself technically in the middle, being goaded to further action by the far left, and staunchly opposed by the right. This position is always unenviable for a controversial political movement in Latin America, proportionately more so when it is a Marxist-dominated movement. From Allende's standpoint the regime was superficially within constitutional confines and within the gradualist tradition. But he was a political extremist by ideological standards. This dichotomous situation was too much for Chile's sociopolitical and economic system and structure. Allende's position was not altogether unlike that of Arturo Alessandri between 1920 and 1924.

Neither Allende nor Alessandri could effectively control his support groups, overcome political and legislative opposition to his schemes, or cope with serious economic problems. Both fell to the military.

Should we consider the possibility that some constants in the political system of Chile in certain circumstances provoke civil-military crisis? If so, the list might begin with the nature of coalition politics, the executive-legislative rivalry, the difficulties of coalitions made up of parties or factions hitherto untested at the highest level of national politics, and the limits of systemic flexibility in Chilean party politics.

In addition it would be wise to survey the difficulties of national-istic leadership with respect to United States and other foreign investment and the international economic situation. Chile's pathetic situation in 1972–73 did not augur well for other Latin American exponents of extremism, within or without constitutional bounds. Are political extremism, championing of economic nationalism, and maintaining close ties with foreign economic interests now mutually exclusive in a superficially democratic ambience? Are they more compatible in an authoritarian ambience? Does what happened in Chile show that authoritarianism is a more effective road to moder-nity and social justice than what passes for democracy in Latin America, or does authoritarianism truly function as a brake on progress?

To the military, democracy is a frustrating, bewildering, and almost alien concept. Because of the strength and flexibility of Chile's political system and the absence of obvious structural weakness until 1972–73, the armed forces did not openly express hostility toward civilian direction of national affairs the way the armed forces of Argentina, Brazil, and Peru have in the past half-century. Yet, ominously, there did exist a critical attitude about democracy among Chilean military leaders: "Democracy carries within its breast the seed of its own destruction. There is a saying that 'democracy has to be bathed occasionally in blood so that it can continue to be democracy.' Fortunately this is not our case. There have been only a few drops." Ten years ago a Chilean officer might have been retired on the spot for such a statement. It was attributed to General Pinochet soon after formation of the junta of September 11, 1973!

If the golpe of September 11, 1973, was uncharacteristic of Chilean political tradition, might not the Allende regime have been sufficiently uncharacteristic to render tradition meaningless? Can two uncharacteristic phenomena provide conditions propitious for a return to the norm? Probably not, for the armed forces appear to favor a restructuring of both the political system and civil-military relations. Between 1932 and 1970, as we have seen, national leadership passed constitutionally from right to center to left. Was this the limit of the system? Perhaps it could sustain no more, just as it could sustain no more under the conditions prevalent between 1891 and the golpes of 1924 and 1925. Probably so, for by 1973 the military saw no alternative.

Comparisons and Some
Thoughts on Chilean Civil-Military Relations

We also compare military golpes and their ensuing regimes. Two speculative comparisons come to mind here, based on early press and observers' reports on what happened in Chile. First is a comparison of the Chilean golpe and formation of the junta with the situation in Greece from 1967 to 1974 (and even with the anti-Communist crusade of 1965–66 in Indonesia). This is a cumbersome and unlikely comparison but it has been made—on the basis of superficial examination. To the viewer of *Z* and *State of Siege* (the latter filmed in Chile) what went on during and after September 11, 1973, seemed a corroboration of supposed military attitudes toward democracy, reform, and liberty. Brutality, book burning, mandatory haircuts for young men whose hair length was judged unseemly, outlawing of the word *compañero* (comrade), the specious rumor that women could not wear pantsuits in public—all these contributed to opinions that Chilean officers were like Greeks. So did the order to paint over all political slogans on walls and buildings. To many this confirmed that it was indeed the cloud of fascism that loomed in the air about Santiago and the rest of Chile.

The "macrocomparison" between Chile and Greece can go that far but no further. It is indeed cumbersome and superficial, but the similarities may have much to do with professional military reactions to Marxism and to social, political, and economic situations seen as anarchic, deteriorating, or destructive. What happened in Chile, though hardly inevitable, was to be expected given the ad hoc development of a professional military ideological stance. Chaos, corruption, politiquería, ineffective government, extralegal measures, executive-legislative impasse, the foreign-influenced menace to Chilenidad, and Marxism, were simply unacceptable to the military.

The second comparison, less cumbersome and superficial than that of Chile with Greece, somewhat more attractive, and surely more productive, is that of Chile with Argentina, Brazil, and Peru. This comparison is especially stimulating because of similar military experiences with professionalism and because of the long absence in Chile of the type of thought that led to the repeated assumption of a political role by the armed forces in Argentina, Brazil, and Peru. The Chilean military's attitude toward males with long hair is reminiscent of General Juan Carlos Onganía's 1966 stand against necking in public parks. More seriously, the hostility toward Marxism and the labor left in Chile recalls similar attitudes in Brazil and Peru, as well as Argentina. The violence, brutality, and alleged torture in Chile remind us of the violence, brutality, and torture in post-1964 Brazil. The infusion of military personnel into municipal and provisional administrations (not to mention the cabinet), CORFO, railway administration, banking operations, university administration, and other state activities is analogous to what has happened recently in Brazil and even more so to events in Peru since 1968. Furthermore, by the end of 1973 it was apparent that Chile's military leaders (none of whom could qualify as an economist) were seriously considering economic measures similar to those adopted in Brazil since 1964. Finally, the attempts by MIR, Socialists, and Communists to subvert military discipline in Chile are also points for comparison, for both the Brazilian and Peruvian military have faced similar problems.

Chile, however, is unique among Latin American nations, for there Marxism was legal and in power. It took Marxism to provoke a civil-military crisis in Chile; in Argentina, Brazil, and Peru it took less, from a strictly ideological standpoint.

Whereas military golpistas in Argentina, Brazil, and Peru pointed out the existence of civilian terrorist and paramilitary groups, only in Chile did civilians cache arms in order to launch a civil war and destroy the military. Only in Chile has there been such convincing proof of plots, including what appear to be a number of proposals for action, collectively called "Plan Zeta," to create a clandestine "parallel, irregular, socialist, revolutionary people's army" and to liquidate high-ranking military leaders and opposition politicians.[66] The day of the golpe, *El Mercurio* carried a story criticizing the government for its own criticism on television of army operations in Temuco that uncovered an arsenal of automatic weapons, land mines, grenades, ammunition, and a sophisticated arms factory run by a MIR guerrilla group. On September 14, 1973, *El Mercurio* again published stories and photos of arms found during the golpe in La Moneda, in Allende's private residence (Tomás Moro), and in his mountain retreat. Czech and Russian automatic weapons, grenades, bazookas, rocket launchers, recoilless rifles, mortars, ammunition, and spare parts were displayed. Never in Argentina, Brazil, or Peru was the military faced with a menace of such proportions.

If the 1973 golpe in Chile cannot be categorized as rightist or leftist, if it cannot be specifically compared to any other similar phenomena in Latin America or elsewhere, was it, then, centrist? Was it a middle-class golpe? This view will probably obtain for some time, given the popularity of aligning the military with the middle sectors, and given the support for the golpe voiced by socioeconomic groups generally placed in a middle category. Nevertheless, this view is also subject to scrutiny. Is the officer class indeed representative of the middle sectors? If it is, are the troops who did the real work and who maintained the junta after September 11 also representatives of the middle class? Was the Allende regime truly representative of the lower classes or just of portions of that socioeconomic group? Until 1970, we ought to bear in mind, the Chilean lower classes were the socioeconomic group most favorably disposed toward military political participation. We should avoid considering social classes or sectors as monolithic groups, for the Allende regime and the golpe that ended it demonstrated otherwise.

The middle sectors of Chilean society are not homogeneous or cohesive. The army officer class, and probably that of the navy and air force, is not homogeneous either. But military men are probably more closely knit because of professional interests (and the development of military families) than are their civilian counterparts. The Chilean middle sectors did not demonstrate support for, or reliance on, the military between 1932 and 1970, for they did not need to; did they back the military in desperation in 1973? For a week (September 11–18) maybe, but then leaders and organizations of middle-sector interests began to take a second look.

The Chilean military probably reflects middle-sector values more than values of the upper class or lower class, for the majority of officers at all ranks are middle-sector in origin, coming from families in business, the professions, the military, or agriculture. But in ousting Allende the military also represented the attitudes of nearly 63 percent of the 1970 electorate. In ousting Marxists from power the military represented over 54 percent of the 1973 electorate. In short, the golpe can be considered responsive to a majority made up of all classes or sectors, for surely the Chilean middle sectors do not account for such a high percentage of voters.

The Chilean middle sectors disdain authoritarianism more than their counterparts in Argentina, Brazil, and Peru. Their years of participation and influence in the Chilean political system and the libertarian nature of Chilean society are responsible for this. The Chilean middle sectors zealously cherish civilian control of politics. The military has become highly critical of the polity and the 1925 Constitution—the Constitution it helped to impose on the country. The military does not oppose social change, limitations on private property, or restructuring of the economy. Middle-sector attitudes on these views do not necessarily mesh with those of the military, especially when it comes down to libertarianism versus authoritarianism as the structure within which policy is made and carried out. We cannot be sure, moreover, that in the event of economic collapse and political stalemate the military would not have overthrown an Alessandri or a Tomic. To dismiss the Chilean golpe of 1973 as a response to the desires of the middle sectors is at once to obfuscate and to dissemble.

Obviously the Chilean military would not long tolerate the existence of armed groups that threatened its existence or that of the order it was charged with defending. In the 1930s, when the government of Arturo Alessandri tacitly supported the Republican Militia, the army was shaken. It could do nothing about this insult to its honor, for it had no civilian support group. It would have nothing to do with the far left, the only civilian group that strongly opposed the militia. In the 1970s, when arms were distributed to peasants and workers and stored in government buildings and union headquarters, and when PL engaged in rightist terrorism, the army, navy, air force, and carabineros found that they did have civilian allies who opposed the creation of paramilitary organizations.

In the final analysis the constitutional proscription of deliberation was simply not sufficient to hold the Chilean armed forces in line. When it became apparent that civilians were arming themselves, the armed forces halted the process before civil war broke out.

Some military leaders have long considered that the upper classes are tied to outside interests. They obviously believed by 1973 that UP political parties, labor, and peasant organizations were also tied to international interests. It may be that in Chile any military–middle sector alliance is based on intangible Chilenidad, not on ideological, economic, or philosophical affinities.

This conclusion appears reasonable upon examining the positions of those immediately in charge of Chilean affairs as of September 11, 1973. Their careers and the attitudes they expressed on the overthrow of Allende made it abundantly clear that they were military professionals first, politicized citizens second. Pinochet, Leigh, Merino, and Mendoza are ideal examples of that breed of Chilean whose sociopolitical ideas may be influenced by their family origins or their friendships with civilians, but whose actions are based on the military ethos.

When Tobías Barros wrote *Vigilia de armas* in 1920, little did he suspect that it would be reissued in early 1973 and made available to all army officers.[67] In his foreword to the second edition, the now-venerable Barros explained that "the author would not have written at this time this *Vigilia de armas!* Nevertheless, he could not fail to deny authorization for its [re]publication, because he thinks that its reading offers a view of the army of a half-century ago and of the problems that troubled young officers at that time." "At that time," he said, "the armed forces and especially the officer class constituted sectors strictly delineated, and to a certain degree isolated from the civilian milieu. This gave to the life of the young officers . . . characteristics that we at times compare to those of religious communities. This is no longer true."[68] Or is it?

As well as the term *"pueblo en armas," Vigilia de armas* contains the phrase *"brazos armados del organismo social."* It repeats the criticisms leveled over half a century ago of civilian mismanagement of national affairs with particular stress on failures to ameliorate social conditions and modernize the country in an orderly fashion.

The reissuing of *Vigilia de armas* at this time was not coincidental. It was a purposeful gesture designed to disseminate among officers serving in the 1970s nationalistic ideas that had been popular in the 1920s. The names of General Pinochet, while he was chief of staff and head of the *MECH* "consulting council," and Colonel Pedro Ewing Hodar, head of army public relations and later public relations chief for the 1973 junta, appear in the imprimatur. This piece of militaristic propaganda may be even more indicative of Chilean military thought in the 1970s than of the militarism of fifty years ago.

Pinochet, Leigh, Merino, and Mendoza are intensively nationalistic and highly critical of what happened to their country between 1970 and 1973. To them Allende and UP, MIR, VOP, and PL were directly to blame, but the system that allowed Allende and UP to assume power—and that system's inability or unwillingness to cope with MIR, VOP, and PL—is the consummate culprit.

General Pinochet, a *porteño* by birth ("as was Allende," many journalists reported), is a pre–World War II product of the Escuela who, during his twenty-seven-year career (1936–73) rose from second lieutenant to division general to junta chief. He has been described as quiet, tough-minded, serious, critical of the civilian right and left, sympathetic to Christian Democrats, lacking humor, and a rigid disciplinarian. He taught geopolitics and artillery at army schools, and in his widely used (and rather well-written) *Geopolítica: Diferentes etapas para el estudio geopolítico de los estados*[69] concluded that "every state must maintain constant control of its own development, in order to influence opportunely whatever situation affects its growth. The state's cultural objectives and civilization, the increase in national power by way of augmenting the capacity of its citizens, and permanent regard for national security are the bases for harmonious progress of the state; in planning its growth it must clearly establish what is to be accomplished, always considering that every state should aspire to attain the greatest possible extension and capacity."[70] Clearly the Allende-UP regime did not measure up to this rigid code, so derivative of Haushofer and other geopoliticians. But it is Pinochet's code and by extension that of the Chilean Army. Within a year of the golpe, Pinochet became the dominant figure of the junta, even assuming the titles President of Chile and Supreme Chief of the Nation.

Gustavo Leigh has been characterized as outgoing, suave, debonair, worldly—a stark contrast to Pinochet. Leigh, born in Santiago, turned fifty-three on September 19, 1973, a fitting birthday for a career officer. He became a second lieutenant in 1941 and rose to chief of the general staff of the air force by 1972, then became commander in chief in 1973. Like Pinochet (and Merino, for that matter), he had various tours of duty in the United States. Alleged to have ties to the discredited, divided PDC, Leigh emerged early on as the ideologue of the junta—or at least as the most controversially vocal. According to

Leigh's version of what happened on September 11, he initiated the golpe (intimating that there was no previous plotting) by contacting Pinochet after hearing Carlos Altamirano's radio broadcast of September 9. It was he who publicly advocated constitutional reform to restructure the political system, allow for military participation in politics (specifically in parliamentary activities), and create a new economic structure. His statements immediately caused Christian Democrats to fear the creation of a corporate state.[71] He was called more than once a "Creole Falangist." The National Party gleefully (at first) supported his proposals for constitutional reform by fiat. Owing to the rise of Pinochet, Leigh ceased to be so vocal during 1974, but he has by no means faded from the scene.

Admiral Merino has been a naval officer since 1936. He was born in La Serena in 1915, and has been called cosmopolitan, articulate, serious, and very conservative in his political ideas. In addition, journalists tell us, he is an avid philatelist, indicating what some journalists consider to be a significant attribute for a political officer. He represents traditional naval conservatism, and if categorization is possible he would probably be placed to the right of Leigh. The necessity of naval support notwithstanding, Merino's role cannot be as critical as that of Pinochet and Leigh.

The same holds for General Mendoza, the fifty-five-year-old commander in chief of the carabineros. He became a junta member not because of his political ideas but because, like Pinochet, Leigh, and Merino, he was made commander in chief in 1973. Mendoza is athletic, a world-class equestrian, and probably the most down-to-earth of the junta lot. Because of his police functions, he may be closer to some Chilean social problems than the other service chiefs, but this may not increase his importance within the junta, given the professional military orientation of the group.

The primary thing to be remembered about the junta is that each of its members has over thirty years of military career behind him. This means education, service, advanced training, and staff and command training and experience. It is hard to believe that this background will not be the primary influence in their thinking and action. Too, it should be remembered that these men are essentially products of pre–World War II initial training and intellectual formation and that their ideas on civilian politics and democracy are affected by those of the military generation to which they belong and the epoch in which they were career oriented and reached maturity.

Finally, we should made some conclusions on Chilean civil-military relations as interpreted in this work. The first of these conclusions is obvious: taken as a set, those factors utilized in assessing Chilean civil-military relations from independence until 1970 were of little significance, if any, by 1973. The golpe of September 11 did not negate their significance for the past. Rather, it indicated their collective lack of significance in the face of political and economic collapse and social tensions, much as did the military political actions of 1924–32. This fact should make observers of civil-military relations in Latin America take notice.

Next, we ought to consider carefully the relative similarities of conditions between 1970 and 1973, and between 1920 and 1924. To reiterate, outright comparisons of Alessandri and Allende, the problems of the Liberal Alliance and UP, professional military attitudes of 1920 and 1970, and the like must be made carefully. Nevertheless, there may be some factors—like the strength and flexibility of the political system, economic dislocation, unresolved social problems, the military's corporate self-interest and perception of its own role, the degree to which the military is integrated or coopted by a regime, the executive-legislative conflict, ministerial irresponsibility or lack of continuity, political extremism and internal and external (to Chile as well as to the military) influences—that warrant examination as long-term constants in the study of civil-military relations in Chile.

Further, there is the fact that as late as 1970 the Chilean armed forces (in these pages the army has been the prime example) had developed no discernible ideological stance, no profile, no set of priorities, comparable to those so evident in Argentina, Brazil, and Peru. But this was no deterrent to political action, given the circumstances of 1973. We must conclude that no matter how professionally developed the Chilean military, and no matter how apolitical that development, the military was able to become intensely political, and in a rather short time.[72] We must also conclude (as many have already done) that professionalism, whatever its specific characteristics, is by no means a barrier to political participation. Because of these conclusions, we can venture another: It may be that factors external to the military are far more important in determining political action by the military than are strictly intramilitary attitudes. Moreover, methods utilized by the Chilean military in carrying out its political role will probably be based on the military ethos, but that role may have been cast from outside the profession. Here the Chilean military's lack of experience as a political force is important, especially in the formulation of economic policy.

In this vein, the lack of a discernible ideological stance or profile as well as the sheer lack of sophistication and experience in political affairs may influence profoundly the way in which a Chilean military government behaves, who it can be influenced by, who it emulates, the degree of authoritarianism and repression that develops, and what the junta does either to stabilize its control or to create a new political system. For although we can see traces of influence from Argentina, Brazil, and Peru in this Chilean phenomenon, what we see ultimately will be something notably different for Chile, if not for Latin America as a whole.

It is obvious that tradition will bind as long as the components of tradition remain relatively proportionate with respect to civil-military relations. The components of traditional Chilean civil-military relations underwent profound alteration during the late nineteenth century and particularly between 1891 and 1924. Once the traditional relationship was reestablished in 1932, alterations were not readily discernible until 1972, when the components of tradition were no longer proportional, extant, or valid.

The net result of the golpe of September 11, 1973, is another inversion of Chilean civil-military relations. Neither the normalcy of 1831–1924 nor that of 1932–73 can be reestablished without dramatic action. It is unlikely that the Chilean armed forces will ever again represent politically what they represented during those epochs. It is unlikely that they can conduct national affairs or extricate themselves from involvement without gaining new enemies.

The minimal result of the inversion of 1973, obviously, was military rule. The duration of military rule will depend on many things. Whether it will result in a new Constitution and massive restructuring will also depend on many things, as will the specific style of that Constitution and restructuring.

In Chile it took Marxism—the stretching of a flexible political system to its functional and ideological limits—to create conditions propitious to military political action. It may be that Marxism and all the ways in which it manifested itself in Chile will be the most telling influence on the actions of military policy makers. It is not at all surprising that, despite the military's hard-line anticommunism,

Communists appear to have weathered the storms of 1973 better than their erstwhile UP comrades. Nor is it a source of wonder that Marxists of all parties and organizations have themselves debated the failures of the Chilean political system and the Allende administration almost as much as they have blamed "counterrevolutionary" forces for the golpe. Whatever the ultimate results of the military overthrow of Salvador Allende Gossens and the new inversion in Chilean civil-military relations, it is certain that those relations, as defined and discussed in this study, entered a new phase on September 11, 1973.

Bibliographical Notes

The following notes are select and restrictive. Because there is no great body of literature on Chilean civil-military relations per se, it has been necessary to use various types of source material. I have endeavored to hold documentation to a reasonable level, consistent with scholarly standards, and have also attempted to provide the reader with potential sources of diverging interpretation and analysis. While relying in some places on standard sources of information, I have made it a point to indicate alternate materials of high quality that are important to a more sophisticated view of the subject. I have purposely utilized some of my own earlier research and publications where applicable. And I have pointedly cited some sources not concerned with Chilean civil-military relations in order to indicate how this subject fits into the overall topic of civil-military relations.

Chapter 1

1. "The primary task of any government is the maintenance of some measure of peace and order within a given community. This *civil imperative* holds for any political grouping, . . . and unless it is met no organized society can exist. In addition to regulating the internal affairs of a community, the government may also be required to provide for its defense against external foes." David B. Ralston, ed., *Soldiers and States: Civil-Military Relations in Modern Europe* (Boston: D. C. Heath and Co., 1966), p. vii.

2. Particularly useful for the following paragraphs is Robert N. Burr's classic study, *By Reason or Force: Chile and the Balancing of Power in South America, 1830–1905* (Berkeley and Los Angeles: University of California Press, 1965), especially chap. 1, pp. 1–11; note Burr's comments on the proper framework for the study of South American "intrarelations," pp. 3–4.

3. Armies in Latin America, for example, could not be said to have existed for the purpose of maintaining a specific "legitimacy" in the post-1815 sense. As a military organization capable of securing a country's foreign policy objectives, no Latin American army, save possibly Chile's (1837–39), proved truly successful in the field on foreign territory in the years following the achievement of independence. The Chilean and Paraguayan armies at midcentury were the only two in South America that should not be classified as anachronistic products of the independence movements, far from being adjuncts of legitimate political systems.

4. In this vein see the following works in English: José Félix Estigarribia, *The Epic of the Chaco: Marshal Estigarribia's Memoirs of the Chaco War, 1932–1935* (Austin: University of Texas Press, 1950); Charles J. Kolinski, *Independence or Death!: The Story of the Paraguayan War* (Gainesville: University of Florida Press, 1965); Leslie B. Rout, *The Politics of the Chaco Peace Conference, 1935–1939* (Austin: University of Texas Press, 1970); Bryce Wood, *The United States and Latin American Wars, 1932–1942* (New York: Columbia University Press, 1966); David H. Zook, Jr., *The Conduct of the Chaco War* (New York: Bookman Associates, 1960); and Zook's *Zarumilla-Marañón: The Ecuador-Peru Boundary Dispute* (New York: Bookman Associates, 1964). There is a dearth of English-language sources specifically concerned with nineteenth-century armed conflict.

5. See Burr's comments on this point as a cause of diplomatic conflict in *By Reason or Force*, pp. 4–5.

6. See Kolinski, *Independence or Death,* and Estigarribia, *Epic of the Chaco,* for Paraguay's historic concerns. Ernesto Barros Jarpa's *La segunda independencia* (Santiago: Editorial Universitaria, 1956) treats the 1836–39 war from the standpoint of an Andean threat to Chilean sovereignty and continued existence.

7. See Adam Szászdi, "The Historiography of the Republic of Ecuador," *Hispanic American Historical Review* 44, no. 4 (November 1964):503–50; and Frederick M. Nunn, "Chile and the Andean Republics: The National Period," in Roberto Esquenazi-Mayo and Michael C. Meyer, eds., *Latin American Scholarship Since World War II* (Lincoln: University of Nebraska Press, 1971), pp. 73–102.

8. By *aristocracy* in these essays I mean the wealthy and upper class of Chilean society, not the government dominated by them; *oligarchy* is used to refer to the form of government, though the terms can be used interchangeably.

9. Some conclusions reached in the following paragraphs are drawn from portions of Burr's approach to Chilean diplomatic history in the examination of civil-military relations. See Burr, *By Reason or Force,* chap. 1, and chap. 2, especially pp. 12–17.

10. On this see Gaetano Mosca, *The Ruling Class* (New York: McGraw-Hill, 1939), especially chap. 9, "Standing Armies."

11. With respect to ideas presented in the following sections, see the stimulating book by Karl Deutsch, *Nationalism and Its Alternatives* (New York: Alfred A. Knopf, 1969), particularly where Deutsch deals with Latin American settlement patterns and their similarity to or difference from those in Europe. Deutsch notes the importance in the overall development of nationalism and national integration of "wheel structures" of communications and transportation (that is, the radiation of these from Paris or Buenos Aires) and "grid structures" of communications and transportation such as those that developed in Germany and the United States. Because of its configuration, Chile can be cited as an example of a "spinal structure" of communications and transportation, a structure no less conducive to national integration and the development of nationalism.

Other works used in framing this portion of the essay are Mosca's *The Ruling Class;* and Stanislaw Andrjewski's *Military Organization and Society* (Berkeley and Los Angeles: University of California Press, 1968).

12. Chile is today larger than any European country with the exception of Germany and Russia; it is smaller than Argentina and Brazil. Gilbert Butland calls the Chile of the early nineteenth century the "birth region" of the modern country and emphasizes the enclosed, isolated nature of the Central Valley prior to territorial expansion. See the various editions of his *Chile: An Outline of Its Geography, Economics and Politics* (London: Royal Institute of International Affairs). Similar emphasis is made by Harold Blakemore in "Chile," in Blakemore and Clifford T. Smith, eds., *Latin America: Geographical Perspectives* (London: Methuen and Co., 1971). This is an especially valuable work.

13. Robert A. Potash notes that as late as 1880 the Argentine provinces were entitled to maintain armed forces independent of the "national army." See his *The Army and Politics in Argentina, 1928–1945: From Irigoyen to Perón* (Stanford, Calif.: Stanford University Press, 1968). On Brazil's centrifugal politics and centripetal military see Frederick M. Nunn, "Military Professionalism and Professional Militarism in Brazil, 1870–1970: Historical Perspectives and Political Implications," *Journal of Latin American Studies* 4, no. 1 (May 1972):38.

14. A good recent source on Chilean independence is Simon Collier's *Ideas and Politics of Chilean Independence, 1808–1833* (Cambridge: Cambridge University Press, 1967). This work also has a solid discussion of the postindependence period to 1833.

15. The Spanish general Mariano Ossorio opined bluntly in a proclamation of November 8, 1814, that the rebels had "oppressed" Chile since 1810. They still operated "in disguise" and were being manipulated by the Buenos Aires insurgents. They had run away (to Mendoza, Argentina) after "sacking churches, robbing the treasury and their neighbors." Ossorio called them "barbarians," "assassins," "thieves," "firebrands," "blasphemers," "pirates," "to whom

there is no right of refuge in civilized society [but] who have received it in Mendoza." Audiencia de Chile, Legajo 315, Archivo General de Indias, Seville.

10. A provocative discussion of the Chilean political system is Maurice Zeitlin's "The Social Determinants of Political Democracy in Chile," in James Petras and Maurice Zeitlin, eds., *Latin America: Reform or Revolution?* (New York: Fawcett Publications, 1968), pp. 220–34. See especially pp. 223–34, where Zeitlin indicates that what we accept as *explanations* for the development of political democracy in Chile are really *descriptions;* one such so-called explanation is "that the military has not intervened . . . in politics. . . ." This is not even a good description, and I have attempted in this essay to provide more thoughtful descriptions and better explanations of civil-military relations.

17. On doctrinaire politics, parties, and factions to midcentury see the perceptive Alberto Edwards Vives, *La fronda aristocrática: Historia política de Chile* (Santiago: Editorial del Pacífico, 1928), pp. 15–112.

18. The most popular recent Marxist interpretation of Chilean history is Luis Vitale's *Interpretación marxista de la historia de Chile*, 3 vols. (Santiago: Prensa Latinoamericana, 1967–71). Volume 3, pp. 176–99 deals with nineteenth-century society. A good, succinct characterization of the nineteenth-century Chilean peasant is that offered by James Petras in his *Politics and Social Forces in Chilean Development* (Berkeley and Los Angeles: University of California Press, 1969). Petras terms the Chilean peasant, "servile," and "dependent." See pp. 74–75.

Chapter 2

1. There is no good study in print of nineteenth-century Chilean civil-military relations. Material must be gleaned from historical treatments of the period and from military histories, which themselves do not discuss military political action as such. The most competent recent military history of Chile is the official *Historia militar de Chile* prepared under the direction of the Comité de Historia Militar del Ejército of the General Staff, 2 vols. (Santiago: Estado Mayor General del Ejército, 1969). The *Historia* has a good working bibliography of printed sources. Volume 1, part 2 deals with the independence campaigns and the formative years of the army. Civil-military relations to 1830 are treated in Diego Barros Arana, *Historia general de Chile*, 16 vols. (Fiago, 1884–1902), vols. 7–14, and more succinctly in Fernando Campos Harriet, *Historia constitucional de Chile* (Santiago: Editorial Jurídica de Chile, 1969), pp. 69–142. One should also consult *Las fuerzas armadas de Chile: Album histórico* (Santiago: Empresa Editora Atenas, 1930), p. 5.

2. The reader should refer to the bibliography in vol. 1 of the official *Historia militar* for works dealing with the military's role in independence.

3. The best biographical treatment of O'Higgins by a Chilean is Jaime Eyzaguirre, *O'Higgins* (Santiago: Empresa Editora Zig-Zag, 1968). An earlier study, still worthy of note, is Benjamín Vicuña Mackenna, *Vida de O'Higgins* (Santiago, 1882). In English, see Stephen Clissold, *Bernardo O'Higgins and the Independence of Chile* (New York: Frederick A. Praeger, 1969); and Jay Kinsbruner, *Bernardo O'Higgins* (New York: Twayne Publishers, 1968).

4. The early history of military training is discussed in Frederick M. Nunn, "Emil Körner and the Prussianization of the Chilean Army: Origins, Process, and Consequences, 1885–1920," *Hispanic American Historical Review* 50, no. 2 (May 1970): 300–322. This essay is based on many primary and some secondary sources.

5. On civil-military collusion in the downfall of O'Higgins see the biographical sources cited above in note 3. A major nineteenth-century work lays O'Higgins's downfall to his dictatorial ways, and was indeed directed against the autocratic president Manuel Montt Torres (1851–61). See Miguel Luis Amunátegui, *La dictadura de O'Higgins* (Santiago, 1853), p. 10.

6. One of the better (though somewhat dated) works to be consulted on military involvement

in politics during the 1820s is Domingo Amunátegui Solar, *Pipiolos y pelucones* (Santiago: Editorial Nascimento, 1939). See also Alberto Edwards Vives, *La fronda aristocrática: Historia política de Chile* (Santiago: Editorial del Pacífico, 1928), chap. 6, pp. 41–44.

7. Two good modern discussions of Liberalism (*pipiolismo*) and Conservatism (*peluconismo*) in the early years of Chilean nationhood are found in René León Echaiz, *Evolución histórica de los partidos políticos chilenos*, 2d ed. (Santiago: Editorial Francisco de Aguirre, 1971), pp. 3–20; and Germán Urzúa Valenzuela, *Los partidos políticos chilenos* (Santiago: Editorial Jurídica de Chile, 1968), pp. 23–28. Both works are interpretive and based on printed sources. In English see Jay Kinsbruner, *Chile: A Historical Interpretation* (New York: Harper and Row, 1973), esp. pp. 49–69. This work is a succinct, readable, scholarly treatment from colonial times to the present, and contains valuable insights on constitutional issues.

8. Barros Arana, *Historia general*, 15:131.

9. For source materials on issues treated in the following section see nn. 6 and 7 above.

Chapter 3

1. On Portales see Benjamín Vicuña Mackenna, *Don Diego Portales*, 2d ed. (Santiago: Universidad de Chile, 1937); Aurelio Díaz Mesa, *El advenimiento de Portales*, 2d ed. (Santiago: Editorial del Pacífico, 1960). In English see the classic Agustín Edwards, *The Dawn, 1810–1841* (London: Ernest Benn, 1931), and Jay Kinsbruner, *Diego Portales: Interpretive Essays on the Man and His Times* (The Hague: Martinus Nijhoff, 1967). The reader would do well to consult the bibliographic references on Portales and his times in Fredrick B. Pike, *Chile and the United States, 1880–1962: The Emergence of Chile's Social Crisis and the Challenge to United States Diplomacy* (Notre Dame., Ind.: University of Notre Dame Press, 1963), pp. 308–9. The political relationship between Portales and Prieto is revealed in Academia Chilena de Historia, *Cartas de don Joaquín Prieto a don Diego Portales* (Santiago: Universidad Católica de Chile, 1960).

2. On this subject see Frederick M. Nunn, "Emil Körner and the Prussianization of the Chilean Army: Origins, Process, and Consequences, 1885–1920," *Hispanic American Historical Review* 50, no. 2 (May 1970):302. See also Jorge Boonen Rivera, *Participación del ejército en el desarrollo y progreso del país* (Santiago: Imprenta del Globo, 1917) and Fabio Galdámez Lastra, *Historia militar de Chile: Estudio crítico de la campaña de 1838–1839* (Santiago: Estado Mayor Jeneral del Ejército, 1910), pp. 35–42.

3. By 1832 Chile's military school had "eighty cadets who, under the direction of French [and] English instructors, receive instruction in all that pertains to military science" (William S. W. Ruschenberger, *Noticias de Chile, 1831–1832* [*Three Years in the Pacific; including Notices of Brazil, Chile, Bolivia and Peru*] [Santiago: Editorial del Pacífico, 1956], p. 86).

4. Fernando Campos Harriet, *Historia constitucional de Chile* (Santiago: Editorial Jurídica de Chile, 1969), pp. 144–54, stresses the austerity and probity of the Portalian creation. This source is especially good for the following paragraphs.

5. "Portales ordered the public offices, filthy, littered with cigar butts, and smelling of liquor, swept clean. He himself inspected when he was least expected. Every custodian in Santiago knew don Diego Portales" (Campos, *Historia constitucional*, p. 148).

6. A good work on the Constitution of 1833 is Alberto Edwards Vives, *Páginas históricas* (Santiago: Editorial Difusión Chilena, 1945). See also Campos, *Historia constitucional*, pp. 331–40; and the standard Julio Heise González, *Chile: 1810 a 1960: 150 años de evolución constitucional* (Santiago: Editorial Andrés Bello, 1960).

7. On the 1836–39 war see the standard Ernesto Barros Jarpa, *La segunda independencia* (Santiago: Editorial Universitaria, 1956), chap. 1; and Galdámez, *Historia militar*. Particularly good on the war, but mainly concerned with the Prieto decade, is the now dated and strictly conservative Domingo Amunátegui Solar, *Historia de Chile bajo el gobierno del general don*

Joaquín Prieto, 4 vols. (Santiago: Imprenta Barcelona, 1900–1903). See also the official *Historia militar de Chile,* 2 vols. (Santiago: Estado Mayor General del Ejército, 1969), 2:7–52.

8. Cited in Campos, *Historia constitucional,* pp. 117–40.

9. Ibid., p. 149.

10. As Francisco Antonio Encina puts it, "The image of Portales, with chains on his feet, led to martyrdom by a drunk through desolate hills during a gloomy night and cruelly assassinated . . . by the order of his most favored friend, profoundly influenced the national imagination" (*Resumen de la historia de Chile,* 3 vols. [Santiago: Empresa Editora Zig-Zag, 1950], 2:917).

11. Covering the forty years 1831–71 is Ramón Sotomayor Valdés, *Historia de Chile durante los cuarenta años transcurridos desde 1831 hasta 1871,* 2 vols. (Santiago, 1875). This work is particularly helpful on the years 1831–51. Still the standard work on Manuel Bulnes's presidency is Diego Barros Arana, *Un decenio de la historia de Chile, 1841–1851,* 2 vols. (Santiago: Imprenta Barcelona, 1913).

12. See Germán Urzúa Valenzuela, *Los partidos políticos chilenos* (Santiago: Editorial Jurídica de Chile, 1968), pp. 29–30.

13. On La Fronda, the resurgence of Chilean Liberalism and Filopolitismo as well, see René León Echaiz, *Evolución histórica de los partidos políticos chilenos,* 2d ed. (Santiago: Editorial Francisco de Aguirre, 1971), pp. 21–34; and Alberto Edwards Vives, *La fronda aristocrática: Historia política de Chile* (Santiago: Editorial del Pacífico, 1928), pp. 65–102. Pike's bibliographical citations (*Chile and the United States,* pp. 310–11) are valuable for these subjects and general political trends, 1830–80.

14. Still the standard biography of Montt is *El gobierno de don Manuel Montt* by Alberto Edwards Vives (Santiago: Editorial Nascimento, 1933).

15. On the revolt of 1851 see the Marxist version by Luis Vitale, *Las guerras civiles de 1851 y 1859 en Chile* (Concepción: Universidad de Concepción, 1971), pp. 5–36. Vitale stresses the importance of the popular movement of the ultraliberal Society of Equality and considers the Cruz pronunciamento of secondary importance. This work has a good bibliography. See also Antonio Iñíguez Vicuña, *Historia del período revolucionario, 1848–1851* (Santiago: Imprenta del Comercio, 1905).

16. Chile's status as a power is ably treated in Robert N. Burr, *By Reason or Force: Chile and the Balancing of Power in South America, 1830–1905* (Berkeley and Los Angeles: University of California Press, 1965), chaps. 3, 4, pp. 33–72.

17. On the revolt of 1859 see Vitale, *Las guerras civiles,* pp. 37–74; Pedro Pablo Figueroa, *Historia de la revolución constituyente, 1858–59* (Santiago, 1889); and the military version of the conflict by Francisco Javier Díaz, *La guerra civil de 1859* (Santiago: Imprenta de la Fuerza Aérea, 1947).

18. See William Columbus Davis, *The Last Conquistadors: The Spanish Intervention in Peru and Chile, 1863–1866* (Athens, Ga.: University of Georgia Press, 1950).

Chapter 4

1. Valuable for a study of politics during this period are Fernando Campos Harriet, *Historia constitucional de Chile* (Santiago: Editorial Jurídica de Chile, 1969), René León Echaiz, *Evolución histórica de los partidos políticos chilenos,* 2d ed. (Santiago: Editorial Francisco de Aguirre, 1971), Germán Urzúa Valenzuela, *Los partidos políticos chilenos* (Santiago: Editorial Jurídica de Chile, 1968), and Francisco Antonio Encina, *Resumen de la historia de Chile,* 3 vols. (Santiago: Empresa Editora Zig-Zag, 1950), vol. 2. There are no first-rate studies of the Pérez decade or the presidency of Federico Errázuriz Zañartu. Albert Edwards Vives, *La fronda aristocrática: Historia política de Chile* (Santiago: Editorial del Pacífico, 1928), pp. 113–62 should be consulted for an interpretive view of oligarchic fission and politics at midcentury. The

impressive bibliographic citations of Fredrick B. Pike, *Chile and the United States, 1880–1962: The Emergence of Chile's Social Crisis and the Challenge to United States Diplomacy* (Notre Dame, Ind.: University of Notre Dame Press, 1963), chap. 1, pp. 312–15 provide a wealth of material.

2. An excellent study of the Pinto administration, and one of the most important recent works on nineteenth-century Chilean political history, is Cristián Zegers A., *Aníbal Pinto: Historia política de su gobierno* (Santiago: Editorial Universitaria, 1969).

3. There is no better source on Chilean foreign affairs than Robert N. Burr, *By Reason or Force: Chile and the Balancing of Power in South America, 1830–1905* (Berkeley and Los Angeles: University of California Press, 1965). Like Pike's *Chile and the United States,* Burr's study has an ample bibliography of basic sources. For information on the decade preceding the War of the Pacific see Burr, pp. 117–35.

4. The standard version of the War of the Pacific is found in the official *Historia militar de Chile* (Santiago: Estado Mayor General del Ejército, 1969), vol. 2, pp. 64–196. The most widely read Chilean version is by Manuel Bulnes's son, Gonzalo Bulnes *Guerra del Pacífico,* 3 vols., 2d ed. (Valparaíso: Imprenta Universo, 1919). It is better military history than his *Historia de la campaña del Peru en 1838* (Santiago, 1878). Wilhelm Ekdahl, member of a German military mission, wrote a technical version of the war, *Historia militar de la guerra del Pacífico entre Chile, Perú y Bolivia,* 3 vols. (Santiago: Instituto Geográfico Militar, 1919). See also the longtime standard Indalicio Téllez, *Historia militar* (Santiago: Instituto Geográfico Militar, 1925). The Bulnes work on the War of the Pacific is the most documented, thorough, and trustworthy of Chilean sources. There is a plethora of mediocre works on this international conflict written from the standpoint of each participant. The best Peruvian version (and a solid work from the Peruvian view) is Carlos Dellepiane, *Historia militar del Perú,* 2 vols. (Buenos Aires: Talleres Gráficos Luis Bertrand, 1941). Volume 2 deals with the War of the Pacific.

5. Dellepiane, *Historia militar del Peru,* stresses Chile's military and naval buildup before the war and the aggressive diplomacy of the Santiago government. Dellepiane, like all Peruvian sources before and since, repeatedly asserts that Chile's navy was the stronger.

6. The commemoration of the Battle of Iquique held annually on May 21 is one of the most important Chilean holidays. Congress begins its yearly sessions on this date, there are speeches and a parade, and wreaths are placed on the graves of heroes and at the feet of monuments. The papers all run editorials and special articles, sometimes supplements. The martyrs and heroes of Iquique and other battles of Chile's own "Great War" figuratively live again. In what at times seems a frenzy of nationalism, Chileans of all classes momentarily forget their problems and vicariously relive Chile's past. A recent scholarly treatment of one aspect of Chilean devotion to the memory of War of the Pacific heroes is William F. Sater's *The Heroic Image in Chile: Arturo Prat, Secular Saint* (Berkeley and Los Angeles: University of California Press, 1973).

7. On the army in the wake of the war see Gerardo Zúñiga Montúfar, *El ejército de Chile: Impresiones y apuntes* (Santiago: Imprenta Universo, 1904); Gustavo Walker Martínez, *Estudios militares* (Santiago: Imprenta Barcelona, 1901); Francisco Javier Díaz, *A propósito de nuestra política militar* (Santiago: Imprenta Jeneral Díaz, 1938); Jorge Boonen Rivera, *Participación del ejército en el desarrollo y progreso del país* (Santiago: Imprenta del Globo, 1917); Indalicio Téllez, *Recuerdos Militares* (Santiago: Instituto Geográfico Militar, 1945); and Armando Donoso, *Recuerdos de cincuenta años* (Santiago: Editorial Nascimento, 1947). Donoso interviewed General Boonen for the chapter on him in this book. A solid article covering the second half of the nineteenth century is José M. Barceló Lira, "La evolución del ejército chileno desde la ocupación del territorio araucano (1859–1879) hasta nuestros días," *Memorial del Ejército de Chile (MECH)* 28 (March–April 1935):199–218.

8. On Chilean society at this time see Fredrick B. Pike, "Aspects of Class Relations in Chile, 1850–1960," *Hispanic American Historical Review* 43, no. 1 (February 1963):14–33.

9. For information and bibliography on Körner see Frederick M. Nunn, "Emil Körner and

of the civilian sector most similar to them economically, educationally, and socially. I believe this tendency grows more important year by year in twentieth-century Latin America where military organizations are professional.

6. See Carlos López Urrutia, *Historia de la marina de Chile* (Santiago: Editorial Andrés Bello, 1969), chap. 16, "Cuarenta años de paz," pp. 311–32.

7. On population and demographic shifts during these years see Julio Heise González, *Chile: 1810 a 1960: 150 años de evolución constitucional* (Santiago: Editorial Andrés Bello, 1960), pp. 70–87.

8. See Samuel P. Huntington, "The Role of Military Influence in Foreign and Domestic Policy: Europe, Latin America and the United States," in *The Working Papers from the 1970 Atlantic Conference* (New York: Center for Inter-American Relations, 1971), pp. 61–86.

9. One of Chile's most politically minded officers, Marmaduke Grove, studied in Germany, and his reaction was typical. Jack Ray Thomas tells us that "Kaiser Wilhelm's Germany impressed Marmaduke, particularly the German people. . . . Grove compared his Chile to every European state he visited and Chile always came out second best in the comparison . . . he wanted to see improvements made so that Chile could favorably compare with any European nation." See Thomas's "Marmaduke Grove: A Political Biography" (Ph.D. diss., Ohio State University, 1962), p. 39. See also Marmaduke Grove Vallejo, "Estudios militares en Alemania," *Claridad*, February 5, 1938.

10. An ample bibliography on labor and socioeconomic questions of late nineteenth and early twentieth-century Chile appears in Campos, *Historia constitucional*, pp. 271–72.

11. As examples see Florentino Abarca, *La decadencia de Chile* (Santiago, 1904); the novel by Luis Orrego Luco, *Casa Grande* (Santiago, 1908); and the essays of Alejandro Venegas, *Sinceridad: Chile íntimo en 1910* (Santiago, 1910).

12. Karl Liebknecht, *Militarismus und Anti-Militarismus*, published in English as *Militarism and Anti-Militarism* (Glasgow: Socialist Labour Press, 1917), and reissued (New York: Dover Publications, 1972).

Chapter 6

1. The fact that the Chilean Army was apolitical when the professionalization process began supports this conclusion. As has been shown, there were close personal ties between state and army under Prieto and Bulnes, but thereafter there can be no doubt that the military was attached to the office of the president, but to no individual. Balmaceda did attempt to coopt the army, but too late, and to no avail. Moreover, the decline of personalism did not result in Chile because of close relations between civilian political leaders and officers.

2. Professionalization, resulting as it did from concern over future defense needs in the post–War of the Pacific years was by no means seen as a vehicle for removing the army from politics. As has been shown, the army was not politically involved.

3. The best study of the Civil War period is Harold Blakemore, *British Nitrates and Chilean Politics, 1886–1896: Balmaceda and North* (London: Athlone Press, 1974). There is a plethora of literature on the war itself. For a competent discussion of sources and points of view see Blakemore, "The Chilean Revolution of 1891 and Its Historiography," *Hispanic American Historical Review* 45, no. 3 (August 1965):393–421. Two official publications detail the role of the armed forces with ample documentation: *Memorandum de la guerra civil de 1891* (Santiago, 1892); and *La guerra civil de 1891: Relación historia militar* (Santiago: Estado Mayor Jeneral, 1917). See also Frederick M. Nunn, "Emil Körner and the Prussianization of the Chilean Arr Origins, Process, and Consequences, 1885–1920," *Hispanic American Historical Review* 50, (May 1970):305–6.

4. Nunn, "Emil Körner," pp. 305–6. See also *Para la historia: Algunas piezas d/ seguido a 118 capitanes del ejército de Chile por el tribunal militar, 2 de noviem/* (Santiago, 1891), for data on army purges after the Civil War.

the Prussianization of the Chilean Army: Origins, Process, and Consequences, 1885
Hispanic American Historical Review 50, no. 2 (May 1970):300–322.

10. Ibid., p. 304.

11. See, for example, Walker Martínez, *Estudios militares*, pp. 174–75.

12. An excellent, succinct study of the Chilean Navy is the Mahanesque Luis L
Influencia del poder naval en la historia de Chile desde 1810 hasta 1910 (Valparaíso: Ir
de la Marina, 1911). A solid, recent study is Carlos López Urrutia, *Historia de la marina ι*
(Santiago: Editorial Andrés Bello, 1969). Chapter 15 (pp. 311–33) deals with the post-18
and with the Civil War of 1891.

13. Körner's self-seeking motives and the Anglo-German conspiracy premise are de
(respectively) by Julio César Jobet, "El nacionalismo creador de José Manuel Balm
Combate (San José, C. R.) 4, no. 23 (July–August 1962) and in the dispatches from Unite
Minister to Chile Patrick Egan to Secretary of State James G. Blaine, U.S. Department
Files, Dispatches Received by the Department of State from United States Ministers
(1823–1906), #143 (March 17, 1891)–#154 (April 23, 1891).

Chapter 5

1. Professionalism is discussed here in the same context that I have treated it elsewh
Frederick M. Nunn, "The Latin American Military Establishment: Some Thoughts
Origins of its Socio-Political Role and an Illustrative Bibliographical Essay," *The Amer*
no. 2 (October 1971):135–51; "Military Professionalism and Professional Militarism in
1870–1970: Historical Perspectives and Political Implications," *Journal of Latin A*
Studies 4, no. 1 (May 1972):29–54; and "The Impact of European Military Training ο
American Armies: Aspects of Military Modernization in Argentina, Brazil, Chile an
1890–1940," *Military Affairs* 39, no. 1 (February 1975):1–7.

2. Pertinent to this section is chapter 4 of Edwin Lieuwen's pioneering *Arms and Pο
Latin America*, rev. ed. (New York: Frederick A. Praeger, 1961), pp. 36–58, especial
portions dealing with the effects of World War I and the Great Depression. See also
Johnson, *The Military and Society in Latin America* (Stanford, Calif.: Stanford Universit
1964), chaps. 4, 5, and 6, passim.

3. Data on the Extended Presidential Family have been assembled from app
biographies in Virgilio Figueroa, *Diccionario histórico y biográfico de Chile, 1800–1925*
in 4 (Santiago: Imprenta y Litografía La Ilustración, 1925–31). On the reinterpretation
Chilean Constitution of 1833 important during the Parliamentary Republic see F
Campos Harriet, *Historia constitucional de Chile* (Santiago: Editorial Jurídica de Chile
pp. 259–81. See also Julio Heise González, *La constitución de 1925 y las nuevas ter
sociales* (Santiago: Editorial Jurídica, 1951). See also Fredrick B. Pike's useful biblic
citations in his *Chile and the United States, 1880–1962: The Emergence of Chile's Soci
and the Challenge to United States Diplomacy* (Notre Dame, Ind.: University of Notr
Press, 1963), pp. 336–37.

4. It is fair to say that as of 1970 approximately 30 percent of the army officer class w
up of descendants or near relatives of army officers.

5. I believe this should be obvious upon examining the yearly *Escalafón*, the officer r
the Chilean Army for selected years beginning ca. 1900. While one must take care to a
possible family relationships, aristocratic surnames such as those prominent in politics,
and business prior to 1900 and in the army prior to 1879 appear only rarely in the arr
1891.

This does not mean that subordinate officers necessarily identified with middle-class iι
Rather, they identified with the interests of their profession first, and second, if at all, wi

5. A roster of Germans serving in Chile in the 1890s can be found in Gerardo Zúñiga Montúfar, *El ejército de Chile: Impresiones y apuntes* (Santiago: Imprenta Universo, 1904), pp. 57–60. A scholarly discussion of Germany's motives for encouraging military modernization can be found in Jürgen Schaefer, *Deutsche Militärhilfe an Sudamerika: Militär und Rüstungsinteressen in Argentinien, Bolivien, und Chile vor 1914* (Düsseldorf: Bertelsmann Universitäts-Verlag, 1974).

6. I have used available yearly *escalafones* (title varies from year to year); the annual *Memoria del ministerio de guerra* and *Memoria del estado mayor del ejército de Chile*, the *Reglamentos* of both the Escuela and Academia, and the annual *informes* presented by Academia and Escuela administrators from 1889 to 1914. Conclusions reached in this section are based on these sources and on those cited in Nunn, "Emil Körner."

7. Especially good military sources on the beginnings of military political interest are Arturo Ahumada, *El ejército y la revolución del 5 de septiembre,1924: Reminiscencias* (Santiago: Imprenta La Tracción, 1931), pp. 21–25; and Carlos Sáez Morales, *Recuerdos de un soldado*, vol. 1: *El ejército y la política* (Santiago: Editorial Ercilla, 1933), pp. 37–40. The diplomat Emilio Rodríguez Mendoza, in his *Como si fuera ahora* (Santiago: Editorial Nascimento, 1929), pp. 220–48 also covers this subject well.

8. To Barros Luco is ascribed the aphorism: *"No hay más que dos clases de problemas en la política: los que se resuelven solos y los que no tienen solución"* ("There are only two kinds of problems in politics: those which resolve themselves and those which have no solution.") Needless to say, the venerable Barros was not thought to be a forceful administrator!

9. See Rodríguez, *Como si fuera ahora*, pp. 216–17.

10. See table 2, above, p. 90.

11. Aníbal Riquelme, "Relación que debe existir entre la política de un estado i el alto comando del ejército," *Memorial del Estado Mayor del Ejército de Chile* 9, no. 9 (September 1914):638–50.

12. Manuel Moore Bravo, *Instrucciones para el desarrollo de las virtudes militares del cuerpo de oficiales de la IV división del ejército* (Valdivia: Imprenta Central E. Lampert, 1917). See especially pp. 5–25.

13. Domingo L. Terán, *Tema militar* (Santiago: Imprenta del Ministerio de Guerra, 1917).

14. On military plotting in 1919 see Columbano Millas P., *Los secretos que divulga un secretario privado de los ministros de guerra* (Santiago: Imprenta Universitaria, 1923); Alejandro Walker Valdez *¿Revolución? La verdad sobre el motín militar* (Santiago: Imprenta y Litografía Selecta, 1919); Román Calvo, *El motín militar: Anotaciones del dietario de una mosca* (Santiago: Imprenta Sud América, n.d.).

15. See Millas, *Los secretos*, p. 157; Sáez, *Recuerdos*, 1:45–50; Walker Valdez, *¿Revolución?*, pp. 35–40, 78–81; and Ricardo Donoso, *Alessandri, agitador y demoledor: Cincuenta años de historia política de Chile*, 2 vols. (Mexico City and Buenos Aires: Fondo de Cultura Económica, 1952–54), 1.227.

16. Official information on the 1920 mobilization (which must be used carefully and compared with press accounts) can be found in *La llamada movilización de 1920: Antecedentes y documentos* (Santiago: Escuela Tipográfica La Gratitud Nacional, 1923).

17. Joseph Shea to Bainbridge Colby, July 1, 1920, U.S. Department of State Files, 825.00/137. Hereafter cited as DSF.

Chapter 7

1. For a narrative, descriptive treatment of this period see Frederick M. Nunn, *Chilean Politics, 1920–1931: The Honorable Mission of the Armed Forces* (Albuquerque: University of New Mexico Press, 1970), pp. 7–113.

2. On Alessandri's career in politics see Arturo Alessandri Palma, *Recuerdos de gobierno*, 3

vols. (Santiago: Editorial Nascimento, 1967). Vol. 1 deals with 1920–25; vol. 2 covers events from 1924 to 1932; and vol. 3 treats the 1932–38 administration. Portions of vol. 1 of Arturo Olavarría Bravo's *Chile entre dos Alessandri*, 4 vols. (Santiago: Editorial Nascimento, 1962–65) deal with the 1920s. See also the favorable treatment by Augusto Iglesias, *Alessandri, una etapa de la democracia en América: Tiempo, vida y acción* (Santiago: Editorial Andrés Bello, 1960). Ricardo Donoso's scathing study, *Alessandri, agitador y demoledor: Cincuenta años de historia política de Chile*, 2 vols. (Mexico City and Buenos Aires: Fondo de Cultura Económica, 1952–54) is a necessary tool for the study of Alessandri and his times. In English see James O. Morris, *Elites, Intellectuals, and Consensus: A Study of the Industrial Relations System in Chile* (Ithaca, N.Y.: New York State School of Industrial and Labor Relations, 1966); and a solid, objective M.A. thesis, Sally Ann Jones, "Arturo Alessandri and the Chilean Presidential Elections of 1920" (Portland State University, 1968).

3. René Montero Moreno, *Orígenes del problema social en Chile: Tema de invierno* (Santiago: N. Avaria, 1926) and "Los principios comunistas frente a las leyes biológicas y la estructura espiritual de la sociedad moderna," *MECH* 26, no. 1 (January 1932):45–53; Oscar Fenner Marín, *Observaciones sobre la labor que corresponderá a la comisión revisora de las leyes de justicia militar* (Santiago: Imprenta del Ministerio de Guerra, 1922); David Bari Menezes, *El ejército ante las nuevas doctrinas sociales* (Santiago: Estado Mayor General del Ejército, 1922); Bartolomé Blanche Espejo, *Heridas abiertas* (Santiago: n.p., 1924); Carlos Sáez Morales, *Y así vamos: Ensayo crítico* (Santiago: Editorial Ercilla, 1938); Tobías Barros Ortiz, *Vigilia de armas: Charlas sobre la vida militar* (Santiago: Estado Mayor General del Ejército, 1920); Gaspar Mora Sotomayor, "El ejército y la opinión pública," *MECH* 21, no. 2 (October 1926); Agustín P. Benedicto, *El ejército en el estado moderno* (Santiago: Editorial A. Bruce R., 1929).

4. Material on the Chilean political officers of the 1920s can be found in the bibliography of Nunn, *Chilean Politics, 1920–1931*, especially pp. 208–10. Chapters 3–4, pp. 28–87, treat the 1920–25 period.

5. This table is based on the *Escalafón por grados y antigüedad de los oficiales de guerra y mayores del ejército y empleados militares* (Santiago: Imprenta del Ministerio de Guerra, 1925).

6. Carlos Sáez Morales, *Recuerdos de un soldado*, vols. 1, *El ejército y la política*, and 2, *Génesis y derrumbe de la dictadura* (Santiago: Editorial Ercilla, 1933) is an excellent source for information on military politics, 1924–25. See also Arturo Ahumada, *El ejército y la revolución del 5 de septiembre, 1924: Reminiscencias* (Santiago: Imprenta La Tracción, 1931); Juan Bennett A., *La revolución del 5 de setiembre de 1924* (Santiago: Balcells y Compañía, 1925); and Frederick M. Nunn, "A Latin American State within the State: The Politics of the Chilean Army, 1924–1927," *The Americas* 27, no. 1 (July 1970):40–55.

7. For this section I have utilized chiefly Luis Correa Prieto, *El presidente Ibáñez, la política y los políticos: Apuntes para la historia* (Santiago: Editorial Orbe, 1962); Enrique Blanche Northcote, "General de división don Bartolomé Blanche Espejo" (unpublished notes in possession of the author, Santiago, 1962); and Marmaduke Grove Vallejo, *Toda la verdad* (Paris and Buenos Aires: n.p., 1929). In English see Jack Ray Thomas, "The Evolution of a Chilean Socialist: Marmaduke Grove," *Hispanic American Historical Review* 47, no. 1 (February 1967):22–37.

8. On the further development of military political interest during 1925–26 see Nunn, "A Latin American State within the State."

Chapter 8

1. For the following section I have relied on essentially the same materials utilized in composing chaps. 7 and 8 (pp. 115–59) of my *Chilean Politics, 1920–1931: The Honorable Mission of the Armed Forces* (Albuquerque: University of New Mexico Press, 1970), making an effort at analysis and interpretation rather than narration and description of specific events.

2. Ibañismo is treated best in two works by René Montero Moreno, a longtime Ibañista: *La verdad sobre Ibáñez* (Santiago: Empresa Editora Zig Zag, 1952) and *Confesiones políticas: Autobiografía civil* (Santiago: Empresa Editora Zig-Zag, 1959).

3. See Nunn, *Chilean Politics, 1920–1931*, pp. 117–21.

4. Ibid., pp. 123–25, 136–37.

5. Ibid., pp. 128–29.

6. Enrique Balmaceda Toro, as quoted in *El Mercurio* (Santiago), July 21, 1927.

7. Novelist Eduardo Barrios Hudtwalcker compared Ibáñez to both O'Higgins and Balmaceda in his preface (pp. 9–11) to Montero Moreno's *La verdad sobre Ibáñez:* "Just as Balmaceda was idealized, 'he who loved Chile more than anything else in life' so is this Chilean [Ibáñez] of today. . . . If O'Higgins had governed again, more would have been his greatness. With the return of Ibáñez we can expect a return of O'Higgins."

8. Anti-Ibáñez individuals, groups, and plots are discussed in Nunn, *Chilean Politics, 1920–1931*, pp. 138–42. See also Marmaduke Grove Vallejo, *Toda la verdad* (Paris and Buenos Aires: n.p., 1929); Agustín Edwards, *Recuerdos de mi persecución* (Santiago: Editorial Ercilla, 1931); Ernesto Würth Rojas, *Ibáñez: Caudillo enigmático* (Santiago: Editorial del Pacífico, 1958); and Aquiles Vergara Vicuña, *Ibáñez: César criollo*, 2 vols. (Santiago: Imprenta La Maestranza, 1931).

9. Table 4 is based on materials utilized in Nunn, *Chilean Politics, 1920–1931*, pp. 123–25, 136–37.

10. Ibid., chap. 8, "The Institutionalized Mission," pp. 134–59.

11. Ibid.

Chapter 9

1. On Chilean politics in the recent period see the following sources: Fredrick B. Pike, *Chile and the United States, 1880–1962: The Emergence of Chile's Social Crisis and the Challenge to United States Diplomacy* (Notre Dame, Ind.: University of Notre Dame Press, 1963), chaps. 8–9, pp. 243–304; Federico G. Gil, *Genesis and Modernization of Political Parties in Chile* (Gainesville: University of Florida Press, 1962) and *The Political System of Chile* (Boston: Houghton Mifflin Co., 1966); James Petras, *Politics and Social Forces in Chilean Development* (Berkeley and Los Angeles: University of California Press, 1969); Germán Urzúa Valenzuela, *Los partidos políticos chilenos* (Santiago: Editorial Jurídica de Chile, 1968); Ernst Halperin, *Nationalism and Communism in Chile* (Cambridge, Mass.: M.I.T. Press, 1965); Peter G. Snow, "The Political Party Spectrum in Chile," *South Atlantic Quarterly* (Autumn 1963):474–87; Ben G. Burnett, *Political Groups in Chile* (Austin: University of Texas Press, 1971); and Mario Zañartu and John J. Kennedy, eds., *The Overall Development of Chile* (Notre Dame, Ind.: University of Notre Dame Press, 1969).

2. Peruvian military literature, for example, abounds with material on the subject of what kind of infrastructure that country ought to have and how it ought to be developed. See the following recent examples published prior to the golpe of 1968: Francisco Morales Bermúdez, "Pensamiento estratégico," *Revista de la Escuela Superior de Guerra* (*RESG*) 10, no. 1 (January–March 1963):7–12; Napoleón Urbina Abanto, "La regionalización del país y el desarrollo económico nacional," *RESG* 14, no. 1 (January–March 1967):7–12; Carlos Bobbio Centurión, "¿Que ejército necesita el Perú?," *Revista Militar del Perú* (*RMP*) 58, no. 675 (March–April 1963):132–36; Edgardo Mercado Jarrín, "El ejército de hoy y su proyección en nuestra sociedad en período de transición," *RMP* 59, no. 685 (November–December 1964):1–20. See also the reprint of a portion of *A Program for the Industrial and Regional Development of Peru: A Report to the Government of Peru* (Cambridge, Mass.: Arthur D. Little, Inc., 1960): "Programa de desarrollo nacional y regional para el Perú," *RESG* 8, no. 2 (April–June 1961):7–38.

The adamant insistence on a trans-Amazon road system stands as evidence of the Brazilian Army's position on infrastructural needs and "interiorization."

3. On Chilean nationalism, see Halperin, *Nationalism and Communism.*

4. See the candid remarks made by John J. Johnson on the shortcomings of Chilean democracy and civilian rule in this sphere in 1968: U.S., Congress, Senate, Committee on Foreign Relations, *Survey of the Alliance for Progress: Hearings Before the Subcommittee on American Republics Affairs,* 90th Cong., 2d sess., February 28, 1968, pp. 74–75, 80–81.

Johnson concluded his testimony this way: "There is no question but what the Chileans have a great interest in political processes. The point is that nothing comes of it. At the national level they can elect liberal presidents, but the political structure of the country is such that at the local and provincial level conditions remain very much the same as they were a century ago."

5. Here I am limiting my opinions strictly to Chile, and in no way am I suggesting that situations elsewhere may be considered identical. Argentina, like Chile, has a wide political spectrum and heavy political participation, but civilianism, nevertheless, is not a firmly established tradition in Argentina.

6. "Painful but necessary measures" was the term used by Ibáñez in 1927 to describe his regime's deportation policy. See Frederick M. Nunn, *Chilean Politics, 1920–1931: The Honorable Mission of the Armed Forces* (Albuquerque: University of New Mexico Press, 1970), p. 138.

7. I am not at all convinced of the validity for Chile of the "middle class military coup" thesis advanced by José Nun in his "A Latin American Phenomenon: The Middle Class Military Coup," in *Trends in Social Science Research in Latin American Studies: A Conference Report* (Berkeley, Calif.: Institute of International Studies, 1965), pp. 55–99.

8. Conclusions reached in the following section are based on materials cited in Nunn, *Chilean Politics, 1920–1931,* chap. 9, pp. 160–76.

9. For sources dealing with the following paragraphs see n. 1 above.

10. See Ricardo Donoso, *Alessandri, agitador y demoledor; Cincuenta años de historia política de Chile,* 2 vols. (Mexico City and Buenos Aires: Fondo de Cultura Económica, 1952–54), 2:120–41.

11. This section is based on examination of articles dealing with political, social, and economic themes appearing in the pages of the *Revista Militar* (Argentina), *Revista Militar Brasileira, Revista de la Escuela Superior de Guerra* (Peru), and *Revista Militar del Perú* through the last four decades. I have made no attempt to record the actual number of pages devoted to such themes, nor have I computed the number of articles. However, I can state that Argentine, Brazilian, and Peruvian military authors have outproduced their Chilean counterparts at approximately a 10 to 1 ratio in dealing with "extraprofessional" matters.

Chapter 10

1. On the fall of Ibáñez and the ensuing political instability, see Frederick M. Nunn, *Chilean Politics, 1920–1931: The Honorable Mission of the Armed Forces* (Albuquerque: University of New Mexico Press, 1970), pp. 160–68. See also Raúl Marín Balmaceda, *La caída de un regimen: Julio de 1931* (Santiago: Imprenta Universitaria, 1931); H. Ochoa Mena, *La revolucion en Chile: La caída de la tirania militar* (Santiago: Imprenta Cisneros, 1931); Víctor Contreras Guzmán, *Bitácora de la dictadura: Administración Ibáñez, 1927–1931* (Santiago: Imprenta Cultura, 1942), pp. 230–45; Ricardo Donoso, *Alessandri, agitador y demoledor: Cincuenta años de historia política de Chile,* 2 vols. (Mexico City and Buenos Aires: Fondo de Cultura Económica, 1952–54), 2: chaps. 1–3, pp. 12–74; René Montero Moreno, *Confesiones políticas: Autobiografía civil* (Santiago: Empresa Editorial Zig-Zag, 1952), pp. 71–75; and Carlos Sáez Morales, *Recuerdos de un soldado 2: Genésis y derrumbe de la dictadura* (Santiago: Editorial Ercilla, 1933), pp. 115–30.

2. See Sáez, *Recuerdos de un soldado* 3: *26 de julio de 1931 al 24 de diciembre de 1932*, pp. 1–42, for material on the reactions against Ibañistas after the fall of their leader.

3. A comprehensive treatment of the mutiny is still needed. The following sources treat aspects of this curious episode: José M. Cerda, *Relación histórica de la revolución de la armada de Chile* (Concepción: Rafael Merino H., 1934), is an eyewitness account by one of the mutineers; Leonardo Guzmán, *Un episodio olvidado de la historia nacional (Julio–noviembre de 1931)* (Santiago: Editorial Andrés Bello, 1966), pp. 39–134, gives a semiofficial view by a cabinet member at the time of the mutiny and was the best narrative description available until the publication of Carlos López Urrutia, *Historia de la marina de Chile* (Santiago: Editorial Andrés Bello, 1969). See López's chap. 17, pp. 359–76. See also Ramón Vergara Montero, *Por rutas extraviadas* (Santiago: Imprenta Universitaria, 1933); and Edgardo von Schroeders, *El delegado del gobierno y el motín de la escuadra* (Santiago: Imprenta y Litografía Universo, 1933); Vergara and Schroeders provide military-loyalist versions.

4. Schroeders talked with Communist organizers in Coquimbo and believed them when they claimed that the sailors were not *"compañeros"* but *"pancistas"*—in other words, that they were primarily interested in their stomachs, not ideological matters. Schroeders, *El delegado*, p. 28.

5. But cf. William Culbertson to Henry Stimson, September 9, 1931, DSF, 825.00/REVOLU-TIONS/42, wherein the thesis that Marxists inspired the sailors to mutiny, then lost control of the affair is advanced.

6. The best sources on this period are Sáez, *Recuerdos*, 3:48–140; Donoso, *Alessandri*, 2:75–87; Arturo Alessandri Palma, *Recuerdos de gobierno*, 3 vols. (Santiago: Editorial Nascimento, 1967), 2:447–50; Domingo Melfi, *Sin brújula* (Santiago: n.p., 1932).

7. The names of those accused of violating the Constitution between 1927 and 1931 have been mentioned elsewhere. Some civilians were found guilty and lightly punished, while military personnel were merely attacked harshly in public sessions and in the press. There were no courts martial held to judge accused officers.

8. I have based this version of the golpe of June 4, 1932, and the Socialist Republic on the following sources: Manuel Aránguiz Latorre (Montero's private secretary), *El 4 de junio* (Santiago: Empresa Editora Zig-Zag, 1932); Alfredo Guillermo Bravo, *El 4 de junio: El festín de los audaces* (Santiago: Imprenta Universitaria, 1933); Raul Marín Balmaceda, *El 4 de junio de 1932* (Santiago: Imprenta Universitaria, 1933); Jorge Grove V. (Marmaduke's brother), *Descorriendo el velo: Episodio de los doce días de la república socialista* (Valparaíso: Imprenta Aurora de Chile, 1933); *¿Porque cayó Grove? Declaraciones sensacionales* (Santiago: La Nación, 1933); Jack Ray Thomas, "The Socialist Republic of Chile," *Journal of Inter-American Studies* 6, no. 2 (April 1964):203–20; Alessandri, *Recuerdos*, 2:141–271; and Culbertson to Stimson, DSF, 825/REVOLUTIONS/72, June 6, 1932–825.00/REVOLUTIONS/174, July 29, 1932.

9. I have discussed this in my *Chilean Politics*, p. 171. What Alessandri did or said that day at El Bosque is today a moot point but haunted don Arturo until his death.

10. On the June 10 golpe see Mario Bravo Lavín, *Chile frente al comunismo y al socialismo* (Santiago: Editorial Ercilla, 1934); and Sáez, *Recuerdos*, 3:195–215.

11. See Sáez, *Recuerdos*, 3:225–30.

12. Sáez, *Recuerdos*, 3:270–94, is particularly good on the ultimate ouster of the military from political power in 1932.

Chapter 11

1. Two useful studies dealing with recent Chilean civil-military relations which should be consulted are: Alain Joxe, *Las fuerzas armadas en el sistema político de Chile* (Santiago: Editorial Universitaria, 1970); and Liisa North, *Civil-Military Relations in Argentina, Chile, and Peru* (Berkeley, Calif.: Institute of International Studies, 1966). These should be used with care. The Joxe work is an attempt by a sociologist to assess historical civil-military relationships, and is

lacking in historical perspective. Nevertheless, Joxe makes some worthwhile contributions. North's work is an effort at comparative analysis but suffers from a lack of depth in dealing with Argentina and Chile. Like the Joxe work, it is really more an exercise in methodology than a contribution to knowledge. Both studies suffer from an overreliance on secondary source material.

2. On the reelection of Alessandri see Arturo Alessandri Palma, *Recuerdos de gobierno*, 3 vols. (Santiago: Editorial Nascimento, 1967), 2: chaps. 1 and 2, pp. 1–16; and Ricardo Donoso, *Alessandri, agitador y demoledor: Cincuenta años de historia política de Chile*, 2 vols. (Mexico City and Buenos Aires: Fondo de Cultura Económica, 1952–54), 2: chaps. 7 and 8, pp. 120–62.

3. Conclusions reached in the following section are based on extensive interviews with General (ret.) Oscar Novoa Fuentes, Santiago, September 12 and October 24, 1962; and numerous interviews and conversations with Defense Ministry officials, both civilian and military, March–December 1962, September 1969, and May 1972. These last go unnamed for obvious reasons.

4. An incomplete listing of defense ministers supplied by the Defense Ministry indicates that of twenty ministers since 1932, twelve have been civilians. General Arnaldo Carrasco served as minister under President Ríos; General Guillermo Barrios served under President González; and five officers (three generals, two admirals), served under Ibáñez in his second presidency: Generals Adrián Barrientos, Luis Vidal, and Abdón Parra (promoted after appointment), and Admirals Francisco O'Ryan and Vicente Merino. General (ret.) Tulio Marambio served briefly under Eduardo Frei. The second Ibáñez presidency is the only time military figures dominated the ministerial scene, and they were not popular.

5. More often than not, defense ministers have come from the president's own party. Only Liberal Manuel Bulnes Sanfuentes, who served under the Radical González, Conservative Julio Pereira Larraín, who served under Liberal Jorge Alessandri, and Radical Alejandro Ríos Valdivia, who served as Salvador Allende's first defense minister, did not come from the chief executive's party. Bulnes, of course, had a magic name for military men, and his political affiliation was secondary. Ríos was a one-time instructor at the Escuela, and had numerous friends and former students in the officer corps.

6. None of Jorge Alessandri's appointees from 1958 to 1964, for example, could be considered a major political figure when compared to his appointees in other ministerial positions.

7. For example, Juan de Dios Carmona, Eduardo Frei's first (and best) defense minister. Though Frei was not at all popular with army leaders, his defense minister was recognized as able, energetic, and sympathetic to the needs of the military.

8. Emilio Bello is the best example of a civilian popular with military men. He was also uncontroversial and a capable administrator.

9. The following section is based on the aforementioned interviews and conversations with Defense Ministry officials and with General Novoa, and an interview with General (ret.) Bartolomé Blanche Espejo, Santiago, September 10, 1969.

10. In my *Chilean Politics, 1920–1931: The Honorable Mission of the Armed Forces* (Albuquerque: University of New Mexico Press), p. 203, n.53, I have stated: "Their names were lined out or marked retired on a copy of the *Escalafón* for 1931 seen by the writer in August 1962 in the Ministry of Defense. . . ."

11. The best source in Spanish or English on the Republican Militia is Terence Stephen Tarr, "Military Intervention and Civilian Reaction in Chile, 1924–1936" (Ph.D. diss., University of Florida, 1960). See also Jorge de la Cuadra Poissón, *La verdad sobre las incidencias milicianas* (Santiago: La Nación, 1935).

12. At its height the Militia reputedly had a membership of 40,000! Henry Norweb to Cordell Hull, October 2, 1933, DSF, 825.00/GENERAL CONDITIONS/64.

13. See Norweb to Stimson, October 11, 1932, DSF, 825.00/815.

14. But the militia staunchly defended itself as "apolitical," "composed of elements of all social and professional classes," "the most diverse political groups (Radicals, Conservatives,

Socialists)," and "citizens who never joined any of the existent parties." In an official statement of October 29, 1933, the militia proclaimed its essential purpose: "It will battle tyranny, civil or military" (*El Mercurio*, October 29, 1933).

15. "Furthermore the government which permitted [the militia] to exist was never the object of favorable consideration in army circles" (Leonidas Bravo Ríos, *Lo que supo un auditor de guerra* [Santiago: Editorial del Pacífico, 1955], p. 54).

16. See William Phillips to Hull, March 2, 1936, DSF, 825.00/REVOLUTIONS/242.

17. *El Mercurio*, May 19, 1933.

18. On the resurgence of Ibañismo in the 1930s see the appropriate chapters in René Montero Moreno, *La verdad sobre Ibáñez* (Santiago: Empresa Editora Zig-Zag, 1952) and *Confesiones políticas: Autobiografía civil* (Santiago: Empresa Editora Zig-Zag, 1959). See also Carlos Ibáñez del Campo, *Programa presidencial* (Santiago: Empresa Editora Zig-Zag, 1938). Grovismo's resurgence can be assessed by examining Partido Socialista, *Grove a la presidencia* (Santiago: Imprenta Cóndor, 1937); *Lo que dijo Grove: Lo que respondieron sus contradictores* (Santiago: La Nación, 1934); Manuel Bedoya, *Grove: Su vida, su ejemplo, su obra* (Santiago: Imprenta y Litografía Casa Amarilla, n.d.).

19. On the 1932–38 Alessandri presidency see Michael Potashnik, "The Role of the Right in the Modernization of Chile, 1932–38" (Ph.D. diss., University of California, Los Angeles, 1966); and John Reese Stevenson, *The Chilean Popular Front* (Philadelphia: University of Pennsylvania Press, 1942).

20. Barros's views on Ibáñez and the issues at stake in the 1920s and 1930s are found in his *Recuerdos oportunos* (Santiago: n.p., 1938); See also Marta Infante Barros, *Testigos del treinta y ocho* (Santiago: Editorial Andrés Bello, 1972), pp. 55–64.

21. The Infante book is the best available treatment of the 1938 campaign. It is based on newspaper coverage of the period, and is a balanced and incisive study. See also Alessandri, *Recuerdos*, 3:179–302. Alessandri's account contains documents pertinent to the president's role in the resistance to the putsch. Ricardo Donoso, *Alessandri*, 2:256–68, presents an anti-Alessandri version of the putsch.

22. See the records of the investigation of Arriagada's conduct in Donoso, *Alessandri*, 2:303–17.

23. Official returns for the 1938 presidential contest are reproduced in Infante, *Testigos*, p. 194.

24. The Edwards-Arriagada confrontation is treated in Donoso, *Alessandri*, 2:269–97.

25. The letter is cited in Donoso, *Alessandri*, 2:297 and Infante, *Testigos*, pp. 100–101.

26. There are numerous works on Chilean politics in recent times, in addition to those cited in chap. 9, n. 1. Two of the best and most informative on the Christian Democrats are: George W. Grayson, Jr., *El partido demócrata cristiano chileno* (Buenos Aires and Santiago: Editorial Francisco de Aguirre, 1968); and Arturo Olavarría Bravo, *Chile bajo la democracia cristiana*, 5 vols. (Santiago: Editorial Nascimento, 1964–68). Grayson's is by far the more objective and scholarly of the two. Olavarría's *Chile entre dos Alessandri*, 4 vols. (Santiago: Editorial Nascimento, 1962–65) covers the years 1938–58. For works on Carlos Ibáñez's second term of office see works on Ibáñez by Montero Moreno cited previously. Donoso, *Alessandri*, 2:295–512 continues the attack on Alessandri to the latter's death in 1950.

27. Election data have been assembled and interpreted from the following: Institute for the Comparative Study of Political Systems, *Chile Election Factbook, September 4, 1964* (Washington, D.C.: Operations and Policy Research, 1964), and *The Chilean Presidential Election of September 4, 1964* (Washington, D.C.: Operations and Policy Research, 1965); Frederick M. Nunn, "Chile's Government in Perspective: Political Change or More of the Same?" *Inter-American Economic Affairs* 20, no. 4 (Spring 1967):73–90; and various mimeographed materials supplied by the Dirección del Registro Electoral, Santiago.

28. The following sources have information on military interest in politics from the late 1930s to the early 1950s: Bravo Ríos, *Un auditor de guerra;* Ernesto Würth Rojas, *Ibáñez:*

Caudillo enigmático (Santiago: Editorial del Pacífico, 1958); the Montero Moreno volumes on Ibáñez; Alberto Cabero, *Recuerdos de don Pedro Aguirre Cerda* (Santiago: Editorial Nascimento, 1948); and Horacio Gamboa Núñez, *En la ruta del 2 de abril* (Santiago: Imprenta Fantasía, 1962).

29. An especially good analysis of the Ariostazo can be found in Attaché's Report #3068, August 26, 1939, DSF, 825.00/REVOLUTIONS/267, G-2 Report #3020-d.

30. See Cabero, *Recuerdos de don Pedro Aguirre Cerda*, p. 287, and Montero Moreno, *Confesiones políticas*, p. 111.

31. The "Pig's Feet Plot" is discussed in Bravo Ríos, *Un auditor de guerra*, pp. 200–212.

32. The following section is based heavily on Luis Correa Prieto, *El presidente Ibáñez, la política y los políticos: Apuntes para la historia* (Santiago: Editorial Orbe, 1962); Gamboa, *En la ruta del 2 de abril;* Bravo Ríos, *Un auditor de guerra;* Würth, *Ibáñez;* and Raúl Silva Maturana, *Camino al abismo: Lo que no se ha dicho sobre el proceso de la línea recta* (Santiago: Editorial Universitaria, 1955). The best treatment in English is by Donald W. Bray, "Chilean Politics During the Second Ibáñez Administration" (Ph.D. diss., Stanford University, 1961). See also Bray's "Peronism in Chile," *Hispanic American Historical Review* 47 (February 1967):38–49. The weekly *Ercilla* from February 25 to June 7, 1955, covered the episode more completely than any of the Santiago newspapers.

33. Full title: *Bases para una acción política de contenido nacional y popular: Plan línea recta* (Santiago, 1955).

34. The following section is based on Gertrude E. Heare, *Trends in Latin American Military Expenditures, 1940–1970* (Washington, D.C.: U.S. Government Printing Office, 1971); Joseph Loftus, *Latin American Defense Expenditures, 1938–1965* (Santa Monica, Calif.: Rand Corporation, 1968); Edwin Lieuwen, *Survey of the Alliance for Progress: The Latin American Military: A Study Prepared at the Request of the Subcommittee on American Republics Affairs of the Committee on Foreign Relations, United States Senate* (Ninetieth Congress, First Session) (Washington, D.C.: U.S. Government Printing Office, 1967). See also U.S. Arms Control and Disarmament Agency, *World Military Expenditures and Arms Trade, 1963–73* (Washington, D.C.: U.S. Government Printing Office, 1973). The dangers of relying too heavily on these kinds of data in reaching conclusions on the political behavior of the military in Latin America have been ably pointed out by Martin C. Needler in his "United States Government Figures on Latin American Military Expenditures," *Latin American Research Review* 8, no. 2 (Summer 1973):101–3.

Chapter 12

1. From the burgeoning list of materials on the Allende regime, its inheritance, and its problems see Ana Lía Payró et al., *Chile: ¿Cambio de gobierno o toma del poder?* (Mexico City: Editorial Extemporaneos, 1971); Regis Debray, *The Chilean Revolution: Conversations with Salvador Allende* (New York: Pantheon Books, 1971); Les Evans, *Disaster in Chile: Allende's Strategy and Why It Failed* (New York: Pathfinder Press, 1974); Michael J. Francis, *The Allende Victory: An Analysis of the 1970 Chilean Presidential Election* (Tucson: University of Arizona Press, 1973); Kenneth Medhurst, ed., *Allende's Chile* (New York: St. Martin's Press, 1972); David J. Morris, *We Must Make Haste—Slowly: The Process of Revolution in Chile* (New York: Vintage Books, 1973); Gary McLoin, *No Peaceful Way: The Chilean Struggle for Dignity* (New York: Sheed and Ward, 1974); North American Congress on Latin America, *New Chile* (Berkeley, Calif.: NACLA, 1972); ODEPLAN-IDS, *The Chilean Road to Socialism* (Austin: University of Texas Press, 1973); Gustavo Canihuante, *La revolución chilena* (Santiago: Editorial Nascimento, 1971); Hernan Godoy Urzúa, ed., *Estructura social de Chile* (Santiago: Editorial Universitaria, 1971); Catherine Lamour, *Allende: La nueva sociedad chilena* (Barcelona: Editorial Dopesa, 1972); MAPU, *El segundo año de la revolución popular* (Santiago: Editorial Unidad Proletaria,

1972); Luis Maura, *Chile: Dos años de unidad popular* (Santiago: Editorial Quimantú, 1973); a special issue of the Chilean Jesuit journal *Mensaje* (September–October 1971); Carlos Neely, *Cambios políticos para el desarrollo: El caso de Chile* (Santiago: Editorial Universitaria, 1968); Aníbal Pinto et al., *Chile hoy* (Mexico City: Siglo Veintiuno Editores, 1970); Hernán Ramírez Necochea, *Historia del imperialismo en Chile* (Santiago: Editora Austral, 1970); Robert Moss, *Chile's Marxist Experiment* (Newton Abbot, Devon: David and Charles, 1973) and his "The Santiago Model-1 Revolution within Democracy?" *Conflict Studies*, no. 31 and "The Santiago Model-2 Polarisation of Politics," *Conflict Studies*, no. 32 (both January 1973); Paul M. Sweezy and Harry Magdoff, eds., *Revolution and Counter-Revolution in Chile* (New York: Monthly Review Press, 1974); Richard E. Feinberg, *The Triumph of Allende: Chile's Legal Revolution* (New York: New American Library, 1972); and Arturo Valenzuela and J. Samuel Valenzuela, eds., *Chilean Socialism?* (New York: E. P. Dutton, 1974).

2. See Charles J. Parrish, *Bureaucracy, Democracy, and Development: Some Considerations Based on the Chilean Case*, LADAC Occasional Papers, series 2, no. 1 (Austin: University of Texas Press, 1970).

3. The army consists of 38,000 officers and men, the navy has 15,000 and the air force 8,000. There are 15,000 carabineros.

4. On Allende's attempts to step up military expenditures see Cristián Zegers Ariztía, "The Armed Forces: Support of a Democratic Institutionality," in Tomás P. MacHale et al., *Chile: A Critical Survey* (Santiago: Institute of General Studies, 1972), pp. 311–24.

Official government figures, however, would lead us to think otherwise. Chilean Senate computations indicate a decline in military expenditures (as a percentage of the national budget) since 1956, with only slight upward deviations, from 26.4 percent (1956) to 7.8 percent (1971). See *Chile* (Embassy of Chile newsletter, Washington, D.C.), no. 250 (January 20, 1973). One of the "slight upward deviations" was indeed in 1971. These figures do not at all coincide with those discussed in chap. 11, leading one to concur with Martin Needler on the dangers of relying too heavily on statistical explanations for military attitudes and behavior.

5. "1971: La inflación del tacnazo," *Panorama Económico*, no. 251 (December 1969–January 1970):3–7

6. Luis Soza, "Papel de la industria militar en la movilización de la industria civil," *MECH*, May–June 1931, pp. 539–53. There are several errors in *MECH* volume numbers beginning in the 1930s, so to avoid confusion in notes from this point forward only months of issue will be given. Unless marked with an asterisk (*), all authors are military figures.

7. Ramón Cañas Montalva, "Petróleo, el oro negro magallánico," *MECH*, August 1931, pp. 163–67. Thirty-one years earlier Lieutenant Colonel Manuel Moore's book-length essay on Magallanes, *Estudios militares hechos en el territorio de Magallanes* (Santiago: Estado Mayor Jeneral del Ejército, 1900), concerned itself with strategic matters (at the insistence of General Körner). At the time no one knew of Magallanes' value in other than geographical or strategic terms. The Cañas essay did indicate a shift in emphasis from military matters to economic development of Chile's Far South.

8. Jorge Carmona, "¡Hacia la economía! La racionalización de nuestra instrucción militar," *MECH*, November 1931, pp. 587–93; "Reclutador," "La educación militar del país," *MECH*, January 1932, pp. 39–44.

9. René Montero Moreno, "Los principios comunistas frente a las leyes biológicas y la estructura espiritual de la sociedad moderna," *MECH*, January 1932, pp. 45–53.

10. Ramón Cañas Montalva, "Fuerzas morales," *MECH*, October 1932, pp. 369–74.

11. Barceló Lira, "La evolución del ejército chileno desde la ocupación del territorio araucano (1859–1879) hasta nuestros días," *MECH*, March–April 1935, pp. 199–218.

12. Angel Varela R., "La instrucción escolar en el ejército," *MECH*, May–June 1935, pp. 395–400. See also Víctor Molina Pino, "El ejército y su función social de acuerdo con la necesidad de capacitar al individuo en un oficio que le permita desempeñarse en forma más eficiente al ser restituido a la sociedad civil," *MECH*, September–October 1935, pp. 833–41.

13. See Eduardo Guerra, "Algo de lo que significa la movilización civil y militar," *MECH*, July–August 1936, pp. 563–68; Guillermo Barrios T., "Consideraciones generales sobre la movilización," *MECH*, July–August 1936, pp. 533–47 and September–October 1936, pp. 665–73.

14. Barros Ortiz, "Apuntes y notas sobre la formación del oficial de hoy," *MECH*, January–February 1937, pp. 1–28. I refer to Baron Colmar von der Goltz, *The Nation in Arms: A Treatise on Modern Military Systems and the Conduct of War* (1883), tr. Phillip A. Ashworth (London: Hugh Reese, 1913).

15. Germán Reinhardt R., "La influencia militar en la formación y desarrollo del territorio de Magallanes," *MECH*, July–August 1937, pp. 665–67 and September–October 1937, pp. 849–60.

16. Arturo Fuentes Rabé (tr.), "Generalidades sobre movilización industrial," *MECH*, January–February 1938, pp. 5–27.

17. Maxime Weygand, "Como educar a nuestra juventud," *MECH*, May–June 1938, pp. 453–67 and July–August 1938, pp. 585–602. I refer to Lyautey's "Du rôle social de l'officier," *Revue des deux mondes*, March 15, 1891, pp. 443–59, translated and published in Chile as "La función social del oficial," *MECH*, November–December 1939, pp. 851–67. That the idea that the military had an educative function appealed to Chilean officers was evidenced by the publishing of an article by Francisco Castillo Nájera (Mexican ambassador to the United States), "El ejército como instrumento de educación," *MECH*, March–April 1940, pp. 271–76. This is a remarkable piece of pro-military propaganda presented by Castillo as an address to the American Legion convention, Washington, D.C., November 28, 1939!

18. Guillermo Aldona, "El ejército: Escuela de civismo e institución de equilibrio social," *MECH*, September–October 1940, pp. 687–709.

19. *MECH*, July–August 1941, pp. 489–93.

20. Guillermo Toro Concha, "Algunos aspectos de la misión militar y social de las fuerzas armadas de la república," *MECH*, November–December 1942, pp. 221–28.

21. On military training see Enrique Bollmann Mora, "La instrucción escolar pre-militar," *MECH*, January–February 1943, pp. 51–56; on economic mobilization see Aniceto Muñoz F., "El departamento de movilización económica y los problemas de la defensa nacional," *MECH*, March–April 1943, pp. 239–42.

On political events in Argentina, see *MECH*, July–August 1943, pp. 555–72; Luis Vargas Feliú, "Chile y Argentina," *MECH*, March–April 1944, pp. 305–6.

On geopolitics see Joseph J. Thorndike, Jr., "Geopolítica: La fantástica carrera de un sistema científico que un británico inventó, los alemanes usaron, y los americanos necesitan estudiar," *MECH*, September–December 1943, pp. 881–901. This piece appeared in *Life* (December 21, 1942), and was translated and published in the *Revista Militar del Perú* before appearing in *MECH*. It is the first thoughtful work on geopolitics to appear in *MECH*.

Examples of earlier Chilean works that can be considered derivative of classical geopolitics include Moore, *Estudios militares;* Jorge Boonen Rivera, *Ensayo sobre la geografía militar de Chile* (Santiago: Imprenta del Ministerio de Guerra, 1905); Enrique Monreal, *"Nuestras provincias septentrionales y la seguridad nacional* (Concepción: n.p., 1923); and Carlos Sáez Morales, *Estudios militares* (Santiago: Imprenta del Ministerio de Guerra, 1933).

On the steel industry see Enrique Alvarez Vásquez de Prada,° "El problema del fierro en la economía chilena," *MECH*, March–April 1944, pp. 225–91.

22. As examples see Armando Bueno Ortiz,° "Algunos aspectos geopolíticos del Perú y la defensa nacional," *MECH*, January–February 1946, pp. 77–90; Bernardino Parada Moreno, "El ejército potencial," *MECH*, March–April 1946, pp. 11–26; Marcial Delgado Lazcano, "La instrucción primaria en el ejército: Su evolución metodológica y pedagógica que hay que tener en cuenta para su desarrollo," *MECH*, March–April 1946, pp. 41–56; and Cañas Montalva, "Zona austral antártica" (in all 1945 issues).

23. A significant example would be Eduardo Saavedra R., "Aspecto geopolítico de la

Antártica chilena," *MECH*, September–October 1948, pp. 95–99. This brief essay included maps showing the center of the Pacific Ocean and Antarctica as center points, and emphasizing Chile's strategic location in relation to both. To my knowledge, this was the first example of alternate cartographic projections used by Chilean geopoliticians to draw attention to Chile's national interests. See also Cañas Montalva, "Reflexiones geopolíticas sobre el presente y el futuro de América y de Chile," *MECH*, November–December 1948, pp. 1–26. Cañas's approach here was much the same as that of Saavedra.

24. Benjamín Videla V., "La intervención del ejército en obras de beneficio público," *MECH*, September–October 1947, pp. 64–80.

25. Montaldo Bustos, "Ningun cuerpo armado puede deliberar," *MECH*, July–August 1953, pp. 79–84. See also Horacio Arce Fernández, "La fuerza armada y la seguridad nacional," the prologue to *Estatuto jurídico de las fuerzas armadas* (Santiago, 1957); "Inquietud profesional," an editorial in *MECH*, May–June 1958, pp. 3–4; and in the same issue, Luis Valenzuela Reyes, "Misión de las fuerzas armadas y su participación en el desenvolvimiento normal de nuestra vida democrática," pp. 22–29.

26. *Archivo de don Bernardo O'Higgins* (Santiago: Instituto Geográfico Militar, 1964), vol. 25.

27. Hernán Hiriart Laval, "La política militar y la opinión pública," *MECH*, May–June 1964, pp. 15–19.

28. Raúl Poblete Vergara, "Recursos naturales de la provincia de Aisén," *MECH*, September–October 1967, especially pp. 137–48. Nevertheless, in 1965 appeared Rene González Rojas's book-length *Contribución de las fuerzas armadas al desarrollo económico: Hacia una revisión de conceptos conveniente para países sub-desarrollados* (Santiago: Editorial Universitaria, 1965). This is a general work.

29. Between 1970 and 1973 several *MECH* articles may have indicated a change in attitude on the part of the army. See Claudio López Silva, "Las fuerzas armadas en el tercer mundo," *MECH*, July–August 1970, pp. 11–51, in which the author seeks to explain the "internally oriented" role of the military in developing countries; Gustavo A. Díaz Feliú, "El soldado alemán: El ejército chileno debe conservar su tradición prusiana," *MECH*, May–June 1971, pp. 126–27, a troubled little essay in which the author yearns for the "good old days" and considers the army to be the "people in arms" (*pueblo en armas*); Giancarlo Fortunato, ° "Sociología militar," *MECH*, November–December 1971, pp. 44–68. The translation from Italian and publication of this essay indicates, I believe, a resurgence of interest in the army's position with regard to the society around it. *MECH*, November–December 1970, devoted 148 pages to coverage of the funeral of René Schneider, and made no bones about the high command's shock at his assassination.

30. The Academias are, however, referred to collectively as the Centro de Altos Estudios Militares.

31. See Roy Allen Hansen, "Military Culture and Organizational Decline: A Study of the Chilean Army" (Ph.D. diss., University of California, Los Angeles, 1967).

32. Much of the following section has been based on Chilean press reports and opinions of the Schneider assassination, particularly as expressed in *El Mercurio*, *La Nación*, *Clarín*, *El Siglo*, and *Ercilla;* material in *MECH* cited in n. 29 above; and on Chile: General Secretariat of Government, *Documentos secretos de la ITT* (Santiago: Editorial Quimantú, 1972). See also *El caso Schneider* (Santiago: Editorial Quimantú, 1972).

33. As quoted in a memorandum, To: E.[dward] J. Gerrity, From: H.[al] Hendrix and R.[obert] Berellez, September 10, 1970. *Documentos secretos de la ITT*, pp. 10–17.

34. Ibid., passim.

35. The following paragraphs are based on Chilean press reports, especially *El Mercurio* and *Ercilla*.

36. In his *Estados Unidos y las fuerzas armadas de América Latina* (Buenos Aires: Editorial Periferia, S. R. L., 1971), Horacio L. Veneroni asserts that United States military aid is designed to maintain all Latin American military organizations as pawns of United States interests in the

area. Whether or not this is true, Chilean military leaders repeatedly expressed preference for United States armaments (in one case for Northrop F5E "Freedom Fighters" and A-37 light-attack bombers) over Soviet Union products being urged on them by the administration.

37. *MECH*, July–September 1972, p. 19.

38. Apparent normalcy in executive-military relations during 1970–71 is evident upon reading various essays in *MECH*, September–October 1971.

39. Salvador Allende Gossens, "Fuerzas armadas y carabineros," in *Nuestro camino al socialismo: La vía chilena* (Buenos Aires: Ediciones Papiro, 1971), p. 128.

40. In a press conference, May 5, 1971 (ibid., p. 125). These remarks appear in an English language version, *Chile's Road to Socialism* (Baltimore, Md.: Penguin Books, 1973).

41. For examples see n. 29 above.

42. Zegers Ariztía, "The Armed Forces," p. 314.

43. On the controversial Tohá's role as interior minister, the accusations against him for violations of the Constitution in 1971, and his removal from Interior, see Joan E. Garcés, *Revolución, congreso y constitución: El caso Tohá* (Santiago: Editorial Quimantú, 1972).

44. The following paragraphs are based on Pablo Piacentini, "La doctrina Schneider-Prats y el gobierno de la unidad popular," *Estrategia* (Buenos Aires), 3, no. 17 (July–August 1972):24–28.

45. In army circles the story goes that Allende wanted Canales retired as early as April 1972 and ordered Prats to take the necessary steps. Prats demurred, telling the president that he (Prats) could not be responsible for the high command's response to such an act. Allende wisely waited until enough evidence of wrongdoing could be assembled. This incident may have been the basis for rumors that a golpe plot existed as early as April 1972. See the report by Marcel Niedergang in *Le Monde*, March 15, 1974.

46. In the March 2, 3, 4, and 5 editions.

47. See Zegers Ariztía, "The Armed Forces," p. 318; and Ted Córdova-Claure, "Las fuerzas armadas de Chile ante el proceso de cambio," *Estrategia* 3, no. 17 (July–August 1972):20–23.

48. See Robinson Rojas, "The Chilean Armed Forces: The Role of the Military in the Popular Unity Government," in Dale L. Johnson, ed., *The Chilean Road to Socialism* (Garden City, N.Y.: Doubleday & Co., 1973), pp. 310–22. This volume contains valuable essays on all facets of the 1970–73 experience.

49. Much of the following section is based on interviews conducted in Santiago, and on Santiago, Lima, and Buenos Aires press coverage. See also "Las fuerzas armadas en 1972," *Portada*, no. 35 (October–December 1972):36–38; Ricardo Claro Valdés, "La participación de las fuerzas armadas," in José Garrido Rojas et al., *Participación para una nueva sociedad* (Santiago: Ediciones Portada, 1973[?]); and H. E. Bicheno, "Las fuerzas armadas en el sistema político de Chile," *MECH*, May–June 1972, pp. 26–37. This is a harsh critique of Alain Joxe, *Las fuerzas armadas en el sistema político de Chile* (Santiago: Editorial Universitaria, 1970).

50. Cited in Córdova-Claure, "Las fuerzas armadas," p. 20.

51. During March 1972 General Pedro Palacios served briefly as minister of mines, and rumor had it that General Orlando Urbina Herrera would be named interior minister in an attempt to show the administration's willingness to act against civil disorder. See the interview with Urbina, "Un hogar chileno para la humanidad," *MECH*, May–June 1972, pp. 72–76. Urbina was actively involved in planning the 1972 UNCTAD meeting.

52. In *CER (Centro de Estudios de la Revolución)* 3, no. 9 (February 1973). Such "difficulties" were the subject of a timely essay on Chile's socioeconomic problems, heretofore uncharacteristic of *MECH*: Guido Serrano,° "Economía internacional y desarrollo económico," *MECH*, January–April 1973, pp. 3–17.

53. *El Mercurio*, December 3, 1972.

54. The following section dealing with the 1973 elections and the aftermath is based heavily on Chilean press sources. For data on the elections see *CER* 3, no. 10 (March 1973); *Chile Economic News*, no. 16/38 (March 15, 1973); *Chile*, no. 252 (March 6, 1973); *Latin America* 7, nos. 10 and 11 (March 9 and 16, 1973).

55. See *CER* 3, no. 12 (May 1973); *Chile Economic News*, no. 23/46–47 (August 1, 1973); *Latin America* 7, no. 21 (May 25, 1973); and *El Mercurio*, May 22, 1973.

56. See *El Mercurio*, June 30, 1973. Chile's leading newspaper had only barely recovered from a six-day government-imposed suspension of publication. The June 30 edition contained empty spaces where coverage of the putsch would have appeared!

57. On September 9, just two days before the golpe, Socialist Party Secretary General Carlos Altamirano candidly admitted in a radio broadcast that he had pressed sailors to mutiny.

58. See *El Mercurio*, July 13, 14, and 15, 1973; *CER* 3, no. 14 (July 1973).

59. This section is also based on Chilean and foreign press reports. See also Juan E. Guglialmelli et al., "Chile: Los sucesos del 11 de setiembre," *Estrategia* 5, no. 24 (September–October 1973):49–120; and Instituto de Estudios Generales, *Fuerzas armadas y seguridad nacional* (Santiago: Editorial Portada, 1973). The official view is presented by Hernán Millas and Emilio Filippi in their *Anatomía de un fracaso: La experiencia socialista chilena* (Santiago: Empresa Editora Zig-Zag, 1973), and *Chile, 70–73: Crónica de una experiencia* (Santiago: Empresa Editora Zig-Zag, 1974). For impressionistic views see Gabriel García Márquez, "The Death of Salvador Allende," tr. Gregory Rabassa, *Harper's*, March 1974; and Robert F. Kennedy, Jr., "Chile," *The Atlantic Monthly*, February 1974. Of the two, García is decidedly the more knowledgeable about Chilean affairs. For those who fancy the melodramatic, the golpe is staunchly defended in U.S., Congress, House, Committee on Internal Security, *The Theory and Practice of Communism, Part 5 (Marxism Imposed on Chile–Allende Regime)*, *Hearings before the Committee*, 93d Cong., 1st sess., November 15, 1973 and March 7, 13, 1974; and denounced vehemently in Heynowski and Scheumann, *Operación silencio* (Berlin, D.D.R.: Verlag der Nation, 1974). The former is widely distributed by the Chilean Embassy in Washington, D.C., and the latter is available in translations throughout Eastern Europe, e.g., *A "Hallgatás Hadművelet"; Chile Salvador Allende után* (Budapest: Magvető Könyvkiadó, 1974). On economic problems of the Allende regime and their significance in its downfall see two articles by Paul E. Sigmund, "The Invisible Blockade and the Overthrow of Allende," *Foreign Affairs* (January 1974):322–40; and "Allende in Retrospect," *Problems of Communism* (May–June 1974):45–62. On United States policy toward Allende see U.S., Congress, House, Committee on Foreign Affairs, *United States and Chile during the Allende Years, 1970–73: Hearings before the Subcommittee on Inter-American Affairs* (Washington, D.C.: U.S. Government Printing Office, 1975). For a sharp criticism of the recent Chilean policy of the United States see James Petras and Morris Morley, *The United States and Chile: Imperialism and the Overthrow of the Allende Government* (New York: Monthly Review Press, 1975).

60. *Chile*, no. 257 (September 24, 1973). To indicate the lengths to which the junta goes to disseminate these assertions, they also appear in such inappropriate places as the slick magazine-style public relations brochure freely distributed during the 1974 Pacific cruise of the navy's training ship *Esmeralda*. See *Armada de Chile, XIX crucero de instrucción 1974, "buque escuela" Esmeralda* (Santiago: Ministerio de Relaciones Exteriores, Editorial Lord Cochrane, 1974).

61. For a documented discussion of repression following September 11, see *Report of the Chicago Commission of Inquiry into the Status of Human Rights in Chile* (Chicago, 1974).

62. The burning of Greene's works may have been coincidence or he may have incurred wrath for his pro-Allende piece, "Chile: The Dangerous Edge," *Harper's*, March 1972.

63. Everett G. Martin correctly, and with nine months of perspective, analyzes the foregoing points in an article in the *Wall Street Journal*, June 3, 1974. See also the earlier analysis by Richard Gott in the *Manchester Guardian*, November 21, 1973.

64. But not to the point where the United States military professes no interest! See Air Force Reserve, Element Training, Staff Development: Academic Year 1973–74 Course, No. 45-004: *Significant Factors in U.S. Foreign Policy: Chile Since 1970* (Robins Air Force Base, Ga., 1974).

65. See the *Wall Street Journal*, November 2, 1973. Other especially good discussions of the post-Allende economic transition appeared in editions of April 19, May 13, and June 3, 1974.

66. "Plan Zeta" is included in the official *White Book of the Change of Government in Chile* (Santiago: Empresa Editora Nacional Gabriela Mistral, 1973). Though portions of the *White Book* may be *ex post facto* fabrication, the evidence points to a large-scale conspiracy on the left to seize power by force of arms. Much of the *White Book*'s tone is comparable, however, to that of the official Soviet line explaining the "restoration of rights and liberties" (to the people of Czechoslovakia in 1968), as expressed in *On Events in Czechoslovakia* (Moscow: Press Group of Soviet Journalists, 1965). Much new information on "Plan Zeta" was revealed in the trials of alleged air force conspirators in April 1974. See *Chile*, no. 263 (April–May 1974). See also Ricardo Boizard (Picotón), *Proceso a una traición: Detalles íntimos del sumario de la FACH* (Santiago: Ediciones Encina, 1974); Genaro Arriagada Herrera, *De la vía chilena a la vía insurreccional* (Santiago: Editorial del Pacífico, 1974); Lautaro Silva, *Allende: El fin de una aventura* (Santiago: Ediciones Patria Nueva, 1974); and the special edition of *El Mercurio*, September 11, 1974, for information on conspiracies to subvert the discipline of the armed forces and destroy their "hierarchical" and "professional" characteristics guaranteed by a 1971 insertion in the Constitution.

67. Tobías Barros Ortiz, *Vigilia de armas*, 2d ed. (Santiago: Estado Mayor General del Ejército, 1973).

68. Barros Ortiz, "Advertencia necesaria," ibid., pp. 9–10. On this theme see the recent Horacio Polloni, *Las fuerzas armadas de Chile en la vida nacional* (Santiago: Editorial Andrés Bello, 1972); and Sergio Miranda Carrington, "Las fuerzas armadas en el ordenamiento jurídico," in *Fuerzas armadas y seguridad nacional*, pp. 34–70, cited in n. 59 above. Contributors to the latter work readily admit that their purpose in writing was to encourage the armed forces to overthrow Allende by pointing out the military's multifaceted role in national life. Equally inciting were the tabloid-magazine publications of 1972–73, *Tacna* and *Tizona*, written and published by civilians and distributed to officers.

69. Augusto Pinochet Ugarte, *Geopolítica: Diferentes etapas para el estudio geopolítico de los estados* (Santiago: Estado Mayor General del Ejército, 1968).

70. Ibid., p. 241.

71. The junta later "categorically denied" this, announced a committee of jurists would "update" the 1925 Constitution, and proposed a plebiscite on constitutional changes. Soon after the golpe, with those favoring corporatist models in leadership positions, it became clear that a junta-sponsored constitutional revision would, if enacted, ban antidemocratic (Marxist) political organization, reorganize Congress and limit its powers by making it subordinate to the executive branch, reorganize the judiciary along what are termed "pyramidic" lines, provide for plebiscites to resolve executive-legislative conflicts, and do away with those features of the electoral system which permit (indeed, foster) election by plurality instead of majority. Such constitutional reforms have appealed to a broad spectrum of military men for years. For civilian opinion on constitutional problems between 1970 and 1973 see "El derecho chileno y el presidente Allende, I–II," *Revista chilena de derecho* 1, nos. 3–4 (June–August 1974):414–547; nos. 5–6 (October–December 1974):707–59.

The junta's attraction to corporatist models becomes obvious on reading the *Declaración de principios del gobierno de Chile* (Santiago: n.p., 1974). Very attractively published in a four-language translation (Spanish, English, French, German), the *Declaración* makes it clear that Chile needs purging, the introduction of new elements into government, civil-military equilibrium, and a return to the veneration of historical figures in order to emerge from the recent crisis. The government promises "authoritarian, impersonal and just government . . . guided by the inspiration of Portales." I believe this corroborates the importance of the themes discussed in the opening pages of chap. 8.

The junta's efforts in these directions are documented in Gobierno de Chile, *Un año de construcción, 11 septiembre 1973–11 septiembre 1974: El jefe supremo de la nación, general de ejército, Augusto Pinochet Ugarte informa al país* (Santiago: Talleres Gráficos del Servicio de

Prisiones, 1974). See also República de Chile 1974, *Primer año de reconstrucción nacional* (Santiago: Empresa Editora Nacional Gabriela Mistral, 1974).

72. Writing in the *New York Review of Books*, Laurence Birns claimed what the Chilean armed forces did on September 11, 1973, may have surprised or astonished the "student of Chilean history and society." I would reply that despite many indicators, no serious "student of Chilean history and society" should be amazed at all. An alarming degree of naïveté and subjectivity are manifested by Birns's insistence that the Chilean military acted as a tool of the upper classes (Laurence Birns, "The Death of Chile," *New York Review of Books*, November 1, 1973). A more balanced account is found in the Birns-edited special issue of *IDOC*, no. 58 (December 1973): *Chile, The Allende Years, The Coup, Under the Junta.* Condemnation by the left or by those sympathetic with the Allende regime has not abated but increased with the passage of time. See Pablo Díaz et al., *Chile: Una tragedia americana* (Buenos Aires: Editorial Crisis, 1974); Pío García, ed., *Las fuerzas armadas y el golpe de estado en Chile* (Mexico City: Siglo Veintiuno Editores, 1974); Pablo Santillana, ed., *Chile: Análisis de un año de gobierno militar* (Buenos Aires: Prensa Latinoamericana, 1974); and Oscar Barros, *El revés de la moneda* (Buenos Aires: Editorial El Lorraine, 1974). These works all consider the military as an extension of upper-class, imperialist, capitalist interests because of the fall of Allende, thus ignoring the more far-reaching aspects of recent civil-military relations.

Index

Academia de Defensa Nacional. *See* National Defense Academy
Academia de Guerra. *See* War Academy
Academia Militar. *See* Military Academy
Academia Politécnica Militar. *See* Military Polytechnic Academy
ACHA. *See* Chilean Anticommunist Action
Aconcagua Province, 34
Acosta, Ambrosio, 31
Admiralty, 168, 201, 230. *See also* Navy of Chile
Agrarian Labor Party, 189, 222, 239, 244
agrarian reform, 191
Aguilar, Mario, 283
Aguirre, Manuel, 114
Aguirre Bernal, Sócrates, 137, 140, 141, 148, 162, 170
Aguirre Cerda, Pedro, 187, 189, 234–36, 240, 242, 263
Ahumada Bascuñán, Arturo, 114, 128, 137, 138, 141, 143, 149
Air Force of Chile, 180, 185, 186, 202, 226–27, 293
Air Force School, 208, 269
Aldea, 169
Aldea, Juan de Dios, 69
Aldona, Guillermo, 263
Alemparte, Arturo, 160
Alessandri, Gustavo, 229
Alessandri Palma, Arturo: biographical data, 9; political involvement, 171, 187, 197, 198, 202, 203, 221–22, 243; presidency (1920–25), 89, 92, 98, 107, 124–25, 131–33, 134, 135, 141, 143, 146–49; presidency (1932–38), 180, 183, 188–89, 195, 221, 223–36; reform program, 132, 136; relations with military, 127, 130, 136, 163, 168, 185, 202, 223–24, 226–30, 233; resignations, 127, 136, 140, 144, 146; mentioned, 206, 209, 255, 257, 272, 283, 285, 297, 300, 306
Alessandri Palma, José Pedro, 134
Alessandri Rodríguez, Jorge, 187, 189, 224, 237–38, 239, 240, 267, 302
Alessandristas, 140, 141, 149, 162, 163, 170, 185, 205, 213. *See also* Alessandri Palma, Arturo
Alfonso Barrios, Pedro Enrique, 239, 244

Aliancistas. *See* Liberal Alliance
Allende Gossens, Salvador: overthrown, xi, 151; political involvement, 158, 188, 189, 239–40, 244; presidency (1970–73), 177, 241, 253–308; relations with military, 224, 268–89
Allendistas, 254, 273, 285, 293. *See also* Allende Gossens, Salvador
Almirante Blanco Encalada, 67, 118
Almirante Cochrane, 67
Altamirano, Carlos, 305
Altamirano, Luis, 227
Altamirano Talavera, Luis, 124, 134–35, 136, 138, 140, 143, 146, 148, 149, 168, 169
Alvarez Goldsack, Ramón, 246
American and Foreign Power Company, 190
American Popular Revolutionary Alliance (Alianza Popular Revolucionaria Americana), 190, 204, 297
Anaconda Copper Company, 277
Ancón, Treaty of, 68, 70
Antarctica, Chilean, 264
antimilitarism, 31–33, 120–21, 183–84, 197–98, 202, 203–4
Antofagasta: city, 65, 67, 95, 96, 103, 118, 124, 125, 191, 201, 217, 256; province, 12, 65, 69, 71
Antofagasta Nitrate Company (Compañía de Salitre de Antofagasta), 65
API. *See* Independent Popular Action
APRA. *See* American Popular Revolutionary Alliance
Araucania, 7, 12, 14, 54, 69
Araucanians, 6–7, 11, 27, 68
Araya Peters, Arturo, 253, 285
Archivo de don Bernardo O'Higgins, 264
Arellano, Daniel, 286
Arequipa, battle of, 48
Argentina: boundary disputes, 65, 70–71, 142, 143; "Conquest of the Desert," 6; military, 85, 86, 112, 127, 186, 190, 193–94, 204, 237, 243, 249–52, 261, 262, 265, 292, 295, 298, 300–302, 306–7; mentioned, 14, 46, 55, 118, 177, 178, 181, 184, 191, 218, 219, 248
Arica: city, 67, 69, 125, 256; province, 12, 68, 69
Ariostazo. *See* Herrera Ramírez, Ariosto